Drawn from the Classics

Drawn from the Classics

*Essays on Graphic
Adaptations of Literary Works*

Edited by STEPHEN E. TABACHNICK
and ESTHER BENDIT SALTZMAN

McFarland & Company, Inc., Publishers
Jefferson, North Carolina

LIBRARY OF CONGRESS CATALOGUING-IN-PUBLICATION DATA

Drawn from the classics : essays on graphic adaptations of literary works / edited by Stephen E. Tabachnick and Esther Bendit Saltzman.
  p.   cm.

Includes bibliographical references and index.

ISBN 978-0-7864-7879-8 (softcover : acid free paper) ∞
ISBN 978-1-4766-1976-7 (ebook)

1. Literature—Adaptations—History and criticism. 2. Graphic novels—History and criticism. 3. Literature—Study and teaching. 4. Graphic novels—Study and teaching.   I. Tabachnick, Stephen Ely, editor.   II. Saltzman, Esther Bendit, editor.

PN171.A33D73 2015
809—dc23   2015008556

BRITISH LIBRARY CATALOGUING DATA ARE AVAILABLE

© 2015 Stephen E. Tabachnick and Esther Bendit Saltzman. All rights reserved

No part of this book may be reproduced or transmitted in any form or by any means, electronic or mechanical, including photocopying or recording, or by any information storage and retrieval system, without permission in writing from the publisher.

Front cover image from *Alice in Wonderland* © 2015 Shutterstock

Printed in the United States of America

McFarland & Company, Inc., Publishers
  Box 611, Jefferson, North Carolina 28640
    www.mcfarlandpub.com

To our families
Sharon, Daphne, Orrin, and Laurie Tabachnick
Joel, Samantha, and Zachary Saltzman
for your loving encouragement and support

Table of Contents

Preface	1
Introduction	3
Here There Be Monsters (and Heroes): Homer's *Odyssey* and the Graphic Novel—PAUL D. STREUFERT	19
Hwaet If? *Beowulf* in Comics—JASON TONDRO	33
Killing Desdemona: Staging Sexual Violence in *Othello* Graphic Novels—J. CAITLIN FINLAYSON	46
Illustrating the Uncertainty Within: Recent Comics Adaptations of Edgar Allan Poe—DEREK PARKER ROYAL	60
The Good, the Bad and the Parodic in Graphic Adaptation—ERIC S. RABKIN	82
In Search of the White Whale: Adaptations of *Moby-Dick*—DIRK VANDERBEKE	96
"I don't see what good a book is without pictures or conversations": Imaginary Worlds and Intertextuality in *Alice in Wonderland* and *Alice in Sunderland*—MATTHEW J. A. GREEN	110
"Does That Change Anything?" (Post)Feminist Implications of *Gemma Bovery*—ERIC L. BERLATSKY	127
Drawing Style, Genre and the Destabilization of Register in a Graphic Adaptation of Trollope's 1878 Novel *John Caldigate*—DAVID SKILTON and SIMON GRENNAN	147

The Masks of Dracula: In Search of the Authentic Performative
    Vampire in Three Graphic Novel Adaptations of
    Bram Stoker's *Dracula*—Ana G. Gal   161

The Picture *and* Dorian Gray: Interpretive Pluralism
    in Graphic Adaptations of Wilde's Novel—
    Esther Bendit Saltzman   177

Illustrating the Abyss: An Interview with Catherine Anyango
    on *Heart of Darkness* —Christine Ferguson   194

Visualizing the Unrepresentable: Graphic Novel Adaptations
    of Kafka's *Metamorphosis*—Martha Kuhlman   205

An Unusual Adaptation of F. Scott Fitzgerald's *The Great Gatsby*—
    Stephen E. Tabachnick   221

Not Telling, but Retelling: From Raymond Queneau's
    Exercises in Style to Matt Madden's *99 Ways to
    Tell a Story* and Back—Jan Baetens   235

Illustrated Man: Ray Bradbury, Comics and the Authorized
    Graphic Novels—Darren Harris-Fain   249

Bibliography   263
About the Contributors   267
Index   271

Preface

We embarked on this work because there is and has been no other collection dealing exclusively with graphic novel adaptations of literary works. We felt that such a collection would be useful not only to scholars but to high school and university teachers, especially since such works are already being used in the classroom, including ours. We have learned that students are very enthusiastic about this hybrid form of reading at least in part because it matches the current cognitive environment of both reading text and viewing pictures at the same time, as on the internet and in many print media today. And although the graphic novel grows out of the traditional comics, it embodies a depth and subtlety that was previously unavailable in the comics because of those comics' commercial constraints on both content and form, limited production values, and lack of a serious audience. Even though the graphic novel is based on the traditional comics, it is so different in these respects that it amounts to a new literary/artistic form, and there is very little more exciting in the humanities than the emergence of a new form in our own time. But over and above the current situation, the graphic novel has already produced works, including adaptations, that promise to become classics. Moreover, like adaptations of literary works into film or dramatic format, graphic novel adaptations add another interpretive dimension to the works adapted, and that extra dimension helps students as well as scholars visualize the given work in a new way.

Each of the contributors to this collection is an academic specialist very familiar with this new genre, and each analyzes the adaptations of a different author's work and explains what is unique and valuable about the adaptations and what each adds to a given work, or why a certain adaptation does not succeed in doing so. Each contributor uses his or her own method to analyze the works, ranging from close reading to more theoretical approaches, thus allowing for a variety of critical techniques as well as a variety of perspectives on the contents of the works. In addition, in two cases the artists who have created graphic novel adaptations are participants in the collection, and bring their unique insights to illuminate their work.

The study of the graphic novel continues to expand at a great rate, in large part because of the opportunities for new research and perspectives, and so does the investigation of adaptations in all media, which is itself a recent field of study. By bringing together the fields of graphic novel and adaptation studies, it is hoped that this collection will help advance both of these fields. Moreover, the original works themselves will profit from the new interpretations provided by their graphic novel adapters, and this will help advance the field of literary studies, with which we, like our contributors, are deeply involved. Adaptations have often been undervalued and we hope that this collection will illuminate their value for both scholarship and teaching.

We also hope that general readers, who may have enjoyed graphic novel adaptations just as they have cinematic adaptations, will gain a deeper sense of just why they have enjoyed these adaptations from this collection. We feel gratified that readers of these essays, whether specialists or general educated readers, will enter into a mental dialogue with the contributors, and feel themselves enriched whether they agree or disagree with them. Ultimately, our hope is that the excitement that the contributors obviously feel about this new field of mental endeavor will be experienced by all readers of this collection, and that they in their turn will embark on their own voyages into this new territory.

Introduction

On display at the George Frederick Watts Gallery in Guildford, UK, is his portrait of a tree trunk with a vine gently curving up the trunk. As the observer approaches the painting, the title, "A Parasite," becomes visible. This title then affects the viewer's interpretation of the image; it re-directs the viewer's gaze, emphasizing the vine over the tree trunk. Just as the title changes the perception of this painting, the addition of a visual image or series of images to a verbal text can affect its interpretation as well.

Similarly, excellent adaptations of literary works into visual media, such as film, theater or graphic novels, inevitably provide new interpretations. And a new interpretation of a literary classic enhances the narrative for the student or scholar. We can compare such an interpretation to a gifted pianist's playing of a composer's work and bringing his or her own perspective to that work. But in comparison with a pianist, the graphic novel, like film and theater, is often the product not only of one writer/artist but of a collaboration between writer(s) and visual artist(s), so the interpretive process is enriched by the sensibilities of both literary and visual contributors.

In her discussion of adaptation, Julie Sanders calls attention to J. Hillis Miller's claim for the potential of a text to be "inhabited ... by a long chain of parasitical presences, echoes, allusions, guests, ghosts of previous texts" (qtd. in Sanders 4). The inspiration for this collection is the idea that adaptations are not parasites on their adapted texts, but that they are in a symbiotic relationship with them. The adapted text and its adaptation(s) are at once intimately related and separate and unique entities. Not only can scholars and students benefit from the comparison of these adaptations with the original texts, but the adapted texts can contribute to an expansion of the already-existing interest in these texts.

Although there have been individual studies of some graphic novel adaptations, there has been no collection devoted solely to such adaptations. It is our contention that these adaptations, when studied alongside their adapted texts, provide unique opportunities for understanding those texts more fully as well as offering a unique reading experience in themselves. Consequently, one goal for this collection is to demonstrate the wide range of research and pedagogical opportunities that graphic novel adaptations of literary classics offer to scholars and teachers. The collection covers examples of literary classics from antiquity to the modern period, and our contributors apply many different approaches to their chosen texts. It is our hope that this collection will be found useful for high school and university teachers, as well as for scholars working on these texts, and that the collection will inspire use of these adaptations in literary scholarship and research.

To examine precisely how the study of graphic novel adaptations can contribute to the study of literature, this collection seeks to consider the following questions: How does the graphic novel reading experience differ from the reading of the text-only work? How does the combination of image and word create a new perception and interpretation of a prose text? What makes a graphic novel adaptation effective or ineffective? What can theory add to an understanding of these adaptations? And most of all, how can graphic novel adaptations contribute to an understanding of the adapted texts? Each contributor's essay helps to answer one or more of these questions by providing a detailed analysis of the adaptation(s) in comparison with the original text(s).

The increasing production of graphic novel adaptations of literary classics makes this collection timely because such adaptations are progressively becoming the subject of scholarly research and required reading in high school and university classrooms. Historically, illustrations accompanying a written text have played the major role in the visual expression of literature; they have been credited with adding what is largely a descriptive element, presenting details of a scene or character that are described in the original text. More recently, comics art has been used not merely to illustrate, but to employ the combination of image and text to fully communicate and even expand upon ideas and meaning rather than to merely visually reproduce detailed descriptions of a written text. Thus, comics, or sequential art as it is sometimes called today, has opened up new avenues of discourse about literary classics.

The original *Classics Illustrated* series, begun in 1941 by Albert Kanter and continuing until 1971, attempted to bring the classics to a young group of readers who did not yet have the skills to read a complex text. To that end, the *Classics Illustrated* adaptations of classic texts were simplified and abridged in terms of both incident and language, to the extent that the adaptation sometimes bore little resemblance to the original outside of basic plot and characters. This was a worthy enough goal at the time, and comics art itself had not progressed to the point that a more ambitious program of adaptation was possible. Only in the 1970s did the comics themselves evolve to the extent that an extended prose work containing all possible subtleties of expression and idea could be rendered in a fully compatible comics format—the graphic novel. The graphic novel represents the development of the comic book into an extended art form no longer constricted by commercial limitations of form and content. Essentially, the graphic novel as it was developed in the hands of Will Eisner, Alan Moore, and Art Spiegelman among others, is a full-length artistic form combining all of the subtle tools of verbal and visual art available to creators in all fields of literature and art. Instead of simplified content and a limited number of standardized panels, the graphic novel offers sophisticated content, high quality paper and ink, varied panel sizes and shapes, and original and striking combinations of word and image. Graphic novel adaptations have grown in number and scope in parallel with the development of the graphic novel itself into a full-fledged literary/artistic genre, which includes original works as well as adaptations. For instance, Russ Kick's three-volume series, *The Graphic Canon*, contains excerpts from many important literary works rendered by multiple adapters.

The study of graphic novel adaptations incorporates the new fields of comics studies and adaptation studies. The contributors to this collection often avail themselves of the insights of these fields as well as the perspectives provided by literary and art criticism, cultural studies, narratology (or the study of the many dimensions involved in the narration of a story), and (since graphic novels are being created in many countries today) international studies, among other areas. The insights of comics studies and adaptation studies, as well as these other fields, have proven fundamental for the study of graphic novel adaptations.

Comics Studies

In their introduction to *A Comics Studies Reader*, Jeet Heer and Kent Worcester survey current trends in comics studies scholarship:

> The burgeoning of comics studies is testified to by a wide array of evidence: impressive new biographies and monographs; the construction of a scholarly infrastructure (archives, conferences, journals, listserv groups, and so on); greater

theoretical ambition and sophistication; the internationalization of comics scholarship (facilitated by the web); the recovery of lost classics; and the growing audience for talks, books, and articles on the history, aesthetics, craft, and politics of comics. While the best of the new comics scholarship is eclectic in approach and foci, it consistently returns to certain core themes: the history and genealogy of comics, the inner workings of comics, the social significance of comics, and the close scrutiny and evaluation of comics [xi].

Will Eisner and Scott McCloud are ground-breakers responsible for initiating comics theory. In his acknowledgments, McCloud credits Eisner with "the first book to examine the art-form of comics," *Comics and Sequential Art*. Eisner also explains the narrative aspects of comics in *Graphic Storytelling and Visual Narrative*. He discusses symbolism, artistic style, reader emotional response, and sequence. Of the medium itself, he says:

> The reading process in comics is an extension of text. In text alone the process of reading involves word-to-image conversion. Comics accelerates that by providing the image. When properly executed, it goes beyond conversion and speed and becomes a seamless whole.... [Comics] is entitled to be regarded as literature because the images are employed as a language.... When this language is employed as a conveyance of ideas and information, it separates itself from mindless entertainment. This makes comics a storytelling medium [Eisner 5–6].

McCloud's *Understanding Comics* has insightfully illuminated critical aspects specific to the comics medium. His book assists the reader with the skills necessary to read comics with an analytical eye. He also provides some key concepts that demonstrate the sophistication of the comics medium as a unique communicator of ideas. First, just as Eisner explains that reading comics is a dynamic process, McCloud explains the importance of the gutter, or place between comics frames, as the area in which the reader actively participates through the process of "closure." In this way, McCloud states that comics is "...a medium where the audience is a willing and conscious collaborator and closure is the agent of change, time and motion" (McCloud 65). Active interpretation, then, is a natural consequence of this reader participation.

A second concept that is critical to viewing comics is McCloud's idea that often comics are a form of "amplification through simplification." Cartoon art, he says, "[strips] down an image to its essential 'meaning,'" and "an artist can amplify that meaning in a way that realistic art can't" (McCloud 30). In this way, along with the use of realistic techniques, the graphic novel artist can emphasize concepts through the use of this specialized type of visual art, thereby communicating his or her interpretive reading.

Another concept that is important for our understanding of comics and adaptation is McCloud's contention that "by de-emphasizing the appearance of the physical world in favor of the idea of form, the cartoon places itself in the world of concepts" (McCloud 41). By translating a verbal text into the comics medium, then, the artist necessarily conceptualizes the narrative as he or she adapts it. Conversely, the reader will also conceptualize the translation of the text and be able to make his or her own interpretations.

Additional scholarship addresses comics theory from varying perspectives and approaches. Thierry Groensteen, for instance, in *The System of Comics*, argues for the primacy of the image, and presents comics as a "collection of codes" forming a comics "system." These codes include "visual and discursive" elements that work simultaneously. All aspects of the visual are important, including not only images within the frames, but also the layout, proportion, and sequence of the frames. Pascal Lefèvre also emphasizes the various components of comics, and states that:

> As a hybrid medium, the graphic narrative shares many features with other media, but uses those features in unique ways; think of drawing styles, the *mise en scène* in panels, the way verbal and visual elements are combined (e.g., in speech or thought balloons), the breakdown (or "*découpage*") of story elements into distinct panels, and the interaction between individual panels and page layouts [Lefèvre 1].

It is precisely these combinations of features that make the adaptation of texts into the graphic medium so inviting for analysis.

Narrative theory also provides important connections to comics scholarship. Jared Gardner and David Herman refer to comics as "one of the world's most vibrant and compelling forms of narrative practice," and demonstrate the significance of the graphic novel as an important storytelling medium (1).

Adaptation Studies

Adaptation studies as a theoretical entity is relatively new. Although stage and visual art have been discussed theoretically since ancient times, the acknowledgement of adaptation as a process encompassing multiple media is recent, but several scholars have begun writing about this important aspect of the humanities, and a journal, *Adaptation*, is now devoted to it. Julie Sanders, in *Adaptation and Appropriation*, stresses the enjoyment of literature and the ability of adaptation and appropriation to facilitate that. She addresses types and degrees of adaptations and appropriations, as well as their ability to enhance exploration of textual meanings created by author, adapter, and reader. Both Sanders and Linda Hutcheon address the inadequacy of fidelity as a gauge of adaptation quality; they both discuss the wide spectrum of adaptations and the degree to which they reproduce aspects of their adapted sources. They both also address intertextuality as an important aspect of adaptation. In *A Theory of Adaptation*, Hutcheon states:

> For the reader, spectator, or listener, adaptation *as adaptation* is unavoidably a kind of intertextuality *if the receiver is acquainted with the adapted text*. It is an ongoing dialogical process, as Mikhail Bakhtin would have said, in which we compare the work we already know with the one we are experiencing....[1] [21].

Similarly, the reader of the graphic novel adaptation engages in a dialogue with both texts, as Hutcheon explains that "...adaptation *as adaptation* involves, for its knowing audience, an interpretive doubling, a conceptual flipping back and forth between the work we know and the work we are experiencing" (Hutcheon 139). Both Hutcheon and Sanders explain that adaptations become new works of art, and the new work then reflects its textual inspiration. The graphic adapter and reader can then re-examine the adapted text using the questions and ideas brought out in the adaptation. The analysis of adaptations, therefore, requires sophisticated comparisons that go beyond what is included and what is left out. While these aspects of analysis are indeed important, the visual techniques that the adapters use give added insight into how we interpret meaning. Indeed, the graphic novel's introduction of telling visual images, in combination with intelligently selected text, can direct the reader toward themes, motifs, metaphors, and background issues present but not always apparent in the original versions of classic literature.

Hutcheon also explains that most of the work on adaptation has been done in the field of cinema (Hutcheon xii). In "Twelve Fallacies in Contemporary Adaptation Theory," Thomas Leitch discusses the need for theory in film adaptation studies. He cites previous works on film adaptation, George Bluestone's 1957 *Novels into Film*, and Brian McFarlane's 1996 *Novel to Film*, but maintains that most studies of film adaptation are based on individual examples rather than on more generalized theory (Leitch 150), and he explains the need for such theory. Hutcheon also cites Bluestone and McFarlane and agrees with Leitch that a comprehensive theory of adaptation is necessary.

Where Hutcheon differs, though, is her multimedia approach to adaptation. Her stated purpose in writing *A Theory of Adaptation* is "to derive theory from practice," and to address a wide variety of contemporary media, including film, graphic novels, "performance media," and media she deems "interactive," such as video games and amusement parks (Hutcheon xii). While her primary purpose is to develop a comprehensive theory, she explains that she is also indirectly arguing for the legitimacy of adaptation (Hutcheon xii-xiii). Hutcheon examines adaptations as "deliberate, announced, and extended revisitations of prior works" (xiii-xiv). Preferring the term "adapted text" to "original," she describes adaptation as "an acknowledged transposition of a recognizable other work or works," "a creative and interpretive act of appropriation/salvaging," and "an extended intertextual engagement with the adapted work" (8). Finally, Hutcheon emphasizes the importance of the creative process in adaptation, and discusses the importance of intentionality in the analysis of it "in the interpretations of meaning and the assignment of value" (107). The adapter's interpretation of a given text can follow or expand on accepted historical meanings of texts or provide material for possible new meanings that might be embedded in them. Furthermore, the adapter can add potential new meanings or, through ambiguity or word/image choice, can facilitate the graphic novel reader's own interpretations of meaning. The potential for new interpretations and the discussion of established ones then adds to the value of these graphic novels for scholarship.

Since graphic novels engage their readers through use of printed words and images that work together, they communicate as a distinct medium. In *Understanding Media*, Marshall McLuhan states that "'...the medium is the message' because it is the medium that shapes and controls the scale and form of human association and action" (McLuhan 24). Consequently, if the graphic novel medium forms an association between the adapted text and the reader, understanding how the medium communicates will, in turn, facilitate the reader's understanding of both texts.

Graphic Novel Adaptations

Bringing the various fields of study together, scholarship on graphic novel adaptations can take many directions. One area of scholarship focuses on pedagogy, aimed at teaching the graphic novel and teaching with graphic novels. Some of this scholarship deals with using graphic novels to improve literacy and comprehension; some of it deals with the use of graphic novels in higher education. Stephen Tabachnick's *Teaching the Graphic Novel* collection addresses the use of graphic novels, including some graphic novel adaptations of literary texts, at the university level for both undergraduate and graduate studies. There are also a number of literature studies available on individual graphic novel adaptations. Marion Perret, in "Not Just Condensation: How Comic Books Interpret Shakespeare," states that these adaptations "interpret as well as inform" (Perret 73). She also points out that "sophisticated readers recognize that visual perspective may convey an intellectual or emotional point of view," and that "interpretation may be blatant or surprisingly subtle, visual or verbal" (Perret 74). Her statement communicates the importance of visual literacy in reading comics effectively.

In "The Graphic Novel and the Age of Transition: A Survey and Analysis," Stephen Tabachnick addresses some adaptations of late nineteenth century and early twentieth century literary works. Tabachnick explains that many texts of the period are strongly visual within the verbal narrative and thus lend themselves to graphic novel adaptation. These adaptations, he says, "allow us to see the original novels in new and different ways," and allow us to reach a "broader audience" (Tabachnick 25).

The graphic novel adaptation—as opposed to, for instance, a film or theatrical adaptation—is particularly appropriate to the classroom because the graphic novel is above all a reading experience. We read from left to right and top to bottom of a graphic novel page, paying careful attention not only to the page layout as a whole but to the combination of word and image in each panel on the page. In addition, the graphic novel reader, like any reader of prose text, can linger over a given passage, or look backward or forward; the reader is under no constraint or time pressure, as is the viewer of a film who of necessity must constantly move forward with the images on the screen. And, the graphic novel can offer the reader a panel consisting of a page or a two-page spread with large or many images, or smaller panels focusing on a few images or a single image. Obviously, this is an augmented reading experience compared to the reading of text alone. This particular kind of augmented reading seems a perfect fit for the cognitive abilities of today's students, who are used to viewing pictures and reading text at the same time in the context of the internet, cell phones, and even newspapers, which now seem to have pictures on every page. This too makes the graphic novel a form suitable for our age, and one particularly appropriate for contemporary adaptations of classic texts. Given the graphic novel's sophistication, in excellent adaptations few or no subtleties are lost in translation from the prose text, and the reader reads the graphic novel and meditates upon it at his or her own speed.

Moreover, as in case of other visual media such as film or drama, the use of images in the graphic novel adaptation reduces the necessity for prose descriptions of characters, actions, and settings, which makes the adaptation shorter than the original text, with the possible exception of graphic novel adaptations of plays, which may contain the complete original play. A novel or non-fictional work which would take many hours to read can be read in one or two hours in its adapted form. Characters whose looks the reader has to imagine are visualized by the adaptation's artist instead. If the reader is not blessed with a strong visual imagination, he or she will be grateful for the artist's sharper perception of a given character. In addition, the artist will show a gesture or other element of body language, or an item of dress, that the reader had not thought of. All of these elements contribute to the perception and therefore to the interpretation of a given text. Similarly, a given setting visualized by the artist of an adaptation will provide a fuller picture than is likely to be imagined by the reader of the prose text, no matter how detailed its description. Or the artist may choose to more fully illustrate a passage that is only briefly rendered in the original. In this sense, the saying that one picture is worth a thousand words is realized. If, of course, the reader has a strong visual imagination, he or she may be disappointed in the artist's rendering. But in either case, a new element has been added to the original text which has an impact on its interpretation by the reader, and which sharpens his or her perception of the original, whether he or she regards the artist's rendering positively or negatively. A definite limitation of adaptations, however, is that the graphic novel, because of its use of panels with speech bubbles or even more lengthy narrative passages included on the page, cannot reproduce the long philosophical discourses which are common in classic literature, despite the skill of the adapting writer. Here the question of whether or not the adapter uses the same wording as the original text also becomes important, because any change in the original language or style can obviously influence the interpretation of a text, and the reader may regard such changes positively or negatively. As Roy Thomas, the adapting writer, has stated in his introduction to the Marvel graphic novel of Oscar Wilde's *The Picture of Dorian Gray*,

> Naturally, there were problem areas. There always are, when adapting a work from one medium to another.... The problems are always different, but they are always there ... and they're part and parcel of what makes adaptation work interesting and a challenge all on its own.

He explains how he had to reduce the philosophical discourses in the novel while at the same time adding scenes only briefly described by Wilde's narrator. How each adapting writer and artist attempts to solve the inevitable problems of adaptation is itself an interesting study.

Thus, the reader or critic of a graphic novel adaptation has much to consider. This survey of the graphic novel adaptation of classic literary texts from the earliest times to the present will be useful not only to educated readers who want to select the best adaptations for their own reading, but also to scholars and teachers who want to use such works in their own research or in the classroom. In the case of there being several adaptations of the same work, our contributors have tried to indicate which one or ones would be best, and for which uses. The variety of approaches brought by our contributors will ensure a lively interaction with readers, who will find many ways of approaching graphic novel adaptations here.

The Collection

For ease of use, the collection is arranged chronologically starting with the earliest original texts and proceeding to the most recent. To compare each original text with the graphic novel adaptation or adaptations, each contributor has used his or her own method of analysis, ranging from theoretical considerations of the differences between pure text and the graphic novel through close reading of the given graphic novel adaptation. Because it considers graphic novel adaptations from many different aspects, the collection provides the reader with knowledge of different methods of adaptation analysis as well as some of the new perspectives that an excellent adaptation can bring to the original prose text.

The ancient and medieval periods are represented by Paul D. Streufert and Jason Tondro, respectively. Streufert, who sees ancient epics as having much in common with modern superhero comics, compares three graphic novel adaptations of Homer's work: Hinds' *The Odyssey*, Jolley and Yeates's *Odysseus: Escaping Poseidon's Curse*, and Thomas and Tocchini's *The Odyssey*. He concludes that in its own special way each graphic novel adaptation features a confrontation between older visions of heroism and monstrosity in terms that the modern reader can appreciate, and that the adaptations "draw clear lines of connection between our fears and those of the ancients."

From ancient times we progress to the medieval as Jason Tondro differentiates between several adaptations of *Beowulf*. Perhaps because it is so visual, this work has appealed to many graphic novel (as well as film) adapters. Tondro addresses artistic representation, faithfulness, context, and the application of these issues in the teaching of the poem and its adaptations. He finds that the confrontation between Grendel's mother and Beowulf, which students often find boring in the original text, becomes exciting when portrayed in graphic novel format, although not all adaptations do so. He concludes that when "students think they know a poem like Beowulf, that is precisely when they are best primed to see what other creators have made of it—how adaptation, alteration, cutting, and re-interpretation change what the text is saying."

J. Caitlin Finlayson examines two adaptations of Shakespeare's *Othello*. Finlayson discusses these adaptations in terms of style, treatment of the passage of time, and the representation of the tropes of race, gender and sexual violence in the murder scene (Act V, scene 2). She finds that the particular graphic novels that are now available are not excellent adaptations, and bowdlerize the content of the original. So, unlike the other contributors to this volume, she concludes that the adaptations—while often following theatrical precedent—do not add anything new to the interpretations of the play.

Since nineteenth century literature has a very large number of works featuring strikingly visual characters, from Melville's white whale to Dorian Gray and his portrait and the monster-like Kurtz in Conrad's *Heart of Darkness*, this century's literature has inspired more graphic novel adaptations than that of any other century, and that is reflected in the number of essays in the collection based on this literature.

Edgar Allan Poe's work has probably been more often adapted into all forms of media than that of any writer except Shakespeare, and the graphic novel is no exception. Supplementing a previous article of his on earlier adaptations, Derek Parker Royal takes us on a comprehensive tour of the numerous comics and graphic novel adaptations of Poe's work created since 2008. Using Linda Hutcheon's adaptation classification system, he shows how the Poe adaptations fall into several major categories, and he discusses the positive and negative characteristics of each adaptation.

Eric S. Rabkin's discussion of the interpretive value of graphic novel adaptations of literary works focuses particularly (but not only) on a parody of Bronte's *Wuthering Heights* in R. Sikoryak's *Masterpiece Comics*, a collection of comics parodies of classic literary works. Rabkin provides an insightful view into precisely what three specific types of graphic novel adaptations contribute to our understanding of prose texts. He makes the point that "parody need not be profound and profundity does not require parody, but when the two align, as Sikoryak has contrived, we encounter adaptations that both illuminate what we knew and give us something marvelous and new," and he emphasizes the fact that the comics medium makes parody all the more powerful.

Dirk Vanderbeke surveys several adaptations, both serious and parodic, of *Moby Dick*, and the suitability of each for its intended audience. He discusses the varying expectations that audiences have of adaptations, and finds that each of the adaptations he discusses has its strengths and weaknesses, but that all of them show the unique characteristics of the graphic novel, especially "its persistent tendency to fall back on established and commercially successful imagery, styles and formats, and its ability, nevertheless, to transgress previous patterns and to find new and exciting artistic techniques and narrative strategies for the advancement of comics and graphic novels as an art, and sometimes even for creative re-interpretations of Melville's inscrutable white whale."

Matthew J. A. Green examines several graphic novel versions of *Alice in Wonderland* according to various theoretical criteria in order to decide which would be the most useful in the classroom and elsewhere. He focuses particularly on Bryan Talbot's *Alice in Sunderland: An Entertainment* which, using a variety of techniques including a mixture of black-and-white and colored panels, interweaves and extends Carroll's original work into the present, commenting on many facets of contemporary society as it does so. He concludes that Talbot's *Alice* reasserts "the value of fantasy, humor and other popular ephemera in creating art that unwinds and rewinds the weave and woof of a broader social tapestry."

Eric L. Berlatsky deals with a contemporary retelling of Flaubert's *Madame Bovary*, showing us what graphic novel creator Posy Simmonds has contributed to our understanding of the protagonist in that tale by creating a new character based on her, Gemma Bovery. By comparing the gender-based and cultural perspectives of nineteenth century France to those of the present period, Berlatsky shows what has changed in Western culture since *Madame Bovary* was written. He also reveals how the use of comics techniques helps the reader to understand Flaubert's story in a new way.

Simon Grennan, who is now working on an adaptation of Trollope's novel *John Caldigate*, has teamed up with David Skilton, a Trollope expert, to discuss the problems involved in this and to some degree in all adaptations. They offer us a detailed explication of Trollope's style, including his frequent use of equivocation, and they explore the problem of bridging time periods in an adaptation. One answer to this problem is that Grennan has chosen a type font and drawing style that will remind readers of nineteenth century illustrators such as Honoré Daumier. But beyond that, they write that the adaptation attempts to achieve a situation in the graphic novel "...where the view always seems trustworthy and verisimilar, literally revealing the plot by accumulation of views, repetition and the slightest variations" in a way that will remind the reader of the original text.

Ana G. Gal tackles three graphic novel renditions of Bram Stoker's *Dracula*, pointing out the importance of the resurrection of the original novel in the wake of such popular contemporary vampire phenomena as *Twilight*. Gal informs us on the basis of an analytical discussion which of the adaptations does the best job of rendering Dracula's "otherness" and capturing the emotions associated with it, as well as why all of the adaptations fall short of capturing Dracula's inner world. She also explains how and why the graphic novel adaptations contribute to the reader's horror at Dracula's appearance, often in subtle ways. According to Gal, the Marvel Comics adaptation by Roy Thomas and Dick Giordano in particular captures the Count's ability to horrify us.

Esther Bendit Saltzman compares three versions—by Thomas and Fiumara, Edginton and Culbard, and John Coulthart—of Wilde's *The Picture of Dorian Gray* in order to show what each contributes to the interpretation of Wilde's work. She demonstrates that both the aesthetic and the moral sides of Wilde's work are emphasized by each of the versions but often in strikingly different ways that offer multiple opportunities for interpretation. The comparison of two graphic novels in comics format with Coulthart's shorter collage-style depiction of story elements gives us an idea of how the format of the different types of graphic adaptations can also bring out specific emphases and meanings.

Christine Ferguson, in her chapter on *Heart of Darkness,* interviews Catherine Anyango, the artist of an outstanding adaptation of Conrad's *Heart of Darkness* with a script by David Mairowitz. In Anyango's studio in north London, Ferguson discusses the way in which Anyango worked with Mairowitz, and the unique artistic features of this adaptation, including the use of Conrad's facial features in her rendition of the character Marlow's face. Ferguson and Anyango also explore some of the cultural and aesthetic difficulties of rendering *Heart of Darkness* as a graphic novel, including ways of dealing with charges of racism against Conrad and methods of rendering the book's horrors in a way that will draw the reader in rather than repel him or her. In particular, Anyango describes her use of cinematic techniques in this, her first graphic novel venture.

Moving into the twentieth century, Martha Kuhlman addresses the problem of representation, or "visualizing the unrepresentable," in Kafka's *Metamorphosis*, and the importance of the comics medium in the transformation of this narrative. Kuhlman examines three graphic novel adaptations of Kafka's work, including David Mairowitz and Robert Crumb's "melodramatic metamorphosis" showing Gregor as a beetle, Peter Kuper's "alienated Gregor" depicting him as an insect with a human head, and Václav Gatarik's Czech-language version in which Gregor appears as "grotesque," with an insect's body and an exaggerated and distorted human head. She concludes that "the variety of graphic interpretations demonstrates how readings of the text change depending upon the time and place."

Stephen E. Tabachnick provides a close reading of Australian artist Nicki

Greenberg's adaptation of F. Scott Fitzgerald's *The Great Gatsby*. He carefully examines this striking and unusual adaptation, which features invented creatures, rather than human beings, to represent the characters, and which uses the imagery of a photo album throughout to represent Nick's memory of past events. According to Tabachnick, the result is an adaptation with much "value added," which offers a completely original interpretation of Fitzgerald's classic novel.

In a departure from the adaptation of novels, Jan Baetens discusses Raymond Queneau's classic 1947 text *Exercises in Style*, and compares it with Matt Madden's adaptation, entitled *99 Ways to Tell a Story*. Queneau was one of the founders of the OuLiPo (Ouvrage de Littérature Potentialle, or workshop of potential literature) school of French literature, which imposed fantastic constraints on itself, such as writer Georges Perec's not using the letter "e" in an entire novel, for instance. Baetens examines Queneau's work in terms of verbal constraint, and Madden's work in terms of visual constraint, in order to compare the pedagogical and other differences between Queneau's prose text and Madden's graphic novel. He concludes that Madden's book is a "love song addressed to the comics medium," and that like Queneau's original, it is a classic work.

Darren Harris-Fain's analysis of graphic novel adaptations of Ray Bradbury's science fiction novels closes the collection. Harris-Fain, taking an historical approach, points out that Bradbury had a lifelong love of comics and authorized several graphic novel adaptations of his work, including *Fahrenheit 451*. He explores the ways in which Bradbury's original vision was influenced by comics as well as the ways in which graphic novel adaptations of his work helped realize the goals of Bradbury's prose writing in striking new ways.

As all of these essays demonstrate, while pure literary texts will always have their unique merits, graphic novel adaptations can bring a new vision and a new interpretation to the works upon which they are based. We hope that readers will enjoy and profit from reading these individual scholarly perspectives on such adaptations, all of which aim to show just how exciting a form the graphic novel has become.

Note

1. Hutcheon cites Robert Stam, "Beyond Fidelity: The Dialogics of Adaptation," 2000, p. 64.

Works Cited

Eisner, Will. *Graphic Storytelling and Visual Narrative*. Tamarac: Poorhouse Press, 1996. Print.

Heer, Jeet, and Kent Worcester. "Introduction." *A Comics Studies Reader*. Ed. Jeet Heer and Kent Worcester. Jackson: University Press of Mississippi, 2009. Print.

Hutcheon, Linda. *A Theory of Adaptation*. New York: Routledge, 2006. Print.

Leitch, Thomas. "Twelve Fallacies in Contemporary Adaptation Theory." *Criticism*. 45.2 (2003): 149–171. *Wilson OmniFile*. Web. 27 February 2011.

McCloud, Scott. *Understanding Comics*. Lettering by Bob Lappan. New York: HarperCollins, 1993. Print.

McLuhan, Marshall. *Understanding Media: The Extensions of Man*. New York: Signet, 1964. Print.

Perret, Marion. "Not Just Condensation: How Comic Books Interpret Shakespeare." *College Literature*. 31.4 (2004): 72–93. *Project Muse*. Web. 5 May 2011.

Stam, Robert. "Beyond Fidelity: The Dialogics of Adaptation," *Film Adaptation*. James Naremore (ed.), New Brunswick, NJ: Rutgers University Press, 2000, 54–76. Print.

Tabachnick, Stephen E. "The Graphic Novel and the Age of Transition: A Survey and Analysis." *English Literature in Transition*, 1880–1920 53.1 (2010): 3–28. *Project Muse*. Web. 5 May 2011.

_____. *Teaching the Graphic Novel*. New York: MLA, 2009. Print.

Thomas, Roy, adapt. *The Picture of Dorian Gray. By Oscar Wilde.* Illustrated by Sebastian Fiumara. New York: Marvel Illustrated, 2009. N.p. Print.

Here There Be Monsters (and Heroes)
Homer's *Odyssey* and the Graphic Novel

Paul D. Streufert

As a professor of literature who works primarily on the Greco-Roman classics, I enjoy engaging my students in questions of canonicity. In survey classes where students read and discuss authors like Homer and Shakespeare, perhaps two of the most revered literary figures in the popular imagination, they are often surprised to learn that texts like *Iliad* and *Hamlet* had wide appeal in their original performative contexts. They come to recognize even the plays of Sophocles, with their philosophical ambiguities and elevated language, were viewed at the Civic Dionysia by thousands of Athenians of varying levels of class and education. Though traditional biases towards or against high and low literature have been fading for decades, at a university like mine, a state school in East Texas, I am often surprised by the conversations I have with students and colleagues about the value of studying graphic texts, which many still consider undeserving of serious academic attention. Finding and investigating the nexus between classic literature and visual texts has proven to be a useful piece of evidence in arguing for the significance of popular forms of storytelling. Of all the works in the canon of Greek mythology, Homer's *Odyssey* provides a story well suited to visual narrative. With its heroes and villains, magic and violence, and overt sexuality, it reads much like a superhero comic of the mid to late twentieth century. Illustrators and writers have acknowledged its adaptability, as *Odyssey* has inspired at least five graphic novel versions in the past five years. This essay will focus on three: Gareth Hinds's *The Odyssey* (2010), Dan Jolley and Thomas Yeates's *Odysseus: Escaping Poseidon's Curse* (2008), and Roy Thomas and Greg Tocchini's *The Odyssey*, published by Marvel Comics in 2010. Using books 9–12, the so-called "travels of Odysseus," the essay will compare the treatment of the hero figure and his conquering of monstrous villains, specifically the Cyclops Polyphemus and the witch Circe. These three graphic novels deconstruct and refigure the heroic and monstrous as they target younger readers, many of whom, presumably, are encountering Homer's story for the first time. Yet each text reveals a deft understanding of one of Homer's central themes: the relationship between monstrosity and social connection. The authors and illustrators of the graphic texts highlight the social disconnection of Polyphemus and Circe, much like the villains in superhero comics. The Homeric poets emphasized this trope through the ancient Greek concept of *xenia* or "hospitality." Each graphic novel gestures towards this idea, reinforcing its prominence in Homer's original as well as its resonance for modern readers.

Hinds's graphic novel *The Odyssey* ranks as the most narratively detailed and thorough of the recent graphic adaptations. It includes both the most popular stories, such as Odysseus's embarrassing nude encounter with the princess Nausicaa and his massacre of Penelope's suitors, as well as more obscure ones, such as the Telemachy—the stories of Odysseus's son in the first four books of Homer—and the often omitted book 24, in which Odysseus makes peace with the suitors' families. For his visual media, Hinds works with watercolors and pencil, creating a dream-like atmosphere of shadow and light, particularly useful in the seascapes and Odysseus's trip to the Underworld in book 11. The verbal text, for which Hinds credits inspiration from a variety of translators including Butler, Rieu, and Fitzgerald (Brannon 45), appears in computer-generated rather than hand-lettered form. Unsurprisingly, his graphic novel works best when it tells the story visually, which he does admirably for all 24 books of the original. Published the same year, Thomas and Tocchini's *The Odyssey* includes fewer narrative details than Hinds, yet keeps the overall structure of the story intact. Thomas, who wrote *Conan the Barbarian* among other titles for Marvel (Thomas and Tocchini 5), emphasizes the heroic attitudes and actions of Odysseus, making him less self-aware and more confident than in Hinds or Homer. Tocchini's illustrations support this masculine heroic ideal as well, showing Odysseus as virile and youthful, while portraying nearly every female character as full-figured and thin. His portrayal of the goddess Athena ranks as the most innovative of the portrayals of the original cast. In the Homeric original, in other classical sources like the tragedian Aeschylus, and in Greek visual art, Athena appears androgynous. She is the chaste virgin goddess, resembling her father Zeus more than her half-sister Artemis or Aphrodite, the goddess of sexuality. In his graphic novel, Tocchini portrays her as full-figured and barely dressed, a young, lithe divinity with Nordic features. Eschewing historical conventions and context, Thomas and Tocchini clearly indicate that Odysseus's story rests easily in the tradition of superhero comics, a fact underpinned by its publication by Marvel Comics.

Published two years earlier than these graphic novels and aimed at the youngest readers, *Odysseus: Escaping Poseidon's Curse* tells just a small part of the ancient original. As part of the Graphic Universe series under Lerner Publishing, *Escaping Poseidon's Curse* is restricted by a forty page limit, necessitating writer Dan Jolley and illustrator Thomas Yeates to keep the story simple and focused on action. They confine their story to books 9–12, the so-called "travels of Odysseus," and highlight his slaying of monsters like Scylla, a dog-faced hybrid creature featured on their cover. Due to space restraints, Jolley and Yeates pass over the more contemplative moments of the hero's journey, such as the trip to the Underworld, where Odysseus interviews a long-dead prophet Teiresias, as well as family members and colleagues from the Trojan War. Like Thomas and Tocchini, they play up the story's comic book themes, while keeping more of the narrative and historical consistencies of the original, an approach supported by an academic consultant credited by the editors (Jolley and Yeates 4).

All three graphic novel adaptations share a concern with the heroic response to monstrosity and explore it through the common use of the episodes with the Cyclops Polyphemus and the witch Circe. Like comic book super-villains, their lack of connection to others and their anti-social behavior mark them as monstrous, even as much as or more so than their appearance. Lack of connectedness, both for the ancient readers of the *Odyssey* and contemporary comic book readers, defines a character as a monster or a villain, a point emphasized in a recent study of the Marvel Universe. In 2007, physicist P.M. Gleiser and his team analyzed the social network "formed by 6,486 characters and 12,942 books" (1). They observed that heroes in Marvel comics are richly connected in a community, while villains lack commensurate connection and have little sense of unity (4). The replaying of these anxieties in the ancient source and its modern graphic adaptations supports the idea that social disconnection and the subsequent breakdown of civility are a shared concern. As James Twitchell argues in his reading of visual horror, "People ... have been drawn to recreate their fears in pictures and then pass those images on, almost as if they believed that art could control present and future anxiety" (4). Though contemporary audiences might not literally fear witches or one-eyed monsters, a fascination with their disruption to society plays a major part in the retelling of the ancient myth.

As a verbal text, Homer's original description of Polyphemus and the Cyclopes focuses much more on their lack of civilized behavior rather than their terrifying appearance. They neither farm nor manufacture, two key functions of civilization. Homer calls them *athemistoi*, "lawless," and describes them primarily in political terms:

> They have no assemblies or laws but live
> In high mountain caves, ruling their own
> Children and wives and ignoring each other [Lombardo 9.110–12].

Of particular note in this description is the Cyclopes' unwillingness to collaborate with each other, an unthinkable lifestyle for the Greeks of the Homeric Archaic Age and beyond. As Aristotle reminds us, humans need a *polis*, a city which affords protection and connection. The Cyclopes' refusal to assemble or engage in other forms of government marks them as monstrous, more animal than human. After Odysseus and his men meet Polyphemus, Homer spends surprisingly little time explicitly describing the Cyclops's physical appearance and does not mention his unnatural single eye. Instead, the poet focuses on the monster's uncivilized behavior in terms of *xenia* or "hospitality." According to the *xenia* code, the Greek visitors who have come to Polyphemus's cave have a right to expect food, shelter, and protection from their would-be host, yet he does not follow these conventions, asking the Greeks to identify themselves upon first seeing them—a faux pas in terms of *xenia*—and then cruelly eating six of them. Odysseus, trying to modify the behavior, invokes Zeus, the Greek father-god and guarantor of *xenia*, but Polyphemus refuses to follow the rules of hospitality, the cornerstone of civilization in the ancient world. Not surprisingly, the graphic novel versions of this episode highlight Polyphemus's intimidating appearance, yet each keeps a subtle focus on the lawlessness so terrifying to Homer's original audience.

Hinds's version of the episode begins with the Greeks on the island of the Cyclopes, unaware of the anarchy they are about to encounter. On the bottom panel of page 93, Hinds shows Odysseus and his crew eating and drinking alongside their boat, a foreshadow of the feast they will become, but more significantly the panel highlights the markers of civilization they will soon leave behind. Odysseus holds a skin of wine, something the Cyclopes do not make and cannot handle, the very tool the hero will use to outsmart the monster in the near future. Hinds also highlights the ship in this panel, a clear indicator of the collective effort of civilization, and the means by which the Greeks will escape the monster's island. Two panels later, as they are about to enter Polyphemus's cave, Hinds shows the Greeks going from a place of order—their beach camp and even a fenced-off pen, presumably for the Cyclops's livestock—to one of darkness and chaos. The cave entrance is painted in black, and Odysseus and his men approach it tentatively (94).

Several panels later, the monster appears and readers get a sense of his physical, rather than political, monstrosity. As in the ancient source, Hinds's Polyphemus is huge, at least four or five times as tall as Odysseus. In style and body type, he is clearly other to the civilized Greeks. He is hairless, and his lack of a beard stands in stark contrast to the sailors. His nipples are pierced and he has multiple scars on his chest and arms (95). In later panels, Hinds underscores his animal nature with sharp fangs, nowhere mentioned in Homer (100). In his dialogue and narration, Hinds keeps the idea of *xenia* and its violation at the forefront, exploring the idea in much the same way as the original, but in his visuals, he ensures that modern readers see and fear the Polyphemus's anarchy. As if to highlight these points, he washes all the panels which take place in the cave in a orange-red hue, ostensibly the glow of Cyclops's fire.

While Hinds takes a conservative approach to his source material concerning the violation of hospitality, covering nearly all of the same plot points as Homer, he also plays with forms and techniques traditionally found in comics. He uses onomatopoeia, sound words included to enliven the action of the visuals, throughout *The Odyssey*, but relies on them heavily in this particular episode. The words, which layer the text with a dark humor, invoke the fight scenes between heroes and villains in comic books. When Polyphemus kills the first of Odysseus's men by smashing the victim's head on a rock, his first aggressive anti-social act, Hinds approximates the sound with the word "SPLURNCH" (97). In retaliation, Odysseus and the other Greeks blind him with a wooden shaft heated in the fire. Hinds underscores the visceral nature of this act with the word "KSSSSS" and shows the victim responding with the comic book interjection "EEEARGGH!," both of which he hand letters rather than employing the computer generated font used for dialogue (102–3). While Hinds explores Homer's ancient ideas, he never loses sight of the narrative possibilities of hero meeting and defeating monster.

Thomas and Tocchini's treatment of the Cyclops episode varies in several significant ways from Hinds's, though the theme of hospitality and its violation remains at the forefront. In this version, Polyphemus looks even more animalistic. Like Hinds and Homer, he towers over the humans, carrying a tree trunk and three mature sheep from his flock in his first appearance (55). Tocchini's illustration here evokes a world of otherness, both for the Greek characters and the modern audience. This muscular Polyphemus wears decoration meant to terrify and intimidate. A blue-grey tribal tattoo covers the purple skin on his skin and shoulders, while a gigantic chain adorns his neck, prominently displaying a charm in the shape of an eyeball (55). His own eye, bright red and disproportionately large, along with fangs, suggest savagery and a predatory nature.

To complement Tocchini's vision of the Cyclops, Thomas weaves the *xenia* theme carefully throughout the scene. When Odysseus asks for hospitality, the monster screams, "We Cyclopes care nothing for Zeus or any of your blessed gods, for we are stronger than they," coupling his lawlessness with hubris (56). On seeing his men killed "as though they had been puppies," Odysseus prays, "Father Zeus, preserve us!" (58). Even as the monster scares through appearance, he also reminds readers of the importance of civilized, polite behavior. As in superhero comic books, those who break the law often pay a price, and Polyphemus suffers eye-gouging and blindness for his crime. Though few would debate that Polyphemus got what he deserved, Thomas and Tocchini make a significant narrative and artistic choice to play up the pathos at the end of this episode. In the Homeric version, Odysseus sneaks out of the cave tied to the underbelly of the giant's biggest ram. The blind Cyclops checks the top of each animal which exits the cave, and pauses when he stops the ram carrying Odysseus. He addresses the ram:

> My poor ram, why are you leaving the cave
> Last of all? You've never lagged behind before.
> [...] Now you're last of all. Are you sad
> About your master's eye? A bad man blinded me,
> Him and his nasty friends, getting me drunk,
> Noman—but he's not out of trouble yet!
> If only you could understand and talk,
> You could tell me where he's hiding. I would
> Smash him to bits and spatter his brains
> All over the cave [9.445–46; 450b–457a].

Though all three graphic novel versions contain this narrative moment, Thomas and Tocchini develop it more than the others, juxtaposing their Polyphemus's animalistic visage with his vulnerability. A pathetic bandage, tied like a blindfold, encircles his head, and he imagines the sadness of his prime ram as he lifts it off ground, exposing the hero beneath (68–9). His speech follows Homer closely, revealing a connection between Polyphemus and his livestock, a reminder that the monster is himself more animal than human.

In *Escaping Poseidon's Curse*, Jolley and Yeates take a much different approach to Polyphemus, portraying him less as an animal, preferring instead to draw him as a sort of caveman, a word used by Odysseus before he even sees the Cyclops (14). Though he wears an animal skin, his beard identifies him as human and not unlike the Greeks. Yet Jolley and Yeates use the *xenia* theme throughout the episode, including one ironic detail omitted by the graphic novel versions. After Odysseus and his men blind the Cyclops, the victim's neighbors gather around his cave, alarmed by his cries and offering to help. Odysseus had already set up his most famous trick—introducing himself as "Nobody" to the mentally slow creature. In this version, the Cyclopes ask Polyphemus "What has happened? Are you hurt?" When he responds that Nobody is hurting him, they tell him, "If Nobody has hurt you, it must be Lord Zeus who has caused your pain" (19). Though the neighboring creatures do not realize it, they have assessed the situation accurately, as Zeus punishes those who break the *xenia* code. Though Odysseus had blinded him, ancient audiences would have known the blinding to have been directed by the father-god. Hinds and Thomas and Tocchini skip this detail, but Jolley and Yeates's inclusion of it reinforces the primacy of the hospitality idea for their younger, modern readers. They create a monstrosity that is both visual and cultural, playing on tropes of otherness that operate in the modern world. As Stephen T. Asma argues in *On Monsters*, "The idea that foreign cultures are threatening because their cultural values exclude or compete with one's own is certainly contentious, but it is, rightly or wrongly, a dominant position of late" (241). Polyphemus's lack of civilized behavior and its correction by the hero Odysseus drives this scene as much as the monster's appearance or cannibalism, and graphic novel artists have explored this ancient idea in their own translations of the work.

After two brief incidents, one with the helpful king, Aeolus, and another with the barbaric Laestrygonians, the next monstrous villain the Greeks encounter is the witch Circe. Like the Cyclops narrative before it, this story focuses on hospitality and its violation, yet Circe's monstrosity emerges in much more subtle ways. Creatures like Polyphemus, which look monstrous, allow characters and audience to read the hero/villain dichotomy quickly and easily. According to the Homeric account, Odysseus and what remains of his team land on the island of Aeaea, and, after becoming aware of Circe's presence, Odysseus sends out half of the men for reconnaissance. They find Circe "singing in a lovely voice / As she moved about weaving a great tapestry" (Lombardo 10.237–38). Circe's appearance, one of proper civilized behavior, particularly in terms of gender roles, calms the men and keeps them off guard (Buitron-Oliver and Cohen 36). Unlike Polyphemus, who reveals himself as monstrous by his appearance and breach of *xenia*, Circe looks appealing and follows the hospitality code. She invites them in and serves wine, the proper sequence for hosts entertaining guests. This hospitable act disguises her violation of *xenia*, as she had laced the wine with a drug that transforms the men into pigs. One survivor, the cautious Eurylochus, had suspected a trap and reports to Odysseus, who in turn goes to confront Circe. Along the way he is intercepted by the god Hermes, who gives him a magical plant which will protect him from the witch's magic. When he faces Circe, she tries to transform him; Odysseus threatens to kill her with his sword, and after making her swear an oath not to hurt him, the encounter turns sexual. Afterwards she returns the pigs to their prior form, and Odysseus and the crew enjoy Circe's generous hospitality for an entire year.

This narrative moment in Homer offers a unique opportunity for comparison between modern graphic novel illustrators and artists from the ancient world, as it was an extremely popular subject for vase painters from the Archaic through the Classical periods—roughly the seventh through the fourth centuries BCE (Buitron-Oliver and Cohen 36). Of particular interest are those pieces that depict the moment when Circe tries to transform Odysseus, and his masculine, action-hero response. In Homer's text, the event is subtly charged in terms of gender and sexuality: "At this, I drew the sharp sword that hung by my thigh / And lunged at Circe as if I meant to kill her" (Lombardo 10.342–43). A fifth-century Attic krater, a wine-mixing bowl, in the National Museum in Warsaw (140352) preserves one of the best examples of this encounter (Reeder 405–406). The vase depicts Odysseus lunging at the retreating Circe in an attempt to dominate. The hero's hands display two obvious markers of his masculinity: in his right hand he holds a sword near his thigh, just as described by Homer, but in his right he grips what appears to be a scabbard (Benson 405). Both images are phallic, with the sword positioned in such a way as to indicate the sexual dominance to come. The scabbard too appears as a signifier of male dominance, though it is less clear why Odysseus would thrust the weapon's case towards Circe's face. In contrast, Circe drops her only defense, the poisoned wine cup, leaving her vulnerable and empty handed in front of her attacker. Her dress marks her as non–Greek (Benson 406), a sort of villain in the world of the Greek hero. The implicit action on this vase, with one dominant character advancing and another timidly retreating, both with weapons signifying their fighting style, shares some commonalities with comic book art. Like a superhero out of the mid-twentieth century, Odysseus wears a cape with a hood, which provides a sense of his movement. Circe's flowing skirt too implies motion, as she runs from the hero. As in many other ancient depictions of Circe (see Cohen, plates 31 and 32), she is usually shown with her cup, the physical token of her villainous identity in ancient art. Like the Joker's playing cards or the Green Goblin's pumpkin bombs, this accessory at once identifies her and, in its abandonment in the Warsaw krater, marks her failure in besting the hero.

Though Hinds, Tocchini, and Yeates showed a great deal of variance in their illustrations of Polyphemus, a consistency appears in their portrayal of Circe. All three include a scene similar to that on the Warsaw krater, yet emphasize different details. Hinds, who throughout his text prefers an earthy and historically accurate approach, dresses Circe in white, with a chastely covered head. Like the painter of the Warsaw krater, he keeps the phallic imagery at the forefront, showing both Odysseus's sword near his thigh, as well as his scabbard in a prominent position. Circe crouches at his knees in the traditional pose of supplication, without her wand or her cup of poison, tokens of her power (fig. 1). While this panel establishes the dominance of the hero, Hinds intriguingly juxtaposes it with another panel on the subsequent page, separated by images of Odysseus and his men enjoying the *xenia* of the witch's household. Four panels later, Odysseus himself kneels before the naked Circe asking her for help with his return to Ithaca (125). She brushes her hair as she listens to him, her head now uncovered, as she now holds equal power with the hero. Hinds explores the multiple layers of this complex relationship, as they interact as enemies, lovers, and finally partners in preparing Odysseus for the next step in his journey, a trip to the Underworld. Hinds's vision of this moment in the hero's story demonstrates a sort of equality between the genders, as well as between hero and villain.

Thomas and Tocchini's telling of the scene hits many of the same notes, especially in terms of *xenia* and the seduction of Odysseus and his men by Circe. Yet they do find other points to emphasize as well, particularly the use of the witch's wand as an instrument of her magic. The device is mentioned in Homer; the Greek term he uses is *rhabdos*, which can denote a stick used in sorcery, or, in a less fantastic context, simply a rod used for corporal punishment, both of which apply to Circe's actions here. In Tocchini's action sequence of her attempt to transform Odysseus, thereby taking his manhood and his hope of returning home, she clearly uses it as both a physical weapon to direct his body and signifier of her own mystical power. After giving Odysseus the drink that should turn him into a pig, she grabs the

Figure 1. Circe swears an oath in Gareth Hinds's *The Odyssey* (124).

stick while he looks away and attacks him with it, only to lose it to him and his drawn sword (87). In figure 2, Odysseus is shown with two weapons, his sword, in the traditional place near his thigh, as described by Homer, and her magic *rhabdos*. In this illustration, much like the War-saw krater, Odysseus holds two phallic symbols, and his taking Circe's wand clearly establishes her defeat at his heroic hands. Tocchini's Circe bends and twists in every panel, giving a sense of motion with her contrapposto positioning. Unlike Hinds, who works for a stronger sense of historical

Figure 2. Odysseus negotiates with Circe in Thomas and Tocchini's *The Odyssey* (88).

accuracy, Circe's immodest dress invokes present-day costuming, surely marking her as foreign to Odysseus and making her body one of the very devices she uses to conquer men. Gone also is the sense of collaboration and trust developed in Hinds, as Tocchini keeps the two characters visually at odds throughout their year-long encounter. Given these emphases, Tocchini's illus-

Figure 3. Jolley and Yeates include Odysseus's crew, transformed into pigs, observing his encounter with Circe (25).

tration may be the closest to the Warsaw krater than any of the three graphic novels.

    Jolley and Yeates's account of Odysseus's encounter with Circe reinforces many of the traditional elements found in Homer. The crew discovers her singing and weaving, luring the men in with promises of safety and domesticity. She invokes hospitality directly, both to the men as they eat, and as she welcomes Odysseus several panels later. Though she uses no poison in their version, her glowing magic wand appears throughout, and, in its ability to transform men, serves as the chief sign of her villainous power. Present too is the scene of aggression, when Odysseus draws his weapon and advances as if to attack her. They rely less on explicit metaphors than the other graphic novels, but like the others, this Odysseus establishes his authority and demands the return of his crew as he holds a spear to Circe's throat. In their telling, Jolley and Yeates include a detail in the story that Hinds and Thomas and Tocchini do not, which keeps their version consistent with ancient vase paintings of the Circe scene. They take care to show the victims of the witch's magic and the stakes for which the hero is fighting. When Odysseus first encounters Circe at her doorway, he stands in an aggressive pose, spear and shield up (25). Her pose is seductive, with her arms extended and her right leg slightly forward. To the right of Odysseus, penned in Circe's yard, stand his men, now a herd of muddy pigs (fig. 3). Though not usually the most expressive of animals, Yeates anthropomorphizes them, drawing some with sad faces, while others oink in distress. Homer makes no mention of the transformed companions watching Odysseus confront Circe, yet ancient artists often included them in vase paintings of this scene. On the Warsaw krater, a pig-headed man cowers behind Odysseus as the hero attacks the witch. Numerous other examples from Attic, Etruscan, and Boeotian art indicate its common usage across the ancient world (Cohen plates 32, 34, 36, and 38). By reminding their readers of Circe's victims, men made into monsters and kept from their journey home, Jolley and Yeates invoke an ancient tradition while emphasizing a different theme than Hinds or Thomas and Tocchini.

In its treatment of heroes and monsters, Homer's *Odyssey* fits quite well thematically in the world of the present-day graphic text. Like a comic book, its action sequences thrill readers even as the story explores constructions of power, gender, and selfhood's relationship with otherness. As Gareth Hinds asserts, "it is THE perfect book to make into a graphic novel" (Brannon 44). The hero's defeat of monsters like Polyphemus and Circe, who flout Zeus's laws of hospitality, reinforces the value of civilized behavior in our own time and circumstances. The term itself reveals this idea, as "*Monster* derives from the Latin word *monstrum*, which in turn derives from the root *monere* (to warn). To be a monster is to be an omen" (Asma 13). Civilization and its rules still matter to readers, and the creators of these *Odyssey* adaptations recognize and tease out the nuances of this idea. Other excellent graphic novel versions of Homer's work have appeared in recent years, most notably Seymour Chwast's *Homer: The Odyssey* (2012) and Christopher Ford's *Stickman Odyssey: An Epic Doodle Book One* (2011), both of which take a more playful and less textually conservative approach to the original. Their lighthearted and humorous approach to the story reminds us how funny and entertaining Homer can be, while in contrast Hinds, Thomas and Tocchini, and Jolley and Yeates draw clear lines of connection between our fears and those of the ancients.

Works Cited

Asma, Stephen T. *On Monsters: An Unnatural History of Our Worst Fears.* Oxford: Oxford University Press, 2009. Print.

Benson, Carol. "Krater with Circe and Odysseus." *Pandora: Women in Classical Greece.* Ed. Ellen D. Reeder. Princeton: Princeton University Press, 1995. 405–406. Print.

Brannon, April. "Seeing The Odyssey: An Interview with Gareth Hinds." *Signal* 35.2 (2012): 44–45. Print.

Buitron-Oliver, Diana, and Beth Cohen. "Between Skylla and Penelope: Female Characters of the Odyssey in Archaic and Classica Greek Art." *The Distaff Side: Representing the Female in Homer's Odyssey.* Ed. Beth Cohen. Oxford: Oxford University Press, 1995. 29–58. Print.

Chwast, Seymour. *Homer: The Odyssey.* New York: Bloomsbury, 2012. Print.

Cohen, Beth, ed. *The Distaff Side: Representing the Female in Homer's Odyssey*. Oxford: Oxford University Press, 1995. Print.
Ford, Christopher. *Stickman Odyssey: An Epic Doodle Book One*. New York: Philomel, 2011. Print.
Gleiser, P.M. "How to Become a Superhero." arXiv.org Cornell University, 12 Feb. 2013. Web. 18 Sept. 2013 http://arxiv.org/abs/0708.2410.
Hinds, Gareth, and Homer. *The Odyssey: A Graphic Novel*. Somerville, Mass: Candlewick, 2010 Print.
Jolley, Dan and Thomas Yeates. *Odysseus: Escaping Poseidon's Curse: A Greek Legend*. Minneapolis: Lerner, 2008. Print.
Lombardo, Stanley, trans. *Odyssey*. Indianapolis: Hackett, 2000. Print.
Reeder, Ellen D., ed. *Pandora: Women in Classical Greece*. Princeton: Princeton University Press, 1995. Print.
Thomas, Roy, and Greg Tocchini. *The Odyssey*. New York: Marvel, 2010. Print.
Twitchell, James B. *Dreadful Pleasures: An Anatomy of Modern Horror*. Oxford: Oxford University Press, 1985. Print.

Hwaet If? Beowulf *in Comics*
Jason Tondro

Once held up as the archetypal academic text—a story no one read unless it was assigned in class—*Beowulf* has become more popular in the last fifteen years. Some of the credit for this must be granted to Heaney's wonderful translation, which has given classrooms "poetry that means business." The impact of Heaney's edition made Beowulf a marketable property again, resulting in a wave of Hollywood adaptations. But Beowulf comics have—with notable exceptions—been driven by personal artistic vision rather than by the twin idols of Heaney and Hollywood. It has often been noted (perhaps best by Scott McCloud in his follow-up book *Making Comics*) that one of the things that makes comics production so exciting is its relatively low entry fee; it can take tens of thousands of dollars to make the cheapest of films, but a writer and artist with the time and dedication can create a comic for almost nothing (McCloud 184–187). This has allowed talented individuals who have a keen personal interest in the Beowulf story to create idiosyncratic adaptations and appropriations of the original poem, almost all of which have some use in the classroom.

This particular study will focus on three especially interesting and pedagogically lucrative texts: Jerry Bingham's single volume *Beowulf* from 1984; Gareth Hinds's three-issue *Beowulf*, eventually collected into a single-volume edition; and IDW's 6-issue adaptation of Neil Gaiman and Roger Avery's cinematic *Beowulf* from 2007, also collected into a single volume. Along the way, two other versions of the character will also be discussed: the unfortunate *Beowulf: Dragon Slayer* from DC's Silver Age; and *Kid Beowulf*, a recent, thoughtful, and fun "prequel" for middle-school readers.[1]

Jerry Bingham's Beowulf

Jerry Bingham's comics reputation will always rest on the memorable and influential *Batman: Son of the Demon*, but he is an astonishingly prolific creator who has worked in many fields, from illustration and fine art to a stint as a Disney "Imagineer." In the early 1980s, before his landmark Batman story, Bingham pitched a single-volume adaptation of *Beowulf* to Marvel and DC. Ralph Bakshi's animated adaptation of *Lord of the Rings* had revitalized interest in fantasy, but the "Big Two" would not touch the project, and it eventually landed at First Comics (Bingham, "Mileage"). This was in the early years of the independent comics movement; First, Eclipse, Comico, and other publishers were competing with Marvel and DC for shelf-space at dedicated comic book shops. Despite the many rejections Bingham's proposal had earned, the book was exceedingly well received upon release and won the first Kirby award for "Graphic Album."[2]

Bingham's Beowulf is "freely translated and adapted," (1) but faithful to the text as far as it goes. He has made alliteration a priority, so the poem maintains some of its distinctive sound. The differences lie in the many cuts to the tale necessary to bring the project in at 42 pages. Both Wealtheow and Unferth are entirely absent, for example, as are the instructive (some would say distracting) interludes by bards which shed light on the social customs and internecine concerns of the feuding Danes. These cuts are especially disappointing because they leave Grendel's mother as the only feminine presence in the book. There are many challenges to teaching *Beowulf*, but one of them is the fact that the poem is written for, and largely concerns, warrior men; half our modern audience thus begins the reading from a point of exclusion. Some adaptations of *Beowulf* address this, but Bingham's edition is not one of them. There are no sympathetic women in this book. The end of the story, while suitably tragic thanks to Beowulf's death, also makes no mention of the greater, looming tragedy of the certain destruction of Beowulf's realm and the enslavement of the Geats. In that sense, it is a simpler tale; unsurprising, given its brevity.

Visually, Bingham is consciously tapping Frank Frazetta, John Buscema, and Hal Foster (fig. 1). Rather than create an authentic representation of 8th century Scandinavians, Bingham is drawing on a tradition of heroic fantasy fiction that makes every Geat and Dane look like a barbarian from the wilds of Cimmeria. Faithful reproductions of 7th century Anglo-Saxon helms are drawn alongside Viking horned helmets from a Wagnerian epic (11). Wiglaf is visually indistinguishable from Conan (40). The debt to *Prince Valiant* is found not only in the art style but also in the use of narrative captions through-

Figure 1. In these panels from p. 31 of Jerry Bingham's *Beowulf*, the hero emerges from the lair of Grendel's mother. First Comics.

out instead of more traditional speech balloons. The result is a comic that feels more like an "illustrated story" and less like "a comic book," which can make it more accessible and friendly to a student audience with little or no exposure to comics.

All this may make a Beowulf scholar cringe, but the book remains very loyal to the primary narrative of the tale and has been used to teach *Beowulf* in classrooms from elementary school all the way to research universities. The larger social context of *Beowulf*, cut from the comic, can be introduced through more traditional means while Bingham's graphic novel carries the main weight of the plot. Bingham, who is very approachable and has both a Facebook presence and an active blog, has very fond memories of this book and likes to tell the story of the day he got a box full of art made by elementary school students who had just read *Beowulf* and drawn their own versions inspired by his pages (Bingham, "Mileage"). He is also the first to admit he did not do enough historical research before making the book which was, after all, a product of his early career. After he became aware of increasing scholarly interest in his book (including the research that would lead to this article), Bingham wrote a long blog essay about how his *Beowulf* came to be. There, he cites Tolkien's interest in the poem and reveals his own surprise that the book was well received, considering the fact that some of the Kirby Award judges were the same people who rejected the book when he first pitched it (Bingham, "Mileage"). It is *Beowulf*, not Batman, which Bingham cites as the favorite comics project of his career.

This may be the best use of Bingham's graphic novel version: An instructor and her class could read the book and post questions or comments directly to Bingham, and he will answer them in a generous and charitable voice. This level of engagement with a creator is not usually possible when we're teaching, especially when we're teaching Medieval literature. Bingham's *Beowulf* is out of print and First Comics long out of business, but single copies can be found for very affordable prices on eBay or Amazon; an instructor would then need to scan each page in color and distribute this electronic edition to students.

Beowulf: Dragon Slayer

A decade before Bingham's book, DC published *Beowulf: Dragon Slayer*. The Comics Code Authority had just been revised (Nyberg 170–174), allowing for the depiction of horror and of monsters previously banned; this resulted in a rush of new titles like Marvel's *Tomb of Dracula* and DC's *House of Mystery*. Conan proved very successful over at Marvel, and DC responded with a raft of competing titles, the most interesting of which was Mike Grell's *Warlord*. But one of these books was *Beowulf: Dragon Slayer*, written by Michael Uslan and drawn by Peruvian artist Ricardo Villamonte. Uslan was already known for teaching a course on comics and American culture at Indiana University, but the *Batman* films which he would go on to produce were a decade in the future; Villamonte would later go on to do a long stint on Marvel's series *Power Man & Iron Fist*.

The protagonist of *Beowulf: Dragon Slayer* is unrecognizable to readers of the original poem. He is part Conan, part Tarzan: A "noble savage" with an "ape-beast" for a father (1: 7), who wields a massive club and whose helmet is adorned with silver horns recovered from a battle with a minotaur. With its confused story and a hodgepodge of antagonists that include everything from Dracula to Satan to flying saucers, *Beowulf: Dragon Slayer* is a truly execrable comic. This has not prevented scholars from writing about it, however, thanks largely to the influence of John Gardner's 1971 novel *Grendel* on writer Michael Uslan (1: 19).[3] In *Beowulf: Dragon Slayer*, Grendel spends much of his time shouting at the sky and lamenting life's injustices in a mode lifted from Gardner's novel. Beowulf himself is accompanied by "The Shaper" (1: 7), whose name is a direct translation of the Scandinavian bard, or "scop," and another reference to Gardner's book. But this Shaper is also portrayed with a maniacal laugh lifted from the Joker, and he works his magic by intoning spells backwards, a motif lifted from DC's character Zatanna. The fact that these "incantations" are all self-referential in-jokes (the first example, from page 17 of issue 1: "ARTSUH TARAZ HCARPS OSLA") does nothing to endear the character to critics. While Beowulf experiences picaresque adventures in which he drinks the venom of the black viper or fetches "the ambrosia of the zumak fruit," Grendel kills Satan (!) and takes over Hell.

Despite an attempt by DC to re-launch the title as part of its "New 52" initiative, the original run of *Beowulf: Dragon Slayer* has never been reprinted; because *Beowulf: Dragon Slayer* is a book best forgotten once read, this becomes a fortunate coincidence.

Gareth Hinds' Beowulf

Gareth Hinds's ambitious three issue adaptation of *Beowulf* was originally self published under the imprint THECOMIC.COM, but has since been reprinted by Candlewick. Both versions are available in single volume editions and in quantity directly from Hinds through his website. When Hinds first did this book, he used an abridged version of the century-old Francis Gummere translation of the poem, and an authorial note at the end of the project voices Hinds's appreciation for this version, which he calls "the most poetic, most authentic, and all-around best English translation ever produced," at least at the time of the book's composition in 1998 (2: inside back cover). This translation is not as accessible to students as Heaney's, but it is more loyal to the syntax and structure of the Anglo-Saxon line; this creates useful moments of comparison in the classroom when placed alongside a more contemporary translation. Despite his love of Gummere, Hinds swapped it out for A.J. Church's prose text when Candlewick published its second edition, also correcting some printing problems with the color of Hinds's first issue.

In a very real sense, however, it doesn't much matter which translation of *Beowulf* Hinds is using, because his is a version based on artistic vision rather than the poet's ear. There are long sequences of this *Beowulf* with no text at all—just dynamic panels and pages which detail Beowulf's struggle with Grendel or his mother in a way that is both human and physically accurate while still stylized and idiosyncratic. Hinds's Grendel looks like a Giger alien, and his Beowulf moves like an Ultimate Fighter. Hinds makes Beowulf his own, in the best sense, and in this way he inspires students. He shows us that it's all right to take possession of a canon text and make it your own. This is what medievalism does on its best days: resuscitating a text students perceive as "dead" and giving it breathtaking life.

This is not to say that the book is not historically researched; in vivid contrast to Bingham's edition, Hinds's *Beowulf* is firmly anchored in anthropological and archeological detail, creating a sensually stimulating world through which his fantastic monsters prowl and proud Christian heroes do battle. A useful example is the cover to the second issue, depicting Beowulf as he descends into the lake to fight Grendel's mother. (This entire sequence was painted not on the Bristol boards that make up a traditional comic, but on wooden panels.) Beowulf's helmet, with its nose guard, decorative panels marked with boars, and distinctive ridge, invites comparison with the Sutton Hoo helmet without being a copy of it. His sword, visible in the foreground, even bears Futhark runes that spell out HRUNTING for all our students to see and decipher. Hinds's detail work is especially lucrative when partnered with the illustrated edition of Heaney's translation, which replaces facing pages of Anglo-Saxon text with photographs of the Danish countryside, archeological relics, and medieval illustration (fig. 2).

The tale of theft

Figure 2. This page from the second issue of Gareth Hinds' *Beowulf* depicts the descent into the lake. Candlewick.

from the dragon's lair and the dragon's subsequent awakening is told entirely without words. At the same time, it is given lavish pages far more numerous than in Bingham's exposition. The fate of the Geats and the larger political and social concerns of the Beowulf author are present in this comic, but summarized in text rather than illustrated. This facilitates an instructor going "off script" to provide context and elaboration through the use of passages from a text-only translation. When questions of adaptation are raised with Bingham's text, we almost always begin from a position of "what got left out," but when using Hinds's version, the pervasive gloom of the final end of the Geats is there on the page; it's just not entirely clear, and clarity is something an instructor can readily provide.

The publication of the Candlewick edition of *Beowulf* also prompted the creation of a "Reader's Guide" intended for use by teaching faculty. This is a very brief document, only two pages, but it does include discussion questions which can provide an instructor with seed material for her own course. It can be found on the Candlewick website.

Beowulf *at IDW*

All of the texts we have thus far examined predate Heaney's translation; the extraordinary reception of this edition actually made *Beowulf* into something of a fad, as evidenced by multiple film projects in the years that followed. But one of these film projects had its genesis in an earlier time, and in writer Neil Gaiman's personal interest in the poem. Gaiman has used Beowulf in at least two other works (the poem "Bay Wolf," published in the 1998 *Smoke and Mirrors* anthology, and *The Monarch of the Glen*, a novella collected in the 2006 collection *Fragile Things*). The genesis of this 2007 animated film is complex, and it may be impossible to separate Gaiman's contributions from those of his co-author, Roger Avary. Concurrent to the film's release, a four issue adaptation was produced by IDW. This adaptation of an adaptation was written by IDW mainstay Chris Ryall and drawn by Gabriel Rodriguez. The original issues included the complete Gummere translation of the poem, which is especially convenient if your students are also using the first edition of Hinds's *Beowulf*, which cuts from and (in the final chapter) adds to this particular translation. But these single issues are probably too difficult for an entire class roster to find; an instructor would need to acquire them and then scan the pages for distribution. The collected edition, however, is available in electronic and print format.[4]

To call this comic/film a "free adaptation" would be something of an understatement, as unlike both the Bingham and the Hinds version, this text puts dialog into the mouths of the characters, both adds and cuts scenes, and most importantly makes certain interpretive choices which depart—sometimes slightly, sometimes drastically—from the traditional ways of reading this poem. Some of these changes are motivated by the conventions of Hollywood storytelling; it is easier, in a film less than two hours long, for Beowulf to remain in Daneland and marry Wealtheow than for him to travel home and become king of a new country we have never before seen, surrounded by a supporting cast we have never before met. Other changes, however, are driven by Avary and Gaiman's stance on the poem itself. In interviews, the pair made clear their belief that the text of *Beowulf* as we have it is an expurgated version of the poem, censored by a Christian monk from an original which was both raunchier and more morally ambiguous than the version we have today (Smith, "Interview").

Readers of the original poem will recall curious facts from the text which Avary and Gaiman use as evidence for their view; in particular, when Beowulf descends into the den of Grendel's mother, he does not return with a trophy claimed from her. Instead, he brings up the head of Grendel himself. That is, there is no proof that Beowulf killed Grendel's mother at all; there is only Beowulf's testimony that he did so. If we presume that Beowulf is lying, and that he did not kill Grendel's mother, what could she have done to persuade him to spare her life? In Gaiman and Avary's view, Beowulf makes a Faustian bargain with Grendel's mother and is rewarded with everlasting fame (3: 12). Sex seals the pact. The dragon at the end of the poem is not an inhuman force of nature but, instead, Beowulf's own son, engendered by him upon Grendel's mother; it is the personification of his own hubris, out to murder him. Before Beowulf, it was Hrothgar who succumbed to the temptation of Grendel's mother, siring Grendel himself, and after Beowulf, Wiglaf is lured into the water by this same siren. Hrothgar, Beowulf, and Wiglaf are thus pawns in a cyclical tragedy that is doomed to recur as long as men wish for fame—which is to say, forever (fig. 3).

This *Beowulf* is not the first *Beowulf* any serious student of the poem should read. It is imaginative rather than adaptive. But this also makes it of great value to a class which has already read the poem, perhaps even seen other comics adaptations, and who will understand the interpretive choices Gaiman and Avary have made. In this way, the IDW *Beowulf* can help us perceive the mysteries in the poem, its unanswered questions and contradictions. It creates opportunity to discuss the shift from oral to written tradition and the prob-

Figure 3. In IDW's *Beowulf*, adapted by Chris Ryall and Gabriel Rodriguez from Neil Gaiman and Roger Avary's film, Grendel's mother is a Faustian temptress. IDW.

lematic nature of authorial intent. Gaiman and Avary's anxiety over lacunae, their desire to shed light on all facets of the poem, to trace all the monsters back to mortal fathers and connect every character in a familial relationship, highlights those shadowy passages in an especially bright and contrasting way. And, perhaps, it helps modern readers to accept uncertainty, to admit that some questions are better left unanswered.

Likewise, because this book simply has more pages than any previous version, and because Gaiman and Avary feel great liberty to add, subtract, and mutate the original material, supporting characters who suffer in more brief adaptations are instead given luxurious space. Unferth and Wealthow get more pages in the IDW *Beowulf* than they do in all other versions combined. In particular, the use of Unferth as a man who begins the tale a pagan but eventually converts to Christianity (4: 4) can help illustrate both the shift in this character from adversary to ally as well as the social context of a people "who remembered Hell" (Heaney 15). But, ultimately, Unferth and Wealthow, though interesting, are different characters than we have read about in the original poem.

Kid Beowulf

To a critic interested in adaptations of the Beowulf story, Alexis Fajardo's *Kid Beowulf* might not at first appear to be of much interest. It is aimed primarily at a middle-school audience and summarizes the events of the poem in a brief 8-page introduction. With the exception of this summary, the events of *Kid Beowulf* take place before the action of Beowulf itself, technically qualifying it for the category of "prequel." At the time of this writing, it is three volumes in length, adding up to some 650 pages. It is the first volume, *Kid Beowulf and the Blood-Bound Oath*, which is of most interest to Beowulf scholars, because it is in that tale that Beowulf and Grendel are conceived and grow to young adulthood before both are exiled. Later volumes—*Kid Beowulf and the Song of Roland* and *Kid Beowulf and the Rise of El Cid*—portray a Hero's Journey through France and Spain for both Beowulf and Grendel who, in this tale, are twin brothers; that kinship transforms the fated battle inside Heorot into a familial tragedy.

From just this much information, it is clear that Fajardo has taken considerable liberties with the original tale, but fidelity is not the point. Instead, the emphasis is on creating sympathetic characters whose motives both conflict and can be understood. As in Gaiman's text, the mysterious nature of Grendel and his mother cannot be left in shadow. Instead, every stage of an intense family drama is played out before our eyes, with Hrothgar siring Grendel's mother—here named Gertrude—on a beautiful but hapless Heathobard princess (55), and Gertrude in turn using magic to conceal her inhuman appearance when she falls in love with Edgetho (107). Dragon, dam, Grendel and Beowulf himself thus form a bizarre kind of family, with the spirit of Edgetho even in occasional attendance, like Old King Hamlet or the ghost of Anakin Skywalker.

Kid Beowulf thus serves as a useful example of the modern compulsion to explain all unexplained things, to firmly place both Grendel's mother and the dragon into a clear familial relationship with Beowulf himself, and it usefully compares to Gaiman's comic in this way. And, like Gaiman's text, it brings the surrounding characters to vivid life, dramatizing the pagan Geats and Heathobards in a way which can be helpful to a class struggling with, for example, the Finnsburg episode or other historical anecdotes which appear in Beowulf. The portrayal of Gertrude is an unapologetically feminist one; self-reliant, intelligent, and ethically principled, Fajardo's Gertrude is a refreshing antidote to the sexualized Faust found in Gaiman's *Beowulf*. The brief summary of the source poem which appears at the beginning of *Blood-Bound*

Oath is probably too lean to be of much use to students except as a plot crib, but because Fajardo drew this particular sequence in a more detailed style than the rest of the book, it can be constructively compared to Bingham, Hinds and Gabriel Rodriguez's pages.

Finally, *Kid Beowulf* has one other quality which makes it distinct from all the other adaptations here discussed: it has actual teaching tools already prepared. Fajardo has cooperated with Dr. Katie Monnin, an Associate Professor of Literacy at the University of North Florida, to create a long and thorough "Reader's Guide" complete with lesson plans, discussion questions, background information on the design of the characters and Fajardo's creative process, and class projects that are compatible with the Common Core standards. *Kid Beowulf* thus becomes an especially good text to introduce into literature courses designed for Education majors, who have the opportunity to use comics and graphic novels in middle school classrooms.

Conclusions

While students have traditionally seen comics adaptations of canon texts as plot cribs, read before or instead of the source material, instructors who have used comics in the classroom already know that their best use is after the primary text has already been read. When students think they know a poem like *Beowulf*, that is precisely when they are best primed to see what other creators have made of it—how adaptation, alteration, cutting, and reinterpretation changes what the text is saying. This is certainly true of *Beowulf*, and it is not necessary to use any one of the versions here discussed in its entirety. Class time is often at a premium and instructors might be reluctant to assign a collected edition when the book is liable to be discussed in only one class period.

Instead, a very profitable conversation can be had by examining one moment in *Beowulf* from multiple angles; in my experience, that best moment has been the encounter between Beowulf and Grendel's mother. For many students, this is when the poem starts to drag, and comics pages can bring a breath of timely fresh air to the classroom. Perhaps my own interest in feminist discourse is to blame, but I've also found this the precise moment where comics adaptations of *Beowulf* are, for better or worse, most honest. It is here where Hinds's color palette is most vibrant, and because Beowulf is ostensibly underwater for the entire encounter, Hinds's decision to pass page after page without dialog or narrative caption is buttressed by physical laws. Hinds's fidelity to the original text shows Beowulf killing Grendel's mother before he turns to the crippled monster hiding in the corner; Beowulf executes him and brings his head up to the air (2: 18, 21). But it is also here, in this sequence, that Gaiman and Avery's titillating Faust rises from the mere, transforming the poem into another kind of story altogether (3: 11). And this very mystery— that ambiguous space created in the poem by Beowulf's decision to claim his trophy from Grendel instead of the monster's mother—is elided and edited out of Bingham's 42-page version; there, Beowulf returns to the surface with the head of Grendel's mother carried proudly before him! (31). It is a shift which simplifies and clarifies the poem, but in which something valuable is lost. Were I to add anything else to these three perspectives, it might be to show a page or two of the character of Gertrude from Fajardo's *Kid Beowulf*; this bull-headed monster-woman who refuses to lower herself to the savagery of the surrounding Danes and Heathobards makes a useful corrective to Gaiman and Avary's vision of Grendel's mother: a cartoon caricature of Angelina Jolie, wearing nothing but gold paint.

Notes

1. I am indebted to Michael Torregrossa for his invaluable bibliographies on the critical intersection of medievalism and comics.
2. The Kirby Award may not be immediately recognized by non-fans; it existed for only three years (1985–1987) before a dispute over ownership of the award caused it to be discontinued, reborn as the Eisner and Harvey awards. The phrase "graphic novel" had not yet come into popular currency in 1984.
3. For more on *Beowulf: Dragon Slayer* and its debt to Gardner, see Catherine Clarke's, "Re-placing Masculinity: The DC Comics *Beowulf* Series and its Context, 1975–6," in *Anglo-Saxon Culture and the Modern Imagination*, and Michael Livingston and John William Sutton's, "Reinventing the Hero: Gardner's Grendel and the Shifting Face of Beowulf in Popular Culture," in *Studies in Popular Culture* 29.1 (Oct. 2006): 1–16.
4. Issues 3 and 4 of IDW's original *Beowulf* series also contained two of my essays on *Beowulf*, written for a non-academic audience: "A Book on Fire: An Exploration of Beowulf in the Media" and "Hwaet If?: Beowulf as Comic Book Superhero." As my decision to recycle part of this latter title makes clear, these essays helped me determine my own stance on Beowulf as a poem and a popular culture phenomenon. These essays were not reprinted when IDW published a collected edition of *Beowulf*.

Works Cited

Avary, Roger, and Neil Gaiman. *Beowulf: The Script Book*. New York: William Morrow Paperbacks, 2007. Print.
Barr, Mike and Jerry Bingham. *Batman: Son of the Demon*. New York: DC Comics, 1987. Print.
Beowulf: An Illustrated Edition. Trans. Seamus Heaney. New York: W.W. Norton, 2008. Print.
"Beowulf Teachers' Guide." Candlewick Press, n.d. Web. 12/22/2013
Bingham, Jerry. *Beowulf*. Evanston: First Comics, 1984. Print.

_____. "Beowulf: A Lot of Mileage Since 1984." *Scribbler*. Blogspot, 3/11/2013. Web. 12/21/2013.
Clarke, Catherine A. M. "Re-placing Masculinity: The DC Comics Beowulf Series and its Context." In *Anglo-Saxon Culture and the Modern Imagination*. Eds. David Clark and Nicholas Perkins. Cambridge: D.S. Brewer, 2010. Pp. 165–182. Print.
Echard, Siân. "BOOM: Seeing Beowulf in Pictures and Print." In *Anglo-Saxon Culture and the Modern Imagination*. Eds. David Clark and Nicholas Perkins. Cambridge: D.S. Brewer, 2010. Pp. 129–45, plates I–III. Print.
Fajardo, Alexis E. *Kid Beowulf and the Blood-Bound Oath*. Portland: Bowler Hat, 2008. Print.
_____. *Kid Beowulf and the Song of Roland*. Portland: Bowler Hat, 2010. Print.
_____. *Kid Beowulf and the Rise of El Cid*. Portland: Bowler Hat, 2013. Print.
_____, and Katie Monnin. *The Kid Beowulf Reader*. Unpublished. Web. 10/18/2013.
Gaiman, Neil. *Fragile Things: Short Fictions and Wonders*. New York: Harper, 2010. Print.
_____. *Smoke and Mirrors: Short Fictions and Illusions*. New York: Harper Perennial, 2008. Print.
Hinds, Gareth. *Beowulf*. Cambridge: TheComic.Com, 1999. Print.
_____. *Beowulf: A Graphic Novel*. GarethHinds.com, n.d. Web. 12/22/2013
Livingston, Michael, and John William Sutton. "Reinventing the Hero: Gardner's Grendel and the Shifting Face of Beowulf in Popular Culture." *Studies in Popular Culture* 29.1 (Oct. 2006): 1–16. Print.
McCloud, Scott. *Making Comics: Storytelling Secrets of Comics, Manga and Graphic Novels*. New York: HarperCollins, 2006. Print.
Nyberg, Amy. *Seal of Approval: The History of the Comics Code*. Jackson: University Press of Mississippi, 1998. Print.
Osborn, Marijane. "Translations, Versions, Illustrations." In *A Beowulf Handbook*. Eds. Robert E. Bjork and John D. Niles. Lincoln: University of Nebraska Press, 1998. Pp. 341–359, plates 1–13. Print.
Ryall, Chris, and Gabriel Rodriguez. *Beowulf 1–4*. San Diego: IDW 2007. Print.
Schraffenberger, J. D. "Visualizing Beowulf: Old English Gets Graphic." In *Building Literary Connections with Graphic Novels: Page by Page, Panel by Panel*. Ed. James Bucky Carter. Urbana, IL: National Council of Teachers of English, 2007. Print.
Smith, Jeremy. "Interview: Neil Gaiman and Roger Avary (Beowulf)." Chud.com, 7/30/2007. Web. 12/22/2013.
Uslan, Michael, and Ricardo Villamonte. *Beowulf: Dragon Slayer 1–6*. New York: DC Comics, 1975–1976. Print.

Killing Desdemona
Staging Sexual Violence in *Othello* Graphic Novels

J. Caitlin Finlayson

The most common image from *Othello* contained in the Folger Shakespeare's Library's *Picturing Shakespeare* project is of the murder of Desdemona in Act 5, scene 2 (hereafter 5.2). While this archive is not exhaustive, the fact that the murder scene is the most common subject to be depicted in this representative collection testifies to the scene's imaginative and theatrical significance.[1] The key subject materials of this scene are fairly consistent: a bed, a curtain, the figure of Desdemona (often with one breast suggestively exposed for the pleasure of the male viewer),[2] and a glowering or contemplative Othello. In every image, Othello is poised in the forefront, sometimes clearly contemplative, sometimes lurking sinisterly above Desdemona, and sometimes posed dynamically mid-strike. Though Othello's attitude might vary, he is consistently placed in the forefront of the image with his full standing figure facing the viewer.[3] Consequently, the viewer focuses on his facial expression and physical posture/attitude and thus his psychological state; the "story" of the scene is Othello's story and one we view from his vantage point. Desdemona, framed in by the bed's curtains, lies in the background somewhat obscured by the body of Othello and/or the curtains. The focus of these images is squarely on Othello with a secondary nod to a most often sexualized Desdemona (fig. 1). Not much has changed (since the height of illustrating the play-text in the 19th century) in the visual depiction of this scene, even in contemporary comic books.

The murder of Desdemona in 5.2 presents one of the key staging challenges of *Othello*. The director must decide how explicit the violence should be; whether the scene should have a sense of eroticism; whether to cut Desdemona's resurrection scene; and whether Desdemona will vigorously plead for her life, forcefully rebuff her attacker, or passively accept her own murder. These staging choices, among a myriad of others for this scene, determine the audience's reception of the racial, gender, and sexual politics of the play, as well as Othello's self-justification and our allocation of culpability among Desdemona, Iago, and Othello. The staging of the murder also significantly crafts our final impression of Othello's character, depending on whether the director focuses on Othello's humanity; his brutality; his status as "other"; or on the defiled marriage bed as a central image, etc. Shifting these considerations to the graphic novel medium, this paper will address the textual staging of 5.2's death scene in two adaptations: the full text *Othello* illustrated by Oscar Zarate; and *Manga Shakespeare Othello*, adapted by Richard Appignanesi and illustrated by Ryuta Osada. Focusing on this discrete scene in the graphic novel by Zarate as well as that by Appignanesi and Osada, this paper will address more broadly how graphic novels tackle the issue of sexual violence and how these texts' pictorial renderings can be read in the light of the performance history of *Othello*. In particular, both graphic novels employ (to a degree) visual techniques analogous to 19th century staging practices used to veil and distance the violence of 5.2, while concurrently directing our focus to Othello's psychological state and heroic downfall.

Figure 1. A typical example of the depiction of 5.2 from Tonson's edition of Shakespeare, 1709 (Folger Shakespeare Library).

This essay seeks to elucidate the strategies Osada, Zarate, and other illustrators use to depict the scene and control our response, and to explore how these graphic novels partake in the tradition of editing, staging, and picturing Shakespeare's *Othello*, while directing our attention to notable features in these graphic representations. Ultimately, although they are contemporary visual culture depictions of this scene, these graphic novels rehash old theatrical practices. Zarate's comic treads the familiar ground of the male gaze and the stylized eroticism of killing Desdemona. Zarate also emphasizes Othello's face in his sequence of panels that unfold the scene, thus providing a typical visual representation of Othello as a tragic, sympathetic hero rather than brutal, misogynistic murderer. Osada's manga, on the other hand, continues a long established pattern of obviating domestic violence against women in *Othello* to largely the same end goal—producing a tragic, sympathetic Othello. In neither case do these modern popular culture adaptations present us with new interpretive possibilities or with anything other than the predictable objectified and ancillary Desdemona. Altering the visual medium has done little to alter our ingrained cultural-performative interpretation of the death scene.

"the object poisons the sight, / let it be hid" 5.2.360–61

Shakespeare's text demands that 5.2 opens with Desdemona in bed. The bed, a symbol of marital union, betrayal, pollution, and taboo, would seem an essential visual (and narrative) feature of the scene; yet many contemporary graphic novels displace, minimize, or veil its presence, following (perhaps for some of the same reasons) late 18th and 19th century theatrical practice. While the staging of Othello has long abandoned this aesthetic tradition of *hiding* the murder, many graphic novels still enact visual conventions that distance the viewer/reader from the stage property (the bed) and the act (the murder). This is not to suggest that some graphic novels do not forefront the bed, the brutality, or the peep show eroticism of the scene, but most employ veiling techniques to some degree to avoid thrusting every gratuitous detail of Desdemona's death on our senses. Graphic novel versions negotiate between our desire to see (or the graphic novel's desire to reveal) and, as James Siemon remarks of stage productions, "the need to be protected from unmediated vision" (40). Moreover, graphic novel versions generally attempt to locate the tragedy of this scene *visually* in Othello's psychological turmoil and devastation; the wife-murderer is never merely a monster but is always tragic and sympathetic.

In the late 18th and 19th centuries, it was a common theatrical practice to close the curtains of the marital bed, turned deathbed, to shield the audience from the actual moment of murder (Neill 385). Similarly, as Neill remarks: "late eighteenth-and nineteenth-century editors sought to restrict the curiosity that the final scene gratifies and to obscure its most threatening meanings by progressively excising from the text every explicit reference to the bed" and the consummation of the wedding night; moreover, in editions from the late 18th century up until the early part of the 20th century "not one Desdemona ... was permitted to greet Othello in the murder scene with 'Will you come to bed, my lord?'" (5.2.24) (Neill 385 n10). These attempts to sanitize, conceal, and obviate the murder and its sexual tenor have much in common with modern graphic novel depictions of 5.2. As in these earlier textual editions, Richard Appignanesi's manga adaptation cuts Desdemona's plea for Othello to "come to bed." Notably, this line is absent from many other graphic novel versions such as Vincent Godwin (adapter) and Chris Allen's (illustrator), Dorothy Calhoun Fago (adapter) and Vicatan's (illustrator), and Saddleback's *Illustrated Classics* version[4]; though, as a complete text version, illustrator Oscar Zarate includes the line. This is one of many textual and illustrative moves to desexualize and sanitize the violent scene in contemporary graphic novels due in part, no doubt, to the fact that the majority of graphic novel adaptations of *Othello* (including *Manga Shakespeare*) are parts of series aimed explicitly at younger readers and marketed as teaching texts.

Fago's black and white adaptation erases not only the sexual component of the tragedy but the racial component as well. In Fago's version he is not the "old black ram ... tupping the white ewe" (1.1.97–98) nor does Barbantio remark on his "sooty bosom" (1.32.89) or Othello refer to himself as "Haply for I am black" (3.3.304). With race and sex removed as driving forces for the plot from Fago's adaptation, little else of critical interest or complexity remains and one wonders what the purpose is of teaching such a text, and more importantly, presenting it as "Shakespeare." While Appignanesi retains textual references to the "Moor" and blackness, Osada's illustrations are not racially or ethnically specific (though Othello's features are often darkened); Osada's drawings employ the animalistic caricatures common in manga, and both a figurative and literal masking, drawn from the play-script's Venetian setting but these obviations are by no means as extensive as Fago's.

Osada's illustration of the murder scene in the *Manga Shakespeare Othello* is portrayed in a two-page spread (188–189) and, although the scene does depict a modest degree of brutality, the bed in which the murder takes place and the murder itself are conspicuously minimized. The death bed scene in

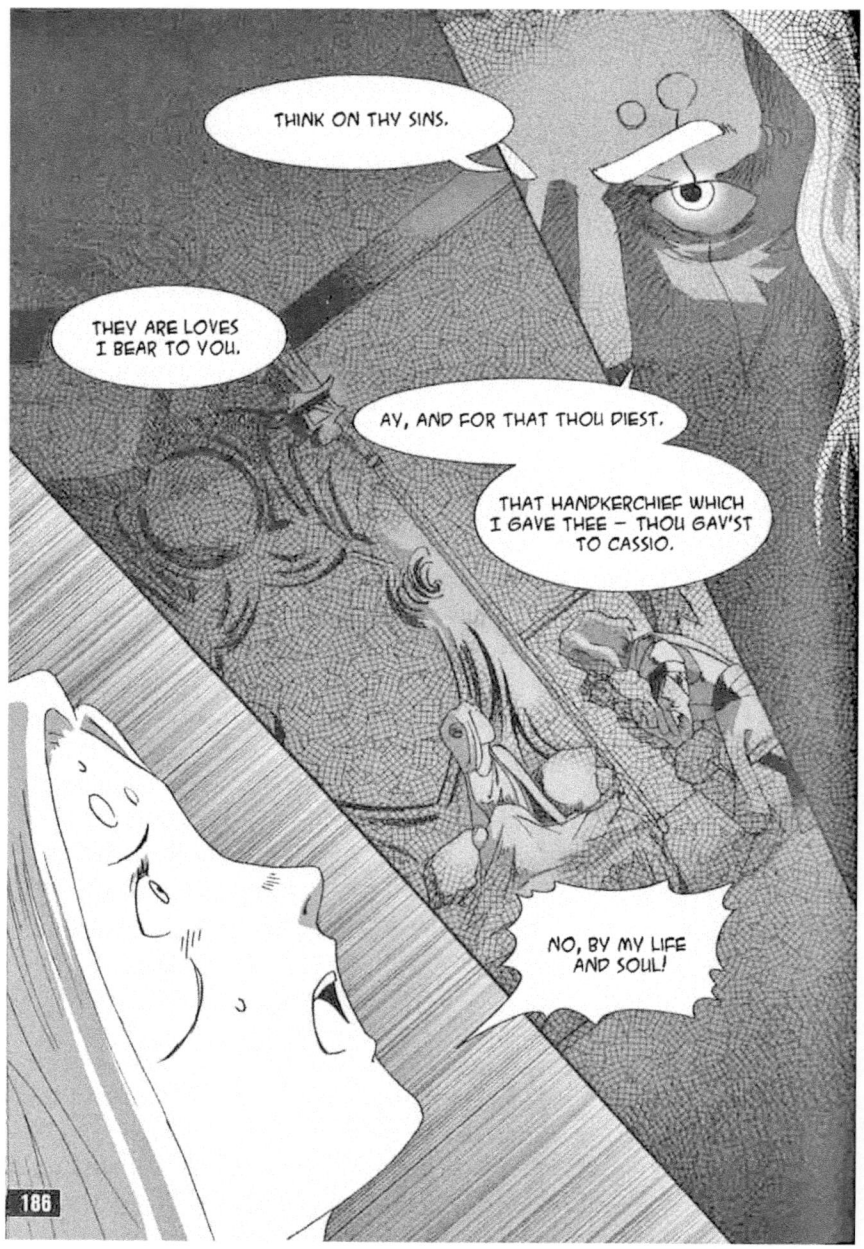

Figure 2. Ryuta Osada's *Othello* downplays eroticism and the marriage bed. SelfMade-Hero, p. 186.

Othello is a key moment of racial-sexual taboo, theatrical revelation and titillation; when the bed is pushed out from the discovery space in 5.2, the audience finally tangibly witnesses what Iago has been asking us to repeatedly imagine throughout the play: a white woman and a Moor in bed. However, in 5.2 the taboo of interracial sex is sublimated into a violent, eroticized death. Yet, in Osada's illustrations of the scene, only one panel displays the key theatrical property of the bed and then it is only as background, with the characters and bed vaguely depicted in broad representational penciling (186, fig. 2). This single depiction of the marital bed by Osada is part of the visual lead-in to the two-page spread of the murder itself. As shown in fig. 2, the full-page bleed that displays the key theatrical property and multivalent symbol of the bed is set up as a triptych with one detailed close-up of Desdemona's face and one of Othello's flanking a middle third panel that depicts Desdemona and Othello kneeling beside her bed (186). In juxtaposition to the detailed close-ups, which frame this singular image of the bed and provide psychological contextualization for both characters, the entire central image is sketched as a wide-angle image (or distance perspective) in which the figures of Desdemona and Othello have no faces. This renders the bed image as indistinct background, and the two close-up panels are essentially blow-ups of the faces of the couple from the central panel. The close-ups and the triptych design focus attention away from the theatrical property that traditionally symbolizes sexual betrayal and taboo—the quintessential image of domestic tragedy—and onto the psychological state of the couple. Desdemona's full face is shown in this full-page bleed with the bed and again in panels on the facing page (187); however, Othello's face is only shown in fragments and shards, close-ups of his eyes and mouth, which in comic book discourse is a traditional method for indicating emotional volatility. This focus on Othello's fractured face as a visual emblem of his fractured psyche, when coupled with four preceding panels (184–185) depicting Othello's hands clutched in contemplative prayer (one of these also displaying the angelic wings that Osada furnishes his protagonist with throughout the manga), craft a typical representation of Othello as a tragic, sympathetic hero.

Similar to the 19th century bowdlerized editions of *Othello* or the strategically employed bed curtain, in his graphic rendition Osada removes the eroticism, the intimacy, and the sexualized components of Desdemona's death. Osada strips the murder of its crucial locale—the bed. Notably, the bed is shown once (192) during Desdemona's resurrection scene but again it is indistinct, drawn from a distance perspective, and marginalized by the fragmented close-up of Othello's face that dominates the panel. Even with Lodovico's invective to "Look on the tragic loading of this bed" (205), Osada denies the reader the image. The reader can't, alas, look at what is not depicted. It is this domestic, sexualized location that even the earliest audience members endowed with the emotional resonance of the scene. Henry Jackson, who witnessed a 1610 performance by the King's Men in Oxford, records his dismay at the intimacy of the murder scene:

> ...the celebrated Desdemona, slayn in our presence by her husband, although she pleaded her case very effectively throughout, yet moved us more after she was dead, when, lying in her bed, she entreated the pity of the spectators by her very countenance [Hanky18].

However, Osada's rendition is dislocated from the intimate, marriage space of the bed and there is only the slightest hint this even happens in a bedroom. There is certainly none of the erotic, physical tug of war we see in Janet Suzman's 1989 production staged at the Market Theatre in Johannesburg in which a shirtless John Kani (Othello) straddles Joanna Weinberg (Desdemona) as he suffocates her. The whole scene is staged with a high level of eroticism as Desdemona embraces Othello only to be repeatedly pushed back down on to the bed, not with violent force, as in director Oliver Parker's film (1995), but with long languid strokes to the front of Desdemona's chest. This back and forth between the actors in Suzman's production blatantly evokes the sexual intercourse of the play's central taboo for the viewer.

In terms of Osada's visual style in his depiction of the murder, it is worth noting that the illustrator generally uses framed, square panels in neat, ordered succession; however, in 5.2 (and in a limited number of other discrete scenes) Osada overlaps uneven, shard-like panels, employs full-page bleeds, and leaves other panels unframed to reflect the scene's heightened emotion and tension. It is the death of Desdemona that restores the panels to the more typical framed, progressive, and symmetrical order. Osada also effectively employs this breakdown in the panels' structure with the other domestic murder—Emilia's (198–99). Again, in this instance, the overlapping and unstructured panels create an emotional intensity in the scene. Moreover, in both cases this chaotic panel design has the effect of hiding or minimizing the actual murders themselves. As with the endpoint of Desdemona's murder scene, with the slaying of Emilia complete, the order and integrity of the panels are restored, perhaps suggesting the men's emotional releases and their resumption of patriarchal control achieved by killing their wives. More disturbingly, this disruption to the regular, ordered design and flow of the panels may suggest that these women are the cause of the disorder, disharmony, and breakdown; only their eradication restores visual order to the composition of the manga.

This disturbing logic is also apparent in the relative visual blocking of Othello and Desdemona in the panels depicting the murder scene. Here too the chaotic and variable panel design continues. It is not until the following two-page spread (188–189) that Othello strikes out and Osada provides a dynamic image of Othello with his hand around Desdemona's throat (188). The vigorous radiating penciling behind the figure of Othello, crafts his grip as a dynamic, powerful action. Notably, the strangulation is initially depicted from a vantage point behind Desdemona, so that the reader sees the back of Desdemona's head with the focus on Othello's darkened, enraged face, his eyes gleaming white and inhuman. Osada then moves to a close-up, frontal view of Desdemona, eyes wide with a hand round her throat. "Banish me, my lord, but kill me not" (188) she pleads, but in this panel we do not see the murderer, only the vice-like grip on his wife's throat. This is followed by a panel featuring a close-up profile view of a tear streaming down Desdemona's frightened face (188), as Othello's second hand reaches out to "stop her mouth" as he has Cassio's. Notably, it is only Othello's hands that are pictured in this panel so the action is essentially disembodied and distanced from the person of Othello.

What follows is erasure, an absence. The climatic fourth panel on this page is entirely black and unframed, with a bold white bubble in which is written: "IT IS TOO LATE" (188). The murder is literally eradicated. It becomes a visual emptiness or void, an absence, a blacked-out panel. This is analogous to the 19th century practice of drawing the bed curtain for the murder, but as Neill remarks these practices may not have the desired effect of sanitizing or diminishing the racial and sexual anxieties of the scene. How do we, the audience, react to the now invisible scene? Are our imaginings worse than the image the illustrator might conjure? Does the blacked-out panel leave us to range over our own sexual and racialized violent fantasies and fears? Students in my *Shakespeare on Page, Stage and Screen* seminar routinely indicate that imagining the scene was more visceral and disturbing than the representations they viewed in Suzman's and Parker's versions. In Neill's terms, "the effect of such erasure [is] only to give play to the fantasy it was designed to check" (Neil 390). Osada's manga, like Iago's repeated evocations to imagine Desdemona and Othello "making the beast with two backs" (1.1.130–131), asks us to imagine that which we fear, revile and/or fantasize about. Perhaps in trying to appeal to a younger reading audience (and the teachers who might use these texts in a class), Osada has diminished the visual representation of sex and violence, only to increase our fascination with these forbidden elements, just as Iago has enjoined us to imagine the sexual taboo of the white Venetian woman and the Moor throughout.

This erasure of the murder is highlighted by the next set of panels in this two-page spread in which Othello says: "NOT YET QUITE DEAD" (Osada 189), pulling a dagger from his armband. The following line, "I WOULD NOT HAVE THEE LINGER IN THY PAIN. SO, SO" (189), is accompanied by an image of a hand grasping a knife hilt with the blade projecting downward as if about to strike the next panel, which is a long, coffin-like blank, all black panel (189). Once again, violence, the sexualized bed, the victim, and the murder are conspicuously absent. This panel signals the end of the murder scene, before the action of the graphic novel moves back into the room with Emilia's knocking at the chamber door. The erasure of the bed as a central prop and the absence of the murder itself in Osada's graphic rendition move against the most common strains of contemporary film and stage representation which generally foreground the bed, presenting a disheveled, sexualized Desdemona and a brutal or tortured Othello (e.g. director Oliver Parker's film). The scene remains problematic across visual media because it refers so explicitly to the underpinnings of Euro-Western visual culture (e.g. the male gaze, the post-colonial gaze, etc.). A traditional response such as crafting a heroic, tragic Othello runs the risk of diminishing the domestic violence and misogyny of the scene, while producing a typically Freudian passive, masochistic female "object." On the other hand, focusing on the eroticism of the murder scene often leads to little more than prurient titillation; while ramping up the violence can render Othello merely a brutal, uncivilized, "other," with no doubt, more prurient titillation of the "violence porn" variety. Given that *Manga Shakespeare* aims to appeal to young readers and educators,[5] removing the murder itself and the more erotic aspects of the scene is an intelligent (if disappointing) tactical move.

"I kissed thee ere I killed thee" 5.2.420

Zarate's color pictorial representation of 5.2 is more overtly sexual, intimate, and violent. Unlike in Osada's, the bed is a focal point of this scene, highlighted by the use of purple for the bed-curtains, which provides a contrast to the predominately black and grey tones of the images in this sequence. A warm yellow glow from the bedside candle envelops the sleeping Desdemona and is picked up in her shock of yellow hair. The purple of the curtains frames in the bed, and is a characteristic color for this scene. The limited color pallet sets 5.2 apart from the rest of the graphic novel, which has a more varied and vibrant color scheme: bright blues, greens, and reds dominate, all in Technicolor brilliance.

Zarate's illustrations of the unabridged play employ conventional, square panels with gutters, avoiding any full page bleeds or overlapping panels, as are seen in Osada's illustrations. All Zarate's panels are neatly framed and in a clear, progressive order. The graphic novel presents the unabridged text, so 5.2 comprises many more individual panels as Zarate parses out the dialogue and action slowly. Osada's manga uses fewer panels and only a fraction of the dialogue in a more quickly paced and stylized scene; for instance, adapter Appignanesi includes only eight of the twenty-two lines of Othello's opening soliloquy in 5.2. While Osada's is in black and white as is typical for manga, Zarate exploits the possibility of color illustrations. Although he employs a limited color pallet in this scene—black, white, purple, and yellow—he exploits this pallet to highlight the bed; Desdemona, who has a shock of yellow hair with purple highlights shadowing her face and lips; and the pillow, which is stark white.

The first full-page of Zarate's depiction of 5.2. is dedicated to Othello's soliloquy, parsed out over six panels (114). The scene opens with a large panel with Othello in the foreground, speaking the opening lines of his soliloquy, as he gazes upon Desdemona asleep in bed in the background of the panel. The next panel, illuminated in a yellow haze of candlelight, reveals Othello contemplating "put[ting] out the light" (5.2.7) before a statue of the Madonna and Child. The subsequent panel depicts a close-up of Othello's face looming over the puffed out candle, trailing smoke. A sequence of three panels show, in intimate close-up, Othello slowly leaning in to kiss Desdemona, the second panel of which is an extreme close-up of just the couple's lips, highlighted by purple tones, tantalizingly on the verge of touching as Othello says: "I WILL KILL THEE AND LOVE THEE AFTER" (114). Their lips, however, never touch and we are denied the fulfillment and sensuality of the kiss. A tear runs down Othello's face as he finishes his soliloquy in the sixth panel, completing the sequence of panels on this page (114). This moment of explicit emotion by Othello, in combination with the image of the Madonna and Child, and the three panels extending his motion to kiss Desdemona, creates a sympathetic, romantic figure of Othello. Like William Satchwell Leney's and Adolph Closs' pictorial renderings of the scene or William Salter's painting *Othello's Lamentation*, Zarate's depiction of the soliloquy in 6 panels, focuses on the emotionally stricken hero. As in the playscript, the viewer is introduced to the murder scene through Othello's soliloquy and thus the viewer is directed to follow the story of the scene from Othello's perspective. Zarate's rendition stresses this concept by having Othello's physical presence dominate the panels and, in a nod to the dramatic convention of the soliloquy, foregrounding Othello's facial expressions and exploiting his physical posture to convey further his psychological state.

Throughout the sequence of panels that make up 5.2, the bed is made a focal point as are Othello's facial expressions. After Desdemona awakes, the bed is repeatedly referenced visually either through the prop itself or a flash of purple curtain draping across the top of a panel helping to frame in visually as well as contextually the scene in each panel (115–117). At one point, Othello begins to climb onto the bed over several panels as he inches towards killing her (115–117). Repeatedly in the sequence of panels between the opening of the scene and Desdemona's death, the figure of Othello is placed in the foreground (Desdemona is only in the forefront in two panels), thus focusing our attention on his facial expressions and body language, and hence his psychological state. In three panels, Othello hovers on the edge of the bed, his arms flung wide as he grips each bedpost in a dominating, cruciform posture (made more explicit by the repeated visual reference to the statue of the Madonna and Child). During the act of suffocation itself, Othello straddles Desdemona on the bed (117, fig. 3). The actual smothering scene is parsed across seven panels (117, fig. 3). The first displays Othello's back as he climbs across the bed towards Desdemona's horrified face. The second panel shifts our focus so that we are viewing Othello's face as he straddles Desdemona, smothering her with a pillow; it is the largest panel on the page. Our focus, however, is quickly shifted away from the murder as the following panel relocates the scene to outside the bedchamber as Emilia knocks upon the door. After this, we are not explicitly shown Desdemona again until her resurrection scene. Instead, the following three panels at the bottom of this page focus once more on close-ups of Othello's face with the final panel of the page depicting only Desdemona's hand with a figurative "voice over" by Emilia calling out to Othello: "WHAT HO! MY LORD, MY LORD!" (117). In the next sequence of panels on page 118, Zarate avoids displaying the body of the dead Desdemona, instead focusing on the stricken face of Othello as over 9 panels he pulls the purple bed curtains shut to hide the body ostensibly from Emilia, but also significantly from the reader-viewer much like 19th century theater practice. Between the literal hiding of the murdered wife behind a curtain to the more figurative veiling of the murder by depicting only Othello's face and Desdemona's hand in the final 4 panels on page 117, by failing to show the murdered body in any of the subsequent panels after the murder until Desdemona's brief resurrection,

Figure 3. In Oscar Zarate's *Othello*, Desdemona is visually subsidiary to a sympathetically rendered Othello. Workman Publishing, p. 117.

and by interpreting the flow of action by interjecting a panel depicting Emilia outside the bedchamber, Zarate's rendition, while sexualized and violent, still participates extensively in the various distancing and veiling techniques seen on stage to handle the scene.

"Look on the tragic loading of this bed" 5.2.426

Lodovico's invective to Iago, and to us, to "Look at the tragic loading of this bed" exemplifies the continuing awkwardness of portraying the central subject matter of *Othello:* interracial sex, domestic violence, and murder. How each author handles this statement by Lodovico is telling. Osada in his graphic rendering of the final moments of 5.2 once again denies us the context of the bed, instead covering the image of the "loaded bed" with a text balloon. Though Osada does provide an image of Othello's face lying next to Desdemona in the following panel, the couple looks merely asleep. There is no evidence of violence in the image and nothing sexually tantalizing either. Zarate does little better. Although in Zarate's rendition Othello strips off his shirt before stabbing himself and then falling onto the bed, the final image is awkward and Othello's body is wooden in its depiction. In one panel, Othello provocatively hovers just above the lips of Desdemona: "I KISSED THEE BEFORE I KILLED THEE" (129); but their lips do not touch, and then next panel shows a dead Othello lying atop Desdemona's corpse with Emilia's dead body leaning onto the bed as well; however, Othello's figure is drawn in a stilted, rigid and in no way sexual manner. The scene is certainly more pointed than Osada's (and at least the context of the bed is apparent), but it is far from the eroticized, chaotic, and bloody loaded deathbed in Oliver Parker's film. Zarate completes the scene with the bed curtains once again being drawn to hide the bodies, with Lodovico's "LET IT BE HID" (129). The last page of the graphic novel is a full page, framed panel showing the bed curtain, the hand of Othello, and Desdemona peaking through the curtain, hinting provocatively at what we can't see behind (130).

Clearly, these two adaptations, while well within the theatrical tradition of staging *Othello*, are competent and at points stylistically interesting renditions; however, they do not bring any new interpretations to the text because they bowdlerize the sexual, racial, violent, and misogynistic aspects of the play. While these adaptations do not challenge traditional visualizations of 5.2., they do not necessarily reflect on the medium itself, and the reader longs for a graphic novel that more explicitly confronts the troubling aspects of this scene and of the scene's performance traditions. The pursuit of visual depictions that navigate less comfortable aspects of the play would maximize the potential experience for readers of Shakespeare.

Notes

1. See Folger Shakespeare Library Digital Image Collection, luna.folger.edu. Web. 24 June 2014.
2. Examples include 18th and 19th century depictions by William Satchwell Leney (Art File S528o1 no.93), John Massey Wright (Art Box Wa51 no. 2), Henri Gauguin (Art File S528o1 no. 48), Dambrusi (Art file S528o1 no. 63), Charles Taylor (Art File S528o1 no.53), Jean François Ducis (PQ1981. D6A1 1813), Taylor (Art File S528o1 no.62), and (attributed to) François Boitard in Tonson's 1709 edition of Shakespeare (Art File S528o1 no.51).
3. In only three illustrations/paintings, he kneels before the bed but in these Othello is still in the forefront of the image: Richard Rhodes (ART File S528o1 no.65), A. Delvaux (ART File S528o1 no.67), and William Salter (FPa50).
4. No illustrator or adapter is listed for Saddleback's *Illustrated Classics Othello*.
5. See marketing materials at: http://www.mangashakespeare.com/free_resources.html.

Works Consulted

Allen, Chris, and Vincent Goodwin. *Othello*. Graphic Shakespeare. Edina, MN: Abdo, 2009. Print.
Boitard, François (attributed to). *Othello 5.2*. 1709. Engraving. Folger Shakespeare Library, Washington, D.C.
Closs, Adolf. *Othello 5.2*. c. Mid-late 19th cent. Engraving. Folger Shakespeare Library, Washington, D.C.
Hankey, Julie, ed. *Othello: Shakespeare in Production*. Cambridge: Cambridge University Press, 2005. Print.
Kaplan, Paul. "The Earliest Images of *Othello*." *Shakespeare Quarterly* 39.2 (1988): 171–186. Print.
Leney, William. *Othello 5.2*. 1803. Engraving. Folger Shakespeare Library, Washington, D.C.
Neill, Michael. "Unproper Beds: Race, Adultery, and the Hideous in Othello." *Shakespeare Quarterly* 40.4 (1989): 383–412. Print.
Osada, Ryuta and Richard Appignanesi. *Manga Shakespeare Othello*. London: SelfMadeHero, 2008. Print.
Salter, William. *Othello's Lamentation*. 1857. Oil on Canvas. Folger Shakespeare Library, Washington, D.C.
Shakespeare, William. *Othello*. The New Folger Library Shakespeare. New York: Simon & Schuster, 1993. Print.
Siemon, James R. "'Nay, that's not next': *Othello*, V.ii in performance, 1760–1900," *Shakespeare Quarterly*, 37.1 (1986), 38–51. Print.
Vaughan, Virginia M. *Othello: A Contextual History*. Cambridge: Cambridge University Press, 1994. Print.
Vicatan and Dorothy Calhoun Fago. *Othello*. West Haven CT: Pendulum Press, 1980. Print.
Zarate, Oscar. *Othello: Complete and Unabridged*. New York: Workman Publishing, 1983. Print.

Illustrating the Uncertainty Within
Recent Comics Adaptations of Edgar Allan Poe

Derek Parker Royal

Perhaps no other American author has sparked the adaptive imagination of popular culture like Edgar Allan Poe. More than any other writer, he has served as the inspiration for everything from films to video games, from toy action figures to young adult paranormal romance fiction, from television cartoons to concept albums or CDs. Within the medium of comics, the examples are truly staggering with multifaceted adaptations that are faithful to the original texts, politicized and polemical, deconstructive or parodic, satiric as well as irreverent, and appropriative of the Poe persona. Indeed, M. Thomas Inge has argued that Poe has been adapted to the comics medium more than any other American writer, well over three-hundred times as of 2008 (*Incredible Mr. Poe* 14).[1] If in studying comics, one were to limit oneself to those adapted from other media—a gargantuan and formidable task—then one would find the graphic devotion to Edgar Allan Poe to be an ever-expanding cottage industry.

The focus of this present study will concern these comics adaptations of Poe, specifically contemporary manifestations of his work and how the comics form is particularly suited to translate, and even transcend, the conventions in which Poe writes. Here I will follow up on a previous study of Poe adaptations where I investigated (at the time) recent examples of Poe's work in comics form.[2] There, I was especially interested in not only the diverse ways in which Poe's writings had been represented visually, but how the tone of his fiction and poetry had been signified by the various comics artists (for example, uses of romantic irony and the predominance of gothic ambiguity) and how the comics medium is particularly suited to adapt these issues. Since the publication of that essay there have been a significant number of additional Poe adaptations in comics form. In fact, the number of Poe adaptations in comics since 2008 has surpassed that of a previous comparable period, and discussed in the earlier study. For those with a palate for Poe-tinged graphic narrative, the most recent offerings are a veritable smorgasbord.

The examples discussed herein are all clear instances of comics texts, combinations of words and illustrations (although not necessarily a balance of the two) that reveal their narratives through sequential presentation. These are usually multi-paneled pages where the text is inextricably embedded in the graphics, either in speech balloons ("real time" speech action that is part of the diegesis) or extradiegetic "voice-overs," that is, commentary or exposition from a narrator outside of the story's action, usually placed in dialog boxes toward the top of a panel. As such, I am excluding from my analysis those works where the images are merely supplements to the original text, much as you would find in a work of literature decorated with the occasional illustration that carries little, if any, narrative weight. However, in my analysis I will not privilege those comics that are more straightforward or "faithful" to the original, either in form or spirit. Much of the richness to be found in graphic adaptations rests upon the variety of uses to which Poe has been put. Translating into comics form a "true" version of "The Masque of the Red Death" is neither more or less legitimate than using the story as a springboard into an entirely different, and perhaps even contradictory, narrative trajectory.

In this sense, it would be most useful to reference the writings of Linda Hutcheon as a point of departure. In her work on adaptation theory, Hutcheon presents what she calls a "reception continuum" model when defining those cultural productions that deliberately translate, revisit, or remediate a text. At one end of this critical scale are "those forms in which fidelity to the prior work is a theoretical ideal, even if a practical impossibility." At the other end are works that adapt much more loosely, either as "spin-offs"—texts that derive from or offer commentary on a prior work, whether or not that work reuses material from another medium—or "expansions," works that play off of a prior text as a point of departure, such as sequels and prequels, fanzines, and fan fiction (171).[3] Regarding recent comics-based adaptations of Edgar Allan Poe, there are those that fall along the entire spectrum of Hutcheon's model: comics that attempt a faithful translation, those that reinterpret the original narratives in light of more contemporary issues and contexts, graphic novels that use Poe's writings as a springboard for completely original tales, and comics that play off of the iconic status surrounding the nineteenth-century author.

Just as significant as adaptation's relationship with the original is the form of presentation. How the comics are packaged, and made available to the reader, can affect the way we interpret and appreciate the text. The way we read an anthology is different from the manner in which we take in a miniseries (perhaps later collected as a trade) or an original graphic novel. And adaptations written primarily as plot summaries—intended as graphic versions of Cliff Notes—pose different reading assumptions than do translations that are created to stand on their own. Yet, what all of these adaptations have in common is the effort to give graphic expression to the themes that best define Poe's writings: the longings and ambiguities that define the human heart, the dynamics that illustrate the uncertainties within. Over the past several years, these comics adaptations of Poe have taken one of four general forms: multiple stories adapted by various creators in an anthology, an individual tale adapted as a single text, multiple stories adapted by a single artist or creative team into one cohesive volume, and an original fictional narrative where the historical/cultural figure of Edgar Allan Poe serves as the central character.

Adapting the Figure of Edger Allan Poe

Some of the more notable recent adaptations of Poe fall in this latter category, for instead of attempting to translate or remediate his original poems and short stories, they use the *figure* of Edgar Allan Poe as a basis for their own fictional narratives. While this type of appropriation may not be commonly read as an adaptation, it nonetheless functions as one, in that the comics incorporate into their stories references to Poe's literature, which in many ways are inextricable from the persona of Poe himself. When we read of ravens, black cats, pendulums, and haunted palaces, it is difficult not to visualize the actual author behind these creations, a mental image that for many readers has become synonymous with gothic horror. Indeed, several of the more "faithful" adaptations of Poe's stories include frame narrators and even protagonists who bear a striking similarity to popular images we can readily recognize, e.g., middle-aged men with a wide forehead, a parted sweep of hair, a cravat, a smallish mouth, and a moderately shaped moustache.[4]

More to the point are those comics that use the historical figure of Poe as a protagonist without any overt pretense of translating any of his tales. The most liberal use of Poe's persona, and most wildly fantastic, can be found in

Dwight L. MacPherson's *The Surreal Adventures of Edgar Allan Poo* (2007, 2008). Appearing first as a webcomic and then eventually being collected into paperback volumes—two have been published so far—it is the story of a diminutive version of the author who is "expelled" by his larger father figure, Edgar Allan Poe. As the story opens, the writer is exiting an outhouse after having relieved himself, giving birth, so to speak, to the titular character. Master Poo, as he is appropriately named, calls out to his "father" as he is carried away through an underground cesspool—how an outhouse is connected to any kind of sewer system is never explained, one of the many whimsical flourishes that drives this narrative—there meeting a rat by the name of Irving who becomes his devoted travel companion. The actual Poe is suffering from writer's block, losing his inspiration due to the loss of his young wife, Virginia. She visits him in ghostly form, telling the frustrated author that his desire to no longer dream (of her, ostensibly) has resulted in the loss of creativity. MacPherson, here, is equating the miniature Poe/Poo not only with imagination and inspiration, but also (and humorously) with excrement. Yet, this is not a completely irreverent treatment of Poe, as the stakes involved in this strange adventure take on an increasingly philosophical tone.

As the story unfolds, the relationship between Poe and Poo becomes more complicated, with MacPherson embedding into the narrative a number of classic texts, or at least references to them. Many of the adventures take place around large bodies of water, one a literal "city in the sea." On their journey, Poo and Irving travel through dark Raven Forest and meet King Nevermore—a large talking raven, of course—and there are quandaries throughout as to what is actually real. With allusions to "A Dream within a Dream," the "real" Poe asks his ghostly Virginia if he is actually dreaming, to which his departed spouse replies, "We are all but ghosts in the dreamer's dream." Later she insinuates that the true Poe, or at least the imagination that has come to define the author, is like "a little lost lad trying to find his way home" (n.p.). In the second volume, this inspirational relationship is turned on its head, with the "real" Poe melding with the adventuring Poo (referred to at times as the "dream child"), becoming a disembodied guiding force in his quest against the Nightmare King, a nefarious force (apparently created by Poe/Poo himself) plotting to annihilate all creativity. As the title suggests, the events in this comic become increasingly surreal, and as of the time of this writing, MacPherson is still at work on a third volume that will supposedly carry the narrative beyond the temporary victory over the Nightmare King. What is significant here are not so much the labyrinthine, even convoluted, plot twists or the bizarre narrative embellishments, but the ways that MacPherson employs the persona of Edgar Allan Poe to pose the kind of questions and themes embedded in the actual poems and short stories. So while *The Surreal Adventures of Edgar Allan Poo* sits at the "expansions" end of Hutcheon's continuum, more of an inspiration than any act of narrative fidelity, it nonetheless adapts elements of Poe's writings to create something wholly original.

Less surreal but equally fantastical is J. Barton Mitchell and Dean Kotz's four-issue miniseries, *Poe*, later collected as a trade paperback (2010). Much like MacPherson's, this comic takes as its point of departure the death of Poe's wife, Virginia, a loss that has left the author despondent and mentally unstable. His well-being is overseen by an older brother, William, a constable who is currently trying to uncover a series of murders plaguing Baltimore. (The author's real-life brother, William Henry Leonard Poe, was actually a sailor and died at a young age, well before the passing of Virginia.) Poe's writings in mystery and the macabre—he is the originator of the modern detective genre, after all—give him an authority that William reluctantly recognizes, so the brother allows Edgar to accompany him on his investigations. In essence, fiction becomes "reality" as Edgar assumes a role played by one of his most famous creations, C. Auguste Dupin. What he and William uncover is a necromantic scheme perpetrated by someone named Roderick Usher, who uses the life force of others to bring back his dead, beloved sister, Madeline.

Similar to MacPherson, Mitchell and Kotz allude constantly to Poe's famous poems and tales, but using more overtly the imagery and premises as scaffolding upon which to build their narrative. Usher appears throughout most of the story in a death mask and red cloak, embodying the "red death" that, he claims, has largely defined his lineage. He imprisons both Edgar and his brother in a dungeon, a pit, underneath the Usher home, where they are threatened with a bladed pendulum. Poe himself is haunted by dream-like visions of another world, followed constantly by a raven that will not let him forget his departed wife. The ghost of Virginia becomes a character in this narrative, and Mitchell mixes in a variety of other classic horror elements, as well, including mummification, Satanic incantation, and a golem. The literary allusions are both major and minor—at one point, Poe encounters Usher while drunk on Amontillado—and the protagonist is able to free himself of the Usher threat only by relinquishing his obsessions over Virginia, and in doing so says goodbye (literally) to the mysterious raven that has been hounding him throughout the narrative. One of the final images is a "kingdom by the sea" where the spirit of his dead wife finds herself, and the story ends as it begins, with a quote from "Annabel Lee." *Poe* never attempts to remediate or translate with fidelity the actual poetry or stories. Instead, and much more so than do MacPherson, Mitchell and Kotz, it employs the literature loosely to create something like a "spin off," as understood by Hutcheon, that could conceivably have existed as one of Poe's gothic tales or even a conundrum for Dupin.

Adapting Poe in Anthologies and Collections

One of the most innovative, and most varied, means of adapting Poe's writing has been in anthologies. Since Eureka Productions launched Graphic Classics in 2001—indeed, the Edgar Allan Poe volume was the very first in the series—Tom Pomplun, the editor, has offered contemporary artists the opportunity to adapt classic texts in unique ways. As a result, every volume of Graphic Classics provides a multifaceted reading of a single author, or a single literary theme, that challenges traditional interpretive strategies. The latter can best be exemplified through the original *Classics Illustrated* comic-book series (1941–1971), where the adapters followed closely the original storyline, presented the narrative in a straightforward manner, left little in the way of narrative nuance or ambiguity, and rarely represented anything other than a detached omniscient perspective, with almost all visuals at eye-level and panels presented in medium to long shots. It was a kind of "factory" formula that, according to Geoffrey O'Brien, resulted in "officially sanctioned blandness" (qtd. in Richardson 81). Pomplun's *Graphic Classics: Edgar Allan Poe* editions—there have been four so far, each subsequent one containing new adaptations not found in the previous ones—employ a multitude of creators, each with his or her own style and narrative philosophy, so that the art and visual character vary from one adaptation to the next.

In the most recent fourth edition, there are three new adaptations of Poe's short fiction, all of which are rendered in a more or less realistic style.[5] Yet, the artist of each is able to provide his own spin on the story's tone, adjusting the illustration style to reflect the setting and set the appropriate tenor. Carlo Vergara's "The Pit and the Pendulum," adapted by David Hontiveros, relies largely on heavy blacks and grays, punctuated with extreme close ups and skewed visual angles, all of which contributes to the uncertainty and impending doom the protagonist experiences. Hontiveros and Vergara even capture the victim's ambiguous psychological state. The opening five panels of the story seamlessly link the seven black-robed judges with the seven candles visible on the courtroom table, and those seven candles become a series of hellish figures, eventually morphing into a swirling vortex that transitions into

Figure 1. Capturing the inner psychological state of Poe's original tale. David Hontiveros and Carlo Vergara, "The Pit and the Pendulum," from *Graphic Classics: Edgar Allan Poe*, 4th edition. Eureka.

utter darkness (fig. 1). If we have any doubts as to the narrator's state of mind—and, accordingly, his ability to reveal and make sense of his surroundings—Vergara's art provides us with no conclusive answers. In this sense, the creators retain a sense of indeterminacy so common to Poe's fiction, a kind of "romantic irony" that encourages multiple, even contradictory, interpretations. As G. R. Thompson has argued,

> Almost everything that Poe wrote is qualified by, indeed controlled by, a prevailing duplicity or irony [serving as a] device that allowed him both to contemplate his obsession with death, murder, torture, insanity, guilt, loss, and fear of total annihilation in a meaningless universe, and also to detach and protect himself from the obsession [*Poe's Fiction* 9].

This ambiguous stance allows the author not only to blur the lines between reality and imagination, but also to undercut any definitive reading that may imply certain intellectual presumptions. The narrator's experiences at the hands of the inquisition are not clear cut, and as such, they beg us to ask for more context before rendering judgment—something his accusers may be denying him.

The other two new stories in this collection are equally revealing. The art in Rod Lott and Gerry Alanguilan's adaptation of "The Black Cat" is similarly realistic—in this instance, with a clear line style—but the frantic state of mind of the narrator is called into question in two ways. The background surrounding the action is often crosshatched and textured, giving the visuals a kinetic energy that underscores the psychological drama. More significantly, Alanguilan's strategic choice of paneling, often irregular and askew, breaks from the traditional nine-panel grid layout, and as such, suggests the narrator's uncertain mental state, made questionable even further by his alcoholism and his obsession over the cat. In other words, the dubious perspective of the narrator finds expression in the graphic layout of the story. In Rafael Nieves and Dan Dougherty's "William Wilson," obscured visuals add to the uncertainty. Throughout much of the comic, the doppelgänger Wilson's face, not that of the narrator Wilson, is hidden from view, concealed partially or entirely. And after the visage of the narrator's classmate is finally revealed, the twin is often presented within, or at least associated with, some kind of physical border: doorways, windows, recessed panels, and picture frames. All of this has the effect of mirroring, as if the narrator is looking at a reflection of and provoking himself (one of the main themes of Poe's original story). Indeed, in the final pages of the story, the lines between reality and fantasy are intentionally blurred when the narrator finally confronts his double, and does so in a mirror. In essence, Nieves and Dougherty use one of comics' most essential features, framing or paneling, as a way of thematically emphasizing the ambiguities embedded in the original.

These examples from the Graphic Classics volume are closer to the fidelity end of Hutcheon's continuum, not only in their adherence to the basic outline of Poe's stories, but in their aesthetic tone. The creators use the elements of the comics form to bring out the original texts' duplicity, or what Thompson has characterized as their "romantic irony" ("Development of Romantic Irony" 267). The same could be said of the stories in another recent Eureka volume, *Graphic Classics: Edgar Allan Poe's Tales of Mystery* (2011). While adaptations such as "The Murders in the Rue Morgue" and "The Facts in the Case of M. Valdemar" are straightforward, realistic, and generally unequivocal in their visual renderings—and in this way, not entirely capturing the spirit of Poe's romances—others use the artist's style to bring out more fully the text's gothic uncertainty.[6] In "Berenice," Tom Pomplun and Nelson Evergreen utilize acute subjective perspectives (the equivalent in film of low-angle and Dutch angle shots) and extreme close ups, especially on mouths and teeth, to bring out the uncanny obsession the narrator, Egaeus, has for his cousin Berenice. The story even ends with an "explosion" of teeth emanating from Egaeus's box as it drops to the floor, the bloodied dentals appearing to leap out toward the reader, accentuating the horrific infatuation. In "The Man of the Crowd," adapted by Rich Rainey, we have another narrator with a monomaniacal obsession. What marks this particular adaptation is Brad Teare's art, which is woodblock-based, and thus, courser and more primitive than others in the collection. This style brings out the psychological nature of the original: the unnamed narrator is inexplicably drawn to a mysterious man as he moves through the crowded streets of London, and whose motives and actions he is unable to decipher. The unknowability of his subject matter—"I can learn no more of him or his deeds. For some secrets do not permit themselves to be told" (93)—is reflected in the ill-defined contours of the illustrations. Indeed, Teare's rough-hewn art and dusky color palette bring out the thematic underpinnings of this story, one (similar to "William Wilson") that suggests a mysterious and dark doubling.

Other stories in this *Tales of Mystery* collection function similarly, and almost all are set in a time period reflected in the original tale. (Despite the thematic twists many creators make when adapting texts in the various Eureka volumes, most are generally true to Poe's temporal setting.) The one exception to this is Ronn Sutton's adaption of "The Tell-Tale Heart," which is placed in more contemporary times. The narrator in this version is a female punk rocker, and Sutton turns it into a gothic confession of generational tensions, where the young daughter becomes obsessed with eliminating her aging father. This translation in time, framing a particular Poe narrative within more contemporary contexts, rests at the heart of another anthology, *Nevermore* (2008). It comprises adaptations of nine classic stories and poems, as well as a two-page biography of Poe that closes out the volume. The stories stand out because of their temporal incongruities, and this, along with the occasional liberties taken with the plots, makes the collection one of the most notable recent examples of Poe translated into other media.

For example, Jamie Delano and Steve Pugh's "The Pit and the Pendulum" is set in a context reminiscent of Orwell's *1984*. The prison has a depersonalizing and eerily antiseptic feel—metal surroundings, smooth steel fixtures, and sharp blades characterize this pit—and whereas Hontiveros and Vergara's adaption in the Graphic Classics collection retains the darkness found in Poe's original tale, with its heavy use of blacks and grays, this version is brightly lit throughout. Delano and Pugh even switch up the perspective of the impending doom. Instead of the classic swinging pendulum being lowered, the victim/narrator himself becomes a pendulum, slowly descending toward a pit of blades. What is more, references to a camera eye and a wall of television screens suggest a kind of Foucauldian surveillance not found in the other adaptation. Ian Edginton and D'Israeli bend their version of "The Murders in the Rue Morgue" to an even greater degree. The story is set in the year 2859, and C. August Dupin's companion and sounding board—the unnamed narrator in Poe's original—is now a cyber being, a "court appointed personal optronic encoder" assigned to keep tabs on the detective (38). The events are revealed from a detached, omniscient point-of-view, thereby enhancing the futuristic and mechanized tone of the narrative. Dupin uses his court-appointed technology to analyze the data he collects at the Rue Morgue crime scene (e.g., run tests on evidence and generate holograms to recall witness testimony and speculate on motive). As if this version of the story were not divergent enough, Edginton and D'Israeli make the offending orangutan the husband and father of the victims, Madame L'Espanaye and her daughter. In the original, M. L'Espanaye has no place in the story. But here, we learn that he has had an acrimonious split from his wife, and that as a result, she conspired to have L'Espanaye's consciousness transferred—via "memory en-gram overlays" (47)—into that of an orangutan. The betrayed husband's fury, coupled with the simian's strength, lead to the brutal murders.

Other stories in the *Nevermore* collection are set in more recognizable, contemporary times. In Dan Whitehead and Shane Ivan Oakley's "The Fall of the House of Usher," Roderick is a former head-banging musician who inherits a fortune and then secludes himself, along with his twin sister, in an old decaying mansion. The narrator of "The Tell-Tale Heart," adapted by Jeremy Slater and drawn by Alice Duke, is a blind volunteer at a community center for the visually impaired—in this way, retaining Poe's original emphasis on eyes—who becomes obsessed with and tormented by her client, whom she claims can actually see. Leah Moore and John Reppion's adaptation of "The Black Cat" (with art by James Fletcher) is set in a carnival, with a degenerate ringmaster who plots to get rid of the show's ineffectual and expensive-to-maintain black panther. "The Masque of the Red Death," adapted by Adam Prosser and illustrated by Erik Rangel, takes place, appropriately enough, at a comics convention, where the organizers attempt to keep out a deadly plague that surrounds them, telling the attending cosplayers—reminiscent of the masked guests in Poe's original tale—to "forget about the nasty ol' reality for a while" and party down at the costume contest (115). But perhaps the most notable adaptation in the collection, certainly one of the most socially conscious, is

David Berner and Natalie Sandells's "The Oval Portrait." Here, we learn the secrets behind a famous movie star, Liliana Kuschke, whose never-aging visage is linked to a photographer obsessed with capturing the true inner beauty of Lily when she was younger. The story's message is similar to that of the original short tale, but in this contemporary retelling, Berner and Sandells effectively contextualize their remediation within our current image-driven culture. Instead of speculating on the aesthetic links between beauty and its representation, this adaptation suggests the grimmer, more deadening impact of celebrity, where subjectivity is all but annihilated.

Adapting Single Tales

The power of anthologies, such as *Nevermore* and the Graphic Classics volumes, rests in the fact that readers are presented with diverse application of interpretation, both narratively and visually. However, in many instances these individual adaptations in a collection are limited in scope, as the creators have only so much space to encapsulate their vision of an Edgar Allan Poe story or poem. They may reveal the gist of the plot, but in the necessary edits they may truncate (intentionally or unintentionally) significant literary elements of the original, even the story's best defining features. Our understanding of Dupin in "The Murders in the Rue Morgue" may be incomplete by radically changing the tale's focalization, and the full impact of imagery could be lost if the "Haunted Palace" section is eliminated from "The Fall of the House of Usher." Such compromises do not necessarily suggest that the adaptations are inferior or secondary to the original, because much of the pleasure derived from transmedia retellings comes from experiencing repetitions with variation (Hutcheon 4). Still, the logistics of an edited collection may necessitate an unfortunate condensation of an adapted narrative, where artists may feel hamstrung and that they could provide a fuller rendering given more page space. In solo-text adaptations, where one story or poem is given a full treatment in a single comic-book issue or graphic novel, these kinds of limitations can become less of an issue. The artists have more room to explore, more of an opportunity not only to tell the story, but to employ a variety of narrative nuances that may or may not have been embedded in the original source. In this way, and based on a different criterion, we may be inclined to judge an adaptation more thoroughly, even more severely, given the expanded creative freedoms.

Since 2008 there have been several solo-text adaptations of Poe, with creators exploring a single work to greater or lesser degrees. The short-lived publisher Powerpop Comics devoted the first and only issue in its "Classics" series to "The Black Cat" (2009). Adapted by Hobby Jones and S. M. Vidaurri, the comic is basically faithful to the original, even to the point of using in places the exact wording, or very close paraphrasing, from the original. In fact, almost the entire story is related through extradiegetic recitation boxes, or the narrator's "voice-overs," as he describes the events leading up to his condemnation. (There are only four panels in the story that include speech balloons.) Other than that, the narrative is carried by the art, which visually reflects and adds little to the text. So although Jones and Vidaurri are able to play out the entire story in this single issue, they never elaborate on or embellish the tale in any way that would make it unique or allow it to vary much from the original.

Similar to the Powerpop Comics adaptation, Bert M. Herholz relies heavily on Poe's original text, telling much of his story through extradiegetic narration boxes. But in *The Casque of Amontillado* (2012), he brings his distinctive gothic style of illustration to the tale so that the adaptation resonates with a unique personal feel. Inspired by both the Mexican Day of the Dead and his friendship with Philadelphia poet of the macabre, Susurrus Din, as he indicates in the book's "Production Notes," Herholz follows Poe's original in its entirety. He does not add anything extraneous, nor does he delete or diminish any major elements. His "spin" on the story is his art, a sparse style that fully utilizes gothic iconography. The dark, ill-defined catacombs—Herholz's backgrounds have a blurred effect—serve as an appropriate environment for his characters with their elongated torsos, emaciated physiques, slim sharp fingers, and tired shadowed eyes.

Less visually distinctive is Matthew K. Manning's *The Fall of the House of Usher* (2013). Much like that of Herholz, this adaptation follows the story closely, residing on the far "fidelity" end of Hutcheon's reception continuum, including references to both "The Haunted Palace" and the *Mad Trist* of Launcelot Canning. Many, if not most, adaptations of "Usher" fail to reference one or both of these intertexts, but Manning devotes several pages to both, particularly the latter. This is significant, in that the violent and absurd action of *Mad Trist* foretells, as well as parallels, the horrific appearance of Madeline, adding to the ambiguous, dream-like tone of this section. (At this point in the story, there is a question as to the narrator's wakefulness.) And while Jim Jimenez's art is not sophisticated, the use of color goes a long way in distinguishing this adaptation. The artist uses color, specifically a sickly lime green, as a visual braiding device, linking together the horrific elements: the tarn, the fog, the Usher mansion windows, Roderick's music and writings, the *Mad Trist* section, the eerie sound effects, and the fissure that runs all the way down the

House of Usher. Indeed, the glowing green crack stands out when the narrator arrives at the house, and it appears prominently at the end before its fall, visually linking the precarious façade of the house and the fractured mental state of Usher.

In addition, Manning and Jimenez's version of Poe's classic story raises the issue of adaptation and its relation to audience. The book is published by Capstone, a producer of educational books for libraries and classrooms, and it is clearly intended for a younger audience. With its simple art and straightforward storytelling, it reads like a study guide, what other publishers such as Cliff Notes and Saddleback have done with classic literature, and similar in tone to the original *Classics Illustrated* comics. (In fact, there is a glossary in the back, as well as study questions, to aid young readers in their comprehension.)

In stark contrast to this, and much further away from the fidelity end of Hutcheon's continuum, is Wendy Pini's webcomic, *Masque of the Red Death* (2007–2010). It is a sophisticated, futuristic, and highly erotic narrative, based largely on "The Masque of the Red Death." Pini, known primarily for *Elfquest*, the long-running series she co-writes with her husband, Richard, applies her fantastical sensibilities to a gothic tale about ego and death (in fact, the original 1842 title of Poe's story was "The Mask of the Red Death: A Fantasy"). In her reinterpretation, Anton Prosper—the Prince Prosper of Poe's original—inherits his father, immense fortune, and then secludes himself on an island. He is a single-minded and uncompromising man of science, and he uses his wealth to develop a nanotechnology that will not only cure disease, but also theoretically extend life indefinitely. He meets another brilliant scientist by the name of Steffan Kabala, someone he first encountered as a youth and who had subsequently possessed a deep infatuation for Anton. The two develop an intense relationship, psychological as well as sexual, until the Prosper family business rival, Tono Trankule, manipulates Steffan in order to obtain Anton's highly secret research. As a result, the nanotechnology becomes corrupted, infects computer systems worldwide, and by interacting with the biological technology already imbedded in most humans, creates a plague that rapidly kills off the population. Only Anton and his isolated guests remain immune from this "red death"—and victims *do* become a deteriorating mass of red meat once afflicted—but, as in Poe's gothic tale, their attempts to live above the disease all come to naught. Anton's mix of idealism, aloofness, and hubris are what eventually bring his end (fig. 2).

What makes Pini's version of "The Masque of the Red Death" so significant is its elaborate nature. Perhaps more effectively than any other adapter, she has created a complex narrative world from a relatively simple premise,

Figure 2. Gothic meets Carnival in Wendy Pini's elaborate adaptation of "The Masque of the Red Death." Father Tree Press.

developing a story to the point that it takes on a life completely outside of Edgar Allan Poe's shadow. All of the principles are there—a detached and self-involved ruler, the frivolity of the privileged class, a disease running rampant, and even the colored chambers—but Pini's *Red Death* is wholly other and stands on its own. Unlike most other adaptations, there are no visual references to the nineteenth-century author, no obligatory allusions to his classic writings, no iconic insertions (e.g., ravens, pendulums, gothic mansions) that have become code imagery for "Poe." In all, Pini's webcomic stands as an illustrative example of how to adapt the classic writer without allowing the narrative to become completely subsumed by the legend.

An Auteur Approach to Adapting Poe

While anthologies provide a multifaceted look at Poe's world, giving readers varied interpretations of the author's subject matter, collections by a single creator (or creative team) allow for a deeper appreciation of a singular vision. Artists can adapt what at first glance may appear to be a dissimilar collection of Poe's poems and stories, and craft a larger work that bears the stamp of an auteur, providing a more unified message and even giving narrative coherency to the various fragments. One such creative team is Denise Despeyroux and Miquel Serratosa. In a series of three adaptations for Enslow Publishers— "The Gold Bug" (sic), "The System of Doctor Tarr and Professor Fether," and "The Fall of the House of Usher"—they provide a sampling of Poe's fiction collected under the publisher's Dark Graphic Novels series (although, arguably, only one of those Poe stories is unambiguously gothic or "dark"). These translations are generally faithful to the originals with a distinctive cartoony art. This makes sense, as the target audience is younger readers. (Similar to Capstone, Enslow is a publisher of K–12 educational books intended for use in classrooms and libraries.) The same is true of Pedro Rodríguez's adaptation of "The Black Cat," part of another Enslow book, *Chilling Tales of Horror: Dark Graphic Short Stories* (2013). Indeed, Rodríguez's art is even more rounded and iconic, or cartoony, than Serratosa's.

A more sophisticated style can be found in the Classics Illustrated Deluxe edition of *The Murders in the Rue Morgue and Other Tales by Edgar Allan Poe* (2013).[7] Originally appearing in French, the title story, along with "The Gold-Bug" and "The Mystery of Marie Rogêt," stand out because they are all tales of mystery or narratives of detection. Poe is most popularly known as a writer of gothic horror, and while "Rue Morgue" has seen quite a number of adaptations over the years, his other detective narratives have received relatively little attention. Even if such a tale is collected, it is usually done within the context of horror, accentuating the terror of the orangutan or the skull-shape of the golden bug. The comics in this Classics Illustrated Deluxe collection, much more so than in other adaptations, are very heavily word-based with multiple expository text boxes, panels filled with handwriting, and extended dialogue contained within word balloons. They would be composed significantly by what Scott McCloud would refer to as "word specific," or perhaps even "additive," text-image arrangements (153–54). This is due to the fact that these are, as Poe referred to them, tales of ratiocination, narratives based on characters' logical thought processes and their abilities to reason conclusions from both observations and deductive premises. As such, it is necessary for the adapters to emphasize intellectual analysis, best represented through dialogue and text, in order to capture the nuances of the mystery. All three stories in the Papercutz edition convey the feeling of "literariness," not only because of the word-specific emphases, but also because of the rich, realistic art as well as the narrative pacing. The adapters resist the temptation to, as well as had no need to, compress the story, letting the events unfold gradually and in their own time—a significant characteristic of a mystery.

However, the clearest and most telling example of an auteur approach to adapting Poe can be found in the work of Richard Corben. In 2012, he began publishing a series of brand new interpretations of the short stories and poems. Indeed, Corben has a long history with Edgar Allan Poe, beginning in the 1970s and his black-and-white work (along with Richard Margopoulos) in the magazines *Creepy* and *Eerie*. In 1984 he released *A Corben Special: House of Usher* from Pacific Comics, and in 2006 he and Margopoulos adapted ten pieces in *Edgar Allan Poe's Haunt of Horror*, published by Marvel Comics. So recently when Corben began revisiting Poe in the pages of the monthly anthology series *Dark Horse Presents*, he came at it with a rich history behind him. Those texts adapted for the anthology include "The City in the Sea," "Berenice," "The Sleeper," "Shadow," "The Assignation," and "Alone" (Feb. 2012–Oct. 2013). He also produced a series of Poe-related comic-book single issues—and in one case, a two-issue story—to supplement and expand upon his contributions to the *Dark Horse* serial: *Edgar Allan Poe's The Conqueror Worm* (Nov. 2012), *Edgar Allan Poe's The Fall of the House of Usher* (May 2013 and Jun. 2013), *Edgar Allan Poe's The Raven and the Red Death* (Oct. 2013), *Edgar Allan Poe's The Premature Burial* (Apr. 2014), and *Edgar Allan Poe's Morella and the Murders in the Rue Morge* (Jun. 2014). All of these recent Poe adaptions, the six short anthology contributions and the issue-length stories, will be collected in a single volume in fall 2014, *Edgar Allan Poe's Spirits of the Dead*.

What is most significant about this burst of adaptive creativity is the artist's choice to stray significantly from the originals, inserting new subject matter into the tales, narrativizing the images and controlling metaphors in the poetry, injecting his stories with subordinate themes, and combining intertextual elements to create new hybrid narratives. Some of Corben's recent adaptations remain faithful to the originals, only slightly altering the action and speech or inserting additional actants. For example, in his retelling of "The Assignation," the artist retains the general outline of the story and only changes a few elements for purposes of brevity and cohesion. Instead of being a completely mysterious figure, in the traditional gothic sense, the rescuer of Marchesa Aphrodite's child is the protagonist's gondolier, and the artistic splendor of his residence—in the original story, its abundance stuns the narrator—is downplayed. And in "Shadow," Corben again follows the outline of Poe's short story, even preserving the number of characters grieving the loss of the young Zoilus. However, one of the seven fellow mourners is Mag the Hag, a figure that the artist created specifically for his recent series of Poe adaptations. In "Shadow," she is primarily a narrative catalyst, inciting Oinos and instigating a fatal encounter with the enigmatic shadow (and ending more violently than in Poe's tale). But in the adaptation series as a whole, Mag serves as a mysterious narrative guide or host who speaks directly to the reader, introduces stories and gives context, provides levity during grim encounters, and generally hovers over the action as an observer or commentator.[8] In this way, she functions as a framing device and a cohesive presence that links together most of Corben's recent Poe adaptations.[9]

However, there are instances where the artist takes significant liberties with his comics translations, especially for thematic impact. One such example is "The City in the Sea," where Corben narrativizes the short poem into a tale of racial violence. In his version, a shipwrecked merchant confronts a group of shrouded characters who inquire of his dilemma. The survivor tells them that he had to dump his merchandise during a violent storm in order to save his ship. When his interlocutors finally reveal themselves, and after the merchant explains that his "stock" was actually captured slaves, we discover that the shrouded figures are all African men in chains, at which point, the entire island falls into the sea. Although critics have read Poe's "The City in the Sea" as a prophetic tale of race in the United States (Erkkila 55), this theme is not apparent, and Corben teases out this message with visuals that are essential to the comics medium. He performs a similar feat with "The Sleeper." Whereas the original visualizes a graveyard and focuses on the loss of a beautiful woman, evolving into a poetic rumination on death, Corben's version is an extended and dramatic tale of adultery, murder, and revenge.

In his comic-book-length adaptations, Corben further embellishes Poe's narratives. With "The Conqueror Worm," he turns the metaphor of the stage into a literal puppet theater and expands the poem into a tale of horror. In

"The Premature Burial" Corben retains the horrific fear of being entombed alive but injects into the story references to romantic betrayal and necrophilia. He employs a similarly deviant premise in "Morella," where he has the widowed protagonist take his wife's daughter, not his own, to bed. In "The Cask of Amontillado," Montressor confesses not to the reader, but to Fortunato's widow (who has no presence in the original) years after the murderous event. What is more, at the end of Corben's version, Montressor's final act is to commit suicide, alluding to a mysterious and incurable ailment: "I've already received my death sentence from a higher authority. I've decided not to wait for the illness ... a dose of morphine, and I'm gone" (n. pag.). In Poe's original, the "sentence" that Montressor receives is his own nagging guilt—there's even the suggestion that the narrator may be confessing his crime to an interested party (Thompson, *Poe's Fiction* 14)—but in Corben's graphic translation, he is unapologetic and pompous. As such, Mag the Hag's parting words in this story, "In pace requiescat," bears less irony.

Yet perhaps the most distinctive feature of Corben's recent Poe adaptations is the interwoven quality of his narratives, where he combines fundamental elements from two (at times, arguably three) different stories or poems to create a wholly original version. He does this with "The Masque of the Red Death." The story begins with Mag the Hag wandering a desolate landscape, "looking for a story" among the ruins (n. pag.). Eventually she finds a disease-ridden soul, one who begins describing a "fair and stately palace" where once "banners yellow, glorious, and golden on its roof did float and flow." This reference to "The Haunted Palace" morphs into the tale of Prince Prospero and his ill-fated celebration. Upon the appearance of the red death, his castle comes crashing down, much as the House of Usher does, with Corben seamlessly interlinking the two narratives of impudence and monomania.

Roderick Usher's fractured mental state is the occasion of yet another Poe mash-up. In his new version of "The Fall of the House of Usher,"[10] Corben combines the oft-adapted tale with the themes undergirding "The Oval Portrait." Indeed, of all the artist's recent revisions, this one is the most ambitious, played out over two comic-book issues. The story begins in a familiar manner, with the story's narrator, here appropriately named Allan, making his way through bleak terrain to the Usher home. He arrives to find Roderick completely consumed by his art, especially when painting a portrait of his sister, Madeline. As the story unfolds, Allan learns that his friend has become obsessed with his sister to the point of incest. Although Madeline eventually dies and is interred, as in Poe's story, she will nonetheless "live on" in Roderick's painting, responding to Roderick's "advances"—yet another creepy sexual

Figure 3. Mash-up "Fall of the House of Usher" and "The Oval Portrait" in Richard Corben's latest adaptation. Corben, *The Fall of the House of Usher* #1. Dark Horse.

twist, similar to those found in "Morella" and "The Premature Burial." The ending of Corben's new tale nonetheless retains the gothic ambiguity embedded in Poe's original. Just as Madeline's return from the dead is intentionally problematized in the 1839 version—the narrator falls asleep just prior to her horrific entrance, thereby introducing the possibility of dreamscape and throwing the entire conclusion into question—Corben is similarly equivocal. Madeline appears to return, taking form after her portrait is destroyed, although there is no explanation or causal links that are graphically presented. The reader can assume, though, given Corben's use of "The Oval Portrait," that she has been "released" from her aesthetic imprisonment. As in Poe's story, the destruction of the Usher estate (and family) is due to Roderick's mania; but in Corben's reinterpretation, those obsessions are inextricably linked to matters of art. It is no accident that the catalyst here is visual representation, making Corben's new "Usher" a self-reflexive discourse on the power, and limitations, of illustrative art (fig. 3).

Richard Corben, in his ongoing engagements with the nineteenth-century writer, stands as perhaps the most exhaustive and most ambitious comics artist adapting the work of Edgar Allan Poe. However, as all of the other creators discussed in this survey demonstrate, the field of comics adaptation as it relates to Poe is rich, vibrant, and truly varied. The success of a graphic translation is not based on its fidelity to plot, its retention of the original themes, or how realistically its visuals are rendered. In fact, straying from authorial intent, bending the narrative to fit particular agendas, and employing a seemingly discrepant style can bring a text to life in unexpected ways. Even when attempted faithfully, new graphic interpretations of classical or other-media texts tell us just as much, if not more, about the adapter than they do about the original author. In comics, part of the thrill of re-visioning texts is discovering their capacities and the weight they can bear. With the literature of Poe, that potential is apparently boundless.

Notes

1. Inge goes on to observe that only Herman Melville and Mark Twain have come closest to Poe's impact in comics, although I would add to that the work of H. P. Lovecraft, whose comics-based adaptations almost rival those of Poe's. For a further analysis of Poe adaptations in comics, see Inge's "Poe and the Comics Connection."

2. See my 2008 essay, "Sequential Poe-try."

3. Traveling along Hutcheon's continuum from the "fidelity" extremity, one finds works that attempt "true" faithfulness to the original, those that condense or truncate the prior text, those that retell or revision popular works (sometimes in parody), and finally on down to those texts that use the originals as jumping off points for something decidedly different (171).

4. Examples here would include the narrators or protagonists in Matthew K. Manning and Jim Jimenz's *The Fall of the House of Usher*, Pedro Rodríguez's "The Black Cat," and various selections from Denise Despeyroux and Miquel Serratosa's *Dark Graphic Tales by Edgar Allan Poe*.

5. Here, I do not consider the adaptations that were included in the previous editions of *Graphic Classics: Edgar Allan Poe*. In my 2008 essay on Poe adaptations in comics, I discussed in some detail "The Imp of the Perverse," "The Premature Burial," "The Tell-Tale Heart," "The Fall of the House of Usher," "The Cask of Amontillado," and "Never Bet the Devil Your Head," all included in the fourth edition.

6. This volume, number twenty-one in the Graphic Classics series, includes texts originally adapted in other Graphic Classics collections, such as "Eldorado," "Hop-Frog," "The Oval Portrait," "King Pest," and "The Masque of the Red Death." As I have discussed many of these stories in my earlier essay on Poe in comics, I will not address them here.

7. Papercutz's Classics Illustrated Deluxe line has a very different format from the original *Classics Illustrated* comic books, although it revives the famous title.

8. Readers will recognize Mag as an allusion to the many narrative hosts who have shepherded readers through classic horror comics. These include, most famously, EC Comics' Crypt-Keeper, Vault-Keeper, and Old Witch, as well as the many characters they inspired, such as Uncle Creepy and Uncle Eerie in Warren Publications' black-and-white comics and DC Comics' Cain, Able, Eve, and Destiny.

9. In a recent interview, Corben describes Mag the Hag as a device of both connection and disassociation. In a collection of adaptations where readers may not know the originals or have many points of reference, she serves as "an element of familiarity. So there is a sense of friendly continuity between stories and books. Also, it is a way of distancing the reader from feeling he is dealing with uncomfortable concepts" (Interview).

10. It is important to note here that in his recent Poe comics, Corben is revisiting texts that he had previously adapted at least once before, and in completely different manners. "Usher," "The Oval Portrait," "The Conqueror Worm," "Berenice," and "Shadow" had all received a graphic treatment prior to Corben's recent Dark Horse comics, and "The Raven" had even been adapted on two different occasions by the artist.

Works Cited

Berner, David and Natalie Sandells. "The Oval Portrait." In *Nevermore: A Graphic Adaptation of Edgar Allan Poe's Short Stories*. Ed. Dan Whitehead. New York: Sterling, 2008. 79–89. Print.

Corben, Richard. "Edgar Allan Poe's The Assignation." *Dark Horse Presents* #28 (Sep. 2013), Dark Horse Comics. 17–24. Print.

_____. "Edgar Allan Poe's Berenice." *Dark Horse Presents* #16 (Sep. 2012), Dark Horse Comics. Print.

_____. *Edgar Allan Poe's Morella and the Murders in the Rue Morgue* (Jun. 2014), Dark Horse Comics. Print.

_____. "Edgar Allan Poe's Shadow." *Dark Horse Presents* #18 (Nov. 2012), Dark Horse Comics. 25–32. Print.

_____. "Edgar Allan Poe's The City in the Sea." *Dark Horse Presents* #9 (Feb. 2012), Dark Horse Comics. 33–40. Print.

_____. *Edgar Allan Poe's The Conqueror Worm* (Nov. 2012), Dark Horse Comics. Print.

_____. *Edgar Allan Poe's The Fall of the House of Usher* #1 (May 2013), Dark Horse Comics. Print.

_____. *Edgar Allan Poe's The Fall of the House of Usher* #2 (Jun. 2013), Dark Horse Comics. Print.

_____. *Edgar Allan Poe's The Premature Burial* (Apr. 2014), Dark Horse Comics. Print.

_____. *Edgar Allan Poe's The Raven and the Red Death* (Oct. 2013), Dark Horse Comics. Print.

_____. "Edgar Allan Poe's The Sleeper." *Dark Horse Presents* #17 (Oct. 2012), Dark Horse Comics. 41–48. Print.

_____. "Interview: Richard Corben." Interview with Derek Royal. *The Comics Alternative*. 8 Jul. 2014. Web. 29 Jul. 2014. http://comicsalternative.com/2014/07/08/interview-richard-corben/.

Delano, Jamie, and Steve Pugh. "The Pit and the Pendulum." In *Nevermore: A Graphic Adaptation of Edgar Allan Poe's Short Stories*. Ed. Dan Whitehead. New York: Sterling, 2008. 13–23. Print.

Despeyroux, Denise and Miquel Serratosa. *Dark Graphic Tales by Edgar Allan Poe*. Berkeley Heights, NJ: Enslow, 2013. Print.

Edginton, Ian, and D'Israeli. "The Murders in the Rue Morgue." In *Nevermore: A Graphic Adaptation of Edgar Allan Poe's Short Stories*. Ed. Dan Whitehead. New York: Sterling, 2008. 37–47. Print.

Erkkila, Betsy. "The Poetics of Whiteness: Poe and the Racial Imagination." In *Romancing the Shadow: Poe and Race*. Ed. J. Gerald Kennedy and Liliane Weissbert. New York: Oxford University Press, 2001. 41–74. Print.

Herholz, Bret M. *The Casque of Amontillado*. Northampton, MA: Soft Shoe P, 2012. Print.

Hontiveros, David, and Carlo Vergara. "The Pit and the Pendulum." In *Graphic Classics:*

Edgar Allan Poe. 4th ed. Ed. Tom Pomplun. Mount Horeb, WI: Eureka Productions, 2010. 4–20. Print.
Hutcheon, Linda. *A Theory of Adaptation*. New York: Routledge, 2006. Print.
Inge, M.Thomas. *The Incredible Mr. Poe: Comic Book Adaptations of Works of Edgar Allan Poe, 1943–2007*. Richmond, VA: Edgar Allan Poe Museum, 2008. Print.
———. "Poe and the Comics Connection." *Edgar Allan Poe Review* 2.1 (2001): 2–29. Print.
Jones, Hobby and S. M. Vidaurri. *Edgar Allan Poe's The Black Cat*. (Summer 2009), Powerpop Comics. Print.
Lott, Rod and Gerry Alanguilan. "The Black Cat." *Graphic Classics: Edgar Allan Poe*. 4th ed. Ed. Tom Pomplun. Mount Horeb, WI: Eureka Productions, 2010. 28–39. Print.
MacPherson, Dwight L. and Thomas Boatwright. *The Surreal Adventures of Edgar Allan Poo*. Berkeley: Image Comics, 2007. Print.
MacPherson, Dwight L. and Avery Butterworth. *The Surreal Adventures of Edgar Allan Poo, Book Two*. Berkeley: Image Comics, 2008. Print.
Manning, Matthew K. and Jim Jimenez. *The Fall of the House of Usher*. North Mankato, MN: Capstone-Stone Arch Books, 2013. Print.
McCloud, Scott. *Understanding Comics: The Invisible Art*. 1993. New York: HarperPerennial, 1994.
Mitchell, J. Barton and Dean Kotz. *Poe*. Los Angeles: BOOM! Studios, 2010. Print.
Moore, Leah, John Reppion, and James Fletcher. "The Black Cat." In *Nevermore: A Graphic Adaptation of Edgar Allan Poe's Short Stories*. Ed. Dan Whitehead. New York: Sterling, 2008. 67–77. Print.
Morvan, Jean David, Corbeyran, Fabrice Druet, and Paul Marcel. *"The Murders in the Rue Morgue" and Other Tales by Edgar Allan Poe*. Trans. Joe Johnson. New York: Papercutz, 2013. Print.
Nieves, Rafael and Dan Dougherty. "William Wilson." In *Graphic Classics: Edgar Allan Poe*. 4th ed. Ed. Tom Pomplun. Mount Horeb, WI: Eureka Productions, 2010. 40–57. Print.
Pini, Wendy. *Masque of the Red Death*. 2010. Web. 20 May 2014. http://www.masque-of-the-red-death.com/gallery/OnlineComics.html.
Pomplun, Tom and Nelson Evergreen. "Berenice." In *Edgar Allan Poe's Tales of Mystery: Graphic Classics*. Ed. Tom Pomplun. Mount Horeb, WI: Eureka Productions, 2011. 44–55. Print.
Prosser, Adam, adapter, and Erik Rangel, illustrator. "The Masque of the Red Death." In *Nevermore: A Graphic Adaptation of Edgar Allan Poe's Short Stories*. Ed. Dan Whitehead. New York: Sterling, 2008. 105–17. Print.
Rainey, Rich and Brad Teare. "The Man of the Crowd." In *Edgar Allan Poe's Tales of Mystery: Graphic Classics*. Ed. Tom Pomplun. Mount Horeb, WI: Eureka Productions, 2011. 80–93. Print.
Richardson, Donna. "Classics Illustrated." *American Heritage* May/June 1993: 78–85. Print.
Rodríguez, Pedro. "The Black Cat." In *Chilling Tales of Horror: Dark Graphic Short Stories*. Berkeley Heights, NJ: Enslow, 2013. 82–95. Print.
Royal, Derek Parker. "Sequential Poe-try: Recent Graphic Narrative Adaptations of Poe." *Poe Studies/Dark Romanticism* 39–40 (2007–2008): 55–67. Print.
Slater, Jeremy and Alice Duke. "The Tell-Tale Heart." In *Nevermore: A Graphic Adaptation of Edgar Allan Poe's Short Stories*. Ed. Dan Whitehead. New York: Sterling, 2008. 91–103. Print.
Thompson, G. R. "The Development of Romantic Irony in the United States." In *Romantic Irony*. Ed. Frederick Garber. Budapest: Akadémiai Kiadó, 1988. 267–89. Print.
———. *Poe's Fiction: Romantic Irony in the Gothic Tales*. Madison, University of Wisconsin Press, 1973. Print.

The Good, the Bad and the Parodic in Graphic Adaptation

Eric S. Rabkin

This essay examines graphic narrative parodies of works, both those originally graphic themselves and those originally text-only, to explore graphic parody in specific and adaptation in general. By definition, adaptation—from the Latin "ad-apt-are," "to make to fit" (*OED "adapt, v."*)—denotes some sort of change of an item from its original context, form, or function into another. One way to think of artistic adaptation is as distributed among three rhetorical classes: *translational, casual,* and *instrumental.* Turning an English novel meant as entertainment for a popular audience into a French novel or into a film each with the same original type of audience and purpose in mind is translational; the rhetorical goal is that the adaptation in some sense give the new audience essentially the same experience as that had by the original audience. (What one means by "essentially" the same, is, of course, a complex question.) Quite different rhetorical aims motivate singing Robert Frost's "Stopping by Woods on a Snowy Evening" to the tune of "Hernando's Hideaway." The melody reminds one of the humor of the song, and of the musical from which it came, *The Pajama Game*. Frost's original poem is far from humorous. The adaptation here may be worth study by those interested in verse forms, but most hearers of the adaptation will simply smile at the oddity of the adaption. The rhetorical goal is to amuse by incongruity; the opportunity to do so is casual. But to belt out, in outline, the story of Oedipus Rex as a honky-tonk melody, as Tom Lehrer has done in his song "Oedipus Rex," makes one realize that jokes, with their inevitable butts, share a structure, if not a tone, with tragedy (Rabkin 152). Lehrer's adaptation is instrumental; it accomplishes something new by enriching our understanding of the original work and of more besides. In general, successful translational adaptation expands the audience of a work; successful casual adaptation exploits a work; and successful instrumental adaptation enriches or essentially alters or comments upon a work, offering us an experience both recalling the original and adding something significant to it. As we will see, R. Sikoryak's graphic narrative "The Crypt of Brontë" involves translational, casual, and all three varieties of instrumental adaptation in his parody of Emily Brontë's *Wuthering Heights*.

In her book-length study of adaptation, Julie Sanders observes that

> ...adaptation studies mobilize a wide vocabulary of active terms: version, variation, interpretation, continuation, transformation, imitation, pastiche, parody, forgery, travesty, transposition, revaluation, revision, rewriting, echo. As this list of terms suggests, adaptations and appropriations can possess starkly different, even opposing, aims and intentions: as a result, adaptation studies often favour a kind of 'open structuralism' along the lines proposed by Gérard Genette in *Palimpsests* [1997: ix], readings which are invested not in proving a text's closure to alternatives, but in celebrating its ongoing interaction with other texts and artistic productions. To this end, sequels, prequels, compression, and amplification all have a role to play at different times in the adaptive mode [18].

It is not clear in what sense these diverse tasks participate in a single "mode," but it is clear that adaptation is a frequent, variable, and important artistic activity. As Sanders herself points out, agreeing with Julia Kristeva, the reuse of well known tropes, the inclusion of allusion, and intertextuality itself—whether in narrative or music or any other art form—can be seen as acts of adaptation (138). I propose that both the enormous variety of adaptation and our understanding of it can be helped by focusing on one particular variety of rhetorical adaptation, parody.

Parody, from the Greek "parodia," a "burlesque" or "song," comes from the roots "para-" and "ode" (*OED* "parody, n.2") meaning, as it were, "a song alongside the song." It is necessarily adaptive:

> A literary composition modelled on and imitating another work, *esp.* a composition in which the characteristic style and themes of a particular author or genre are satirized by being applied to inappropriate or unlikely subjects, or are otherwise exaggerated for comic effect. In later use extended to similar imitations in other artistic fields, as music, painting, film, etc. [*OED*].

This definition implies that parody can occur at multiple levels of generality. A single work can parody another single work and a single work can address the characteristic style or theme or both of a single work or of the work of a single author or of a whole genre. But this multiplicity of generality is not as daunting as may first appear. Lehrer's honky-tonk "Oedipus Rex" does parody Sophocles's, but since the ancient "Oedipus Rex" was itself created in and understandable as an exemplar of the genre of tragedy, Lehrer's modern parody necessarily engages tragedy generically. To put this another way, understanding any given work, we are, even if not consciously, relying on our own sense of what kind of work it is, what context it inhabits, what audience and purpose it originally bore.

Parody, and adaptation in general, can be from a work in one medium to a work in that same medium. Alexander Pope's *The Rape of the Lock* (1712) satirizes the effete and foppish culture of a certain over-privileged class of 18th century English society by telling the story of an unwanted snipping of hair with a mock seriousness appropriate to an act of rape. Pope famously reinforces this incongruity by using a poetic form, "heroic verse" (in English, rhymed iambic couplets), that one associates with great narratives of great events about great people. This formal incongruity underscores how trivial may be the concerns of the privileged. Pope's parody, his adaptation of form, is instrumental; it supports here not the tales of the founding of nations but social criticism.

Aubrey Beardsley created a set of illustrations (1896) for Pope's parody. In the illustration of the snip itself—or the moment just before—Beardsley's meticulous and abundant etching style, from the embroidered drapes to the absurdly architectural coiffures echoing the formal tree-lined avenue seen receding through the salon window, speaks in a way just as does Pope: these people think themselves the grandest in the world, yet their concerns are, from the world's viewpoint, minuscule. Beardsley puts a tiny man with a wry smile in the forefront of the etching, sharing a knowing grin with the viewer. In that sense, Beardsley has created a character in his graphic that offers visually the tone we hear in Pope's narrator's voice. To the extent that we want to see Pope and Beardsley each as satirizing a particular social class, their works are equivalent; Beardsley has translated Pope's satire from verse to etching. But while Pope's work was itself a parody, is Beardsley's? I think it is, but not because we can see the vapid looks of those oh-so-smooth faces of ennui—that would be only to satirize them, and make Beardsley's adaptation across media merely translational. But Beardsley has caught our eye with the knowing eye of his front-and-center little man, someone who asks us implicitly, as does Pope's narrator's use of heroic verse, to see that all that surrounds him is overblown. Through the jester, Beardsley parodies the visual contents themselves: the hairdos, the clothes, the landscape design. The people shown in the

Figure 1. "The Advent'rous Baron the bright locks admir'd; / He saw, he wish'd, and to the prize aspired." From Pope's *The Rape of the Lock*. *The Victorian Web*, http://www.victorianweb.org/art/illustration/beardsley/20.html.

picture go feebly about their little concerns; the jester winks at us (fig. 1). This is not only translational adaptation but instrumental, an adaptation of a parody that is itself a parody.

In *The Kiss V* (1964), Roy Lichtenstein famously exaggerated one of the visual tropes of "true romance" comic books to comment not so much on the comic books as on our culture of the time. His huge blow-up makes the utter uniformity of the Ben-Day dots that mimic human flesh an implicit observation of the sameness popular culture presumes. Yes, the woman's tears are real, but they are the expected tears, the predestined tears, the tears we almost invite by our attempts to find the uniquely valuable in the repetition of authorized emotion. Lichtenstein frames the embrace closely, so we see little of the context except more Ben-Day dots in the yellow background. And, of course, we can tell—from her make-up and well-styled hair and his blue suit shoulder that she grasps—that these are modern Middle Americans of the period of the painting's creation. Lichtenstein and Pope each adapt works from a source medium (graphic art and heroic verse respectively) into new works in their original media. And Lichtenstein, like Pope, offers social criticism. Unlike Pope, however, I think the fidelity of Lichtenstein's work suggests that while his adaptation is instrumental, it is not parodic.

Jeanne Martinet, on the other hand, certainly does satirize—and parody—graphic narratives in *Truer Than True Romance*. She has taken previously published romance comics and reproduced them exactly as they were ... except for the words. Her volume collects many of these extended parodies, often with one or more pages of the original offered for comparison, but the cover alone makes her point.

The cover illustration closely echoes Lichtenstein's kiss, but captures the moment just before the lips touch, just before the blond woman closes her eyes, brings forth tears, and pulls her head toward the man's strong jaw. Because the cover-illustration viewpoint pulls back somewhat from Lichtenstein's, in addition to the hairdos and garb of middle-class life that Lichtenstein depicts, we see that the background here is a commuter train station. We are in suburbia. (The man's suit color is also changed—perhaps suggestively—from Superman blue to fecal brown.) In his word bubble, the man speaks his mind in this transitional time and place: "Wow. You really are clingy and filled with **self-loathing**. No **wonder** I find you so attractive!" This parody of *True Romances* skewers the culture, the men, and the women, and the comics that fed those fantasies. In fact, although the original cover image is not reproduced in Martinet's book, the book's apparatus reports the source as the cover of *Girls' Romances* #36 (December 1955). Martinet has written in the man's revelation of his need to feel superior where the original had a less clear message: "Don't you believe me, Wendy? I **will** come back!" With those words, we can read Wendy's eyes as scared and uncertain, which accords with Martinet's man observing that she—and perhaps Lichtenstein's woman—is "clingy." In the original comic, that uncertainty is soon resolved by another box on the lower-right of the cover where it says, "In this issue: 'Never Lose Heart!'" On Martinet's cover, her name takes the place of the story title's promising admonition. And we do know, in the original, that the promise is meant seriously because there is an empathetic and hopeful tagline across the top of the cover that says, "LOVE STORIES that could happen to YOU!" "Love stories," not "tragedies." What Martinet's parody from 2001 says, of a work and genre in one form as an adaptation of a work and genre from the same form, is that the cultural apparatus that got us to our present should have been suspect all along. This parody is clearly instrumental.

Adaptation, of course, can be from a work in one medium to a work in another, something that usually happens when a novel is filmed. If the adaptation aims to be purely translational, then it may be thought to have failed as we walk out of the theater muttering about how the book was better or they left out the parts we like best. But adaptation from one medium to another can embrace instrumental possibilities. Moving from text-only works to film or to text-and-graphic works can foreground the importance of the visual. A clear example is the successive adaptations of Robert Louis Stevenson's *Strange Case of Dr. Jekyll and Mr. Hyde* (1886). The story, of course, is well known, how the benevolent Dr. Jekyll becomes changed by the potion he experimentally creates and imbibes which causes him to take to the nighttime streets to commit acts of horrible violence, acts that disgust and repel his daytime self, acts he cannot believe he is performing. Stevenson describes this alternation not merely as behavioral but physical, Mr. Hyde looking brutish, Dr. Jekyll refined. The standard reading of the text is that science—which may be pursued as a desire not merely for knowledge but for power—may unleash the beast that lurks in even the best of us. If we hear the words "jecul and hide" we may realize that Mr. Hyde's name is a homophone for "hide," that lurking inner beast. But once we do, if we look at the spelling of the title names, we can see that "kill" hides (or "hydes") in "Jekyll," too. From birth, the man's brutish potential was already present.

In the *Classics Illustrated* version of this story (August 1943), the cover shows a bottom-lit but elegantly dressed man holding a drinking glass of a green liquid. Behind and above him, but in the shadows, a harsher version of his own face looks down. The lighted face looks at the glass, but the shadowed face looks at the man. The slightly waving lines going from the glass up toward the shadowed face may be vapors of some strange liquid or only the cravat of the darker man, a garment that suggests a comparatively casual and self-indulgent smoking jacket while the lighted man is in formal wear with crisp, black bow tie. The visual medium of the *Classics Illustrated* cover—as does the whole work—makes for a powerful translation. But it is not revealing anything not already in the text for a careful reader, especially one who attends to the spelling of surnames.

Inside that comic, we see a picture of a man in a mirror, the well lighted one whose perspective we share, who looks shocked by what he sees, which is the monstrous face—complete with black-ringed eyes—of his inner self.

That image is recalled in a parody from *The Book of Sequels*, a volume with a delightful cover illustration, in the style of Lichtenstein's *The Kiss V*, in which Rhett Butler is embracing Scarlett O'Hara and saying, "On second thought, I **do** give a damn!" One of the one-page items in this collection is a parody of *Classics Illustrated* called *Sequels Illustrated*, and the issue chosen is "The Strange Case of Dr Jekyll and Mr Heckle" (Beard 125). (Frederic Wertham, too, in his notorious anti-comics screed called *Seduction of the Innocent* [1954], had highlighted this issue of *Classics Illustrated*.) The Beard parody is, as all good parodies should be, instrumental, yet it is also translational. The cartoon characters Heckle and Jekyll, who have forever been visually indistinguishable and equally serving as social nuisances, each have the same look of shock in the mirror. Apparently neither had realized how bad they both were. The image picks up the *Classics Illustrated* image's details, including the chemical apparatuses, wafting vapors, and a skull as memento mori. Whether someone reading *The Book of Sequels* would note all those parallels is unclear; however, what is clear is that they would realize that this is a parodic (incongruously using cartoon characters) adaptation of the Stevenson novel and one in which there is no body within which one can "hyde." Scratch the surface ("heckle" originally meant "scratch" [*OED "heckle, v."*]) and the beast is shockingly there. The *Sequels Illustrated* cover suggests that the illusion of civility is itself monstrous. After all, Heckle and Jekyll always have been, and still are, twin pains to all whom they meet.

More than any other graphic collection with which I am familiar, R. Sikoryak's *Masterpiece Comics* mines the instrumental potential of parodic adaptation. The cover of this collection of works that were originally published over a twenty-year period is itself a parody of *Action Comics*. Five figures seem to burst through the page at the reader, a V-shaped phalanx obviously led in the center by a hard-charging William Shakespeare. Although the other figures are not as obviously identifiable, after reading the book one realizes they are Dante Alighieri, Emily Brontë, Voltaire, and Nathaniel Hawthorne. This is rather far from the Avengers. That this is parody is obvious, and hence that this is adaptation.

Sikoryak implies his intention on the copyright page itself where we find an advertisement for "X-Ray Pics," something all readers of the American comics of the couple of decades following World War II would recognize as a parody of advertisements for "X-Ray Specs." Both the verbal and the visual resonances are clear, but so are the thematic ones: "pics" are what we see, and are being offered to us in *Masterpiece Comics;* "specs" are what we see with, and were offered to us in thousands of comics ... for a price. The price here, since we are already holding the book, is only intelligent attention.

Consider the parallels:

1	X-Ray Pics	X-Ray Specs
2	An Amazing Literary Discovery	An Hilarious Optical Illusion
3	Scholarly optical principle really works! Imagine holding a comic book in front of you. Reading closely allows you to "see" beneath the juvenile 4-color images to a world of deep emotional resonance and significant artistic merit. Look at all the friendly characters. Aren't they somehow tragic now? Loads of laughs and fun at cocktail parties. Glasses not required.	Scientific optical principle really works. Imagine—you put on the "X-Ray" Specs and hold your hand in front of you. You seem to be able to look right through the flesh and see the bones underneath. Look at your friend. Is that really his body you "see" under his clothes? Loads of laughs and fun at parties. No. FL7.............................$1
4	Image of a young man with raised hand	Image of a young man with raised hand
5	Image of a book being held	Image of a buxom female almost being touched

Line 1. The words all refer to seeing what is hidden, reference science, and are almost the same in sound.
Line 2. The modern "discovery" is serious, the older "hilarious." *Masterpiece Comics* means to instruct us.
Line 3. The scholarly principle is ours for the taking, requiring only application. That this (critical reading) is an adult—yet still playful—activity is implied by the pleasure it yields at "cocktail parties." Although this is more grown up than the unqualified "parties" of the older advertisement, the newer advertisement still does not take itself completely seriously. There will be drinking.
Line 4. Both ads suggest enablement, empowerment, something "handy."
Line 5. For the "Pics," what comes to hand is literature, and a new way to look

 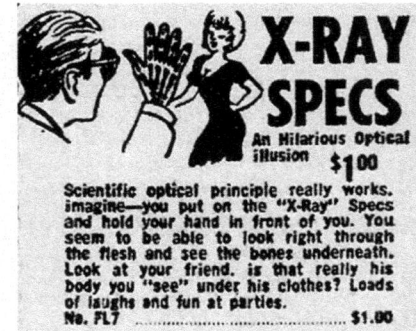

Figure 2. X-Ray Pics from X-Ray Specs. X-Ray Pics from Sikoryak, R. *Masterpiece Comics*, copyright page. X-Ray Specks from zazzle.com, http://www.zazzle.com/x_ray_specs_see_through_clothes_kind_of_sticker–217665619558488771. Drawn and Quarterly.

more deeply into comics as well as the original texts. For "Specs" what comes to hand are our own bones and objects of desire both advertised and obscured by the low-cut dress. Notice that the text (line 3) of the Specs advertisement asks us to imagine the friend as "he" is surprised, but the visual image overcomes the verbal (fig. 2).

At zazzle.com, a gift creation and sales web site that offers, among many options, to make stickers and other objects from the "Specs" advertisement, the site's own copy says, "Not many of us noticed the 'optical illusion' disclaimer ... most of us were focused on the chick in the background. And that is what ripped us off." What Sikoryak wants us to do is refocus, to learn to see more deeply, indeed, to notice the tragic via the world of comics. His parody of the "Specs" advertisement is an instrumental adaptation that comments on the original, creates a new original, and moves the advertisement from something meant to fleece the reader into an integral part of a volume meant to both amuse and instruct the reader. The rest of the volume is one parodic adaptation after another.

Some of those adaptations, like the Pics/Specs parody, take as their originals something from the world of comics, but the extended ones, the ones represented by the literary heroes bursting from the cover, began as text-only works. I am unsure in some cases how far it feels legitimate to push an unpacking of Sikoryak's parodies. In "Blond Eve," for example, his text-to-comic translation creates a casual phonological resonance between "Blondie" (the comic character) and "Eve" (the participant in The Fall) to show us Dagwood as Adam, Blondie as Eve, and Mr. Dithers as God. The original text, of course, was text-only, but it has been translated into more languages than has any other book and illuminated and illustrated and stylistically adapted versions of it abound. In "Blonde Eve," many characteristic actions from the Blondie comics are used, including Dagwood balancing many apples on his arms the way he carries food from the refrigerator to make sandwiches, and Mr. Dithers furiously beating away at Dagwood on top of him with motion lines flying at the moment of condemning him. Did Sikoryak want us to think that Dagwood's greed is the same as the desire for the knowledge of good and evil? Did he want to equate gluttony with lechery, or at least sexual shame, the immediate consequence of eating the apple? Did he want us to see God as cranky and uncaring and unreasonable? I do not find those readings persuasive, but I can't dismiss them because in his adaptation Sikoryak has changed more than the look and feel and narrative tropes of the characters. Blondie/Eve—buxom in the comics and here—is shown in her nakedness with pubic hair. However, picking up an illustration convention that Brian Aldiss names in discussing graphics for classic science fiction magazines, she obviously suffers from the "the Great Nipple Shortage of 1954" (Aldiss 98). This is a Levittown Eve, as we see in the last frame, one in which she and Dagwood have walked directly from Eden into suburbia. In the park-like bushes across the way, we see only the back of Mr. Dither's/God's head as he watches their cookie-cutter home. Is Sikoryak, like Martinet, suggesting that suburban conformity is the condition of The Fall? Sikoryak throughout *Masterpiece Comics* is typically quite accurate with his quotations from his source texts, so his deviations are worth noting. In "Blond Eve," he makes one crucial change from the King James Bible. In Genesis 3:7, we read that "...the eyes of them both were opened, and they knew that they *were* naked; and they sewed fig leaves together, and made themselves aprons." However, Sikoryak has Blondie/Blond Eve shout to Dagwood/Adam, "Quick—gather fig leaves and I'll sew them into aprons" (4). It is true in the Blondie comics that she is always the more sensible of the couple. Is that what the adaptation reflects? Or does it reflect the Levittown stereotype of the stay-at-home mother and homemaker who expects her husband to "bring home the bacon" which she will cook? They are, after all, in the world now. How many readers recall the unmentioned fact that Mr. Dithers's forenames are Julius Caesar? Sikoryak doesn't mention that, but he has asked us to read deeply. Are we being told that to render unto Caesar what is Caesar's (Matthew 22:21) really doesn't do us much good because God and Caesar are, from our viewpoint, the same, and both will only watch and sometimes punish us; both will "dither" about our needs? This would truly exemplify the "Pics" advertisement's suggestion that if we really look at "all the friendly characters" they are "somehow tragic now." "Blond Eve" is, after all, the first full narrative parody in *Masterpiece Comics*. One of the recurring interpretive difficulties with parody, and all adaptation, is how much we can infer was casual, including just our lucky leaps to conclusions, and how much was intentional; how much was a reminder of the source and how much a reworking of the source? The answers to those questions, it seems to me, are easier in what I find to be the most successful of the parodies in *Masterpiece Comics*, "The Crypt of Brontë" (15–29).

Emily Brontë's *Wuthering Heights* was and is a "Gothic novel," which makes it, despite its "classic" status, akin to horror. Sikoryak makes this clear by translating this text-only original into a new version of the infamous EC series *Tales from the Crypt*. And this time, instead of the domestic Nelly Dean as the narrator, we have "The House-Keeper," a visually ghoulish female version of the erstwhile "Crypt-Keeper." At first this adaptation of one character into the other may seem casual, aimed fortuitously at the comedy of incongruity. However, the more closely one attends to the text, the more one sees that much in this parody is warranted translation. Just as many don't read the "he" friend when the chesty female is visible in the Specs advertisement, many don't see the horror in Brontë when they read the text-only original. It is, after all, from a distant and, to many English teachers, revered time. But Sikoryak asks us implicitly to remember that Brontë's 1847 publication came quickly on the heels of Poe's "The Cask of Amontillado" and "The Tell-Tale Heart" and "Ligeia," all works about ghoulishly undying love, works that truly horrified people then but have become familiarized as classics to us. Sikoryak, by getting us to laugh at the silliness of translating a highbrow classic into a pulp format, refreshes our eyes. At the end of his retelling, when she leans over the corpse of Heathcliff—he who has had the side knocked off Catherine's coffin so that when he is buried in an open-sided coffin beside her, their moldering flesh can mingle inseparably for eternity—Nelly asks, "Was he a ghoul or a vampire?" The corpse, in typical EC fashion, is clenched-mouthed, open-eyed, horror-struck, and covered in ichor. Nelly, in typical EC fashion, is grotesque and extending a hesitant, brutish hand toward the body. Surely those words, "ghoul" and "vampire" were, like the images, translations. But they are not. Sikoryak quotes Brontë exactly here. If we take the time to read deeply, we see that the fun of horror has never been, at bottom, fun, but rather whistling by the graveyard. That *Tales from the Crypt* helped us before Congress shut down such "seductive" publications and over a century earlier novelists had as well.

Sikoryak makes us see this. In the novel and the parody, Heathcliff has been horribly ill-treated by Hindley Earnshaw, heir of the man who had taken him in as a youngster and brother of Catherine Earnshaw, the woman who becomes Heathcliff's soul mate. It is their crossed love that provides the armature of the plot. Loving Heathcliff, and knowing he can never advance at Wuthering Heights, the Earnshaw's home, Catherine agrees to marry Edgar Linton of The Grange, a man whose money she intends to use to help Heathcliff. In fact, Heathcliff doesn't realize her motive and, despite his literally undying love, becomes bitter and vengeful. After an absence of years, he returns with money which he lends to a now dissolute Hindley until Wuthering Heights is fully mortgaged to him. Hindley had married a sweet woman, nothing like his unruly sister, but she died soon after bearing their son, Hareton, a weak baby. Catherine and Edgar have a daughter, also named Catherine, who survives, but her mother does not. Heathcliff, ever vengeful, had already taken Isabella, Edgar's sister, forcibly into marriage. Here is Nelly retelling a key moment in this obscene courtship. The text is almost accurate, but the visuals foreground certain matters. Heathcliff is almost always called "Heath," perhaps to update him, as Catherine is called Cathy. But the vision of the dusky Heath

Figure 3. "'Is he a ghoul or a vampire?' I mused." From Bronte's *Wuthering Heights*. Drawn and Quarterly.

here (25), with large hairy hands pulling the struggling Isabel (another updating) toward him, reminds us of a host of filmic hunchbacks, few sweet like Quasimodo, most bitter and "ghoulish," even if, like The Wolfman Heath resembles, they cannot help themselves. Notice that his mouth can as easily be seen as attacking Isabel's throat as her mouth (fig. 3). Nelly does ask, at the end, was he a vampire?

In parodying Brontë, Sikoryak moves us to look more deeply into Brontë, and for some to look for the first time. This parody stops being parodic when we stop being amused at the incongruity and begin to take storytelling in the EC mode seriously. And that teaches us something about the common sources of power for all Gothic art.

But Sikoryak does more. In the original novel, Lockwood, coming to rent Wuthering Heights, where Nelly still works, tells the first few chapters of the story. Only then does Nelly take over. And at the very end, the last words are Lockwood's. A careful reading of the novel lets us know that Nelly is no merely supportive and sympathetic domestic. As the parody highlights, she admonishes, she spies, she carries news. The caption in the frame following this clutching—and it is accurate—begins, "I reported the news to Cathy...." It is easy, reading the novel, and hearing her self-satisfied voice, to forget that Nelly is present and active throughout. Could the original lovers have fared better had she acted differently? To some extent, the novel is not only about crossed love but about observation, and what we make of what we see. And that, of course, is what Sikoryak, by his constant insertion of Nelly into the frames, makes us realize.

At the end of the novel, Isabella's child with Heathcliff is about to marry young Catherine Linton, Catherine Earnshaw's daughter. It seems as if, not only by mingling their spirits and bones but by mingling their offspring, the crossed lovers will find a better fate. The novel ends with Lockwood resuming the narrative and at the very end he leaves Wuthering Heights. It is night. He stops in the churchyard and contemplates the three graves, Edgar Linton on one side, Catherine in the middle, and Heathcliff on the other. "I lingered round them, under that benign sky: watched the moths fluttering among the heath and harebells, listened to the soft wind breathing through the grass, and wondered how any one could ever imagine unquiet slumbers for the sleepers in that quiet earth." Of course, what Brontë is doing here, having just had us read the novel, is letting us know that one could indeed imagine unquiet slumbers, but the impending marriage just might quiet them after all. In the parody, despite "The Tenant" being pictured on the cover (15), Lockwood never appears and never speaks. The last words are those Nelly last speaks in the novel: "I believe the dead are at *peace* ... and it is not right to speak of them with *levity*" (29). This is Nelly, one last time, made to speak in such a way that we know she cannot be trusted, that we must think about her complicity, and wonder about what any story means. That "levity" which we expect with parody can, when made a powerful instrument, fade away.

On the back cover of *Masterpiece Comics*, one of several comic-book style hyper-advertisements claims that this is "Parody & Profundity *in one Package!*" As the works examined here show, parody need not be profound and profundity does not require parody, but when the two align, as Sikoryak has contrived, we encounter adaptations that both illuminate what we knew and give us something marvelous and new.

Works Cited

Aldiss, Brian. *Science Fiction Art: The Fantasies of SF*. New York: Bounty Books, 1975. Print.
Beard, Henry; Christopher Cerf; Sarah Durkee; and Sean Kelly. *The Book of Sequels*. New York: Random House, 1990. Print.
Brontë, Emily. *Wuthering Heights*. Project Gutenberg. [1847]. Web.
Martinet, Jeanne. *Truer Than True Romance: Classic Love Comics Retold!* New York: DC Comics, 2001. Print.
Rabkin, Eric S. *Narrative Suspense: "When Slim Turned Sideways...."* Ann Arbor: University Michigan Press, 1973. Print.
Sanders, Julie. *Adaptation and Appropriation*. London: Routledge, 2006. Print.
Sikoryak, R. (Robert). *Masterpiece Comics*. Montreal: Drawn & Quarterly, 2009 [1989–2009]. Print.

In Search of the White Whale
Adaptations of *Moby-Dick*[1]

Dirk Vanderbeke

Adaptation theory has for a long time grappled with the problem of fidelity and the question of whether adaptations should be judged in relation to their respective originals. Thomas Leitch in his 2008 survey of recent approaches in adaptation studies points out that in spite of the combined efforts of almost every theorist, "the field is still haunted by the notion that adaptations ought to be faithful to their ostensible sourcetexts" (Leitch 64). But then it is not easy to exorcise all demands for fidelity in critical evaluations and also in our own appreciation of adaptations. The expectation that a movie ought to share more with its sourcetext than the title, some basic elements of the plot, and a few overquoted lines, will probably consciously or unconsciously influence the response of most critics and spectators, even if it will prove difficult to pinpoint exactly where artistic freedom ought to yield to considerations of fidelity or accuracy. Robert Stam acknowledges that "the notion of the fidelity of an adaptation to its source novel does contain its grain of truth" (54), but also suggests that "the partial persuasiveness of 'fidelity' should not lead us to endorse it as an exclusive methodological principle" (55).

Inevitably, but also paradoxically, the demand for fidelity will increase in proportion to the artistic complexity of the original; in other words, the more difficult it is to capture the linguistic and metaphorical intricacies of the sourcetext, the higher the expectations will be and the more cruel the verdicts if they are not met. Obviously, no one in his or her right mind would ever criticize Carl Foreman for changing crucial elements in John W. Cunningham's short story "The Tin Star" when he wrote his screenplay for Fred Zinneman's

High Noon. But every attempt at filming any of the "great" canonical works of literature will trigger almost Pavlovian responses of rejection from the literary establishment. Thus it will not come as a surprise that David Lavery's essay on "Melville's *Moby-Dick* and Hollywood," after judging both John Huston's and Franc Roddam's adaptations as merely "superficially faithful" and "failures" (95), culminates in the statement that "*Moby-Dick* has not fared well at the movies" (103). The dismissal of any adaptation seems to have been considered an inevitability, and Elizabeth A. Schultz recounts that "in my junior year at Wellesley college [...] Prof. Patrick Quinn, responding to John Huston's recently released film of *Moby-Dick*, asked us on our final exam to consider why a movie version of Melville's novel would be inadequate" (Schultz xiii).

Presumably, the various comic book adaptations that have been published over the last 70 years[2] would not have met with more grace in the eyes of traditional critics, but then the shift within adaptation studies also informed the perspective on *Moby-Dick* in the comics. In 1982, M. Thomas Inge's survey of Melville adaptations still asked for an evaluation along the usual lines of fidelity:

> Given the popularity and the influence of the comic book, there is an interesting study to be done on the faithfulness of the adaptations of Melville's novels and the influence of the comic book renditions on the public's understanding of Melville [10].

In his later essay "From Ahab to Peg-Leg Pete: A Comic *Cetology*" (2000), however, Inge dismisses the criterion of fidelity and suggests "that the adaptation should be evaluated in terms of its success as a comic book and how creatively it uses and expands on the artistic and technical possibilities of the medium" (158). In this survey, Inge also includes various rather unusual science fiction versions like Rick Veitch's *Abraxas and the Earthman,* a rather weird story culminating in the mystical fusion of whale and human somewhere in outer space, and Alfonso Azpiri's *Lorna: Leviathan*, a softporn variant with a mostly undressed female heroine whose encounter with Ishmael and Queequeg "leaves no doubt about their often questioned heterosexuality in the Melville text" (167).

Over the last two decades, several additional studies of *Moby-Dick* adaptations in the comics have been published, among them Michael C. Berthold's "Color me Ishmael: *Classics Illustrated* Versions of *Moby-Dick*" (1993); Elisabeth A. Schultz's chapter on "Illustrations of Altered Editions of *Moby Dick*" in her comprehensive book *Unpainted to the Last. Moby-Dick and Twentieth Century American Art* (1995); Monika Schmitz-Emans' chapter on heroism and heroes in the comics ("Heldentum und Helden-Comic, Adaptationen von

Herman Melville's *Moby Dick*") in her book *Literatur-Comics*; and Colin E. Beinike's M.A. thesis *Towards a Theory of Comic Book Adaptation* (2011). Of these explorations, Schultz offers a highly informative and perceptive survey of both illustrated versions and comic book adaptations. Schmitz-Emans' approach to the adaptations as instances of hero-comics is peculiar, given that neither the original novel nor most of the adaptations focus on heroism, and the information is occasionally erroneous—e.g. the suggestion that the 1997 recolored and reprinted *Classics Illustrated* edition was a new work by Albert L. Kanter and Louis Zansky fails to take into account that they both died in the 1970s. Berthold focuses on the two *Classics Illustrated* versions (Louis Zansky and Bill Sienkiewicz), Beinike only on Sienkiewicz. Indeed, it is quite obvious that Sienkiewicz receives most critical attention and almost unanimous praise—deservedly, as his version is quite obviously the most ambitious and creative artistic interpretation of Melville's novel as a comic book.

In recent years several new adaptations have also been published, among them works by Will Eisner (1998), Lew Sayre Schwartz / Dick Giordano (2001), Roy Thomas / Pascal Alixe (2008), and Lance Stahlberg / Lalit Kumar Singh (2010); but if Inge assumed that "future artists will [...] find it difficult to escape the power of Sienkiewicz's visual influence" (Inge 2000, 164), this is not really apparent in any of those versions. None of them shows a similar level of symbolic depth and artistic experimentation, and one rather has the impression that the authors deliberately refrained from following Sienkiewicz's example and preferred to stay on the safe side of commercial success, traditional audiences and, in consequence, mainstream formats.

Moby-Dick has a peculiar status. Together with some other works like Homer's *Iliad* and *Odyssey*, Thomas Malory's *Le Morte d'Arthur*, Miguel de Cervantes' *Don Quixote* or Jonathan Swift's *Gulliver's Travels*, *Moby-Dick* is simultaneously popular and unread—at least in the original form. In consequence, these texts are very much in the "public domain," part and parcel of common knowledge, albeit in the form of general associations. As a consequence, *Moby-Dick* has increasingly become a diversified concept; it is no longer one book but an assortment of different versions, ranging from abbreviated adventure tales for children of various ages to the full novel or well-annotated critical editions with lengthy appendices. Moreover, the various movie adaptations have become primary sources for present day audiences; and then, of course, the one-legged captain and his quest for the white whale have become almost proverbial and resurface in the most diverse contexts; for instance, Gary Larson has used the imagery in several cartoons. Ultimately, "Moby Dick" has become a generic term, and every large whale will immediately trigger the name as an automatic response. Similar to *Don Quixote*, a two-part novel of considerable length, which is basically identified with only one episode, the battle with the windmills, *Moby-Dick* is reduced to a core story: Ishmael telling how Ahab chases and fights the whale and how the whale finally sinks the ship. A chase, a fight, a catastrophe—on the one hand simple, on the other hand unreadable. This reduction has also turned Moby Dick into an open metaphor, again similar to other popular literary figures like Don Quixote, Lancelot, Dracula, or Batman. It has been interpreted and re-interpreted so often that it can be used to mean more or less anything—a dumb beast or a sentient being, a symbol of exploited nature or the epitome of evil, Ahab's double, or a metaphor of cosmic ineffability. The book can thus be an adventure tale or a revenge tragedy, an early form of ecocriticism, a psychological study of obsession or insanity, a celebration of homosexual love or male companionship, an instance of racism or antiracism, etc.

In this context, an important point needs to be raised: What is it that a given adaptation actually tries to achieve, and what does it use as its source? I want to argue that five different approaches are possible, which occasionally overlap and may lead to similar results[3]:

1. Of course, an adaptation can set out to achieve a faithful or adequate visualization of Melville's novel—an enormous task, equal to some attempts that have been made over the last decades to offer graphic novel adaptations of works usually considered far beyond such endeavors—e.g. Marcel Proust's *A la recherche du temps perdu* (Stéphane Heuet), James Joyce's *Ulysses* (Rob Berry at http://jamesjoyce.ie/ulysses-seen/) or, distinctly less serious, *The Life and Opinions of Tristram Shandy, Gentleman* (Martin Rowson). The multiple narrative modes—from a seaman's yarn to entries in dictionaries or encyclopae-dias, from discussions about visual representations of the whale to passages in the form of a drama, from semi-academic biological accounts to action packed narrative—demand decisions about their inclusion or exclusion and possibly investigations into their specific malleability for the new medium.

Some specific features of the novel may turn out to be less problematic than expected. The shifting narrative voice and the changes in focalization will, of course, require special attention in any adaptation and may have some impact on the specific handling of the representation of the respective char-acters. Lavery sees this as a crucial aspect for a faithful rendering of *Moby-Dick*, and he demands: "*It must make Ishmael a prominent character and tell the story from his point of view*" (102 italics in the original), even though many incidents in the novel cannot possibly have been witnessed by the ostensible narrator. In graphic novels, however, the unstable narrative situation and focalization do not pose an insurmountable problem, as narration in sequential art frequently changes the point of view, and the audiences have become used to shifting perspectives. The common distinction between captions and speech balloons allows for the necessary differentiation between the narrator and possibly other focalizers, and so Ishmael can tell his part as a voice-over while other episodes lack a recognizable narrator.[4]

Other aspects will prove to be more problematic, for example the dense intertextuality more often than not resists the transfer to the new medium, and while the discussion of pictorial representations of the whale offer themselves to the graphic novel, the almost uncountable biblical and literary allusions would probably defy attempts at visualization.

At present, no "full" version of *Moby-Dick* exists. But then various adaptations grapple with an adequate representation of specific elements, and Elizabeth Schultz approvingly states:

> [T]he illustrations in comic books and abridged versions of *Moby-Dick* also are able to achieve remarkable visual effects that emphasize particular aspects of the novel. However, they render Melville's words irrelevant [80].

From the perspective of recent theoretical approaches to adaptation, the last sentence can be regarded as very high praise.

2. Adaptations address a specific, mostly juvenile readership and offer the basic story as a teaser, hopefully leading to the perusal of the original in some unspecified future. In his 1982 survey, Inge suggested that for his contemporary readers "the introduction to Melville came not in the classroom but by way of the comic book" (9), obviously making a distinction between the ordeal of obligatory school assignments and the fun of voluntary comic book reading. But then it is hard to imagine that Melville's original novel is still high on the agenda of many schools,[5] while *Classics Illustrated/Acclaim Books* presented Zansky's and Kanter's *Moby Dick* in their series of study guides. Most of the existing adaptations emphasize their objective of bringing Melville's novel to a new and young readership—the Pendulum Press series addresses the prospective teacher, Roy Thomas in his "Personal Introduction" to the Marvel edition writes that comic book versions are "appetizers for the bountiful feast to come" (n.p.), the Campfire edition wants to "entertain and educate young minds" (back cover inside), and the Schwarz/Giordano version, first published by the city of Bedford for the 150th anniversary of the novel's first publication, "was created to introduce Melville and *Moby-Dick* to students in the city's elementary school" (48). Of course, the intended audiences can

vary from the rather young to adolescent readers, and this will influence the length and imagery of the adaptation. Shapiro/Nino, Eisner, and Schwarz/Giordano are fairly short and the figures are rather iconic, while Thomas/Alixe and Stahlberg/Singh are longer, darker, but also more realistically executed. Almost each version extends the epilogue to some degree—Thomas/Alixe end with Ishmael being rescued, Shapiro/Nino and Eisner show him safely aboard the *Rachel*, and Schwarz/Giordano even have him back in New Bedford heading for an inland "home" that Melville's novel never mentions. It seems as if the novel's ending is too bleak for the intended audiences and needs some soothing to make it more palatable.

3. Adaptations tend to focus on those aspects of the novel that the audience is already familiar with. In the quest for commercial success, the sourcetext is the public knowledge about *Moby-Dick*, a knowledge based on a melange of associated commonplaces originating in the movies, abbreviated, and usually illustrated, versions for children, and previous adaptations. It is the adaptation of the known that draws a readership, not the adaptation of the unknown, and the successful visualization requires the recognition of what is visualized. Elizabeth Schultz thus suggests a canon of standardized elements in the various adaptations:

> Drawing on the canon of visual narrative episodes, begun by the novel's first illustrators, both the comic-book and children's versions of *Moby-Dick* reinforce the male adventure quest implicit in the novel's chronological narrative. They present sequential tableaux of Ishmael's arrival at a whaleman's inn on a cold night, his terrifying meeting with Queequeg, his emerging friendship with the Polynesian, their meeting with Elijah, their signing on the *Pequod,* Ishmael's anxiety as they wait for Ahab to appear, Ahab's announcement of his quest, his nailing the doubloon to the mast, the pursuit and illustrating cutting up of a whale, the mysterious blazing of St. Elmo's fire, Starbuck's confrontation with Ahab, the pleading of the *Rachel's* captain for help from Ahab, Moby Dick's appearance, the destruction of the *Pequod* by Moby Dick, and Ishmael's survival. Following the first Classics Illustrated edition, Queequeg's rescue of Tashtego becomes a part of the comics' canon [82–83].

Give or take a few short episodes, this is still the plotline of the recent adaptations—and one can imagine a feedback cycle by which the standardized episodes are endlessly retold to juvenile readers and then again to more mature audiences that now expect them in a new movie or graphic novel. Of course, the fight of man and beast is the visual centre of the adaptations, and the covers of the comic book adaptations almost invariably show the confrontation of Ahab and the whale—Sienkiewicz is once more the exception to the rule—sometimes just before the harpoon is thrown and sometimes at the moment when the whaling boat is destroyed. The novel's three chapters about the chase (26 pages) are then very much extended in comparison to the preceding 132 chapters (753 pages). This climax usually takes up between a third and a fourth of the complete adaptation or, in pages, 14–55 in Shapiro/Nino, 9–30 in Eisner, 9–44 in Sienkiewicz, 7–33 in Schwartz/Giordano, 43–132 in Thomas/Alixe, and, slightly less, 10–80 in Stahlberg/Singh. But then the time of the chase is occasionally shortened, and while Shapiro/Nino, Thomas Alixe, and Sienkiewicz maintain the three days, Eisner only has two days and Schwartz/Giordano and Stahlberg/Singh reduce the chase to only one day.

Another aspect in which public "knowledge" may well differ from Melville's novel is the "character" of the whale, and while some of the adaptations retain Starbuck's line that vengeance against a dumb beast is madness or blasphemy (e.g. Thomas/Alixe n.p.), others emphasize the aspect of malice to a degree that indicates that Moby Dick is ultimately endowed with a sentient mind. Most extreme in this respect is Eisner, whose white whale is not travelling the oceans but stationary in the Japan Sea. We are told by Ishmael: "But one did know of *our* coming ... a great white whale. He lurked in wait" (Eisner, n.p., emphasis added), and we are reminded of this two more times. When the chase finally begins and the first harpoon has struck, Moby Dick thinks "This is Ahab.... He is here" (Eisner n.p.). This, of course, may support common notions about Moby Dick as an intelligent being, but it also poses some logical problems: not only does the whale seem to have the gift of clairvoyance, but Ishmael, as the narrator, also seems to know Moby Dick's location, thoughts, and intentions.

4. Adaptations can be influenced by previous visualizations of *Moby-Dick*. Of course, each artist explores the possibilities of his/her chosen medium, and thus responds to previous work on similar subjects. Medieval and Renaissance painters did not only look to the Bible or classical texts as sources for their pictures on religious or mythological topics but also engaged in artistic exchanges and communication with other artists and their creative decisions. Similarly, someone working on *Moby-Dick* will probably be familiar with previous adaptations in the visual media. To varying degrees, the different versions can thus also be regarded as statements within an ongoing discussion, as comments on earlier solutions and suggestions for alternative paths.

In practice, however, the interactions with previous versions are more often than not marked by a lack of radical innovation and show indebtedness to, rather than a departure from, an imagery that has become familiar. As already mentioned, Moby Dick is arguably no longer primarily associated with the novel but rather with the various highly successful adaptations for the screen, in particular the 1953 movie directed by John Huston.[6] While the novel allows and even demands individual imaginative responses to the written text, the movie supplies its audience with images that can quickly become iconic. Public expectations, of course, should not limit the artist to recapitulating pre-existing imagery, but then the iconicity of specific images requires an awareness of their impact on the audience's pre-conceptions and thus the unexpectedness of innovative breaks with such familiar pictures. Most of the comic adaptations shy away from bold experiments, and even though the results can look very different, they usually offer new variants of the traditional mainstream imagery—the same anew, with a twist.

A good example of the impact of the movie is Ahab's appearance. Almost every comic version depicts the captain with some resemblance of the beard made famous by Gregory Peck. This is still true of the most recent versions, and it seems as if Patrick Stewart's celebrated performance in the 1998 TV mini-series has not had a similar impact on the iconography and public perception of Ahab. The image of the bearded captain is actually not supported by the text. In Ishmael's first description of Ahab, no beard is mentioned, and the whitish mark on the face is "[t]hreading its way out from among his grey hairs, and continuing right down one side of his tawny scorched face and neck, till it disappeared in his clothing" (*MD* 122). Close to the end of the book, when the *Pequod* has already passed the Bashee Isles (Philippines), Ahab hands his razors to the blacksmith to forge them into the barbs for his new harpoon, telling Perth that "for now I don't shave, sup, or pray till—" (*MD* 489). It is then stated shortly before the chase that "supper he never touched; nor reaped his beard; which darkly grew all gnarled, as unearthed roots of trees blown over" (*MD* 537). All this indicates that he stopped shaving fairly late in the novel just as he stopped smoking his pipe or discarded the nautical instruments. Rockwell Kent, in consequence, shows him as shaven—but then this does not even change on the last pages when Ahab should have grown a beard after giving away his razors. In the Pendulum Press and Campfire editions, an Ahab with a Gregory Peck beard hands over his razors for the harpoon (Shapiro/Nino 38; Stahlberg/Singh 57), but then the beard does not seem to change afterwards. It is quite possible that the artists, just like Kent, shied away from altering Ahab's image in the course of the adaptation. In the other versions, the scene in the forge is altered, and instead of handing over his razors for the barbs, Ahab now has a new harpoon made from nails or nail stubs (Sienkiewicz 37; Thomas/Alixe, n.p.) or no special material is mentioned. Comic books usually work with a certain level of abstraction and use only a few markers that render faces familiar, and so it is quite possible that a change in Ahab's appearance was considered an impediment to smooth recognition by the readers.

Similarly, none of the comic book versions present Ahab with the slouched hat of the novel (*MD* 130, 537). In Rockwell Kent's illustrations he does, indeed, wear a hat that could be considered slouched, but following Huston's movie he is most frequently depicted with a version of Gregory Peck's top hat (Eisner, Sienkiewicz, Stahlberg/Singh, and Schwartz/Giordano) or no headgear at all (Shapiro/Nino and Thomas/Alixe).

In addition to the impact of Huston's movie, new adaptations are occasionally indebted to earlier adaptations. For example, the layout of Stahlberg/Singh's first two pages indicates an awareness of Shapiro/Nino's opening, even if the content, imagery and atmosphere of the pages are very different.

5. Finally, an adaptation could be primarily interested in its own medium and use the sourcetext only as an impulse to explore innovative possibilities or to join the artistic communication within the medium. And here I have to turn to Bill Sienkiewicz's celebrated work as a possible example. Sienkiewicz obviously departs from the tradition of retelling the story in an easily accessible form. The *Classics Illustrated* series, re-launched in 1990, did not predominantly cater to a young audience but regarded the works as "artistic interpretations" (front cover inside) of canonical works. Indeed, it would be very difficult to imagine how this adaptation could be processed by young minds or pupils in an elementary school.[7] It is even questionable whether the book as an adaptation of *Moby-Dick* can indeed be fully appreciated by readers who do not already know Melville's original text. The episodes are highly condensed and do not really tell a story. They rather trigger recollections or offer artistic comments on aspects of the text the reader is expected to recall. In consequence, Inge questions the status of the adaptation as a graphic novel:

> Given the fact that Sienkiewicz abandons word balloons and the usual panel structure, and he keeps the reader's eye moving mainly from top to bottom in a series of vertical drawings rather than left to right horizontally, one can argue that he has moved in another direction away from the comic book. Since the words and pictures are not always integrated and painting has replaced cartooning, what we may have is an illustrated condensation of the novel—a brilliant one and perhaps a work of art in its own right, but not exactly a version of the pictorial narrative we have come to call the comic book or more recently the graphic novel [Inge 2000, 163].

Regarded primarily as the adaptation of a literary work within the tradition of similar adaptations, Inge's reservation about Sienkiewicz's work may carry some weight, but from the perspective of contemporary developments in comics and graphic novels this evaluation is less convincing. Beineke suggests that:

> Sienkiewicz, along with fellow artist Dave McKean, introduced and popularized the possibility of deviating from the traditional cartooning of comics and bringing to the medium the various techniques, styles, movements, and media utilized and developed in the wider realm of fine and visual art [41–42].

This perceptive point could be carried still further. Comparing Sienkiewicz's *Moby Dick* with Grant Morrison's and Dave McKean's *Arkham Asylum. A Serious House on Serious Earth* (1989), various parallels in the approach are rather striking (see figs. 1 and 2).[8] Especially in the passages from Amadeus Arkham's journals, we find a similar verticality, collages, blurred and smudged images, only captions, and, on one double page, even the rows of pointed triangles that appear repeatedly in Sienkiewicz (most prominently in 16 and 34).[9]

These artistic crossovers are probably motivated by the strong similarity in the topics addressed in the graphic novels— both *Moby Dick* and *Arkham Asylum* deal with trauma, revenge, insanity, the obsession with an animal (whale and bat), and a community of isolates, "each *isolato* living on a separate continent of his own" (*MD* 121, italics in the original). The graphic approach to a canonized work deemed unadaptable turns to an innovative vision of one of the most popular comic book characters and here finds fascinating solutions for its "artistic interpretation." The pictorial allusions and quotations from Morrison/McKean thus present a strong statement

Figure 1. Parallels in artistic approach, including the use of triangles, appear in *Arkham Asylum* and Sienkiewicz's *Moby Dick* (fig 2). Morrison and McKean, *Arkham Asylum*. DC.

Figure 2. The allusion to Murnau's *Nosferatu* is, of course, also quite obvious. Sienkiewiecz, *Moby Dick*, 34. Berkley First.

about the power and potential of an often despised medium. Perhaps, "the great Leviathan is that one creature in the world which must remain unpainted to the last" (*MD* 264), but Sienkiewicz's rather selective and highly condensed adaptation demonstrates that Melville's novel is not beyond creative and captivating visualization. The power of the adaptation, however, does not result from any recognition of the familiar, but from the confrontation with the unexpected which not only offers a new perspective on the original but simultaneously explores the potentials of its own medium and thus also engages in the discussion on the very concept and theory of adaptation.

Moby-Dick is, unquestionably, one of the most often adapted novels in world literature, and each generation of artists adds new versions to the multitude of creative encounters with Melville's novel. These adaptations in the various media have in the course of their history established an alternative sourcetext, a fairly consistent set of narrative and visual elements that have themselves become canonized and now replace the original in public knowledge about *Moby-Dick*. A critical assessment has to take into account that each of these works is not only an adaptation, but also, and perhaps primarily, a contribution to an ongoing series of visualizations of a story that in a feedback loop between popular versions and the collective memory has developed a life of its own and now only shares the title and some basic episodes with the original. The history of the adaptations is, then, a history of repetition with variation, but also of cross-fertilization, of didactical reduction and simplification, but also of the specific developments and changes within comics and graphic novels. Moreover, the different works express the medium's response to commercial demands and reader expectation, but also occasionally the potential for innovative ideas and radical experiment. The works thus allow for a close inspection of the medium as such: its persistent tendency to fall back on established and commercially successful imagery, styles and formats, and its ability, nevertheless, to transgress previous patterns and to find new and exciting artistic techniques and narrative strategies for the advancement of comics and graphic novels as an art, and sometimes even for creative re-interpretations of Melville's inscrutable white whale.

Notes

1. Melville hyphenated the title of his novel, but not the name of the whale within the novel. In secondary literature and in the adaptations, this practice is not always observed. I will follow Melville's usage unless I quote from texts that do not.

2. According to Thomas Inge's 1982 survey, the first was Louis Zansky's 1942 adaptation for *Classic Comics*, later renamed *Classics Illustrated* (9). Jeffrey Levine offers a list of illustrated editions, including comic book adaptations, until 1998.

3. The following observations will necessarily focus on *Moby-Dick* adaptations. For a more general theoretical consideration of literary adaptation in comics and graphic novels, see Vanderbeke, 2010.

4. Sienkiewicz does not use speech balloons but distinguishes narrated passages—which include all instances in which direct speech is accompanied by a narrative formula—including free direct speech near the frames of the banners which are either straight or ragged. This difference seems to have escaped Beinike who claims that "*all* of the text in Sienkiewicz's adaptation appears in captions, even direct statements made by characters that are obviously temporally linked with the respective image" (Beineke 51).

5. Robert Paul Lamb, for example, points out that of the 497 undergraduate students to whom he has taught the novel in the course of thirteen years only 19, i.e. 3.8%, had already read it (42).

6. A direct and acknowledged response to the movie is, of course, Al Feldstein's *MAD* parody "Morbid Dick" from 1956. It is not particularly funny, but the opening line "Call me Fishmeal" (Feldstein 90) is a stroke of genius.

7. It is also the only adaptation I have seen in which Queequeg declares Ishmael and himself "married" (5)—a phrase that might puzzle young readers even more than mature audiences.

8. As Beineke indicates, the influence probably went both ways, and Sienkiewicz had already introduced some of the innovative stylistic elements in his cover for the anniversary issue *Batman #400* (Moench et al. 1986).

9. Elizabeth Schultz reads those convincingly as "sharks' teeth partially fram[ing] characters and objects, conveying the impression of a 'universal cannibalism'" (Schultz 83). In Neil Gaiman's *The Sandman. Endless Nights* (2003) these triangles resurface again in the chapters "Fifteen Portraits of Despair" (art by Barron Storey, designed by Dave McKean, 99) and "Delirium—Going Inside" (art by Bill Sienkiewicz, 117), and in the latter case they are, indeed, linked to sharks.

Works Cited

Azpiri, Alphonso. *Lorna: Leviathan* [1998]. Rockville Center, NY: Heavy Metal, 2000. Print.

Beinike, Colin E. "Towards a Theory of Comic Book Adaptation." MA thesis. University of Nebraska, 2011. Web. 27 August 2013. http://digitalcommons.unl.edu/cgi/viewcontent.cgi?article=1055&context=englishdiss.

Berthold, Michael C. "Color me Ishmael: *Classics Illustrated* Versions of *Moby-Dick*." *Word & Image* vol. 9, January-March 1993, 1–8. Print.

Eisner, Will. *Moby Dick by Herman Melville, retold by Will Eisner*. New York: NBM Publishing, 1998. Print.

Feldstein, Al. "Morbid Dick" [MAD #30, 1956]. *The Organization MAD*. New York: Warner Books, 1973, 88–99. Print.

Gaiman, Neil, et al. *The Sandman. Endless Nights*. London: Titan Books, 2003. Print.

Inge, M. Thomas. "From Ahab to Peg-Leg Pete: A Comic *Cetology*." *Comics & Culture: Analytical and Theoretical Approaches to Comics*. Ed. Magnussen, Anne and Hans-Christian Christiansen.Copenhagen: Museum Tusculanum Press, 2000. 157–176. Print.

_____. "Melville in the Comic Books." *Melville Society Extracts* 50, May 1982, 9–10. Print.

Lamb, Robert Paul. "Fast-Fish and Loose-Fish: Teaching Melville's *Moby-Dick* in the College Classroom." *College Literature* Vol. 32, No. 1 (Winter, 2005), 42–62. Print.

Lavery, David. "Melville's *Moby-Dick*, and Hollywood." *Nineteenth-Century American Fiction on Screen*. R. Barton Plamer (ed.), Cambridge: Cambridge University Press, 2007, 94–105. Print.

Leitch, Thomas. "Adaptation Studies at a Crossroads." *Adaptation* 1, 2008, 63–77. Print.

Levine, Jeffrey. "Illustrated Editions of *Moby-Dick*." *Leviathan* 3.2, 2001, 36. Print.

Melville, Herman. *Moby-Dick or The Whale*. Harrison Hayford, Hershel Parker and G.

Thomas Tanselle (eds.). Evanston and Chicago: Northeastern University Press and The Newberry Library, 1988. Print.
Moench, Doug, et al. *Batman #400. Anniversary Issue*. New York: DC Comics, 1986. Print.
Morrison, Grant, and Dave McKean. *Arkham Asylum. A Serious House on Serious Earth* [1989]. 15th Anniversary Edition. New York: DC Comics, 2004. Print.
Sayre Schwartz, Lew, and Dick Giordano. *Moby Dick. Based on the Novel by Herman Melville* [2001]. Boston: Houghton Mifflin Company, 2002. Print.
Schmitz-Emans, Monika. *Literatur-Comics. Adaptationen und Transformationen der Weltliteratur*, Berlin and Boston: De Gruyter, 2012. Print.
Schultz, Elizabeth. *Unpainted to the Last. Moby-Dick and Twentieth Century American Art.* Lawrence, KS, University Press of Kansas, 1995. Print.
Shapiro, Irwin, and Alex Nino. *Herman Melville. Moby Dick*. West Haven, CT: Pendulum Books, 1973. Print.
Sienkiewicz, Bill, and Dan Chichester. *Herman Melville. Moby Dick*. Classics Illustrated #4. New York: Berkley First Publishing, 1990. Print.
Stahlberg, Lance, and Lalit Kumar Singh. *Moby Dick. Herman. Melville*. New Delhi: Campfire, 2010. Print.
Stam, Robert. "Beyond Fidelity: The Dialogics of Adaptation." *Film Adaptation*. James Naremore (ed.). New Brunswick, NJ: Rutgers University Press: 2000, 54–76. Print.
Thomas, Roy, and Pascal Alixe. *Herman Melville. Moby-Dick*. New York: Marvel Publishing, 2008. Print.
Vanderbeke, Dirk. "It was the best of two worlds, it was the worst of two worlds: The Adaptation of Novels in Comics and Graphic Novels." In *The Rise and Reason of Comics and Graphic Novels. Critical Essays on the Form*. Eds. Dan Hassler-Forest and Joyce Goggin. Jefferson, N.C.: McFarland, 2010, 104–118. Print.
Veitch, Rick. *Abraxas and the Earthman* [1982–83]. West Townshend, VT, 2006. Print.
Zansky, Louis, and Albert L. Kanter. *Herman Melville. Moby Dick* (Classics Illustrated). Recolored and reprinted. Glen Cove, NY: Acclaim Books Study Guides, 1997. Print.

"I don't see what good a book is without pictures or conversations"
Imaginary Worlds and Intertextuality in *Alice in Wonderland* and *Alice in Sunderland*

Matthew J. A. Green

> We all have taken trips in our minds through make-believe lands, where all the queer things we can imagine take place.
> Here is the story of the adventures of a girl named Alice in her wonderland.
> —*Alice in Wonderland*, Classics Illustrated 49

The confluence of a study of "literature based comic books," which are commonly dismissed as failing to faithfully reproduce their source material (Pointner and Boschenhoff 88), and Lewis Carroll's Alice books, which tend not to be read as highly politicized, represents an especially apt site from which to reassert the political bite of intertextuality, a staple concept within Adaptation Studies, and to explore the wider applicability that the idea of the heterocosm or "other world" has for conceiving of the relationship between fantasy and history. While a theoretically informed reading of Bryan Talbot's *Alice in Sunderland* recalls the radical implications once associated with the claim that "any text is constructed as a mosaic of quotations" (Kristeva 66), a nuanced reading of the early *Classics Illustrated* adaptation of *Wonderland* allows for an appreciation of the value placed on imaginary worlds.

The opening caption of the *Classics Illustrated* adaptation of Carroll's classic tale clearly announces its status as a work of fantasy concerned with the "wonderland" of one particular little girl. Notably, the ethos of the series is educational, revolving around the capacity of comics to introduce young readers to canonical literature. Thus, the adaptation's own pedagogical pedigree becomes bound up with that of the earlier work and so, before speaking of Alice or her dreamworld, the editorial voice makes an implicit claim for the value of the fantasy genre based on the universality of imaginative experience. Moreover, while this voice appears at first glance pedantic, if not downright patronizing, things are not quite what they seem. Though the artificiality of such "make-believe" worlds is asserted overtly, these opening two sentences actually begin to blur the line dividing reverie from reality. Imaginary events become substantives, "queer things" coordinated spatially: they "take place." Moreover, even as the existence of a plethora of individualized dreamworlds is announced, the distinction between self-and-other begins to dissolve. The non-sense lands of imagination begin to bleed into the commonsensical world of consensual reality. And the place where this dissolution occurs is precisely at the level of the subject for the caption equates the minds of those reading the text with that of its fictional protagonist: Alice's wonderland becomes a synecdoche standing in for the mental worlds of individual readers. The caption itself, reprinted in all subsequent editions, appears in the first *Classics Illustrated* edition from July 1948, but significantly it replaces an earlier caption from the first page of a preceding edition, serialized in newspaper supplements the previous year under the *Illustrated Classic* title.[1] The *Illustrated Classic* caption asserts the canonical status of *Wonderland* directly and implies that this is the result of a sympathetic rendering of Alice's fantasy world:

> "Alice in Wonderland" has been a perennial favorite among youngsters and oldsters alike for over eight decades. It is a merry story that shows so sympathetically the fancy of a child's imagination [1].

The later caption thus reverses the implicature in this earlier introduction, directly asserting the universality of imaginary worlds while leaving readers to infer for themselves that it will be of interest because it addresses an extraordinary yet not uncommon imaginary experience. The focus has shifted such that the 1948 caption begins not, as the 1947 one does, with an assertion about the text but with a rather bolder claim about the inner lives of its readers. We are no longer asked to sympathize with the non-sensical world of the fictional Alice, but rather to identify with her and to accept fantasy as a constituent part of our daily experience.

The fact that the heroine is herself based on a real person—Alice Liddell—in no way alleviates the complexities involved in effacing the distinction between the text's fictional protagonist and its non-fictional readers. Indeed, if wonderland belongs to the historical Alice at all, it is not because she dreamed it into being but because it was bequeathed to her—first as an oral tale, then as an illustrated and bound manuscript—by Charles Dodgson, the historical figure behind the Lewis Carroll pseudonym.[2] Though not explicit in the story itself, this context is outlined briefly in the biographical notes appended to the main text, in both the *Illustrated Classic* and *Classics Illustrated* editions:

> It was his delightful nonsense told to a child that won the world for Charles Lutwidge Dodgson ... known and loved wherever fairy tales are told as LEWIS CARROLL.
> ...
> Lewis Carroll loved all children, but it was his affection for one child that inspired *Alice in Wonderland*. The little girl's name was Alice Liddell, and she used to visit Carroll at his home. It was on these visits, to the child's delight, that the Oxford professor shed his dignity and spoke of the pompous Walrus, the dour duchess, and the funny mock turtle.
> ...
> Not for the world but for the smile—the laughter of this friend's child—did Lewis Carroll labor on the whimsy and satire contained in his "Alice" [*Classics* 45].

Despite its implicit promise to give us the truth behind the fantasy, the appendix destabilizes the division between fantasy and reality to an extent not actually realized in the narrative itself. The act of unveiling the historical figure behind the nom de plume is accompanied by a similar impetus to reveal the real events behind the fictional story. Initially, this reference to the real is limited to Liddell's role as the inspiration behind Alice before a more sophisticated, though still vague, mapping of the fantastic onto the real appears: "grown-ups read in Carroll's nonsensical verse an amusing indictment of Victorian manners" (45).

Framed in this way, the world beyond the text becomes the source and target of Dodgson's satire. The make-believe world is from the outset populated by figures translated from the pages of history; sense contaminates nonsense from the start, exposing as false the promise of escape offered by the world of reverie. It is precisely Alice's inability to escape the adult world with its contradictions, uncertainties, and lethal arbitrariness that lends her story its dark tincture. But of course the imposition runs both ways for the imaginary world generates a number of real world effects. Not only does satire represent an interventionist genre, seeking both to occasion delight and to reform manners or social practice, but the plethora of adaptations occasioned by the Alice books (which for our purposes include Dodgson's original manuscript

Alice's Adventure Underground, sent to Alice Liddell, *Alice's Adventures in Wonderland*, and its sequel, *Through the Looking Glass, and What Alice Found There*) testify to the extent that Alice's world has entered the popular imagination of the West.

Visually, Alex Blum's artwork in the *Classics* adaptations directly references the artwork of John Tenniel (Jones, *Cultural History* 77), the nineteenth-century illustrator of *Alice in Wonderland*. Less immediately striking, but perhaps even more significant, is the way in which the textual framing outlined above remains faithful to the spirit of the Alice books. Knowingly polyvocal, the published texts deliberately deceive us about their origins through a poetic ascription of their genesis to a boat trip taken by Dodgson and the Liddell sisters:

> Ah, cruel Three! In such an hour,
> Beneath such dreamy weather,
> To beg a tale of breath too weak
> To stir the tiniest feather!
> Yet what can one poor voice avail
> Against three tongues together? [*Wonderland* 5]

That *Underground*, and much less *Wonderland*, did not fly fully formed from Dodgson's lips on that sunny afternoon is a fact well-known to Carroll scholars (Round 183–4); but in an uncanny parallel, the fictitiousness of the *Wonderland's* prefatory poem is mirrored in the historicity of the nonsensical tale that follows, which includes ample references to famous (and not so famous) historical figures, as well as parodies of contemporary attitudes and stereotypes.

Underground, *Wonderland*, and the *Classics'* adaptations dramatize the relationship between fantasy and history in terms of dreaming and wakefulness. All three versions of the story begin with Alice falling asleep and end with her waking up to the sound of her sister calling her name. The *Classics'* Alice responds to her sister's call with a simple "Oh! I've been dreaming!" (*Classics* 44.ii), clearly demarcating the boundary between dream and reality. *Wonderland* and *Underground*, however, end with Alice departing and her sister descending into reverie in a manner that effaces the boundary between the fantasy world and the reader's world. In *Underground*, Alice heads home for tea without communicating her dream to her sister, and the latter dreams not of Wonderland, but of Oxford, "an ancient city, and a quiet river," and of Alice Liddell:

> ... another little Alice, who sat listening with bright eager eyes to a tale that was being told, and she listened for the words of the tale, and lo! it was the dream of her own little sister....
> Then she thought, (in a dream within the dream, as it were) how this same little Alice would, in the after-time, be herself a grown woman: and how she would keep, through her riper years, the simple and loving heart of her childhood: and

how she would gather around her other little children, and make *their* eyes bright and eager with many a wonderful tale, perhaps even with these very adventures of the little Alice of long-ago [89–90; emphasis in original].

Wonderland retains this image of Alice growing older, but in place of the dream-within-a-dream, it introduces the notion that one person's fantasy can come to infect another's. Here Alice recounts her dream before running home and her sister comes to dream first of "little Alice herself," but then of the White Rabbit, the Queen, the Duchess and other characters, before history again intrudes on fantasy and *Wonderland*'s sister, like that of *Underground*, dreams of an older Alice who "would, in the after-time, be herself a grown woman" (110).

In showing the permeability of the boundary between the real and the dream, *Underground* and *Wonderland* call attention to two inter-related aspects of intertextuality, the exchange between text and world and the relationship between texts, both of which are explored by Kristeva in her discussion of "ambivalence." Significantly for the present discussion, Kristeva conceptualizes ambivalence spatially; it "pertains to the permutation of the two spaces observed in novelistic structure: dialogical space and monological space," and temporally, as "the insertion of history (society) into a text and of this text into history" (Kristeva 72, 69). Whereas intertextuality understood as an incorporation of one text within another has become a foundational concept for Adaptation Studies—and indeed is the primary way in which intertextuality has come to be understood—its more radical dimensions, as Worton and Still noted over two decades ago, have tended to be neutralized by subsequent scholars (2). Specifically, the text's ability to intervene in the very historical situation that constrains it, as "writing reads another writing, reads itself and constructs itself through a process of destructive genesis" (Kristeva 77), has tended to be overlooked. A clear example of this neutralization is Gérard Genette's more restrictive definition of intertextuality as "the actual presence of one text within another" in the form of quotation, plagiarism, and allusion (2), which has been generally preferred within Adaptation Studies (Sanders 2; Allen 182).

Carnivalesque Topographics: Alice in Sunderland

That the Alice books themselves stage some of the more radical aspects of intertextuality makes a good deal of sense given that they represent preeminent examples of Menippean satire. The incorporation of the carnivalesque within Menippean discourse links it directly to the concept of intertextuality as developed by Kristeva in her development of Mikhael Bakhtin's exploration of the dialogic dimension of language (Kristeva 79). Describing the process by which "any text is the absorption and transformation of another" (Kristeva 66), intertextuality in this context relates to the iterability of language that makes adaptation possible. In order to speak coherently about adaptations as such, however, the recognition of intertextuality as affecting all texts needs to be qualified with "the added proviso that they are also acknowledged as adaptations *of specific texts*" (Hutcheon 21; see also Allen 180–1). Significantly, as adaptations forsake claims to originality in favor of avowing, with varying degrees of openness, an indebtedness to an earlier text or texts, they have the potential to develop our understanding of intertextuality in creative ways.

Rigorously researched and meticulously executed, Talbot's re-consideration of the Alice books and their legacy amplifies the carnivalesque spirit of his source material to create an alternative social history of Britain. In placing the carnivalesque in the service of a sustained social-commentary, Talbot develops the subversive potential of Dodgson's nonsensical fantasy in a manner that deliberately exceeds the carefully circumscribed satire of the Alice books. As Kristeva notes, "carnivalesque discourse breaks through the laws of a language censored by grammar and semantics and, at the same time, is a social and political protest" (65). That the Alice books clearly draw on Dodgson's expertise as a logician to reprogram the dominant codes (such as causality and non-contradiction) used to structure commonsensical reality is uncontroversial; less obvious, however, is the way in which these books thereby enact a counter-hegemonic position at odds with Dodgson's position in middle-class Victorian society. On a theoretical plane, "there is no equivalence, but rather, identity between challenging official linguistic codes and challenging official law" (Kristeva 65). But what *Sunderland* demonstrates—in its own beautiful exuberance and in the cultural history that it charts—is that the Alice books have proved a longstanding resource across popular culture in general and within counter-cultural productions in particular (257–259, 282, 307).

Sunderland presents a visual and verbal collection of palimpsests in which multiple layers occupy the same frame, a structure that emphasizes its own polyvocality and that of the Alice books. This layering foregrounds an overlapping of fictional and historical worlds that calls into question simplistic distinctions between fantasy and the real. As Round notes, "rather than creating and sustaining a single alternate world on the comics page, Talbot provides us with a range of levels of reality, dreams and imagination, and refuses to validate any one of these levels more than another" (Round 198). Talbot's work enhances our understanding of what Hutcheon describes as a "'palimpsestuous' intertextuality" (21) by fostering a new recognition of the important role the concept of the heterocosm can play in approaching adaptation. An often overlooked mode of adaptation, a heterocosm represents "an 'other world' or cosmos, complete ... with the stuff of a story" and adaptations of a heterocosm transpose "the '*res extensa*' ... of that world, its material, physical dimension" (Hutcheon 14). The most obvious examples of this sort of transposition occur in interactive adaptations like video games and theme park rides or in franchises like *Star Wars* and *Star Trek*, but it also represents a succinct, and hitherto unacknowledged account of the relationship between the worlds of fantasy and of history.

Talbot describes the history of Sunderland as "a little like the history of Britain in microcosm" (Whitson 15) and his rendition of *Alice* explicitly overlays various histories, myths and, significantly, places. As their shared etymological root implies, there exists a strong connection between the representation of a microcosm and the creation of a heterocosm. Talbot reports, "I like to tell stories of parallel worlds where history has taken a different course and can draw from real history for verisimilitude" and he describes *Sunderland* as "an entertainment themed around storytelling, myth and history" (Whitson 13–15). Heterocosmic adaptations have figured widely across Talbot's corpus, ranging from *The Adventures of Luther Arkwright* and its sequel *Heart of Empire*, set across a multitude of parallel universes each including a different history of Britain, to *The Tale of One Bad Rat*, in which elements from the fictional world created by Beatrice Potter overlap with the real world of London and the Lake District. These earlier texts anticipate the deployment of heterocosms in *Sunderland* in various ways. Like the Arkwright books, *Sunderland* celebrates the multiplicity and heterogeneity of history and culture in the face of monologic discourses that work to promote the imperial aims of established interests; *One Bad Rat*, meanwhile, utilizes the overlapping of different worlds to communicate the way post-traumatic stress calls into question the notion of a unified subject, a notion further interrogated through the representations of identity construction and performance that recur throughout *Sunderland*.

Sunderland takes the notion of the imaginary worlds alluded to in the *Classics* adaptations and realizes it visually on the page. Thus pages 115–22 have few panel borders and include overlapping images of scenes from the Alice books, from nineteenth-century Oxford and Sunderland, as well as from

Imaginary Worlds in Alice in Wonderland—GREEN 117

contemporary Sunderland. Similarly, page 174 makes the links between fictional and historical topographies still more explicit by superimposing a number of Tenniel's illustrations across a map of County Durham (see fig. 1).

Nevertheless, pages 68–9 (fig. 2) best exemplify the way in which the combination of multiple worlds facilitates a reconsideration of the official

Figure 1. Overlaying Fictional and Historical Typographies. Talbot, *Alice in Sunderland: An Entertainment.* **Jonathan Cape, p. 174.**

Above and opposite: **Figure 2. A Combination of Multiple Worlds. Talbot,** *Alice in Sunderland: An Entertainment.* **Jonathan Cape, pp. 68–69.**

Imaginary Worlds in Alice in Wonderland—GREEN

pre-history of the Alice books. Here we see various fictional and historical environments and figures associated with the Alice books juxtaposed with a composite image of our narrator, "Pilgrim," walking across Wearmouth Bridge. As Round details, Talbot undermines the myth of Carroll's composition of *Underground* on one golden afternoon, challenging Oxford's monopoly of the

Alice origin story and received representations of Carroll's own sexuality (Round 183–188). Accordingly, the captions on page 68 present a combined narration of the Carroll myth ("according to the myth, the story of *Alice's Adventures in Wonderland* is created spontaneously by Carroll on the 'golden afternoon' of July 4th 1862"), and historical reassessments of his relationship with the Liddell sisters: "There's a popular but unfounded biographical 'fact' that his stutter disappears in their company" (Talbot 68). Visually, this page combines Carroll's photographs of the Liddell girls, facsimile segments from the *Underground* manuscript, a photograph of the *Underground* title page, a wash-drawing of Carroll performing card tricks and one of the celebrated boat trip, Tenniel's illustration of the Dodo from *Wonderland,* and a black-and-white line-drawing of Alice by Talbot that mimics the style of Tenniel's illustrations and Carroll's sketches. This combination of materials foregrounds the dialogic dimension of each of the different literary, historical, and mythic traces that Talbot interweaves, and demonstrates the propensity of texts to exceed their contexts.

Each visual element manifests a different world, and their arrangement makes it clear that they each address themselves to multiple—and very different—audiences. The meanings generated by the presentation of the *Underground* manuscript to Alice Liddell must necessarily have been significantly different from those generated by the inclusion of the facsimile image within *Sunderland*, meanings which vastly exceed the original context of the work. Likewise the photographs of the girls, which as Talbot notes register considerably differently to a post–Freudian audience than it would have to Dodgson's contemporaries (*Sunderland* 115), are here transformed into aesthetic objects that invite additional interpretation. Talbot further emphasizes the polyvalence of images in the top half of the page, digitally altering the photographs of some of the girls to look like paintings. However, while this upper half presents us with an overlapping of different worlds, the bottom half of the page uses the combination of text and image to interrogate notions of authenticity that supposedly underpin these worlds.

The final caption on the page notes that Dodgson "pastes a photograph of Alice Liddell on to the last page [of *Underground*]," a comment that leads into what appears to be the page's only speech bubble, the line-drawn Alice's reiteration of a famous interrogative from the opening of *Underground* and *Wonderland*—"What is the use of a book without pictures?" *Sunderland's* incorporation of this question not only offers a playful nod to the comics medium, but also raises the very serious question of the use to which pictures are put in the creative production or reproduction of various realities within different contexts. The interplay of the photographic portrait pasted into *Underground*, the line-drawings (both Dodgson's and Talbot's), and the photographic facsimile of the *Underground* manuscript, invite a meditation on the authenticity of different visual media. Thus, the simple black-and-white line drawing of Alice announces itself as an artistic (super)imposition, by virtue of its positioning above the other layers, its tonal difference from the wash drawings and photographs, and also because it is a "fake" Tenniel, drawn in his style but in a posture not found in any of the Alice books' illustrations. In contrast, the other line drawings on the bottom half of the page are taken from *Underground*.

This combination of images invites us to draw a hierarchy of authenticity, whereby the photograph takes us closest to Dodgson's source of inspiration; his drawings represent a further abstraction, though still relatively close to the source as they are in the author's hand; and Talbot's image of Alice a further two steps removed, based as it is on Tenniel's adaptation of Dodgson's drawings of the girl. However, the matter is not so straightforward for the photographic portrait was pasted over "the only known sketch Dodgson ever made of the real Alice" (Gardner 132n), an act of obfuscation that necessitated an amendment to the text as it also obscured the final word of the text. Ought we to treat Carroll's photograph of Alice Liddell taken at the same age as his heroine as a more authentic representation of the girl to whom the manuscript was dedicated, or is the drawing in his own hand more in accordance with the original intent and spirit of the piece? While this question is unanswerable, it draws attention to the way in which the various visual elements combine to create an illusion of authenticity that *Sunderland* itself repeatedly exposes as just another stage trick.

This returns us to considerations of intertextual relations rather than a unidirectional relationship between source and adaptation. Specifically, the overt intertextuality of *Sunderland* coincides with a nuanced account of the way in which texts are used, and indeed modified, in order to construct historical realities. Thus, Talbot notes that speculations about Dodgson's sexuality stem from diary and epistolary evidence excised by his family as part of a refashioning of his posthumous reputation (Talbot 115–116). Returning to pages 68 and 69, the page breakdown immediately establishes the search for origins as problematic, with the narrator's voice set in direct opposition to various vignettes depicting a series of historical scenes that the words declare to be fictions. But the visual presentation of this voice draws attention to its own fictionality. Not only is the narrator himself presented as a line drawing, but the background for his panel on the left half of page 69 has clearly been manipulated (it is a digital photograph that has had an artistic filter applied and has been elongated to create an exaggerated perspective). Moreover, while on page 69 the captions clearly lead into, and closely resemble, the narrator's speech balloon, a comparable visual affinity links the captions on page 68 with Alice's speech balloon.

The visual equivalence accorded to narratorial and character speech here develops another of the text's recurrent themes, the presentation of various authorial personas, of various versions of "Bryan Talbot," in different roles throughout. Further, it blurs the boundaries between the domains of thought and speech during the process of transposing Alice's words from Dodgson's manuscript text: "once or twice she had peeped into the book her sister was reading, but it had no pictures or conversations in it, and where is the use of a book, thought Alice, without pictures or conversations" (*Underground* 2). *Wonderland* too has Alice thinking rather than speaking, though minor differences in lexis, punctuation, and formatting indicate that, in keeping with the visual references on the page, Talbot is here working from the earlier text.[3] Talbot's reworking, then, transforms the way in which these words are presented to the reader—no longer is the audience in the position of overhearing Alice's thoughts, but instead these sentiments are addressed overtly to us as the contents of spoken discourse that is visually accorded the same status as that of the author-narrator.

In overriding the distinction between the private, mental world of thought and the public, social world of speech, *Sunderland* shows itself to be compatible with poststructuralist models of identity construction (and it is worth noting that elsewhere in the text, Talbot has considerable fun playing with the concept of performativity); however, this blurring of the boundary between thought and speech also relates to the intercourse between the dream world and the historical, a prominent feature of the carnivalesque and a framing device for *Sunderland* as it is for the Alice books. The text ends with a photorealistic depiction of Bryan awakening in a theatre beside his wife Mary. Again we see a direct overlaying of worlds as Talbot's sleeping body occupies the same geographical and architectural space as the opening frame narrative, the Empire theatre. And once more we are invited to have a laugh at our author's expense as we witness Mary's bemused chastisement of him, "*Really!* I can't believe you slept through *Swan Lake!*" (317). But *Sunderland* is also about the serious effects that dreams and myths can have for those inhabiting the worlds they delineate. The humor of the closing scene arises in part from the suggestion that the author finds himself bored to sleep by high-culture, dreaming instead of various forms of popular entertainment: children's literature, comic books, variety shows, fantasy stories, ballads and dirty jokes. However, just as the airy-nothing of the dreamworld has a direct bearing on historical realities, so too Talbot's project makes it clear that the various ephemera of popular culture have real work to do in defining the sociopolitical landscape.

In fact, *Sunderland* recoups the political force embodied in the Menippean tradition, an impulse seriously attenuated in the Alice books, by seeking to wrest British history and the Union Jack from the allegedly populist discourse of the far right. Full of truly delectable satire, *Sunderland* concludes its performance on page 298 with a clarion call to its audience:

> The extreme right appropriate this flag as an emblem for a small-minded tribal concept of a mythological Britain that has never, nor will ever exist...
> ...except in their dreams.
> This flag is special. It represents our land, our people, our history and our culture.
> All our culture.
> All our people.
> It's the symbol of a story rich in tragedy and heroism [298].

Against the dreams of the far right, based on an exclusionary reading of history, Talbot presents a palimpsestic arrangement of images that visually recall the revisionist history outlined in the previous pages, one which includes battles and monks as well as our erstwhile heroine, Alice (see fig. 3). But even at its most politically sincere, *Sunderland* resists the twin temptations of monologism and univocalism. The historical scenes here depicted evoke a rich cultural fabric and recall preceding instances in which the text has entered into dialogue—often oppositional—with its social contexts. Likewise, the top inset reasserts the artifice that supports this concluding monologue. The player, drawn in black-and-white line art, stands in front of three frames drawn in the same style but presented as draft manuscript artifacts. These frames are themselves repeated from the bottom row of the previous page where they form the conclusion of a four page section in which the panel borders and backgrounds (designed to look like pages torn from a lined notepad), along with the rough draftsmanship, suggest that the historical narrative being conveyed is a work in progress. This visual device returns us to the opening scene, comprised of three full-page panels, in which Talbot the audience member approaches the Empire theatre progressing not through diegetic space or time but rather through various stages of artistic completion. As Round notes these pages "triplicate his opening scene in various states of completion" and thus seem "to expose the processes apparent in creating comics grammar"(192).

Read together, the beginning and end of *Sunderland* thus draw attention to the status of history as a constructed narrative with the production of comics panels serving as a metonym for the imaginative labor involved in any act of storytelling, irrespective of labels such as "fiction" and "non-fiction," "realism," and "fantasy."

Figure 3. A Palimpsestic Arrangement Illustrating History as a Constructed and a Contested Narrative. Talbot, *Alice in Sunderland: An Entertainment*. Jonathan Cape, p. 298.

Véronique Bragard suggests that "comics have become, to use Bakhtin's words, a 'developing genre' whose intrinsic quality is its capacity to create multifarious dialogical forms" (46), while Frank Pointner and Sandra Boschenhoff note that in studying comics adaptations, scholars need to be alert to those "aspects of the act of storytelling that comics are better equipped for than prose" (89). Talbot's focalization of British history through Sunderland/*Sunderland* draws together multiple heterocosms into a palimpsest that both visually and verbally foregrounds a set of dialogical relationships, the traces of which are evident over half a century earlier in the first *Classics* editions. Each of these adaptations in its own way testifies to the propensity of the comics medium to not only depict alternative worlds, but also to bring them into visible juxtaposition with places that are more recognizably "real." Not only is *Sunderland* a work that can only be accomplished in the comics medium, it also demonstrates that adaptations can indeed be understood as "intertextual" in the extended and more radical sense of the word, for it is both polyvocal and dialogical. Kristeva argues, "the poetic word, polyvalent and multi-determined, adheres to a logic exceeding that of the codified discourse and fully comes into being only in the margins of recognized culture" (65). Talbot takes the marginal and repositions it centerstage. In the process, *Sunderland* manages to transport the Alice books from the mainstream canonicity proclaimed by the *Illustrated Classic* adaptation back to the margins, reasserting the capacity of fantasy, humor, and other popular genres to unwind and rewind the weave and woof of a broader social tapestry.

Notes

1. Both titles were owned by the same company (Gilberton) and featured almost identical content, though the stand-alone *Classics Illustrated* titles were shortened from 64 to 48 pages. On the pages that were retained in the 1948 *Wonderland*, the only substantive alterations include changes to the opening caption, as noted, and the addition of a small number of explanatory notes. All illustrations are by Alex Blum, but the scriptwriter is unnamed, though it is likely "the writer would have been one of Jerry Iger's Fiction House regulars, most likely George D. Lipscomb, Harry G. Miller, or John O'Rourke" (Jones, personal communication). For a complete publication history see Jones, "Introduction" loc. 1005

2. Hereafter, in keeping with accepted scholarly practice, all references outside of quotations will be to Dodgson rather than Carroll.

3. The 1897 edition of the novel, revised by Carroll and considered definitive amongst scholars, reproduces this text almost exactly, though it includes quotation marks around Alice's thoughts, replaces "where" with "what" and italicizes "is."

Works Cited

Allen, Graham. *Intertextuality*. 2nd ed. London: Routledge, 2011. *Adobe Digital Editions*. eBook.

Blum, Alex, and Anon. *Alice in Wonderland, Classics Illustrated* 49, Kindle edition (3rd edn). Cambridge, MA: Trajectory, 2013. eBook.
_____. "Alice in Wonderland," Part 1, *Illustrated Classics*, Milwaukee Journal (June 22, 1947). Web. 10 January 2014 http://www.jsonline.com/historicarchive/.
Bragard, Véronique. "Conrad's Two Visions: Intermedial Transgenericity in Anyango and Mairowitz's Graphic Adaptation of *Heart of Darkness*," *European Comic Art*, 6.1 (Spring 2013), 45–65. Print.
Carroll, Lewis. *Alice's Adventures in Wonderland* and *Through the Looking-Glass,* ed. Hugh Haughton. London: Penguin Books, 1998. Print.
_____. *Alice's Adventure Underground*, in *Alice's Adventures in Wonderland* and *Through the Looking-Glass*, ed. Hugh Haughton. London: Penguin Books, 1998. Print.
_____. *Alice's Adventure Underground*, digital facsimile. London: British Library Board, Web. 10 January 2014 www.ebooktreasures.org.
Gardner, Martin, ed. *The Annotated Alice*. Definitive ed. London: Penguin Books, 2001. Print.
Genette, Gérard. *Palimpsests: Literature in the Second Degree*, trans. Channa Newman and Claude Doubinsky. London: University of Nebraska Press, 1997. Print.
Hutcheon, Linda. *A Theory of Adaptation*. London: Routledge, 2006. Print.
Jones, William B., Jr. "*Alice in Wonderland*: Introduction," in Blum, Alex and Anon. *Alice in Wonderland, Classics Illustrated* 49. Cambridge, MA: Trajectory, 2013, loc.1005–1017. *Kindle*. 3rd ed. eBook.
_____. *Classics Illustrated: A Cultural History*, 2d ed. Jefferson NC: McFarland, 2011. Print.
Kristeva, Julia. *Desire in Language: A Semiotic Approach to Literature and Art*, ed. Leon S. Roudiez, trans. Thomas Gora, Alice Jardine, and Leon S. Roudiez. Oxford: Blackwell, 1981. Print.
Pointner, Frank E., and Sandra E. Boschenhoff. "Classics Emulated: Comic Adaptations of Literary Texts," *The CEA Critic* 72.3 (Spring-Summer 2010), 86–106. Print.
Round, Julia. "Contrariwise! Breaking Rules in Bryan Talbot's *Alice in Sunderland*," *Critical Engagements: A Journal of Criticism and Theory* 3.1 (Spring/Summer 2009), 180–201. Print.
Sanders, Julie. *Adaptation and Appropriation*. Abingdon: Routledge, 2006. Print.
Talbot, Bryan. *Alice in Sunderland: An Entertainment*. London: Jonathan Cape, 2007. Print.
Whitson, Roger. "Engraving the Void and Sketching Parallel Worlds: An Interview with Bryan Talbot," *ImageText* 3.1 (Winter 2007). Web. 10 January 2014. http://www.english.ufl.edu/imagetext/archives/v3_2/talbot/.
Worton, Michael, and Judith Still, eds. *Intertextuality: Theories and Practices*. Manchester: Manchester University Press, 1991. Print.

"Does That Change Anything?"
(Post)Feminist Implications of *Gemma Bovery*

Eric L. Berlatsky

Among the handful of most canonical French novels, Gustave Flaubert's *Madame Bovary* (1857) has been praised and critiqued from a variety of vantage points. Persistent among critical readings, however, is the preoccupation with *Bovary*'s treatment of gender. That is, despite Flaubert's claim that his ambition was to write "a book about nothing" (*Letters* 154), in fact, he most certainly wrote a book about the constraints of gender, among other things. As the iconic story of a "tragic adulteress" who embodies a number of female stereotypes while subverting others, it brings into focus the troubled relationship between the supposed universality of canonical literature and the specifics of modern gender politics. One of the longstanding objects of critique of the feminist movement has, of course, been the literary canon, particularly because of its exclusion of female authors and traditionally "feminine" literary forms.[1] Conversely, texts traditionally labeled as "universally" great often display problematic, even misogynistic, attitudes toward women.

These objections themselves are, of course, now long in the proverbial tooth and *Madame Bovary* has certainly met with its share of feminist resistance. From its date of publication, the novel's attitudes towards women have been hotly contested. Flaubert's letters and treatment of his paramour, Louise Colet, display a wide streak of misogyny,[2] but *Bovary* itself is more complicated and has evoked more diverse responses.[3] Therefore, when a contemporary woman cartoonist recasts the novel in the present day, as Posy Simmonds does in her graphic novel, *Gemma Bovery*, it seems destined to interrogate the gender politics of the original and even to expose its failings through feminist critique. Liz Constable's reading of *Gemma* treats it in precisely this fashion, examining the graphic novel's focus on food and eating in order to explore the ways in which society both encourages and polices female "consumption."[4] Despite the validity of this reading, however, to see *Gemma Bovery* as decisively feminist where *Madame Bovary* is not is to substantially misread both texts.

Simmonds' *Gemma,* a cleverly self-reflexive adaptation, was originally published serially, one page at a time, in the *Guardian* in the late 1990s. Simmonds' hybrid text is neither traditional comics, nor an illustrated book, as it intermixes blocks of typed prose with progressions of panels of various sizes and shapes, both framed and not, with hand-lettered captions in a variety of styles, on tall, thin pages reflective of their newspaper origins. It is set in both contemporary London and Normandy, whereas *Madame Bovary* is written, of course, purely in prose, and is set in provincial France a century and a half previous. In making these changes, and others, *Gemma* asks questions about the nature of adaptation and about the significance of alterations to an original with as much cultural capital as *Bovary*. Many of these changes work to point the reader to the substantial differences (and similarities) between gender roles in the two times and places, interrogating whether or not Flaubert's original can be said to speak to us in such different circumstances, even given its reputation as a perennial. While Flaubert can confidently write to Louise Colet that "poor Bovary, without a doubt, is suffering and weeping at this very hour in twenty villages in France" (*Letters* 195), such confidence cannot help but wane when the "hour" is long past.

Likewise, Simmonds' treatment of Flaubert is not a categorically feminist one, as its rejection of *Madame Bovary*'s conclusion surprisingly reasserts the powerlessness of its female protagonist in ways that, if anything, exceed the depiction of Emma Bovary's own lack of agency. *Gemma,* then, suggests that *Madame Bovary* is not sufficiently "universal" to account for the pressures and circumstances that impinge upon the lives of contemporary bourgeois women, but it does not simply reject the novel as so much antiquated patriarchal propaganda. Rather, it reminds us of the ways in which *Madame Bovary* still speaks to us *and* the ways in which its insights must continually be supplemented and/or adjusted for contemporary readers.

Madame Bovary, *Gender Politics and Narrative Ambiguity*

From its inception, *Bovary* was read not only as a formal *tour de force*, as a shockingly realistic depiction of provincial France, and as a legally actionable corruption of its readers' morals, but also as a comment upon contemporary gender roles. In one of the earliest (and most famous) commentaries on the novel, Baudelaire praised Emma Bovary as an exhibition of masculine spirit within a female body, one that resists the social restrictions placed upon it by marriage and community. For Baudelaire, in creating Emma, Flaubert imbues her with his masculine and "virile soul," "relinquish[es] ... his actual sex and make[s] himself into a woman" (339). That is, as the famous, if elusive Flaubertian dicta, "Madame Bovary c'est moi!" indicates, Baudelaire reads Emma as a female Flaubert, but a version invested with his (presumed male) imagination, virility, and intellect. Baudelaire's assumption that imagination, intellect, and sexuality are, by default, masculine prerogatives, is itself sexist, but it is possible to argue that when Flaubert creates a woman with these attributes, he makes an implicit claim that Baudelaire is wrong to jump to that conclusion. For Baudelaire, Emma represents "the perfect human being" (342), combining the best "natural" features of the two genders and raising woman "above the realm of the purely animal and close to the ideal realm of men" (342). His assumption that women need a man like Flaubert to initiate them into the human family could hardly be more condescending, but it does highlight the ways in which *Bovary* depicts Emma as fully human *despite* Baudelaire's, and others', assumptions to the contrary. Likewise, in the eyes of Baudelaire, and later critics like Lawrence Birken (618), Emma approaches the ideal of androgyny, some 70 years before Virginia Woolf expressed it in *A Room of One's Own*.[5]

Subsequent critical conversation has then, not surprisingly, frequently focused on the novel's attitude towards women. Some feminist commentators have castigated the book for its portrayal of a stereotypically "romantic" woman who predictably falls victim to "bovarysm," the "problem of delusional self-perception" (Petruso 46),[6] while others argue that the very notion of "reality" upon which a critique of bovarysm depends is actually an ideological construction of patriarchy (see Small).[7] Nevertheless, the way in which Emma eventually "succumbs" to her "baser" bodily desires is frequently read as a realization and embrace of sexist stereotypes about women's voracious, uncontrollable sexual (and consumer) desires. Insofar as the novel "blames" Emma for her own descent from boredom into infidelity, debt, and, suicide, it collaborates with a variety of patriarchal stereotypes.[8]

Other critics, however, have been quick to note that Flaubert's withering irony applies not only to Emma and her behavior, but also, if not more so, to her plodding, vacuous, incompetent, "officier de santé" (not quite a doctor), husband Charles, and to the hypocrisies of the ostentatiously conventional bourgeois residents of Yonnville (Yawn-ville). Given the failings of those around her, it is not shocking, and perhaps not even blameworthy, that Emma seeks excitement in ways and means that those around her judge harshly. Also, given the restrictions on the options of nineteenth-century bourgeois women in the provinces, actions against the status quo such as those she takes are, perhaps, nearly the only ones possible, in resisting a bourgeois woman's inevitable fate of boring drudgery. Given all of these factors, it is not unreasonable to see Emma as a potential feminist icon, attempting to take control of her life and gain agency in a world where the deck is stacked against her. That the best she can do is engage in adultery and commit suicide can be read more an indictment of the society in which she lives than of Emma,[9] though her eventual fate is itself stereotypical.[10]

Even the moments in the novel that are most critical of patriarchal society are riddled with ambivalence, simultaneously excusing Emma's sins and attributing them to "natural" origins in sexist fashion:

> She wanted a son; ... this idea of having a male child was like an anticipated revenge for the powerlessness of her past. A man, at least, is free; he can explore each passion and every kingdom, conquer obstacles, feast upon the most exotic pleasures. But a woman is continually thwarted. Both inert and yielding, against her are ranged the weakness of the flesh and the inequity of the law. Her will, like the veil strung to her bonnet, flutters in every breeze; always there is the desire urging, always the convention restraining [82].[11]

The passage is typical of *Bovary*'s contradictory treatment of gender. On one hand, it exhibits the awareness that women's subjugated social position is a result of "convention," an "inequity of law" that allows men to pursue their desires and "thwarts" women's efforts to do the same. At the same time, the passage exhibits (stereo)typical attitudes in its description of women (and particularly Emma) as "inert" and "yielding," while simultaneously ruled by a "weakness of the flesh" that results in a (contradictory) overpowering "desire." The passage critiques patriarchy, but it also collaborates with it in its discursive construction of women as simultaneously passive and voraciously passionate.

Complicating matters further is the formal feature for which *Bovary* is best known, and that which has enshrined it in the modernist canon as an essential early influence: its pervasive deployment of *style indirect libre* (or "free indirect discourse"). Free indirect discourse is, of course, characterized by its evasiveness in matters of narratorial attribution.[12] While it maintains a third person point-of-view in pronoun usage, it blends the language, attitudes, and perspectives of an extradiegetic narrator with those of one or more of the novel's characters.[13] Above, the passage reflects Emma's own attitudes (her desire for a son, her belief that men are free, women not), though it is perhaps unlikely that she would express her beliefs in precisely such metaphorical terms ("like the veil strung to her bonnet"). The blending of Emma's emotions, beliefs, and language with that of the narrator makes it even more difficult to pinpoint the novel's attitudes about gender, as about all things. Is it Emma who considers her inability to achieve social and sexual satisfaction as a symptom of a society stacked against her, or does the extradiegetic narrator offer that explanation? Does Emma consider herself to be "inert" and "weak" (rehearsing familiar sexist stereotypes), or are these beliefs strictly those of a (sexist male?) narrator, or merely the "received ideas" of the community? The use of free indirect discourse makes the answers to these questions largely unknowable.[14]

Dominick LaCapra has noted that the most disturbing element of the novel for those who prosecuted it for obscenity was "the absence of an authoritative center of moral and cognitive judgment to serve as a reliable guide for the reader" (119, 127). Flaubert and the publishers, in turn, were able to successfully defend the book, not on the basis of artistic merit, but on the grounds that it was clearly opposed to Emma's adulterous transgressions. The basis for this was not any overt commentary by the narrator, but by the bitter end to which Emma succumbs (LaCapra 34). The painstakingly detailed and stomach-turning description of her suicide by poison was meant, claimed the defense, to warn against Emma's actions and deter women with similar impulses. The claim is, of course, questionable. The scene can just as easily be read as a critique of those who abandon or ignore Emma in her hour of need, of the husband whose idiocy drives her to adultery, of the unctuous Lhereux who preys upon Emma's attempts to alleviate her sorrows with material goods, etc. As the tribunal initially proposed, without a stable narratorial voice, the events described do not clearly indicate one moral/ethical position.

The very thing that disturbed the French legal system is, of course, that which was most likely to make the novel a classic. Where the justice system hates moral and ethical ambiguity, such abstruseness has historically attracted the literary critic, whether in New Critical or poststructuralist mode. In this vein, Baudelaire praised *Bovary*, saying "a true work of art does not need to make moral pleas" and that "it is the reader's task to draw the right conclusions from its outcome" (340). The novel's capacity to both blame Emma for her actions *and* to castigate the circumstances that lead to them, while obscuring any categorical ethical judgment within an evasive, but innovatively precise, formal web contributes heavily to the novel's canonization, particularly insofar as the critical climate which developed over the next century was heavily influenced by Flaubert and his admirers.

Gender and Gemma

Certainly, the questions of "individual responsibility" vs. "social influence" highlighted in *Bovary* continue to be relevant to both life and literature today, and the novel's ambiguous judgment of the origins of Emma's sins are relevant to the contemporary reader. At the same time, given the advancements of feminism and the shifts in gender roles in the West over the past century and a half, certain elements of *Bovary*'s celebrated ambivalence no longer seem as compelling. Certainly, we are no longer inclined to consider seriously the implication that women are naturally "inert," that they are more likely than their male counterparts to mistake romance for reality, or that they are less able to control their bodily impulses. While these stereotypes undoubtedly persist, they are no longer a largely unquestioned assumption, and they can be, in this essay at least, relegated to the category of "sexism," or even "misogyny." Likewise, many of the social and institutional restrictions that exist to "thwart" bourgeois Western women in Flaubert's novel no longer exist in the time and place of Simmonds' *Gemma*. Gemma, as the graphic novel portrays, is not prevented, or even discouraged, from pursuing premarital sex, nor is she forced into her marriage with an undesirable partner. Likewise, Gemma has a series of jobs (graphic designer, interior decorator) and, as such, is more free to pursue her own "desires," both personal and professional, though often those desires are themselves questionable for other reasons.[15] While Emma Bovary is trapped in a marriage she cannot escape through divorce, and her life options do not include professional development, Gemma is free to pursue marriage (and divorce) with whomever she pleases, to pursue employment that is intellectually fulfilling, and even to change her geographical location on a whim, as she does when she abandons London for Normandy. Emma's inverse desire to abandon the provinces for Paris is, of course, "thwarted." The closest she can get is the occasional weekend tryst in Rouen.

With all of these differences, it would be easy to conclude that *Madame Bovary*'s relevance to our times, at least in terms of gender politics, would be minimal at best. Indeed, without the *names* of the characters in *Gemma Bovery*, it might not occur to a reader to link the two texts at all. It is true that Gemma is dissatisfied with her husband and embarks upon an affair, but such a description applies to any number of texts (and "real women") both before and after the publication of *Bovary*. In fact, Simmonds cleverly both encourages readers to, and discourages readers from, connecting the two texts. While both Gemma's first and last names are only one letter removed from her literary precursor, her maiden name is not similarly linked to Emma's. Likewise, while she too marries a "Charlie," it is surprisingly revealed near the close of the book that he is not "Charles Bovery" (as the reader and baker/narrator Joubert expect), but is, in fact, named "Cyril." With this revelation, the book breaks with *Madame Bovary* in significant fashion, as Joubert, up to this point, has been expecting Charlie to die, in accordance with his literary near-namesake, of a broken heart. In the aftermath of Gemma's death, Joubert is convinced that the Bovery family is following the pre-established plot of *Bovary*, but the revelation of Cyril's "real name" breaks the spell, making Joubert realize that there is no inevitability to the "pattern" he has detected. When Charlie asks Joubert, "Does that change anything?" (104), the answer cannot help but be "yes," not only for Charlie's prospects in escaping impending death, but also for women's prospects in our contemporary world.

This is not, however, the first deviation Simmonds' story takes from Flaubert's. Gemma, for instance, does not commit suicide (as Joubert expects), but instead accidentally chokes on a piece of (Joubert's) bread. Also, whereas in *Madame Bovary,* Charles is Emma's first sexual partner, in *Gemma,* Charlie is clearly a "rebound" from her more serious affair with Patrick Large. The two men Gemma has affairs with *after* her marriage (the aristocrat Hervé de Bressigny, and, briefly again, Large, on his visit to France), are not clearly parallel to Emma's lovers (Léon, the student and eventual lawyer, and Rodolphe Boulanger, the aristocrat). Hervé, for instance, is both student *and* aristocrat, combining some distinguishing features of both Léon and Rodolphe. Likewise, while Emma is the victim of Rodolphe's callous and cynical seductions (first), she pursues Léon (second) after loving him platonically before meeting Rodolphe. Gemma, on the other hand, pursues Hervé (first), before briefly falling victim to Large's charms (after already having had a sexual affair with him in England). Even Charlie Bovery himself exchanges places with the Leon side of Hervé at the close of the book, in which Charlie lives on and finds another "suitable" woman (as Leon does), while Hervé (like Charles in Flaubert's novel) is haunted by the loss of Gemma, though unlike Charles he does not die within *Gemma*'s pages. The periodic surfacing of the characteristics of both Léon and Rodolphe in a variety of characters does not stop with Hervé, Large, or even Charlie, as it also extends to Joubert himself, who seems to be a mixture of Rodolphe, Homais, and Flaubert himself. Since Flaubert's Rodolphe's last name is Boulanger ("baker"), he is linked to Joubert's profession, as well as to Joubert's love/obsession for Gemma. Joubert is also linked to Homais, since he, like the pharmacist, is the neighborhood busybody who pokes his nose into the Boverys' business. Despite these connections, Simmonds includes another Homais analogue in a brief visit to the neighborhood pharmacy. Finally, Joubert takes on the role of primary narrator, linking him at least indirectly to Flaubert's ironic narrator, and to Flaubert himself through the close proximity of the sounds of their names. Even this semi-homophonic link is, however, complicated by the reference to another 18th/19th century author, Joseph Joubert, best known for his *Pensées*.

That is, while analogues and connections between the characters in the two books exist, they are not 1:1 connections and, as such, are somewhat tenuous. Certainly, to some degree, this reflects *Bovary* itself, which, as Naomi Schor argues, sees each of Emma's paramours as symbolic substitutions for one another (20). However, Simmonds also plays with these near-correspondences in the context of Joubert and Gemma's relationships to *Madame Bovary* itself. Joubert, a baker only because he is a failed writer/editor, is more than passingly familiar with Flaubert's novel and immediately takes Gemma's name and affairs as evidence of an inescapable pattern that will lead to her doom. Gemma, who has never read the novel, merely finds Joubert's obsession creepy and thinks *Bovary* irrelevant to her own life. Again, here, irony is pervasive, as Emma Bovary is an obsessive reader who mistakes romantic novels for her own provincial existence and is thus (eventually suicidally) disappointed by her life's comparative mundanity. By contrast, it would be possible to argue that Gemma fails to read *enough*, not recognizing the patterns from Flaubert's masterwork that indirectly lead to her own demise.

Both Emma and Gemma, then, are unaware of narratives in which they are to some degree, trapped. For Emma, it is the general "marriage plot" to which she succumbs, supplemented by the "tragic adultress" narrative that, though she sees it as an escape from marriage, is actually a standard part of it. Gemma operates within the same social narrative, of course, but a more specific iteration of it, that of Flaubert's novel itself. Because of the shifting landscape of laws and customs revolving around gender, however, Emma's situation, at least to the modern reader, seems inescapable, while Gemma's appears simply to be a result of a lack of self-awareness. That is, while Emma would be doomed to a crushing life of bourgeois boredom with her husband *even if* she recognized her life as a "typical story," Gemma, from Joubert's perspective, need only recognize her life as a reflection of Emma's in order to change direction. To extend this observation to a meta-fictive level, the graphic novel seems to imply that if modern women (like Gemma) were more aware of, and more attentive to, past oppressions and past social plots, they might be able to extricate themselves from them.

Complicating matters even further, however, is the fact that Joubert's perspective proves to be misguided, since it is not Gemma's affairs, nor her debts, nor her disappointments in life that lead to her death. In fact, Gemma's death seems, at least on its surface, to be a purely random accident that takes place not because of her transgressions, or as a final response to the oppressions of patriarchy, but for no reason at all. Indeed, the most "feminist" elements of the graphic novel seem here to be prematurely short-circuited. After some brief backsliding into an affair with Large, Gemma realizes that he sees her merely as objectified window-dressing, and she elects to exert agency in refusing to have an extended affair with him and, in so doing, be once again defined by her relationship with a man. Along with her rejection of Large, she takes up yoga and meditation, in what could, on one hand, be read as just another of her numerous short-lived hobbies, but might also be seen as an effort to take control of her own body and mind. Similarly, though she has run up sizable debts like Emma, she takes steps to either pay them off or appease her creditors without the desperate begging and descent into near-prostitution that characterizes Emma's final days. Though Gemma considers returning to Charlie, she does so not in pursuit of dreamy romance, but because she realizes that she has never given their relationship a "realistic" chance. Whereas Albert Thibaudet is undoubtedly wrong when he claims that Emma Bovary has "no will power" (381), what is true is that she lives in a world where her will cannot, in and of itself, accomplish her goals. When Gemma asserts her will, belatedly, the world responds, not necessarily (or not only) because she has greater inner strength, but because her world's restrictions on women are less powerful.

These elements of *Gemma Bovery* remind its readers that contemporary women do not face the same inevitable alternatives of an Emma Bovary: either a fulfilling fantasy life, or a frustrated and soul-crushing real one. That is, *Gemma Bovery* seems to move its protagonist through a version of Flaubert's novel in order to allow her to disengage from it, discarding the tragic adulteress plot that leads her to suicide in favor of a different resolution that suggests that, though individual women *may* fall prey to romanticizing love relationships, make poor choices in husbands, and make choices dictated by their bodily desires (and the dictates of consumer society), such eventualities are not "natural" or "essential" inevitabilities and that women (even the *same* woman) may turn away from this path, take control of their lives and escape these "plots' oft-repeated by patriarchy. Certainly, if Gemma emerges from her shadowing of Emma's life into one that is more self-determined and self-directed, we would have no difficulty calling *Gemma Bovery* a feminist book.

It is for this reason that Gemma's ultimate demise is so troubling, and so fascinating. When Gemma chokes on Joubert's bread, it might be possible to see her as the victim of men, or of herself, but it is difficult to do either.

Gemma's death is so contingent and unintentional that the most obvious conclusion is that nobody is to blame and that the death itself is merely a random accident. If this is the case, however, what are the ramifications for the feminist reading of the book that has been building up to this point?

Narrative Form and Female Agency in Gemma Bovery

Many, though not all, iterations of feminism largely center upon female agency. Whether advocating for equality (and thus agency) in the political and social arena, or searching for (and insisting upon) agency in representations of women in cultural texts, the rejection of the stereotypical image of the woman as an irrelevant appendage to a male partner, or as mere body without rational consciousness, is important to feminist thought. Gemma's series of choices near the close of the graphic novel, enumerated above, seem to operate within these feminist parameters. This is particularly the case in Gemma's rejection of Patrick Large. Large sees Gemma as an attractive body which he can first discard and later reclaim without reference to her feelings or wishes. As Gemma herself realizes, Large talks "at" her and not *to* her, treats her like a "piece of [his] kit—like [his] watch or [his] bloody Mont Blanc pen" (87). In short, he treats her like an object rather than a subject. Gemma's ultimate rejection of Large (despite her sexual attraction to him) indicates clearly her capacity to make conscious choices that are explicitly opposed to the pull of the body. This embrace of female rationality and autonomy does not reject sexuality altogether (as some early feminist manifestoes, like Mary Wollstonecraft's, largely did), but merely indicates that Gemma, and women like her, have power over their own lives and are more than capable of making rational decisions.

Female agency is reflected in one of the crucial formal shifts of *Gemma Bovery* as well. While *Madame Bovary* is almost exclusively third person, *Gemma* principally provides a series of overlapping first-person perspectives. The primary narrator, at least in the "word track," is Joubert, who emphasizes his narratorial agency by repeatedly asserting "I, Joubert," before even the most banal observations. Because Joubert steals Gemma's diaries however, the reader is also privy to Gemma's words. Indeed, while a traditional novel might not distinguish between the two narrators typographically, *Gemma* presents Joubert's narration as typed prose, while Gemma's is presented in her own handwritten script. This choice gives the illusion, at least, that while Joubert is the one who is diegetically "presenting" Gemma's diaries to us, we are not only reading her words, but also her handwriting, suggesting that we are, in fact, getting them more or less directly: that she is "speaking" for herself. Indeed, at times, as in the presentation of "Three Seasons" in Bailleville, Normandy, Joubert's voice and presence are nowhere to be found. Rather, an entire page is devoted to Gemma's diary entries (35, fig. 1). Given that the book was originally published one page at a time, it is significant that entire pages can occlude Joubert's presence and instead assert Gemma as narrator, as teller of her own story, and therefore as agent in its transmission. Here, and elsewhere, Joubert's (masculine) "power" over storytelling and meaning-making is dialogically challenged by Gemma's point-of-view.[16]

Narratorial status is also complicated by the deployment of some of the formal strategies of comics. At a Bovery dinner party, Joubert identifies a "love bite" on Gemma's neck, providing him with evidence of Gemma's affair with Hervé (54, fig. 2). On the same page, however, Joubert's reliability, or even status, as narrator is put under pressure. While it is certainly true that Joubert can hear and presumably report the dialogue of the partygoers, this dialogue is not presented in his typewritten narration, but is shown emitting directly from speech balloons. Likewise, Joubert himself is depicted visually from an external vantage point, suggesting that we are not getting "his view" at all, but that there is rather some kind of "third person" *reportáge* accomplished through Simmonds' pencil drawings. Further complicating matters, is the fact that much of the page is occupied by one of Gemma's large thought bubbles, within which Hervé and Gemma embrace before the party and discuss the details of their affair. It would be impossible, of course, for Joubert to accurately report Gemma's thoughts, and there is no clear evidence here that this information is transmitted from her diary. In an even more bravura display of cartooning, Simmonds depicts Hervé's thoughts (in a thought bubble) *within* Gemma's thought bubble, as Hervé thinks of his girlfriend, Delphine. Again, it would be impossible for Gemma to know what Hervé is thinking, and doubly impossible for Joubert to know (and report) what Gemma is thinking about what Hervé may be thinking. On one hand, the nested thought and speech bubbles depict what seems like a transparent representation of what (objectively?) happened in the afternoon before the party. On the other hand, one can read the scene merely as Joubert's guess at what Gemma might have been thinking based on his observation of her at the party and on a reading of her diary.

All of this, then, may be seen as an approximation of the ambiguity of the "free indirect" style, as explored by Kai Mikkonen in his reading of *Gemma*. Mikkonen notes how the juxtaposition of a (first person) word track with an

Figure 1. An entire page of Gemma's first-person handwritten diaries. Simmonds, *Gemma Bovery*. Pantheon, p. 35.

Figure 2. Nested narration in Simmonds' *Gemma Bovery*, approximating the narrative confusion of *Madame Bovary's style indirect libre* (p. 54). Pantheon.

image track that provides a seemingly more "objective" external view, approximates the effect of free indirect discourse, providing "internal and external positions" simultaneously (473).[17] However, though Mikkonen provides a comprehensive account of the various ways in which Simmonds' muddies the narratorial waters (481–484), he does not discuss the ways in which these might impact ideological content, including gender politics.

On one level, the simple inclusion of substantial chunks of first person narration by Gemma seem to provide a more substantial "voice" for women than Flaubert's novel. On the other hand, the "view from outside" provided by the visual depiction in each comics panel reminds the reader that the characters whose voices are seen/heard in the text (including both Gemma's and Joubert's) are not truly presenting themselves, but are always also presented by the controlling hand of the cartoonist.[18] Likewise, and as a corollary, as Mikkonen notes, "It does not seem necessary, in order for us to understand the story, that the verbal narrator is in full control of the image track" (485). That is, narration seems possible, in comics (and film), without reference to the explicit narrator, even when one exists. The mere fact that the reader can see Joubert's eyes is a reminder that we are not merely looking *through* them, despite his role as narrator. In this way, *Gemma Bovery* continuously and subtly reminds its readers that "agency" in a fictional text is always itself a fiction, as all movements of all the characters are determined by the cartoonist. In this context, even when Joubert finally concedes that the lives of Charlie and Gemma are *not* predetermined by their literary predecessor, the reader knows that, in fact, they *are*, insofar as Posy Simmonds takes Flaubert as a model.

"Does That Change Anything?"

The struggle over agency, and especially female agency, exhibited in the form of *Gemma Bovery,* then finds its way back into the plot, as discussed above. Just as Gemma's emerging narratorial voice is subsumed by Simmonds' art and plot, Gemma's "real-life" agency (via the rejection of Large, the turn to yoga, and the attempt to sort out her finances) is stifled by the banal accident of choking on bread. In this, the text seems to remind its readers that Gemma's life is not her own, that any decision she makes is prone to redirection by an "outside" force (diegetically fate/luck and metadiegetically the hand of the cartoonist). Within the logic of the story itself, Gemma's choking seems to suggest that while agency may be asserted to some degree, in the end, in an almost existential fashion, all events are contingent, even absurd, and life itself cannot be bent to the will of individuals. While the power of patriarchy may be diminished in the century and a half since the publication of *Madame Bovary*, other powers, like luck and randomness, continue to restrict the scope of human agency. Insofar as these forces would theoretically apply equally to men and women, however, the book might be said to reflect, if not to promote, an incipient feminism. It is possible to see the emergence of Gemma's autonomy and agency before her banal death, a demise, unlike Emma Bovary's, that cannot logically be linked to her femininity.

At the same time, metadiegetically, it cannot be denied that what kills Gemma is not *actually* a random piece of bread, but the inexorable illogic of Simmonds' plot. Simmonds chooses this fate for Gemma and Gemma, as "only lines on paper," cannot resist.[19] The gendered implications of such a reading are somewhat more disturbing. In *Gemma Bovery*, Gemma dies and Charlie lives, whereas in *Madame Bovary*, both die. On one hand, the deviation from Flaubert seems to suggest a degree of freedom. We, like Gemma and Charlie, are not programmed by previous "plots," and our mortality is more a result of dumb luck than of gendered oppression. On the other hand, whereas in *Madame Bovary* at least, death is the great equalizer, and the suffering and restrictions visited upon Emma in life also catch up to Charles Bovary in the end, driving him into poverty and eventual death. If Emma suffers under patriarchy, at least he suffers its consequences as well (though other men, like Homais and Lheureux, are rewarded). In *Gemma,* Charlie, though saddened in the immediate aftermath of Gemma's death, closes the book with a smile and a friendly kiss from Joubert, homosocial bonding that excludes both Gemma and Joubert's wife. The last mention of Charlie refers to his return to London and to a new girlfriend, something Charles Bovary would never have considered (106). There is something troubling, from a feminist point of view, about the survival and happiness of Charlie Bovery in the aftermath of Gemma's death.

In *Madame Bovary*, it is at least possible to see Emma's demise as both a result of patriarchal oppression and a castigation of it. In *Gemma Bovery,* this possibility is either buried or absent because of the dramatic shift in Gemma's "cause of death." In Simmonds' version, Gemma's demise cannot be perceived as punishment for her own supposed transgressions, but it is also not the (il)logical result of an oppressive society. Its randomness seems to detach it entirely from the world of gender politics, though several men do actually contribute to it. As depicted on the book's penultimate page, Large interrupts Gemma in the act of eating a sandwich with professions of his love. He then attempts to save her by administering the Heimlich maneuver, but is interrupted by

Charlie who believes that Large and Gemma are embracing. The resultant struggle between Charlie and Large prevents either of them from administering to Gemma, holding both of them partially responsible. Likewise Joubert himself feels some responsibility, since it is his bread upon which she chokes. In some ways, then, it is the ways in which these men both compete for Gemma and attempt to administer to her that kills her. Joubert attempts to feed her, Large attempts to love her (and live with her), and Charlie does both of these things, while protectively asserting his marital "rights." Just as Gemma begins to assert her independence (by rejecting Large, in particular), she is engulfed in a sea of male attention and male competition that, at least, indirectly, leads to her death.

It is the "indirectly," of course, that remains the sticking point, and which sheds light upon distinctions between the 19th century French provinces and the situation of contemporary women. At 150 years' remove, it is possible to draw some concrete causal connections between the economic institution of marriage, the near-impossibility of divorce, and the understandable turn to suicide. Conversely, in *Gemma's* turn into the twenty-first century, marriage itself is neither as economically restrictive nor as inescapable, but there are the more "indirect" pressures of patriarchy that come to bear upon Gemma and her contemporaries. Among these, of course, are the body-image pressures reflected in Gemma's fluctuating weight, the pressure to both engage in extra-marital sex *and* to remain faithful,[20] the pressure to earn a living *and* to fulfill more stereotypical/historical domestic roles. These pressures that push and pull modern women in diverse directions could be said to be embodied, in Gemma's final moments, by the three men who demand her attention while failing to "save" her from one another.

While it is possible to read Gemma's men, in her final scene, as quasi-symbolic embodiments of the patriarchal pressures of the modern world, the evidence of the book seems to suggest more that (in Joubert's words): "it really was as accident—No one's to blame" (103). Indeed, the causal connection between such pressures and Gemma's death is undermined, rather than asserted, by Gemma's turn to yoga, debt repayment, and rejection of Large's charms. As Joubert articulates, in the immediate aftermath of Gemma's death, the only imperative that seems to *require* her death is the connection to Flaubert's novel (103), and that too is undercut by the revelation that Charlie is *not* Charles, but Cyril. By emphasizing the differences between Emma and Gemma, by showing Gemma extricating herself from more contemporary patriarchal pressures, and by (finally) refusing any causal connection between *Madame Bovary* and *Gemma Bovery*, Simmonds' graphic novel suggests that it may be possible for women to extricate themselves from patriarchal "plots" and to productively render Flaubert's novel, ultimately, irrelevant for the modern world. However, it seems that it cannot imagine doing so while still leaving its female protagonist alive to tell the tale. Instead, the book closes with an uninterrupted (typed) reverie by Joubert, while Gemma's voice, speech bubbles, and handwriting disappear following her death. Simmonds ultimately asserts her own "freedom" from Flaubert's progenitor text not by allowing Gemma (or Emma) to live, but by allowing Cyril Bovery to walk away, to be happy, and to replace Gemma with another woman, treating her, as Patrick Large does, as a replaceable object. While the graphic novel stresses both the similarities and differences in gender relations between the nineteenth and twentieth (and twenty-first) centuries, and even emphasizes increased agency for its protagonist, its ultimate sacrifice of woman for male pleasure can hardly be seen as indicative of "progress." If anything, it suggests the difficulty in extricating ourselves from patriarchal plots, even in a text that self-consciously explores the possibility of doing so.

Notes

1. In this regard, Naomi Schor's reading of *Bovary* is paradigmatic. Schor emphasizes the fact that Emma Bovary *is* a writer (calling the novel a "portrait of the artist as a young woman" [15]), but that she writes in a genre devalued by patriarchal society, the personal letter. Ironically, Flaubert's own letters have been pored over as expressions of his genius due to his success in more public, and masculine, genres.

2. For useful accounts of Flaubert's misogyny in his life and letters, see Pace and Beizer, the latter of which reads *Bovary* and Flaubert's letters to Louise Colet through the prism of nineteenth-century pathologization of hysteria.

3. A list of feminist/gendered readings of *Bovary* would include: Beizer, Birken, Bronfen, Brooks, Culler ("Uses"), Danahy, Ferguson, Furst, Goodwin, Huyssens, Kapoor, Kelly, McEachern, Orr, Pace, Riffaterre, Sabiston, Schor (3–28), Small, Spacks, Vanderwolk, Williams, and Wolf.

4. Numerous critics have also read *Bovary* itself in the context of food, eating, eating disorders, and/or "consumption" more metaphorically framed. See, for instance, McEachern, Furst, Marder, Petruso, Ronell, Tanner, and Vinken.

5. Though many critics acknowledge Emma's occasional proclivity for masculinity (including dressing as a man and smoking in public), some are less quick to see the behavior as androgynous (Orr 45). Sartre prefers to see Flaubert himself as the androgyne. See Barnes, who reads Sartre's *Flaubert* in light of Baudelaire's.

6. The term originates in Jules de Gaultier's 1902 book of the same name.

7. Still others refuse the notion that the novel is predicated upon reality at all, suggesting that it is almost solely concerned with language itself (see Culler and LaCapra [65–117]).

8. See Pace, who attacks the novel as an exercise in self-hating misogyny; Riffaterre, who reads the novel as a recapitulation of stereotypes about adulteresses; and Wolf who sees the novel as the playing out of "patriarchy's script" (41) and the devaluation of woman as "a castrated version of man" (39). See also Goodwin, Lasch and Huyssens (44–64) who discuss *Bovary's* contrast of low/mass consumer culture (as associated with women) and high culture/modernism (as associated with men).

9. See, for instance, Birken, who reads the novel as a challenge to dominant bourgeois sexuality,

and even to the binary system of gender (618). Others who see the novel as a feminist critique of the society that both produces and punishes Emma are Danahy, Furst, Gerrard, Kapoor, Ronell, Sabiston, Williams, and Winchell.

10. Brooks, following Bronfen and Riffaterre notes that, with her adultery, Emma becomes "no longer Emma, but a member of the genre of adulteresses" (32).

11. This passage is often the lynchpin of feminist readings of *Bovary*. See Schor (22–23), Culler ("Uses" 74–76), Danahy (136), Gerrard (12), Sabiston (345–346), and Spacks (200).

12. For accounts of *Bovary's* complex use of free indirect discourse, see Ginsburg ("Narrative") and LaCapra (126–149).

13. There is one famous exception to the third person narration of the novel, as it opens with a first person plural, "we" (*nous*) narration, seemingly by Charles Bovary's (male) classmates.

14. See Ginsburg ("Narrative" 150–152) and LaCapra (esp. 150–168) for extended readings of *Bovary* passages that reveal their fundamental uncertainty in matters of narratorial attribution. My own lack of fluency in French makes me reliant on earlier critics (and translators) in this regard.

15. This difference between Emma and Gemma is emphasized by the fact that they have similar interests, but Gemma can turn those interests into income, while Emma cannot. See Goodwin (62), who discusses Emma's unpaid preoccupation with interior decoration.

16. Feminist critics of *Bovary* have been quick to note the erasure of Emma's voice. Ginsburg argues that Emma never fully "come[s] into being as a narrator" and is "silenced" by Flaubert ("Narrative" 65). Vanderwolk emphasizes that "Emma is not simply a woman who does not write; she is a fictional character whose creator does not permit her to do so." Constable takes Gemma's "choking" as evidence of a similar, if more obliquely symbolic, silencing of Gemma (66, 80).

17. Mikkonen's observation reflects that of Percy Lubbock on *Bovary's* narrative mode, "...while one aspect of [Flaubert's] matter can only be seen from within, through the eyes of a woman, another must inevitably be seen from without, through nobody's eyes but the author's own" (354).

18. Phillipe Marion's notion of "graphiation" is important here, defined as a "set of graphic markers evoking the presence of a drawing instance" (Surdiacourt 174; Thon 71). For Marion, the mere existence of a hand-drawn picture reminds the viewer of the existence of the artist and the occasion of their drawing. See also Thon for a good overview of the ways in which this "pictorial" representation in comics creates an additional narrator-function that differs from standard prose narration.

19. The reminder that comics are "only lines on paper" is made by Robert Crumb.

20. Ferguson argues that these conflicting pressures originate in 19th-century utilitarian France (and appear in the original *Bovary*), where sex itself is initially configured as "work" whose success is defined by the (orgasmic) "happiness" produced (771–773; 776). Goodwin also observes that Emma is trapped between the stereotypical mass-produced images of the "sweet and virtuous mother, devoted to her accomplished husband; and the glamorous adulteress with dark and passionate secrets" (761).

Works Cited

Barnes, Hazel. "The Biographer as Literary Critic: Sartre's Flaubert." Rpt. in *Gustave Flaubert's Madame Bovary: Modern Critical Interpretations*. Ed. Harold Bloom. New York: Chelsea House, 1988. 83–109. Print.

Baudelaire, Charles. "*Madame Bovary*, by Gustave Flaubert." 1857. Rpt. in *Madame Bovary: Backgrounds and Sources, Essays in Criticsm*. Ed. and Trans. Paul De Man. New York: W. W. Norton, 1965. 336–343. Print.

Beizer, Janet. *Ventriloquized Bodies: Narratives of Hysteria in Nineteenth-Century France*. Ithaca: Cornell University Press, 1994. Print.

Birken, Lawrence. "*Madame Bovary* and the Dissolution of Bourgeois Sexuality." *Journal of the History of Sexuality* 2.4 (April 1992): 609–620. Print.
Bronfen, Elisabeth. *Over Her Dead Body: Death, Femininity, and the Aesthetic.* Manchester: Manchester University Press, 1992. Print.
Brooks, Marilyn, with Nicola Watson. "*Madame Bovary:* Becoming a Heroine." *The Nineteenth-Century Novel: Identities.* Ed. Dennis Walder. London: Routledge, 2001. 29–47. Print.
Constable, Liz. "Consuming Realities: The Engendering of Invisible Violences in Posy Simmonds's *Gemma Bovery. South Central Review* 19.4/20.1 (Winter 2002–Spring 2003): 63–84. Print.
Crumb, Robert. "Drawing Cartoons Is Fun." 1969. Rpt. in *The R. Crumb Handbook.* London: M Q Publications, 2005. Back Cover.
Culler, Jonathan. *Flaubert: The Uses of Uncertainty.* Ithaca: Cornell University Press, 1974. Print.
———. "The Uses of *Madame Bovary.*" *Diacritics* 11 (September 1981): 74–81. Print.
Danahy, Michael. "*Madame Bovary:* A Tongue of One's Own." *The Feminization of the Novel.* Gainesville: University of Florida Press, 1991. 126–158. Print.
Ferguson, Frances. "Emma, or Happiness (or Sex Work)." *Critical Inquiry* 28.3 (Spring 2002): 746–779. Print.
Flaubert, Gustave. *Madame Bovary.* 1857. Trans. Geoffrey Wall. New York: Penguin, 1992, 2003. Print.
———. *The Letters of Gustave Flaubert, 1830–1857.* Ed. and Trans. Frances Steegmuller. Cambridge: Harvard University Press, 1980. Print.
Furst, Lilian. "The Power of the Powerless: A Trio of Nineteenth-Century French Disorderly Eaters." *Disorderly Eaters: Texts in Self-Empowerment.* Eds. Lilian Furst and Peter Graham. University Park: Pennsylvania State University Press, 1992. 153–166. Print.
Gerrard, Lisa. "Romantic Heroines in the Nineteenth-Century Novel: A Feminist View." *International Journal of Women's Studies.* 7.1 (1984): 10–16. Print.
Ginsburg, Michal. "Narrative Strategies in *Madame Bovary.*" Rpt. in *Gustave Flaubert's* Madame Bovary: *Modern Critical Interpretations.* Ed. Harold Bloom. New York: Chelsea House, 1988. 131–152. Print.
———. "Vision and Language: Teaching *Madame Bovary* in a Course on the Novel." *Approaches to Teaching Flaubert's* Madame Bovary. Eds. Laurence Porter and Eugene Gray. New York: MLA, 1995. 61–68. Print.
Goodwin, Sarah Webster. "Libraries, Kitsch, and Gender in *Madame Bovary.*" *L'Esprit créatur* 28.1 (1988): 56–65. Print.
Huyssens, Andreas. *After the Great Divide: Modernism, Mass Culture, Postmodernism.* Bloomington: Indiana University Press, 1986. Print.
Kapoor, Sucheta. "Transgressing Limits: Reading Emma Bovary as a Disguised Prostitute." *Journal of the Department of English* 33.1–2 (2006): 192–215. Print.
Kelly, Dorothy. *Fictional Genders: Role and Representation in Nineteenth-Century French Narrative.* Lincoln: University of Nebraska Press, 1989. Print.
———. *Reconstructing Woman: From Fiction to Reality in the Nineteenth-Century French Novel.* University Park: Pennsylvania State University Press, 2007. Web.
LaCapra, Dominick. *Madame Bovary on Trial.* Ithaca: Cornell University Press, 1982. Print.
Lasch, Christopher. *The Culture of Narcissism: American Life in an Age of Diminishing Expectations.* New York: Warner Books, 1979. Print.
Lubbock, Percy. "[The Craft of Fiction in *Madame Bovary*]." 1924. Rpt. in *Madame Bovary: Backgrounds and Sources, Essays in Criticism.* Ed. and Trans. Paul De Man. New York: W. W. Norton, 1965. 349–357. Print.
Marder, Elissa. "Trauma, Addiction, and Temporal Bulimia in *Madame Bovary.*" *Diacritics* 27.3 (1997): 49–64. Print.

McEachern, Patricia A. "True Lies: Fasting for Force or Fashion in *Madame Bovary*." *Romance Notes* 37.3 (1997): 289–298. Print.

Mikkonen, Kai. "The Implicit Narrator in Comics: Transformation of Free Indirect Discourse in Two Graphic Adaptations of *Madame Bovary*." *International Journal of Comic Art* 13.2 (Fall 2011): 473–487. Print.

Orr, Mary. *Flaubert: Writing the Masculine*. Oxford: Oxford University Press, 2000. Print.

Pace, Jean. "Flaubert's Image of Woman." *The Southern Review* (Winter 1977): 114–130. Print.

Petruso, Michael. "Madame Bovary in the Consumer Society." *Ça Parle* 1.1 (Fall 1985): 46–59.

Riffaterre, Michael. "Flaubert's Presuppositions." *Diacritics* 11 (1981): 2–11. Print.

Ronell, Avital. *Crack Wars: Literature, Addiction, and Mania*. Lincoln: University of Nebraska Press, 1992. Print.

Sabiston, Elizabeth. "The Prison of Womanhood." *Comparative Literature* 25.4 (Autumn 1973): 336–351. Print.

Sartre, Jean-Paul. *The Family Idiot: Gustave Flaubert, 1821–1857*. 4 vols. Trans. Carol Cosman. Chicago: University of Chicago Press, 1981–1991. Print.

Schor, Naomi. *Breaking the Chain: Women, Theory, and French Realist Fiction*. New York: Columbia University Press, 1985. Print.

Simmonds, Posy. *Gemma Bovery*. New York: Pantheon Books, 1999. Print.

Small, Helen. "Feminist Theory and the Return of the Real: 'What We Really Want Most Out Of Realism…'" *Adventures in Realism*. Ed. Matthew Beaumont. Malden: Blackwell, 2007. 224–240. Print.

Spacks, Patricia Meyer. "Women and Boredom: The Two Emmas." *The Yale Journal of Criticism* 2.2 (1989): 191–205. Print.

Surdiacourt, Stephen. "Can You Hear Me Drawing? 'Voice' and the Graphic Novel." *Travelling Concepts, Metaphors, and Narratives: Literary and Cultural Studies in an Age of Interdisciplinary Research*. Eds. Sibylle Baumbach, Beatrice Michaelis, and Ansgar Nünning. Trier: Wissenschaftlicher Verlag Trier, 2012. 165–178. Print.

Tanner, Tony. *Adultery in the Novel: Contract and Transgression*. Baltimore: Johns Hopkins University Press, 1979.

Thibaudet, Albert. "*Madame Bovary*." 1935. Rpt. in *Madame Bovary: Backgrounds and Sources, Essays in Criticism*. Ed. and Trans. Paul De Man. New York: W. W. Norton, 1965. 371–383. Print.

Thon, Jan-Noël. "Who's Telling the Tale: Authors and Narration in Graphic Narrative." *From Comic Strips to Graphic Novels: Contributions to the Theory and History of Graphic Narrative*. Berlin: Walter De Gruyter, 2013. 67–99. Print.

Vanderwolk, William C. "Writing the Masculine: Gender and Creativity in *Madame Bovary*." *Romance Quarterly* 37.2 (May 1990): 147–156. Web.

Vinken, Barbara. "Loving, Reading, Eating: The Passion of Madame Bovary." *Modern Language Notes* 122.4 (September 2007): 759–778. Print.

Williams, Tony. "Gender Stereotypes in *Madame Bovary*." *Forum for Modern Language Studies* 28.2 (1992): 130–139. Print.

Winchell, James. "Reading (in) *Madame Bovary*." *Approaches to Teaching Flaubert's* Madame Bovary. Eds. Laurence Porter and Eugene Gray. New York: MLA, 1995. 98–105. Print.

Wolf, Susan L. "The Same or M(O)ther: A Feminist Reading of *Madame Bovary*." *Approaches to Teaching Flaubert's* Madame Bovary. Eds. Laurence Porter and Eugene Gray. New York: MLA, 1995. 34–41. Print.

Drawing Style, Genre and the Destabilization of Register in a Graphic Adaptation of Trollope's *John Caldigate*

DAVID SKILTON AND SIMON GRENNAN

Although graphic adaptations of literary fiction are commonplace, the great majority have been motivated either by pedagogy or by hagiography. The pedagogic approach assumes that narrative drawing is more accessible to children than text. The hagiographic approach assumes that the source text is an original to which adaptations must aspire by overcoming the assumed limits imposed by their own media.

A number of graphic adaptations of historic fiction interrogate the process of adaptation from literary text to narrative drawing itself, turning the adaptation process into a method of inquiry into some of the central issues of remediation, narrative drawing and historiography: the relationships between specific texts and new images and concepts of authenticity, record and narrative voice.

These make visible the ways in which the process of adaptation engenders an understanding of historic texts and their production. Frequently, they visibly manipulate the reading experience through techniques of juxtaposition, anachronism and visual revision, prompting reflections upon the impact of diverse media on the practice of history, for example: Marcel Broodthaers' 1969 *Un Coup de dés jamais n'abolira le hansard*, Dino Battaglia's adaptations of Maupassant stories and Catherine Anyango's 2010 *Heart of Darkness*. These works are self-aware in eliding categorical expectations of existing registers and genres, or what narratologist Gérard Genette termed works in the "second degree" (5).

It is in the foreground of these observations that a new, 96 page graphic adaptation of Anthony Trollope's 1878–1879 novel *John Caldigate* has been commissioned from artist and comics scholar Simon Grennan by a research team at Katholieke Universiteit Leuven. Titled *Dispossession* in English and *Courir deux lièvres* in French, its publication coincides with a 2015 academic conference on the occasion of the bicentenary of Trollope's birth.

In this context, the new graphic novel will function as a research outcome in the sense that its academic audience is a "knowing one," to use Linda Hutcheon's term (Hutcheon 122). This audience will both expect to read the graphic novel as the product of a self-aware relationship with Trollope's novel and make demands upon the new graphic novel that derive from its members' own, particularly focused, experience of Trollope's novel itself. As a result, the process of making the adaptation has distilled questions about the act of novel/comic adaptation itself that have enabled the emergence of a methodology for the adaptation process and aimed to produce the new book as a comprehensible response.

Two questions have guided the adaptation: 1) What results if the existing generic constraints of graphic novels are self-consciously reformed in the process of adaptation, and the protocol for the new book derives from an analysis of Trollope's text relative to the behaviors of its time and ours? And 2) How can *Dispossession* employ and/or depict equivocation in the style of its facture, distinct from the depiction of the plot?

Following Walter Benjamin's theorization of translation, the process of creating *Dispossession* approaches Trollope's text as the source of a protocol or set of governing rules, including an apprehension of the reading behaviors of his contemporaries and of contemporary graphic novel readers (70). As a result, the relationship between novel and graphic novel constitutes both the process and product of adaptation as an experience for a knowing reader. *Dispossession* developed the following governing rules by which both to produce and rationalize the production of the new graphic novel:

> A limited range of distances between viewer and scene;
> Views of discrete actions, not divisions of actions;
> Rhythmic changes of scene and episode on the page;
> Consistent rhythmic changes of point of view in a visible 1–2–3 rhythm;
> No extradiegetic narrative;
> As small an amount of verbalization in the plot as possible;
> Generalization: this treatment applied in all circumstances.

These rules aim to provide readers with:

> A sense of a materially solid story world;
> A clear sense of the diegetic arthrology of time, place and plot;

An awareness of the importance of material differences to the plot;
A sense that this story-world can only be represented as a graphic novel;
A comprehension of this approach as authorially self-aware.

Figure 1 shows page nine from *Dispossession*. The page exemplifies the application of these rules to a storyboard. In every cell, the characters are seen full-figure. Across the page, the point of view changes methodically in each cell, effectively moving the reader around the perimeter of a single diegetic space in which the action takes place. These changes in successive cells are comprised of only three points of view in total, between which the reader travels, in a sequence that quickly becomes palpable, even on a single page.

This chapter will summarize the rationalization of the governing rules in response to the guiding questions, outlining the ways in which particular theories of register, genre and style have influenced them, relative to text and depiction.

Linguists Douglas Biber and Susan Conrad claim that the analysis of any form of communication begins with the identification of the "situational characteristics" of a register being, in other words, a sociology of the text (Biber and Conrad 2009, 6). With graphic adaptations of historic novels, as with other forms, it is important to make categorical distinctions between register, genre and style in both the graphic novel register and the written register, as it is in the experience of the self-aware manipulation of these distinctions that intertextual analysis occurs. Register correlates with medium in the most encompassing sense of types of form and their associated types of behaviors. Genre, on the other hand, constitutes an approach to the rhetorical organization of expression on the basis of generalized definitions of expectation or conventional use, where rhetoric belongs strictly to *histoire*, to the type of "what is told" rather than *discours*, the situation of "telling to" (Benveniste 110). Style is a systematic variation of expressive form within a genre and register. Style variations are never radical enough to render the genres or registers in which they appear untypical, because typification defines generic comprehension (Biber and Conrad 17).

For example, we encounter figure 1 with a number of sets of expectations that derive from our past experiences of behaving with graphic novels. Our perception of a current ontology of graphic novels underpins our responses: we are able to identify the page as a graphic novel page, encompassing everything that the identification might imply, both formal and social. Further, we understand immediately the diegesis's relationships to established plot genres, or other diegeses in which we have an habitual sense of verisimilitude. Is figure 1 a costume drama? A romance? An adventure? Finally, the page's type of facture might be more unfamiliar than familiar. Its style might appear to belong more

Figure 1. Simon Grennan *Dispossession* page 9, 2013.

to a history of illustration or fine art than to a history of visual narrative, comics and graphic novels, although never so much as to create any confusion about the fact that it is a graphic novel.

Perceiving these distinct levels, it is possible to experience adaptations as the relationships between the contemporary experience of different registers, genres and styles, producing a definition of history as a network of these relationships. For instance, it might seem commonplace to state that, like our age, the nineteenth century was an age of rapid technological and social change in Britain. A primarily rural country became predominantly urban. From 1820 newspapers were printed by steam. However, it is crucial to recognize that technological changes in printing, illustration and transport delivered new, affordable magazines into middle-class homes, mixing fiction and poetry with factual writing on almost any subject. The novelist Anthony Trollope, who rose to popularity in the *Cornhill Magazine* in the 1860s, for example, was a leader among those novelists who presented the middle-class readers of these new magazines with "true-to-life" representations of their own social and domestic lives, in a type of symbiosis that was later defined as "realism," that is, in which readers' expectations were mutually created and fulfilled by a particular form in a particular social milieu (Skilton 149–152).

Thus, registers, genres and styles are distinguishable not primarily on the basis of their formal differences but on the basis of the use that is made of them, the expectations that people bring to them and the situations in which they are produced and encountered. When we read a novel or a graphic novel, our behaviors themselves provide a definition of the type of expression that we encounter and comprehend. According to both philosopher George Dickie and comics scholar Bart Beaty, it is the social behaviors of readers, audiences and participants that define and delimit the expressive forms of registers, genres and styles, resulting in situations in which these forms are reciprocally perpetuated and habituated, in order to access and persuade specific groups (Dickie 34; Beaty 44). For example, Beaty traces the behaviors of an organized comics fan culture as delimiting the typical experience of the Anglophone comics register since the late 1970s (74).

Similarly, in the nineteenth century, many novels appeared as serials, creating as much domestic discussion as serialized television drama does today. Fiction and poetry were shared, and reading aloud in the family was normal practice. New circulating libraries made huge amounts of literature cheaply available to an increasingly literate public, and documented public opinion constrained both writers and publishers. Novelist Walter Scott's historical fiction was a model for many who wanted to explain how the modern age came into being. "Scott's historical investigations are partly driven by his paternalism, which shapes his interest in forms of cultural interaction between social orders in earlier ages," as Andrew Lincoln writes (5). Trollope went further and adapted Scott's methods to write about the exactly contemporary world, reciprocally lending changing social relationships the authority of natural order, of habit and eventually, of typification.

Readers' distinctly different behaviors relative to word and image are characteristics of both the contemporary graphic novel's register and the nineteenth century novel. Pursuing Roland Barthes, Joe Sutliff Sanders points out "...language's ability to reduce the range of meanings in an image..." in text/image relationships across registers (Barthes 1985; Sutliff Sanders 2013, 60). He argues that language, or rather, readers' behavior with language, effectively chaperones readers' behavior with images, and it is the efficacy and types of this chaperoning that underpin relationships between the two. The relative, and unequal, status of images and words is generated by these chaperoning relationships, in which the unruly, that is, multisemic image is meaningfully directed by its relationship with language.

Illustrations in novels were an important feature of nineteenth century fiction with Dickens, Thackeray and Trollope. It was a sign of an author's prestige to have a publisher go to the expense of including images, to be recouped through price or length of print run. Reciprocally, this gave these writers greater prominence. Illustrations in novels were both used as promotional material, and to make the fiction more memorable. Artist John Everett Millais showed Trollope's readers a version of the world they knew visually, as the novelist did verbally. Most illustration was regarded as an art of embellishment rather than a form that produced or helped to produce meaning.

Emerging from this analysis, *Dispossession* provides a knowing reader with a sense that the graphic novel's new story-world is specific to the graphic novel register, in part through the generalization of rationalized depictive techniques, that is, their application in all circumstances.

The central question for the adaptation in the categories of register and genre concerns the possible levels of impact that existing generic constraints might have on the enumeration of the governing rules of this specific adaptation. What results if the existing generic constraints of graphic novels are self-consciously reformed in the process of adaptation, and the protocol for the new book derives from an analysis of Trollope's text relative to the behaviors of its time and ours? With the graphic novel register, as we shall describe, genre and register have a relationship unlike the relationships between the genres of the novel and the writing register.

We have already touched upon some of the ways in which current and historic reading behaviors contribute to the categorization of registers, such as the level of availability of fiction, serialization, family reading aloud and specific approaches to relationships between images and text.

Generically, Trollope defined his type of novel as "realistic" as opposed to "sensational" (Trollope 1996, 146). He meant that readers could accept his fiction as though it were part of their own daily lives, while sensational fiction played with a mystery, exploiting surprises and intricate plots. Early Trollope plots give the impression that nothing is kept from the reader, to focus clearly on how characters deal with things—and the truth as to their actions and motives are very rarely hidden from the reader.

In the 1870s, in contrast, he cultivated an "active reader," who was given the responsibility for making moral and social judgements, instead of having them supplied by the narrator. He made the world and the characters as "real" as before, but only gave his readers the information an intelligent observer could have. The plot of *John Caldigate* follows this model. It is 1873. A young Cambridgeshire gentleman accrues gambling debts while at University and decides to try his luck in the gold fields of New South Wales, Australia. On the ship, he meets and promises to marry Mrs. Smith, a divorced actress. Striking gold, after some time he returns to England and marries Hester, his sweetheart. The actress returns, penniless, and claims that she is already his wife. He is convicted of bigamy and only pardoned when it is proved that an essential piece of evidence (a post-marked envelope) is a forgery. It is never explicit if he and Mrs. Smith were married in Australia or not. *John Caldigate* is not about whether Caldigate committed bigamy in Australia, but about how much we and the other characters can know about what he did there and why.

However, the effect of an exact representation of the verisimilitude of daily life is simply a generic typification, that is, an habitual expectation of reading late Victorian novels presented in this particular way. It is easy to enumerate what remains untold in *John Caldigate* and to identify the rationale of the genre in the process of adaptation. It is not surprising that the 150 years intervening since publication have changed our reading habits.

For example, there are few details about the voyage to Australia. A minority of contemporaneous readers knew these details. Others could perhaps imagine intercontinental travel as less stressful and unhealthy than it was. In *John Caldigate*, Trollope doesn't even tell us the route the ship takes, down into the South Atlantic as far as the icebergs of Antarctica, and returning on the trade winds back up to South Australia. Ships which touched land *en route* had to be quarantined for seven weeks on arrival. Steam ships could not refuel, and wind supplied most of the power. So the recently opened Suez Canal is an irrelevance to the voyages in *John Caldigate*. The rate of infant mortality was shockingly high, even to the novel's contemporary readers. Life on board was morally policed as in the novel, with men and women in separated quarters, but second-class passengers were notorious for stripping off in the tropics, so that near nudity was commonplace on deck.

In *John Caldigate*, Trollope writes: "On board ship there are many sources of joy of which the land knows nothing. You may flirt and dance at sixty; and if you are awkward in the turn of a valse, you may put it down to the motion of the ship. You need wear no gloves, and may drink your soda-and-brandy without being ashamed of it..." (Trollope 1993, 39). However, passengers' accounts are more forthright: "A poor little child died last night ... and the girls said they were going to throw it overboard, but I thought they would be sure to read prayers over it but not so, they opened the Surgeon's window and threw it out" (Haines 55).

Trollope's creation of verisimilitude through omission contributes to the sense that the world of the plot and the world of the reader are indistinguishable and require no dominant narrator to explain or interpret situations and events. In *Dispossession*, this effect is achieved, in part, by excluding extra-diegetic narrative. Everything in the world of *Dispossession* shows itself.

In the case of the graphic novel register, an apprehension of the entire register as a genre provides a deeply rooted, historic characteristic of readers' behaviors. For example, Jeff Winterhart's graphic novel "Days of Bagnold Summer," nominated for a British literary prize in 2012, a Costa Book Award, was described by competition judge Valerie Grove as "...in the graphic genre" (Wild). Grove might be forgiven for her error, given that the Prize's stated focus is "the book," offering an elision of illustrated texts, novels and graphic novels. Her description perpetuates the commonly held idea that graphic novels are a generic subset of writing-register fiction, rather than a distinct set of behaviors constituting another register. However, as Christian Metz notes, registers always offer the potential to express anything about anything, within and often beyond their habitual forms and situations (52).

Trollope's writing style presents the most complex theoretical problems for the adaptation and, hence, opportunities to reflect upon the adaptation process in tracing the new work itself. This complexity arises in the necessity of theorizing the formal aspects of remediation in the greatest detail, that is, the relationships between those technical and material aspects of writing novels and drawing graphic novels that embody meaning in each register.

Writing style, as we have outlined, is categorically distinct from a novel's genre and the register of writing. Categorically, this distinction is mirrored in the graphic novel register by the narrative techniques of drawing and production that are uniquely displayed in the particular layouts, color, typography and drawn trace that we understand as belonging to the graphic novel's author, even though this author is frequently, in some degree, a collective rather than an individual.

In terms of style, the challenge for adaptation lies not only in identifying the existing different behaviors of novels and graphic novels, but in meaningfully producing a new style of drawing relative to an existing writing style. It is not the task of comparing existing styles, but one demanding the speculative creation of new rules within which to draw. As *Dispossession* also has a research function, the process of meaningfully inventing a new style also demands comprehensive rationalization.

It has long been a critical habit in the study of English literature both to consider the verisimilitude of Trollope's novels as an exact representation of the verisimilitude of daily life and to consequently consider his style of writing as self-effacing, autarkic (Skilton 145) or paradoxically non-existent (Booth ix). It is so unobtrusive in effect that some critics claim he "has no style" (Van Dam 12–13). He doesn't "...twist his work to curl papers...," as he said of rival novelist George Meredith (Ellis 175). The spoken dialogue of real life might seem incoherent to read, and so he raises his characters' language a little above the grammatical and logical standard of everyday experience, without making it sound as though it is written by a pedant (Trollope 1993, 154).

His narrative voice is quietly persuasive, and when, as he often does, he tells the reader what were the conventional attitudes to this or that subject or this or that event, he can deceive us into assuming that he entirely subscribes to these conventional views, and has no independent opinions of his own. This is far from true. Closer attention to his mildly ironic tone and his unobtrusive rhetoric reveals that he moves among social attitudes and ideologies, endorsing few, and putting a humorous edge on characters' motives for conforming. Thus conservative critics assume that he thinks like them, and radicals too claim him as their own. It is his particular stylistic achievement as a novelist that he at once belongs and stands a little off.

Trollope himself subscribed to this theoretical transmission model, or what Caroline Abbate has subsequently called "miming mode," in which content, generated solely by an auteur, overrides every formal constraint, in an act of unmediated interpersonal expression (Abbate 27). Trollope writes that the novelist's "...language must come from him as music comes from the rapid touch of the great performer's fingers..." (Trollope 1996, 116).

Such theorizations, including those made by the author himself, are inaccurate. The absence of style is also style, to adapt Paul de Man's idea (Edelman 2010). In fact, Trollope's writing style displays a consistent repetition of rhythms and verbal and grammatical devices that refer to other writing styles, but which are uniquely employed, the whole developing through excision and accretion as the number of his written works increases. As we have noted, this formal methodology of narrative voice is also self-consciously allied to a particular set of socially perpetuated ideas, that readers understand about his characters and plots, not least of which is the unobtrusiveness of Trollope's style itself.

Trollope's writing style formalizes his approach to plot, tying style to genre. In the plot, the narrator both consistently avoids making definitive statements about events and character traits and avoids presenting a definitive opinion. Instead, information is derived from a number of different, and sometimes contradictory, sources and accumulates gradually. Trollope utilizes this technique with great consistency. Over hundreds of pages, the reader effortlessly glimpses situations and people from a number of points of view, over and over again, building a verisimilitude that is neither entirely confirmed nor entirely contradicted by the text.

Trollope rarely describes people or places. If he says that a young man has the qualities of a "swell," it is a warning that he may be unreliable and self-centered. Of course, the narrator may be "setting him up" as unreliable to produce gratification when he later reforms. If Trollope's heroine is "brown" (that is to say a brunette with lightly tanned skin, in contrast to the conventional Victorian beauty with pure white skin and pink highlights), she has a lot of mental and moral strength, and doesn't rely on her looks for her sense of identity. So despite some comments on characters' teeth, eyes and fingernails, appearances are not clearly described. In *Orley Farm* the narrator suggests the reader should turn back to an illustration of Lady Mason chapters before, by Millais, the illustrator of the first edition. Millais, that is to say, has rendered Lady Mason well enough to supplement plot and character, but has not produced a portrait adequate to hang in the home or feature in a police rogues' gallery.

On the other hand Trollope is meticulous about how conversations take place, telling us in detail who is sitting by whom at dinner. In the dining room or the drawing room the scene is set as for a play, and the interaction of the characters is partly determined by where they stand or sit, and whom they can see or hear. So the adaptation concentrates more on the disposition of the characters in each cell, moving around them as events unfurl from cell to cell.

Dispossession maintains a consistent distance, within a small range, between the diegesis and the reader. In this relationship, there are not the extreme changes between one cell and another that characterize movie-influenced graphic novel layouts, for example. Neither is there the fragmentation or multiplication of actions often utilized in graphic novels to alter the pace of reading as dramatic affect. Rather, *Dispossession* uniformly comprises six cell pages in which the reader's feet never leave the ground.

Although equivocation is also strictly unavailable to the facture of the drawings in *Dispossession,* in the sense that drawings always show what they show, the type of marks used are selected relative to known drawing styles that are associated by knowing readers with particular historical periods and ideas. The marks that make *Dispossession*, including the creation of a new typeface for the book, refer explicitly to the styles of marks made by artists such as Gustave Courbet and Honoré Daumier, and rely on readers' association of these artists with a mid–19th century French concept of Realism, or the idea that the artist's mark, not only the image, must communicate the encompassing materiality of the whole scene in view. In movie terminology, this could be described as a type of focalization in which the subject is distinguishable from the background by small degrees of difference only.

Inevitably, this style of facture produces the appearance of a specific atmospheric palette. *Dispossession* consistently seems subfusc and luminous. Whatever the time of day, year or place, everything is clothed in the same generalizing meteorology, an effect that has also been employed by many of Daumier's heirs, for example illustrator Edward Ardizzone.

A novelist can pass over certain things in silence, deciding not to tell about them. Trollope's equivocation perfectly exemplifies the different possibilities of telling and showing. Trollope, who had been to Australia, describes no Chinese workers or aborigines. He knew too little about them. In colonial New South Wales, aboriginals rarely became domestic servants, and were not part of the scene he was portraying. Like all Europeans at the time, he was contemptuous about what he regarded as their passive lives, having no concept of how they lived. Soldiers, convicts and other reminders of colonial repression are not in evidence in *John Caldigate* either. Readers can only speculate on the hardships and morals of the miners and others. Mrs. Smith's life is not described, but the reader understands that it would not be acceptable in England.

When Trollope describes his characters' dress he often gives the contemporary reader clear social or moral messages. A pair of colonial yellow trousers is completely unacceptable to upper-middle class Cambridgeshire, and the person wearing them has to be kitted out as a gentleman before giving evidence in court. Mrs. Smith's costume on board ship is barely described in terms of its low quality. However, a single reference to her straw hat would have identified it to contemporaneous readers as version of a style known as the "Dolly Varden," after a character in Dickens's *Barnaby Rudge*. Varden is young, flirtatious, inexperienced and provocative. Her costume is designed to display her charms as if by accident. Mrs. Smith adopts a persona which, with its pretense of inexperience and apparently unintentional sexuality, suits her requirements as she escapes from whatever scandal has attended her English life: "'Have you observed that woman in the brown straw hat?' Dick said to Caldigate, one morning as they were leaning together on the forepart of the vessel..." Caldigate responds, "I don't recollect her especially. She struck me as talking better than her gown, if you know what I mean" (Trollope 1993, 40).

In the graphic novel register, showing militates against Trollope's technique of equivocal telling. In the twenty-first century, to draw a street in a town in the New South Wales of the 1870s without aboriginal and Chinese people lacks verisimilitude. Showing Mrs. Smith's mode of dress does nothing to create a contemporary sense of the specific character that was obvious to Trollope's contemporaneous readers. Figure 2 is a character drawing of Mrs. Smith. For a late nineteenth century viewer, the mode of dress in which she appears would have been both instantly recognizable as an index of character, an effect that is lost to twenty-first century viewers.

In effect, Trollope's writing style constitutes the careful management of equivocation. It is appropriate that the first word of *John Caldigate* is "Perhaps," a word which is prominent in *John Caldigate* and in several of his other novels of the 1870s: "Perhaps it was more the fault of Daniel Caldigate the father than of his son John Caldigate, that the two could not live together in comfort.... And yet,..." the narrator continues with this language of uncertainly and indirectness: "...he was a man who knew how to live alone," ... "of whom his neighbours said" ... "It was rumoured of him, too, that..." and so forth (Trollope, 1993, 1). This equivocation is not to be confused with any lack of verisimilitude in the plot. Indeed the most profound verisimilitude is required for this effect of equivocation to be achieved and it is the combination of the two that is the root of the ideas both of Trollope's truth to life in his plots and his absence of style.

A corollary of Trollope's consistent use of round after round of accumulated equivocal commentary ("perhaps," "and yet," "it was said of," "it was rumoured of") is the emergence of a specific reading rhythm in *John Caldigate*,

A Graphic Adaptation of John Caldigate—SKILTON & GRENNAN

Figure 2. Simon Grennan *Dispossession* unpublished character drawing of Mrs. Smith, 2013.

to the point where we might claim that this rhythm is a key characteristic of his writing style. It derives entirely from the repetition of equivocal voices to present the plot. Although never mechanical, Trollope's continual round of "perhaps," "and yet," and "it was said of," as it were, creates the pace of the novel, more than any event in the plot itself, dictating both a specific diegetic time and the pace of reading.

Although Trollope eschews visual description, the continual, rhythmic presentation of one opinion after another brings about a distinctive and relatively complex spaciotopia, in which the reader feels positioned relative to the diegesis. In Trollope's text, we do not see, but rather first comprehend, then feel and move around the events of the plot. In retinoscopic terms, this could be described simply as a spaciotopia produced by continually repeating a limited number of changes in point of view.

From this analysis of Trollope's style emerges the question of style in the adaptation, answers to which finalize its governing rules: how does *Dispossession* employ and/or depict equivocation in the style of its facture, distinct from the depiction of the plot? How does the adaptation draw "perhaps"? In *Dispossession*, a sense of the solidity and material specificity of the story-world underwrites the consistent and repeated, that is, rhythmic changes of scene and the use of a limited number of repeated changes in points of view within each scene. This combination moves the reader relative to the view, where the view always seems trustworthy and verisimilar, literally revealing the plot by accumulation of views, repetition and the slightest variations.

Works Cited and Consulted

Abbate, Carolyn. *Unsung Voices: Opera and Musical Narrative in the Nineteenth Century.* Boston: Princeton University, 1996. Print.
Barthes, Roland. *The Responsibility of Forms.* Berkeley: University of California, 1985. Print.
Beaty, Bart. *Comics versus Art.* Toronto: University of Toronto, 2012. Print.
Benjamin, Walter. *Illuminations: Essays and Reflections.* Berlin: Schoken, 1969. Print.
Benveniste, Émile. *Problems in General Linguistics.* Miami: University of Miami, 1971. Print.
Biber, Douglas, and Susan Conrad. *Register, Genre and Style.* London: Cambridge University, 2009. Print.
Booth, Bradford Allen. *Anthony Trollope: Aspects of his Life and Art.* London: Edward Hulton, 1958. Print.
Dickie, George. *Art and the Aesthetic: An Institutional Analysis.* New York: Cornell University, 1975. Print.
Edelman, Lee. "I'm Not There: The Absence of Theory." *Differences* 21.1 (2010): 149–160. Print.
Ellis, Stewart Marsh, ed. *The Hardman Papers.* London: Constable, 1930. Print.
Genette, Gérard. *Palimpsests: Literature in the Second Degree.* Lincoln: University of Nebraska, 1982. Print.
Groensteen, Thierry. "The Current State of French Comics Theory." *Scandinavian Journal of Comic Art* 1.1. (2012) n. p. Web. 01 August 2013.
Haines, Robin. *Life and Death in the Age of Sail: The Passage to Australia.* Sydney: University of New South Wales, 2003. Print.
Hutcheon, Linda. *A Theory of Adaptation.* London: Routledge, 2006. Print.
Lincoln, Andrew. "Walter Scott, Politeness and Patriotism." *Romantic Circles*: Praxis Series (2006) n. p. Web. 10 August 2013 http://www.rc.umd.edu/praxis/patriotism/lincoln/lincoln_essay.html
Metz, Christian. *Psychoanalysis and Cinema: The Imaginary Signifier.* London: Palgrave Macmillan, 1984. Print.
Skilton, David. *Anthony Trollope and his Contemporaries: A Study in the Theory and Conventions of Mid-Victorian Fiction.* New York: St. Martin's, 1996. Print.
Sutliff Sanders, Joe. "Chaperoning Words: Meaning-Making in Comics and Picture Books." *Children's Literature* 41.1 (2013): 57–90. *Project MUSE.* Web. 15 July 2013.
Trollope, Anthony. *John Caldigate.* London: Oxford University, 1993. Print.
_____. *An Autobiography.* London: Penguin Books, 1996. Print.
Van Dam, Frederik. *The Man without Style: Victorian Liberalism and Literary Form in Anthony Trollope's Later Novels.* Diss. Katholieke Universiteit Leuven, 2013. Print.
Wild, Peter. "Two Costa nominations isn't the full picture for comics." *The Guardian* 23 (November 2012) n. pag. Web. 10 August 2013 http://www.theguardian.com/books/booksblog/2012/nov/23/costa-nominations-comics-talbot-winterhard

The Masks of Dracula
In Search of the Authentic Performative Vampire in Three Graphic Novel Adaptations of Bram Stoker's *Dracula*

ANA G. GAL

> [Harker] was very pale, and his eyes seemed bulging out as, half in terror and half in amazement, he gazed at a tall, thin man, with a beaky nose and black moustache and pointed beard.... His face was not a good face; it was hard, and cruel, and sensual, and his big white teeth, that looked all the whiter because his lips were so red, were pointed like an animal's... "It is the man himself!" The poor dear was evidently terrified at something—very greatly terrified.
>
> —Bram Stoker, *Dracula*

In our current fast-paced visual culture, consumers are constantly bombarded with graphic communications that often require not only advanced literacy but also the ability to (re)negotiate the transactions between value and meaning, signifier and signified. Adapting classic literature into graphic novel format through the juxtaposition of written words with static images is a multi-layered process which, when navigated creatively, can extend access to a unique experience without having to minimize the merit of the original text. In the midst of the *Twilight* hysteria, which has dramatically reconfigured the conventions of the "vampire" genre and turned the fanged Other's alterity into a profitable spectacle, nobody seems to care anymore about Bram Stoker's old-fashioned aristocrat who performs tasks that are typical of the working class, roams the streets of London in a "middle-class" costume, and devises his invasion of England in broad daylight, among unsuspecting Londoners. Audiences may remember an elegant, tuxedoed Bela Lugosi staring fixedly into the camera or a long-haired Gary Oldman sporting a top hat and a pair of round blue spectacles. The original Dracula's ability to adopt several (social) masks is generally treated as a relic of the nineteenth-century English culture, primarily because the only vampires that seem to matter today sparkle like diamonds when exposed to sunlight, drink synthetic blood made in Japan, fall madly in love, and repudiate their "condition" to such an extent that they even contemplate suicide.

It is in this vampire-friendly climate that Marvel Comics' *Stoker's Dracula* (2004), Puffin Books' *Bram Stoker's Dracula* (2006), and Classical Comics' *Dracula: The Graphic Novel* (2012) have resurrected the legendary Count in an attempt to introduce audiences, especially new ones, to Bram Stoker's intricate epistolary narrative. The original text is quite problematic due to the textual absence of Dracula's voice, which is primarily inscribed as silence or filtered through the other characters' preconceptions. However, it is this very "present" absence that exposes the intellectual and socio-political framework in which the original *Dracula* functions and that can inspire a new appreciation for Stoker's craft of terror. My intention here is not necessarily to rank the three adaptations in order of preference but rather to discuss the ways in which each graphic rendition attempts to honor, through a diversity of narrative and pictorial techniques, the historical moment and cultural context in which Stoker published his masterpiece. More specifically, I am interested not only in how the script adapters and illustrators from the aforementioned publishers approached the original Dracula's subversive performativity but also how they attempted to repackage nineteenth-century cultural values for a new audience.

The plot of the three adaptations is predictable to readers familiar with the original text: an English lawyer, Jonathan Harker, travels to Transylvania to conduct a business transaction with Count Dracula, an Old-World aristocrat. The first pages of each graphic novel feature the Englishman's encounter with the inhabitants of Transylvania, an encounter that mimics the model established by Stoker in the first chapters of his narrative, though each adaptation illustrates this cultural exchange differently. In the nineteenth century, as many Victorianist scholars contend, a high level of civilization was attainable solely through the rejection of the darkness and tyranny plaguing other corners of the world and consequently, the countries that did not meet the English / Western standards of civilization and progress were represented in the travelogues and literature of the time as harboring unknown threats. According to Ken Gelder in *Reading the Vampire*, the ethnic and cultural diversity of remote and unexplored regions (primarily Eastern nations) was "undesirable in any way other than as a spectacle" (11), a means of experiencing "otherness" critically and detachedly. Due to the rise of nations in Europe and rebellions in Asia and Africa, especially throughout the second half of the nineteenth century, a phobia of the foreign "Other," as Stephen D. Arata notes in his highly influential article "The Occidental Tourist," started coinciding with anxieties about the weakening or disintegration of the British Empire's colonial power—anxieties that were primarily triggered by a paranoid belief in the possibility of "reverse colonization" (623) and that were regulated through a constant demonization of the "Other."

Stoker's novel does not fall within the generic characteristics of the travelogue, yet the popularity it enjoyed (though modest at first) in the late nineteenth century could have been derived from its readers' desire to journey to a geographical location that provided the perfect ingredients for an imaginary, albeit horror-inducing, tourist experience. In his diary entry dated May 3rd, Harker records his passage from Budapest to Transylvania as follows: "The impression I had was that we were leaving the West and entering the East; the most Western of splendid bridges over the Danube [...] took us among the traditions of Turkish rule" (1). A sense of latent horror permeates his account as he conveys his fear of wandering away from the train station without a map ("There are no maps of this country" [2]). Despite his uneasiness, he takes it upon himself to scrutinize, as objectively as possible, the cultural differences displayed by the various populations of Transylvania, more specifically the "Saxons" and "the Wallachs" in the south, the "Magyars in the west," and the "Szekelys in the east and north" (4). In this environment lacking national cohesion, Harker seems unable, if not unwilling, to "understand" the culture and character of the region.

Interestingly, in the Puffin Books adaptation, most of the Transylvanians that Harker briefly interacts with are Slavic-speaking Gypsies—a man with a large moustache and a woman wearing a "bori diklo,"[1] a long skirt, and excessive gold jewelry. Her repertoire includes enormous hoop earrings, a multitude of bracelets on each wrist, and a ring on every finger. In the Marvel Comics and Classical Comics versions, when the inhabitants of Transylvania are not portrayed with their eyes staring wide open or their mouths dropped open in shock at the mere mention of Dracula's name, they are shown clutching crucifixes or desperately begging the foreigner to abandon his plans to visit the castle—a significant narrative moment originally explored by Stoker. What all three graphic novels have in common, though each individual representation proposes distinct levels of detail, is that throughout his stay in Transylvania the Englishman is portrayed with a vexed look or frown on his face, conspicuously elicited by the superstitious nature displayed by the locals. Yet, Harker's obsession with decorum and a devout adherence to a single point of view (the Western/English/Protestant one), implied by several thought bubbles and narrative captions, seem to prevent him from verbalizing his skepticism and self-perceived superiority.

Harker's touristic experience is therefore depicted as a transgression of cultural frontiers from the rationality of the Western civilization to the ordeals and savagery of the East. The Puffin Books Gypsies in particular, with their opulence and constant talk of bloodsucking creatures lurking in the night, conjure up an exotic, colorful Oriental space, despite the stark black-and-white illustrations. In fact, out of the three graphic novels examined here, only Classical Comics has vibrant, color panels. While the use of color allows for a more authentic reproduction of picturesque landscapes, it does not necessarily enhance or shed more light on the Englishman's ethnic insensitivity, though the glossy pages and rich palette, the color red in particular, do intensify the reader's horror in several gory scenes that involve blood shedding, blood sucking, blood spattering, bloodletting, and blood sharing.

Undoubtedly, all three graphic novels feature expert, visually appealing artwork. However, Roy Thomas's and Dick Giordano's Marvel deluxe hardcover edition, consisting of very dynamic and almost life-like black-and-white images, is probably the most effective in preserving the spirit of Harker's journey through its rigor and extensive attention to detail: this version includes over thirty panels depicting the Englishman's perceptions of Transylvania and its inhabitants (before his carriage ride to Dracula's castle), as compared to the twenty-six panels featured in Puffin Books and the twelve in Classical Comics respectively. Both Classical Comics and Marvel rely on excerpts from Stoker's narrative to tell the story, though the latter also engages in hermeneutical acts, such as adding or reformulating thoughts and dialogues, to expand the original meaning. The version published by Puffin Books is a downsized version of Stoker's text, in that the original scenarios and characters are oversimplified to such an extent that they become unilateral and caricaturesque at times, and thus not always apt to inspire lengthy commentaries or reader responses on the political complexities of the age that witnessed the publication of Stoker's text.

The readers familiar with the format and stylistic characteristics of Stoker's novel know that Dracula's consciousness is censored from beginning to end; more specifically, even if the Count is not entirely voiceless, given that his transactions with the other characters are recorded diligently by the latter in their diaries and letters, his speech and perceptions are constantly edited and "transcribed." Thus, how can adapters render, as authentically as possible, an "original" that does not in fact exist in the primary text either? In many ways, the graphic novel format, due to its cinematic quality, fits *Dracula* like a glove, in that it visually translates the original absence into presence or makes manifest *that* which most characters so anxiously think, write, or speak about. The silent monster is endowed with the ability to address readers or at least to produce the impression that he is doing so. For instance, in the Marvel version, the Count's glacial stare seems, at times, to pierce through the pages of the novel. In one instance, he even points a claw-like finger at the reader as if to say, "I am watching you." Nonetheless, even though the illustrators of the three adaptations attempt to fill in the blanks for their readers by giving the unknown or "the unspeakable" a visual representation, they project a self-awareness vis-à-vis the untransferability of certain elements from the original text or the inability to fully close the gap between *what actually is* and *what is represented*.

Firstly, although Marvel pays the biggest tribute to the epistolary form of the original text by adopting specific lettering and frames, in all three graphic novels there is a constant reminder that the monster is *not* supposed to monopolize the truth of the narrative despite the fact that he is present in the majority of the panels. In fact, he is a character that is too many times referred to in the third person within the narrative captions, which in many cases take the shape of letters, telegrams, and even newspaper articles. Secondly, the readers are able to see and "hear" the monster speak, given that he is afforded his own speech bubbles; yet they are almost never privy to his private thoughts and feelings in the same way they are to those of the other characters. That is, even though the writers attempt to verbalize Dracula's interiority based on cues left by Stoker in the original novel, there seem to remain certain aspects of Dracula's inner world that are too ambiguous or unrepresentable, even for the graphic novel medium. For instance, all three adaptations rely on inter-panel gaps or "gutters" to obscure the vampire's intentions, though these panel-to-panel transitions are more masterfully manipulated in Marvel's version. Quite frequently, it incorporates huge blank spaces that serve to discontinue or disrupt the linearity of the narrative right when the Count is ready to act or pursue a course of action. Thirdly and finally, the illustrators in all three graphic novels take some liberties with their representation of Dracula's appearance and body in order to further emphasize his status as "the

Other" of the text. Interestingly, the adaptations by Puffin Books and Classical Comics respectively continue to perpetuate, Hollywood-style, the fictional Dracula's affiliation with Vlad the Impaler, known by Westerners for his sadistic torturing methods and ruthless killings, despite the fact that the novel never claims such associations.[2] Classical Comics even reproduces a portrait of Vlad and the infamous woodcut from a fifteenth-century German pamphlet, showing the Wallachian prince dining among impaled corpses and amputated human limbs.

In Stoker's narrative, Harker's dealings with Dracula elicit dread, discomfort, and a sense of impending doom. For instance, when he meets the Count for the first time, he cannot "repress a shudder" and "a horrible feeling of nausea" (22). It is the vampire's "marked physiognomy"—the "aquiline" face, the hairy temples, the "rather cruel-looking" mouth with "sharp teeth [protruding] over the lips," the hairy palms, the sharp nails (21), and the excessive pallor—that reminds the Englishman that what he is gazing at is not "something" that aligns with familiar images of manhood. In the three graphic novels, the representation of Dracula's appearance in a tangible, image-dependent manner allows readers to discover extra nuances of meaning, which are generally more readily available at the visual level. The original Harker's usage of the word "marked" to describe Dracula's facial traits is remarkably "translated" in the graphic novels, as the authors *show* exactly why the vampire's masculinity is regarded by Harker as unnatural and potentially dangerous. What the visual rendition of Dracula's repugnant body achieves, perhaps even more successfully than the original written text, is to transfer the profound aversion that Harker feels to the readers themselves.

The three visual representations of Dracula, however, are not equal in terms of impact and fidelity to the "original" described by Harker in Stoker's text. Oddly, perhaps in an attempt to lure in the (younger) readers of the *Twilight* generation, the cover of the Puffin Books adaptation is somewhat misleading, in that it features a collage of computer-generated, yet realistic color images that portray a rejuvenated, caped Count with attractive physical attributes, but a ferocious grimace on his face. Yet, what lies beyond the cover is a bleak black-and-white world, where most characters are enveloped in shadows and where danger lurks at every turn (of the page). What readers discover is perhaps the most alienating and sinister visual representation of Stoker's vampire (out of the three). In many instances, even when he is reinvigorated by the blood of his victims, Dracula is so dehumanized that he appears more like an enormous predatory bat wearing a male frock coat than a decrepit aristocrat or a formerly glorious prince. Therefore, what "marks" Dracula's appearance in the Puffin Books version seems to originate first and foremost in the overlapping of two mutually exclusive states of being (being human and being animal)—an in-betweenness that engenders uneasiness specifically because it eludes categorization. This particular visual representation suggests that an unknown threat, not only to individual bodies but also to the integrity of an entire nation, can emanate from such corporeal ambiguity (fig. 1).

Figure 1. A horrified Harker catches his first glimpse of Dracula climbing down the walls of his castle. Reed and Cloonan, *Bram Stoker's Dracula: The Graphic Novel*, Puffin Books.

Like Puffin Books, Classical Comics recycles the Dracula-Vlad the Impaler connection, possibly the only "fact" about the original Count that even individuals who are not familiar with specific aspects of Stoker's work remember or think they know, thanks to Hollywood. Some of the illustrators' aesthetic and coloring choices seem to have been guided by their knowledge vis-à-vis the Wallachian prince's physical idiosyncrasies. Dracula sports a "beaky" nose (Stoker 157), bushy eyebrows and temples, long hair combed backward, and a thick "horseshoe" moustache that is replaced by a slick, pointed goatee when he travels to London. However, what sets this particular Dracula apart is that he also possesses a set of piercing red eyes. If the body can be conceptualized in terms of a topography that can be "marked" to convey meaning or to shed light on what lies within, then the Count's red eyes function here as a warning and constant reminder of his monstrous interiority. On a side note, given Dracula's supposed affiliation with Vlad, this particular physiognomic trait seems adequate here; the name "Dracula" is, after all, a derivation from the Wallachian (Romanian) word "dracul," which means "the devil."

As previously discussed, the Marvel adaptation is very convincing in transferring some aspects of the original text to the new medium, though Thomas and Giordano do incorporate some compelling additions consisting primarily of subtle visual details that are meant to facilitate a rather specific hermeneutical outcome. For instance, their visual rendition of the villain (Dracula) and the hero (Van Helsing) respectively—two prescriptive positions within the genre of comics—is masterfully suggestive, in that the two men constantly mirror each other. In some panels, for instance, the resemblance is so uncanny that readers might find it difficult to distinguish between them. The Puffin Books version is silent about Van Helsing's cultural heritage, while Classical Comics oddly projects the image of an "alien" completely assimilated into English culture, despite his awkward speech. In Stoker's novel, Van Helsing's foreign quirkiness is actually quite problematic and comes across as slightly dubious at times. His experimental dabbling in the occult is, to some extent, as questionable and as unnatural as Dracula's vampirism, yet his overall otherness elicits less anxiety, mainly due to his Western European affiliation, and most importantly, because his actions are ultimately not detrimental to England. Therefore, Marvel does more than just juxtapose the textual with its visual correspondents. By blurring the fine line that separates the two characters, it actually places a magnifying glass over the obscure subtleties of the original text in order to help contemporary audiences appreciate the content of the novel as well as understand the cultural and intellectual framework in which Stoker operated.

The most significant aspect of the original *Dracula* is that the vampire's power derives essentially from his capability to navigate, quite facilely, several social spheres. On the one hand, Dracula belongs to an aristocratic lineage and possesses the capital associated with his rank. Except for the Puffin Books adaptation, whose illustrators give the Count's crumbling castle the appearance of a torture chamber, both Marvel and Classical Comics emphasize how lavishly some portions of the castle are adorned. Despite being in a ruinous state, the rooms that Harker visits, including a forbidden boudoir, feature pompous furniture, albeit outdated and dusty, carpets, heavy curtains, fireplaces, wall ornaments, silverware, and chandeliers. Interestingly, even though Dracula is a foreign aristocrat, he adopts the kind of civility and courtesy that Harker is accustomed to in his home country. Still, in the absence of any servants, he is constrained to perform several menial tasks: firstly, he carries Harker's luggage all the way up to the latter's room; and secondly, he prepares a bedroom and supper for his guest. Marvel is the only one to hint at the Count's gross transgression of his "assigned" social role by including a couple of panels showing him carrying Harker's heavy suitcase up the stairs. In *Making a Man: Gentlemanly Appetites in the Nineteenth-Century British Novel*, Gwen Hyman explains that by engaging in menial activities that are generally performed by the working class, and at the same time by "sucking" Harker's professional abilities (i.e., his linguistic skills and judicial knowledge), Dracula seeks, in fact, to return to the former feudal system and thus to "obviat[e] the need for the hard-working, entrepreneurial-class gentleman" (205).

Stoker's narrative presents two other crucial moments—visually rendered only in the adaptations by Marvel and Classical Comics respectively—in which Dracula is described engaging in some sort of performance. Firstly, Harker spots Dracula climbing down the walls of the castle and wearing his English clothes (fig. 2). Secondly, Dracula travels to London in order to infiltrate its society and invade England from within, which he plans to achieve by spending his capital and engaging in commerce with unsuspecting English agents. A few months after Harker's journey to Transylvania, Mina notices Harker's shock at seeing the Count walk the streets of London disguised as a respectable middle-class Englishman (fig. 3).

In both instances, Dracula is shown attempting to "pass" as a gentleman, which was the most desirable form of masculinity in nineteenth-century England. As Karen Colland Waters notes in *The Perfect Gentleman*, perceptions vis-à-vis a man's social standing were shaped primarily by his external appearance: not wearing the proper clothes or, on the contrary, wearing clothes that did not correspond to his social rank was regarded as a severe transgression

Figure 2. Harker sees the Count climbing the outside walls of the castle dressed in Harker's English clothes. Thomas and Giordano, *Stoker's Dracula*. Marvel Comics.

Figure 3. In London, Harker spots Dracula sporting a frock coat, a cravat, and a walking stick—all essentials in any English gentleman's wardrobe. Cobley et al., *Dracula: The Graphic Novel*. Classical Comics.

in Victorian England (32). As a foreigner in London, Dracula is banished to the margins of English society; yet, as implied in figure 2 and figure 3, he cunningly finds a way to migrate toward the source of power simply by wearing the appropriate "costume." As a gentleman in disguise, the Count can either garner the privileges enjoyed by this particular social category or navigate

English society effortlessly and undetected. His performative resourcefulness or play with various masks is then such an integral part of his character that he cannot function without it, at least not within the context presented by Stoker. Without this ability to camouflage, Dracula loses his power.

The Puffin Books version is the only adaptation that deliberately erases or omits Dracula's performativity, possibly in an attempt to simplify the thematic complexity of the original text. It does not make any references, either visual or textual, to the Count wearing Harker's clothes. Also, the vampire's promenade in London is compressed into one single panel showing a close-up of his eyes and forehead and featuring the following narrative caption: "Jonathan still has nightmares and he even saw the Count in London, but somehow the Count was now younger." However, this kind of (over)simplification does not necessarily lead to a better grasp of the original but in fact widens the distance between the adaptation and its source text. In the graphic novels by Marvel and Classical Comics, the panels addressing the two aforementioned (performative) moments allude to Harker's class anxieties, which the illustrators from Marvel in particular brilliantly represented visually by zooming in on the Englishman's horripilation: his face, drawn from different angles, is frozen into an expression of terror and bewilderment. As figure 2 suggests, when Harker realizes that Dracula is wearing his clothes, evidently to engage in illicit behaviors without raising any suspicions, his most pressing concern is not that the Count is hiding behind a fake identity to divert attention from himself, but rather that this masquerade or mockery of what it means to be a gentleman will end up denigrating the Englishman's status, in which the latter takes a lot of pride: "Any wickedness ... shall be attributed ... to me!" (Marvel; Stoker 46). The better Dracula performs, the more he subverts, and the more he exposes the fact that those at the center of power structures constantly fear a loss of authority once their rules become *too* accessible to outsiders or non-members.

As one can infer from the importance that Marvel and Classical Comics placed on Dracula's performative idiosyncrasies, Harker's almost neurotic backlash is as crucial as Dracula's reactionary response to the environment that stifles his "difference." Because Stoker forbade the Other's unfiltered self-expression, the novel is in many ways *less* about Dracula and *more* about how those who are in a privileged position perceive the vampire. Graphic novel adaptations in particular, as they rely heavily on the marriage between text and the visual performance of that text, can thus facilitate the readers' access to a world of meaning or a certain hermeneutical clarity that the written text may have failed to convey or that the reader may have missed due to his or her insufficient knowledge of the original context. Even though graphic novel adaptations cannot be expected to *fully* deliver the source text with all of its thematic complexities, mostly due to certain constraints dictated by the target audience and the medium in which the transference of the original takes place, graphic renditions that are marketed as "(Bram) Stoker's Dracula," however, do set themselves up for heightened scrutiny, especially by readers who know and appreciate the source text. In *A Theory of Adaptation*, Linda Hutcheon notes that regardless of the medium in which adaptations operate, they are doomed to live in the shadow of the original that they attempted to reproduce (6). However, she also remarks that the process of adaptation is not straightforward but riddled with challenges that may constrain the adapters to alter the original: "Because the adaptation is a form of repetition without replication, change is inevitable [...] and with change come corresponding modifications in the political valence and even the meaning of stories" (xviii). Several questions are worth posing here: How can adapters reproduce a far removed socio-economic, political, and cultural context that the audience, especially young and unfamiliar with the source text, may not fully grasp? How can an adaptation respect the original text but at the same time decode its context in a way that would not completely alienate the target audience? More specifically, can a graphic novel adaptation of a text like Bram Stoker's *Dracula* capture the original response to its publication but at the same time incorporate cultural equivalents that the readers can identify with?

Despite being written two centuries ago, Stoker's novel does not seem to have lost its appeal; it is probably one of the most adapted fictional texts of all time (film, comics, plays, etc.), owing first and foremost to Dracula's ability to infiltrate, blend inconspicuously into his surroundings, and *become* whatever he needs to be—a threat that makes this character as relevant today as he was in the nineteenth century. Both Marvel and Classical Comics seem to have operated with a full understanding of this and thus are more successful than Puffin Books in communicating the original text and connecting with their readers, primarily because their aesthetic choices highlight in fact just how relevant Stoker's text is. Unlike the Puffin Books adaptation, which defangs the Count by reducing him to a mindless beast that audiences cannot decipher, Marvel and Classical Comics include images that allude to more recent mass-hysterias (elicited by the continuous reconfiguration of gender roles, ethnic multiplicity, non-normative sexuality, and even the threat of terrorism). What results is an intellectually stimulating dialogue between the original text and the adaptation, as both graphic novels expose, to some extent, how little Western anxieties seem to have changed since the nineteenth century.

One significant aspect in the adaptations by Marvel and Classical Comics—one that is almost too subtle or tame in Puffin Books—is that some of the Count's interactions with his victims (both male and female) are highly eroticized, and at times sexually and gender-ambiguous. Both Marvel and Classical Comics exacerbate Dracula's masculinity. In numerous panels, his half-nude muscular and densely pilose body inevitably invokes images of extreme virility. Classical Comics even includes an enormous close-up of the Count's blood-dripping nipple when he forces Mina to suck on his breast— a juxtaposition of fatherhood and motherhood that is as disturbing to contemporary audiences as it probably was to nineteenth-century readers. In Stoker's novel, sexual activities of any kind are mostly implied, while in the two graphic novels the sexual energization of Dracula's body (at the visual level) is almost necessary, given the dramatic rise in the sexualization of bodies in the contemporary market. As Feona Attwood points out in *Mainstreaming Sex: The Sexualization of Western Culture*, Western culture has been recently "pornified" to such an extent that it has become obsessed with "self-revelation," "exposure," and sexual self-expression (xiii–xv). One effect of this sexualization is excessive visibility from which consumers derive both pleasure and fear.

One last aspect that I wish to discuss here is that unlike Puffin Books, Marvel and Classical Comics allude to another version of masculinity assumed by the Count in certain instances, one that exists outside of the heteronormative order (i.e., homosexuality). Both adaptations preserve the ambiguity of the original Harker's exchanges with the Count. For instance, when Harker cuts himself while shaving—a scene that is shortened and stripped of any sexual connotations in Puffin Books—the Count's closeness is represented pictorially in a way that is meant to perturb the readers and elicit anxiety. When drops of blood start trickling down on Harker's chin, and this is persuasively illustrated by Classical Comics (due to its use of color), Dracula seems to be overwhelmed by uncontrollable lust. Both Marvel and Classical Comics capture the bestial thirst in Dracula's eyes, just enough to suggest that perhaps it would not be too far-fetched to believe that his intention is to abuse Harker in a sexual way, especially since vampiric feeding is often equated with sexual intercourse. The "shaving" scene is invested with an almost inevitable sexual undertone if considered in conjunction with another scene that takes place when Harker is seduced by Dracula's three vamps and when the Count disrupts the orgy by rushing tumultuously into the room and screaming, "This man belongs to me" (Marvel; Classical Comics 19; Stoker 41).

Despite all of their distinct techniques and levels of content assimilation, all three graphic novels manage to capture the "essence" of the original work, though with varying degrees of complexity. Ultimately, both the source text and its three adaptations project the idea of a nation in a state of crisis due to an unexpected "foreign" invasion—a theme that continues to fascinate popular imagination today. What emerges from all four novels is a white collective that is motivated by (racial and national) solidarity and on which the fate of the entire nation rests. Dracula is the "enemy" out there, always watching and waiting for the opportune moment to strike and seize the power. He stares the reader in the face and forces her to both reconsider and challenge the notion "of everyday life completely secure against threats." As Philip Nickel brilliantly remarks in "Horror and the Idea of Everyday Life":

> As with our purported philosophical solutions to skepticism, the idea of security in the everyday is based on an intellectually dubious but pragmatically attractive construction. We can hardly resist relying on the world not to annihilate us, and we can hardly resist trusting others not to do so. This is not because such reliance is rationally compulsory, but because we choose it as the most easy and natural strategy. One of the best things about horror is that it allows us viscerally to experience this as an epistemological choice [17].

In conclusion, Dracula's re-emergence in graphic novel form makes a lot of sense, as the vampire remains the perfect vehicle to negotiate anxieties during times of cultural stress or shifts. The Count's versatility and ability to assume several "masks" introduces readers to the idea of performance as one of the tactics adopted by those who inhabit the margins to create a space for survival or liberation. Both Marvel and Classical Comics seem to have understood that the original Dracula's power resided, first and foremost, in this ability—to walk among humans and render himself virtually invisible, to infiltrate the human way of life and mind, and finally, to obscure the magnitude of the danger he poses. After all, isn't the very act of not knowing or fully seeing what we are confronted with that our terror feeds on?

Notes

1. According to Harry E. Wedeck in *Dictionary of Gypsy Life and Lore*, "bori diklo" is the term employed by the Romani people to refer to the headscarf or neckerchief worn by their women.
2. In fact, the original Dracula claims to be a Szekely or Magyar (i.e., Atilla the Hun's descendant). In her book *Dracula: Sense and Nonsense,* in a titanic effort to break the myth of the Dracula-Vlad marriage, Elizabeth Miller disputes previous scholarly attempts to generate "artificial links" (180) between the two figures. Her well-documented dissemination leaves little room for doubt as it relies upon a close scrutiny of Stoker's Notes at the Rosenbach Museum and Library.

Works Cited

Arata, Stephen D. "The Occidental Tourist: *Dracula* and the Anxiety of Reverse Colonization." *Victorian Studies* Summer 4.33 (1990): 621–645. *JSTOR*. Web. May 2013.
Attwood, Feona. *Mainstreaming Sex: The Sexualization of Western Culture*. London: I.B. Tauris, 2009. Print.
Cobley, Jason, Jim Campbell, Staz Johnson, James Offredi, Clive Bryant, and Bram Stoker. *Dracula: The Graphic Novel*. Towcester: Classical Comics, 2012. Print.
Gelder, Ken. *Reading the Vampire*. London: Routledge, 1994. Print.
Hutcheon, Linda. *A Theory of Adaptation*. New York: Routledge, 2006. Print.
Hyman, Gwen. *Making a Man: Gentlemanly Appetites in the Nineteenth-century British Novel*. Athens: Ohio University Press, 2009. Print.
Miller, Elizabeth. *Dracula: Sense & Nonsense*. Westcliff-on-Sea: Desert Island, 2000. Print.
Nickel, Phillip J. "Horror and the Idea of Everyday Life." *The Philosophy of Horror*. Ed. Thomas Fahy, Lexington: University Press of Kentucky, 2010. 14–32. Print.
Reed, Gary, Becky Cloonan, and Bram Stoker. *Bram Stoker's Dracula: The Graphic Novel*. New York: Puffin, 2006. Print.
Stoker, Bram, and Leonard Wolf. *Dracula*. New York: Clarkson N. Potter, 1975. Print.
Thomas, Roy, and Dick Giordano. *Stoker's Dracula*. New York: Marvel Comics, 2004. Print.
Waters, Karen Volland. *The Perfect Gentleman: Masculine Control in Victorian Men's Fiction, 1870–1901*. New York: Peter Lang, 1997. Print.
Wedeck, Harry E., and Wade Baskin. *Dictionary of Gypsy Life and Lore*. New York: Philosophical Library, 1973. Print.

The Picture and *Dorian Gray*
Interpretive Pluralism in Graphic Adaptations of Wilde's Novel

Esther Bendit Saltzman

In his preface to the 1891 version of *The Picture of Dorian Gray*, Oscar Wilde states that "diversity of opinion about a work of art shows that the work is new, complex, and vital" (4). Much of the complexity of Wilde's work comes from his paradoxical writing style, which challenges interpretation. Michael Patrick Gillespie argues against singular readings of Wilde's works, emphasizing the "interpretive multiplicities inherent in Wilde's canon, where passages evolve in a fashion that sustains several equally plausible meanings while privileging none" (14). A work as complex as *Dorian Gray*, then, would necessarily challenge its graphic adaptations to exhibit interpretive complexity.

Gillespie offers evidence from Wilde's letter arguing against simple interpretations of his work and suggesting the necessity for a pluralistic approach:

> In a 12 February 1894 letter to Ralph Payne, for example, Wilde neatly summarized the antinomies of *The Picture of Dorian Gray* and gently mocked simplistic reactions to it through a series of concise analogies between himself and the novel's central characters: "I am so glad you like that strange coloured book of mine: it contains much of me in it. Basil Hallward is what I think I am: Lord Henry what the world thinks me: Dorian what I would like to be—in other ages perhaps" [*Letters*, 352] (Gillespie 58).

On the surface a specific analogy, Wilde's statement leaves room for interpretation as does his novel. In the first chapter of *Dorian Gray*, Basil tells Lord Henry, "every portrait painted with feeling is a portrait of the artist, not of the sitter ... it is rather the painter who, on the colored canvas, reveals himself" (Wilde 9). Echoing Wilde's words in the letter to Payne, he explains that he would not exhibit his portrait of Dorian because, he says, "I have put too much of myself into it" (Wilde 7). Readers, therefore, have been reading for evidence of Wilde in his novel since Victorian times.

If we suppose that a work of art is a reflection of the artist rather than only a depiction of its subject, and Wilde is the "painter" of *The Picture of Dorian Gray*, where is he reflected in his novel? Furthermore, if we examine other "painters'" visual adaptations of Wilde's work, where, then, do we see Wilde? Are we looking for Wilde the man, his philosophies, or for the artists adapting his text? Once we compare Wilde's original text to graphic adaptations of it, are we persuaded through the visual elements to "see" him differently, or is there as much room for imaginative interpretation in the graphic adaptations?

In "The Critic as Artist," Wilde states that "the critic will be an interpreter"; he adds that "his object will not always be to explain the work of art," but that "he may seek rather to deepen its mystery" (329). An adapter also functions as interpreter; Stephen Tabachnick explains that adaptations "necessarily represent interpretations of the works adapted" (4). The reader of verbal texts interprets words to determine meaning; the graphic adaptation reader also interprets visual images and their relationships to the verbal text as well.

This chapter examines the interpretive possibilities provided by graphic adaptations of *Dorian Gray*, and argues that these adaptations, especially when analyzed together, can provide pluralistic interpretation of Wilde's complex work of art, adding value to Wilde scholarship. I have selected three graphic adaptations that provide multiple possibilities for interpreting Wilde's presence in *Dorian Gray*. The first is adapted by Roy Thomas and illustrated by Sebastian Fiumara. The second is adapted by Ian Edginton and illustrated by I.N.J. Culbard. Both of these are graphic novel adaptations in comics format. The third, art and adaptation by John Coulthart, is part of the *The Graphic Canon* anthology edited by Russ Kick, and consists of a series of ten pages in collage form using a variety of artistic techniques. These adaptations by Thomas/Fiumara, Edginton/Culbard, and Coulthart help the reader to interpret Wilde's textual presence in unique ways. They differ in their visual depictions of Dorian and in his appearance in relation to the other characters. They all use visual techniques to play upon Wilde's manipulation of art and reality in the novel. Additionally, the adaptations use their visuals to comment on Wilde's views of aesthetics in relation to morality. Ambiguities exist in all versions through the selected verbal text and the graphic artists' renderings, and must in turn depend on each reader's individual interpretation.

Character Representation through Depiction: More Than Just Resemblance

Character appearance is extremely important in *Dorian Gray*, since Dorian's beauty is the catalyst for the events in the novel. Reading Wilde's description of Dorian, as seen through the eyes of Lord Henry, gives us a starting point of expectation:

> Yes, he was certainly wonderfully handsome, with his finely-curved scarlet lips, his frank blue eyes, his crisp gold hair. There was something in his face that made one trust him at once. All the candour of youth was there, as well as all youth's passionate purity. One felt that he had kept himself unspotted from the world. No wonder Basil Hallward worshipped him [17].

From the above description, Dorian should be blond, have rounded reddish lips, and appear youthful if we are looking for mimetic representation. We can also look for signs of the "passionate purity" that is a much less concrete visualization and, consequently, more difficult to show.

Fiumara's depiction of Dorian closely follows Wilde's description (see fig. 1). Dorian appears blond and extremely handsome, even beautiful as one can see in the bottom right frame. We can, though, debate the expression of purity. As Lord Henry suggests that Dorian's cheek may someday show signs of shame, Dorian appears angry, but may actually be expressing "passionate purity" as he reacts. The elusiveness of reading accurate expression maintains ambiguity, especially since it is the expression in the portrait that will first trouble Dorian and will then horrify Basil. Kristian Williams discusses corresponding challenges of visually representing changes in the portrait, and suggests that this is one area in which Wilde's words may do a better job with effect (Part 4).[1]

Fiumara's visual depiction of characters in comparison to one another provides striking opportunities for interpretation. His depiction of Dorian's father links father and son together by making them look similar. Since Dorian's father is the victim of a duel set up by Dorian's grandfather, the depiction uses visual rhetoric to associate Dorian with victimhood. Thus, the depiction provides the reader with the option to read Dorian as a more sympathetic character.

Visual similarities are also evident in the depictions of Dorian's mother and Sibyl Vane. Dorian's mother dies from a broken heart, a victim of her father's class prejudice. Similarly, Sibyl commits suicide, a victim of Dorian's cruelty. The women are drawn to look markedly alike, and both have blond

Figure 1. Innocent Dorian unnerved by Lord Henry. Thomas and Fiumara, *The Picture of Dorian Gray*. Marvel.

hair like Dorian. The similarity between characters leads the reader to question the implications of the depiction, especially since Sibyl Vane has dark brown hair in Wilde's novel. In addition, Adrian Singleton, whose reputation is ruined by Dorian, is also depicted with long blond hair; it would seem that Fiumara is tying together Dorian's victims by depicting them with blond hair and visual similarity.

The appearance of two other characters in the Thomas and Fiumara's version challenges interpretation further. The duchess of Monmouth and Hetty Merton are also drawn to look similar to the other women. Although the duchess flirts with Dorian, there is no significant relationship with him. Hetty Merton is the girl Dorian spares in an effort to reverse the changes in the portrait. However, while Hetty and the Duchess of Monmouth resemble the female victims, they are not victims themselves. The resemblance, then, leaves room for alternative interpretation and makes the victim theme ambiguous. The reader may not see Dorian as victim at all, or may see him as a victim of Lord Henry's influence. And although Dorian sees himself as Basil's victim, he has victims of his own. By visually connecting Dorian with his mother, father, and his victims, Fiumara visually expresses the paradoxical way that Dorian views victimization, and the ambiguous nature of Fiumara's blond motif complements Wilde's paradoxical style.

Edginton and Culbard place an interesting spin on Dorian's appearance in their version. Dorian is depicted with dark hair ending in length at his prominent chin, and his face is markedly rectangular (see fig. 2). Remarkably, this Dorian looks like Wilde; it would, consequently, seem that Culbard is intentionally linking Dorian's character with Wilde's. So, if we accept Dorian as Wilde in this version, are we to interpret Wilde as deficient in morals or even evil, and deserving of his fate? Or, are we to see him as a victim of wrongful public perception? Wilde has been linked with the content of his novel since prosecutors read excerpts from *Dorian Gray* at his trial in 1895. If their visual depiction of Dorian is intended to look like Wilde, Culbard and Edginton are making a statement and seemingly taking a stand. What the statement is, though, is either a clear interpretation of Dorian as Wilde, or a challenge to what Wilde says is the public tendency to link him with Lord Henry. Regardless, there is still room for interpretation.

Interestingly, Dorian appears more innocent in this version, partly due to the artistic style of simple lines and lack of subtle shadowing and intensity of shading. Because of this, Culbard presents a more visible corruption of an innocent Dorian by Lord Henry. The reader must then decide whether the corruption of Dorian reflects suspicion of a morally questionable Wilde, or

Figure 2. Dorian's desperate wish to stay young. Edginton and Culbard, *The Picture of Dorian Gray*. Sterling, p. 15.

whether the play on Wilde's identity demonstrates the difficulties of living in an oppressively strict society. This version includes another reference to Wilde; as Dorian and Lord Henry sit in the garden, they are flanked on either side by the presence of nude male statues. Tabachnick points out that the presence of these statues is evidence of homoerotic allusions that are not present in the Thomas and Fiumara version (Tabachnick 11). The inclusion of homoeroticism further links the Edginton and Culbard depiction of Dorian to Oscar Wilde the man.

Interestingly, a third perspective can be gained from the analysis of John Coulthart's treatment of Dorian. Using a collage style combining different forms of artistic representation, Culthart's treatment provides an interpretive bridge between the other two works by using images associated with Wilde and his era. For his depiction of Dorian, as Coulthart states on his website, he uses John Singer Sargent's painting of W. Graham Robertson. Robertson, according to Couthart, "was a theatre designer and illustrator who Wilde consulted when planning stage designs for what would have been the London debut of *Salomé*. Robertson was also (so far as we know) homosexual which adds an extra resonance" (Coulthart). By using period materials, Coulthart brings an element of authenticity, and explains that "Since I have a lot of Oscar Wilde-related reference material I was able to go further and incorporate details that relate directly to the book and Wilde's life" (Coulthart). In this way, Coulthart brings Wilde into *Dorian Gray* without overtly suggesting where he belongs.

Visual Distinctions: The Blending of Art and Reality

Alison Byerly refers to nineteenth-century aestheticism as the "erasure of the real" (184). Indeed, Wilde's reputation for favoring aesthetics over mimetics is widespread. Gillespie argues that Wilde's argument for aesthetic appreciation of art is not singular:

> First through simple paradoxes and then through more detailed rhetorical strategies that continue the juxtaposition and contrast of different points of view. Wilde developed an artistic format that rejects narrow ideological dispositions and embraces a pluralistic response to reality [36].

In *The Decay of Lying*, Wilde's character Vivian says, "No great artist ever sees things as they really are. If he did he would cease to be an artist" (341). Interpretation, according to Wilde, is a function of aesthetics, and the artist should not represent reality. In a letter responding to critics, Wilde states that a critic should "recognize the essential difference between art and life,"[2] and that a critic should not "confuse the artist with the subject matter."[3] These statements contradict Wilde's description of his presence as variations of his characters.[4] Wilde's statement in a letter dated June 27th provides a possible explanation for the contradiction; he states that the critic should not include "reference to the *personality* [my emphasis] of the author," but does not preclude the philosophies expressed as the subject matter. Even so, Wilde's contradictions are in line with his paradoxical style.

Visual techniques facilitate depictions of the real and the unreal in all three graphic adaptations. Eric Berlatsky discusses the interactions of art and reality in the "'picture frame' model" of literary frame theory, and how the literal frames of the graphic novel format assist in depicting these relationships (Berlatsky 1, 2). The graphic adaptations establish the art versus reality theme by the appearance of the portrait compared to the setting and characters, and by the framing techniques of their depictions.

Thomas and Fiumara begin with a manipulation of the real and imaginary on the second page after the introduction. On the first page, Basil and Lord Henry are discussing the portrait. This page is in comics format using sequential frames. The following page is a single image with no frame; the title of Wilde's novel and a text-box containing "adapted from the novel by Oscar Wilde" are placed on top of the visual narrative in the upper left corner of the page, but in a format that references a title page. Since this is not the actual title page, it is seemingly out of sequence. What it does, though, is add the world of the reader to the world of the characters, as does the departure from sequential framing. The resulting effect is a play on reality mixing the worlds of the picture, the graphic novel, and the reader.

The use of color intensity by colorist Giulia Brusco functions to separate the artificial painting from the world of the characters. The colors of the painting are lighter than the colors in the rest of the page. The "room" and characters around the portrait seem, in relation to the muted colors of the portrait, more realistic. In this way, the artwork establishes a dichotomy between the real and the unreal in the artwork and within the fictional narrative.

In contrast, Culbard achieves the same result by making the portrait look more realistic than the cartoon "real" world outside it (refer back to fig. 2). While the characters will refer to the picture as the "real Dorian" later in the scene (Edginton and Culbard 16), the reader has already perceived the paradox of Dorian's identity by comparing the painting and its subject in different frames on the same page. Kristian Williams also notes the contrast between the different styles of art, stating, "the painting allows us to imagine a real person behind the cartoon image" (Part 2).

Reader perception, though, still has effect here. While I perceive Dorian's painting to be more realistic than the surrounding visuals, Williams perceives it to be "more impressionistic, with full textures and gently faded grays" (Part 2). I believe that these textures and the use of many values of gray are what give the painting its more realistic appearance. Nonetheless, the Dorian in the painting is more attractive than the Dorian viewing it. Williams explains that "Visually speaking, the painting surpasses the man in depth and beauty—thus reflecting both Wilde's metaphysics and his idea that it is art that teaches us to see the world" (Williams, Part 2). Consequently, two readers who agree with an assessment of artistic technique can perceive and categorize effects, and interpretations, differently.

Coulthart also contrasts his realistic depiction of Dorian with the drawn depictions of Basil and Lord Henry. But his most effective presentation of the art and reality issue occurs on page 478 of Russ Kick's anthology. Here Coulthart depicts the scene in which Lord Henry tells Dorian of Sybil Vane's death (see fig. 3). Coulthart visually separates the actress from reality. First, he places her outside the frames, isolating her from the body of the image as she has been removed from life in the novel. Second, she appears as a photographic negative rather than as a fully exposed, realistic photograph. In contrast to the image of Sybil, Dorian appears as a darkened figure without detail and outside his own frame. His gesture depicts his initial alarm upon hearing of Sybil's death. Dorian's frame, bordered by serpents, disappears into the main square containing more serpents as well as a prominent skull, paralleling his subsequent descent into an evil life of cruelty. Thus, Coulthart's use of different media, framing techniques, and strategic design placement play upon Wilde's paradoxical statements concerning reality and life.

Wilde and the Aesthetics/Ethics Balance

The complex nature with which Wilde treats aesthetics and morality in *Dorian Gray* has been a subject of scholarship for years. Even so, Peter Raby articulates the lack of definitive understanding obtained: "In defiance of what might seem critical overkill, Wilde, both as writer and individual, remains as elusive as ever" (xv). This scholarship, however, can assist the graphic adaptation scholar in selecting glimpses of Wilde's character and philosophies present in the adaptations.

Edouard Roditi ties the moral/aesthetic dilemma to the art and reality issue. Addressing Wilde's inclusion of a moral in spite of his belief that art should not be used for moral "propaganda,"[5] Roditi explains that Wilde combined in his works the world that he lived in with an ideal world. Explaining

Figure 3: Dorian learns of Sybil Vane's death. Coulthart, *The Picture of Dorian Gray*. Seven Stories, p. 473.

that Wilde's world of contemplation cannot exist alone in the novel because of the real world that Wilde knew, Roditi maintains, "the dialogues imitate Wilde's ideal world of pure speculation where no action is necessary..." (63–64). The mixing of the real world with one created in *Dorian Gray* allows for Wilde's acknowledgement of ethical standards. Furthermore, Roditi affirms that contemplation becomes corrupted when action is taken. Stephen Tabachnick, citing Roditi, points out that "Dorian has been a bad student of Harry's. Harry never says a moral thing but never actually does an immoral one" (10).

Roditi also indicates the importance of craft in Wilde's aesthetic beliefs, and how Wilde showcases its importance. He explains that Wilde asserted his beliefs, or even those not his own, through his characters' statements or through the crafting of his work (56). To Wilde, Roditi also points out, "form is 'the beginning of things' and 'everything,' but he identifies form with style rather than structure..." (66). It is Wilde's paradoxical style that crafts the novel, bringing ambiguity into it.

Donald Lawler investigates revisions that Wilde made before both the 1890 and 1891 versions.[6] Most of these revisions, he asserts, were done to increase the aesthetics of the work to favor those aesthetics over a moral that was certainly present. Lawler asserts that "for the decadent artist, the experience of beautiful and aesthetic objects is an end to itself.... Above all it is the effect, the aesthetic charm that Wilde wishes to stress as an antidote to the didactic theme" (Lawler 93). Wilde himself admits a moral in the book; in a letter dated June 26, 1890,[7] he states that the public, expecting a "wicked book":

> ... will find that it is a story with a moral. And the moral is this: All excess, as well as all renunciation, brings its own punishment. The painter, Basil Hallward, worshipping physical beauty far too much, as most painters do, dies by the hand of one in whose soul he has created a monstrous and absurd vanity. Dorian Gray, having led a life of mere sensation and pleasure, tries to kill conscience, at that moment kills himself. Lord Henry Wotton seeks to be merely the spectator of life. He finds that those who reject the battle are more deeply wounded than those who take part in it. Yes; there is a terrible moral in Dorian Gray—a moral which the prurient will not be able to find in it, but which will be revealed to all whose minds are healthy. Is this an artistic error? I fear it is. It is the only error in the book [358].

Wilde, then, acknowledges the moral in his story, but explains it as an "error" preventing *Dorian Gray* from being a "useless" piece of art.[8]

By categorizing the moral as an error, though, Wilde may be separating it from the aesthetic value of the book rather than subordinating it. Gillespie explicates Wilde's use of paradox in regard to ethical and aesthetic concerns. Gillespie, stressing the pluralistic nature of aesthetics and morality in Wilde's work, states, "Wilde's canon functions as neither an assault upon nor an apology for conventional morality. Nor does it force one to choose between ethical and aesthetic precepts" (10). Wilde's writing instead allows the reader to examine different viewpoints side by side, allowing for the influence of society on the individual (Gillespie 10). So Gillespie allows for a co-existence between aesthetics and morality that allows the reader freedom to draw his or her own conclusions about Wilde's work.

With these perspectives in mind, one would expect to see applications of Wilde's aesthetic and ethical principles in the conversion to image and word in the graphic adaptations. The addition of visual art to the selected text allows both graphic novels to substitute visual art for some of the novel's literary art. In line with creating an aesthetic work of visual art, the illustrator's style is an important vehicle of aesthetic experience. Thomas and Fiumara craft for the reader a beautiful and detailed rendering of the story. The visuals are done in soft colors,[9] characters are extremely attractive and drawn in a soft, curved-line style, and backgrounds vary in tone with scene and mood; descriptions of past events look somewhat like camera shots taken with a soft lens. The Edginton and Culbard version utilizes a less detailed, sharper-lined, black and white style; even though Dorian resembles Wilde, the use of the black to white spectrum maintains ambiguity by storytelling in shades of grey, and playing on the name of the protagonist.

In addition to aesthetic experience, the graphic adaptations' visual art can provide significant content and affect the ethical ramifications of the representation. Thomas and Fiumara offer a detailed visual representation of Wilde's chapter 11, in which Dorian searches for knowledge and gratification of the senses through studies of history, science, and various forms of the arts. While Edginton and Culbard omit this sequence, its inclusion in Thomas and Fiumara's version serves multiple purposes. First, the chapter is one of those included, as Lawler says, to minimize the moral by the addition of aesthetics. It also provides an extended example of Dorian's contemplative side, which then makes his subsequent action, killing Basil, more striking and effective in eliciting an emotional response from the reader. In turn, it emphasizes the pollution of Dorian's contemplation as he commits murder.

A subtle but important aesthetic technique that Wilde employs in his novel is the use of flower imagery, which connects Dorian's fall to the expulsion from the Garden of Eden, and contributes to the artistry and ethical perspectives of Wilde's novel. The motif enriches the content of the novel and the adaptations. The opening of *Dorian Gray* begins with attention to the strong scent of roses, and Wilde uses the flower motif to add beauty to his physical descriptions of characters as well. Wilde uses roses in his descriptions of Sibyl Vane. Most importantly, he uses flowers to describe Dorian, and incorporates flower imagery into scenes associated with Dorian's victims.

Wilde's entire first paragraph involves flowers and plant life, and contains the first reference to the garden:

> The studio was filled with the rich odour of roses, and when the light summer wind stirred amidst the trees of the garden there came through the open door the heavy scent of the lilac, or the more delicate perfume of the pink-flowering thorn [5].

The graphic novels translate this motif in different ways. Thomas and Fiumara keep the entire text of the paragraph; they do not show the garden or flowers until Henry first warns Dorian about the agonies of aging. Conversely, Edginton and Culbard omit the text of Wilde's first paragraph, but show multitudes of roses in their depiction of the garden scene (Wilde 22; Edginton and Culbard). Just prior to the scene, Henry calls attention to Dorian's "rose-red youth" and his "rose-white boyhood" (Wilde 20). Thomas and Fiumara keep this verbal text as well, incorporating flower imagery and ethical behavior (refer back to fig. 1), while Edginton and Culbard depict the roses visually.

In her 1884 book *The Language of Flowers*, Kate Greenaway lists meanings associated with specific flowers. Deep red roses, in Victorian times, signified bashfulness or shame. While we might associate bashfulness and naiveté with Dorian's youth, he will eventually be ashamed of the deterioration of his soul evidenced by his hiding the portrait; therefore the references to flower meanings contribute to the richness of the narrative.

Flowers also carry out Wilde's philosophy of action as a corruption of contemplation. As the discussion in the garden comes to a close and Dorian contemplates Henry's words, Wilde says that "a spray of lilac [falls] from [Dorian's] hand" (23). The image of the garden and of a fall convey to the reader the imminent fall of Dorian's soul due to the cruelty of his actions. The use of the lilac, as well, reinforces the image, since Victorian connotations of lilacs include "humility, first emotions of love, and youthful innocence" (Greenaway 27). Dorian's cruelty will also show through images of crushed flowers. When Dorian rejects Sibyl, she lays at his feet "like a trampled flower" (Wilde 75). Similarly, just before Dorian kills Basil, he takes "the flower out of his coat," smells it, and crushes it (Wilde 131). Thomas and Fiumara include this action, even devoting a single frame to the crushing of the flower.

Coulthart incorporates flowers in several of his images as well. They are mostly incorporated into Victorian designs in the backgrounds of the collages, and they change with the scene depicted. In the depiction of Sibyl's death in figure 3, the vines become entwined with a skull, adding to the complexity of the image. In depicting Dorian's downward turn to depravity on page 482 of Kick's anthology, the vines are depicted with more thorns than flowers. In the image in which Dorian kills Basil, and in the final image, when Dorian has died, there are no flowers at all.

The ambiguity of Wilde's ending is a final example of Wilde's aesthetic and ethical balance. As Lawler points out, Wilde also paid special attention to the ending to make it less didactic. Lawler explains that the problem with adaptations, up to the time of his 1988 analysis, is their reversal of the art and morality balance. He says:

> It is, perhaps, an additional irony that the continued popularity of Dorian Gray depends on, or at least embraces, a misconception over the way things turn out. The endurance of Dorian Gray as a popular novel ... its adaptation to the stage, as a radio drama, as a motion picture, and as a dramatic tale has continued to fire the imagination after three quarters of a century. In each case of adaptation, however, the conclusion has been altered to make Dorian repentant over his past life. The story has been transformed into precisely the kind of morality tale which Wilde worked so hard to avoid.

The Thomas and Fiumara adaptation maintains the balance as Wilde set it in his original. The selection of text supports a Dorian who is not repentant, and wants to kill his conscience to have a better life. His last chance for hope occurs before he sees the portrait, which he hopes will have reflected his kindness to Hetty Merton. After he sees the portrait, his decision to kill his conscience occurs in two juxtaposed frames. In the first frame, Dorian is bent over as he acknowledges that the picture has been his conscience, and looks as if he has lost hope. It is in the next frame that he makes the decision to kill that conscience. The act of killing his conscience leaves little doubt that he does not repent.

In the Edginton and Culbard version, however, Dorian's last hope for being "good" occurs after seeing the portrait, making this point of hope physically closer to his slashing the portrait. He says he will kill the past, and will start over when the picture is destroyed, but the graphic novel does not include the statements that he is killing his conscience or that he was kind to Hetty Merton because of his own vanity. There is, therefore, a subtle allusion to his hope for redemption and possible repentance in this version. This difference makes a significant change in the moral/didactic balance in the ending. Even so, the discovery of the similarities and differences between the texts requires diligent reading and comparison to determine. Because of the subtlety of the differences, room for interpretation remains in deciding whether or not Dorian actually repents, and ambiguity is maintained.

Coulthart's depiction of the ending, because of the collage format, does not depend on sequence to help interpret Dorian's repentance. His strategy is in his depiction. The image depicts the portrait torn with the knife still in it. But Coulthart omits an image of the young and pure Dorian; the portrait has not changed back and still depicts the old and corrupted Dorian. Furthermore, this Dorian's face is duplicated in close-up at the bottom of the frame. The image, along with a significant amount of Wilde's text included at the top, would seem to favor the view that Dorian has not repented. The reader is also left with the chilling image of a corrupted individual.

Artistic, Interpretive and Scholarly Value

After examining character depiction, the visual representation of reality, and Wilde's preference for aesthetics over morality in art, it is apparent that graphic novel adaptations of *The Picture of Dorian Gray* can encompass and highlight themes and add creative methods to the interpretation of verbal texts. While adaptations can change interpretive options by condensing text and by adding visual images, more value is obtained by comparing them to the original, and to each other.

In terms of character depiction, the use of visuals can make a character more or less sympathetic by individual depiction or by the connections drawn to other characters. While critics have speculated about which parts of Wilde's character are present in his *Dorian Gray* characters, we can make those same speculations by analyzing the adaptations. Even when Dorian is drawn to resemble Wilde, other visuals and selection of text, as in the Edginton and Culbard ending, leave room for interpretation.

The graphic novel genre allows for visual exploration of the real and unreal through implementation of visual techniques that include artistic style and creative use of media. Since an artist can play with visuals that approach degrees of realism, Basil can say with irony that he will stay with the "real Dorian." While Basil refers to the portrait, we can interpret the meaning and ironies for ourselves.

Finally, exploring evidence of Wilde's views on aesthetics and morality in art requires the most stringent analysis, since both aesthetics and a moral exist in *Dorian Gray*. Here again, it is up to the individual reader to decide how moral the story is. The graphic novel adaptations allow the reader to experience visual aesthetics in addition to Wilde's paradoxical wit. Whether we look at Fiumara's soft, beautiful artwork, the additional perspectives that Edginton and Culbard add by making Dorian look like Wilde, or the interpretation of Coulthart's selected scenes in collage form, we gain additional opportunities for interpretation of the narrative.

In looking for evidence of Wilde in the graphic novel versions of *The*

Picture of Dorian Gray, there is evidence for his presence in the adaptations. Thomas and Fiumara, though, show more of Wilde's philosophies, while Edginton and Culbard call attention to Wilde the man. We can view the highlights of the narrative provided by Coulthart's project and linger on particular scenes and artistic nuances. Therefore, strengths or weaknesses of individual adaptations are less important than the artistic value and insight gained from examining them together with the adapted text. The artistic perspectives in multiple adaptations allow the scholar to select strategic points of comparison with which to gain insight, and provide the teacher with opportunities for class examination and discussion. Read individually, but especially together, there is significant opportunity for interpretive pluralism in graphic adaptations of *Dorian Gray*. Although Wilde would probably not have approved of his likeness as a model for Dorian, I hope that he would agree that the graphic novels and graphic interpretations can "deepen [the] mystery" of his work.

Notes

1. Refers to Williams' eight part series for *The Comics Journal* on images related to Dorian Gray. In the series he covers other media representations as well.
2. Letter dated 27, June [1890].
3. Letter to *Scots Observer* dated 9 July 1890.
4. Refer to statement in first paragraph of this paper.
5. "The aim of most of our modern novelists seems to be, not to write good novels, but to write novels that will do good. They wish to reform the morals, rather than to portray the manners of their age. They have made the novel the mode of propaganda." Oscar Wilde quoted in Roditi, p. 59.
6. Lawler argues for the existence of a manuscript pre-existing the 1890 version.
7. Oscar Wilde, "To the Editor of the *St. James's Gazette*."
8. "All art is useless." From the preface to *Dorian Gray*.
9. In Wilde's letter to the *Daily Chronicle*, dated 30 June 1890, he states that "the aesthetic movement produced certain colours, subtle in their loveliness and fascinating in their almost mystical tone."

Works Cited

Berlatsky, Eric. "Lost in the Gutter: Within and Between Frames in Narrative and Narrative Theory." *Narrative* 17.2 (2009): 162–187. Project Muse. Web.
Byerly, Alison. *Realsim, Representation, and the Arts in Nineteenth-Century Literature*. Cambridge: Cambridge University Press, 1997. Print.
Coulthart, John. "The Picture of Dorian Gray." *The Graphic Canon: Volume 2*. Ed. Russ Kick. New York: Seven Stories Press, 2012. 473–483. Print.
Culbard, I.N.J., and Ian Edginton. *Oscar Wilde's The Picture of Dorian Gray: A Graphic Novel*. New York: Sterling, 2008. n.p. Print.
Fiumara, Sebastian, and Roy Thomas. *Oscar Wilde. The Picture of Dorian Gray*. New York: Marvel Illustrated, 2009. n.p. Print.
Gillespie, Michael Patrick. *Oscar Wilde and the Poetics of Ambiguity*. Gainesville: University Press of Florida, 1996. eBook Collection (EBSCOhost). Web. 18 May 2014.

Greenaway, Kate. *The Language of Flowers*. London, 1884. *Illuminated Books*. Web. 13 October 2010.

Lawler, Donald. *An Inquiry into Oscar Wilde's Revisions of The Picture of Dorian Gray*. New York: Garland, 1988.

Raby, Peter. Preface. *The Cambridge Companion to Oscar Wilde*. Ed. Peter Raby. Cambridge: Cambridge University Press, 1997. xv–xvi. Print.

Roditi, Edouard. *Oscar Wilde*. New York: New Directions, 1986. Print.

Tabachnick, Stephen. "The Graphic Novel and the Age of Transition: A Survey and Analysis." *English Literature in Transition*, 1880–1920 53.1 (2010): 3–28. *Project Muse*. 16 September 2010.

Wilde, Oscar. "The Critic as Artist." In *The Picture of Dorian Gray. A Norton Critical Edition*. Ed. Michael Patrick Gillespie. New York: Norton, 2007. 329–336. Print.

———. "The Decay of Lying." In *The Picture of Dorian Gray. A Norton Critical Edition*. Ed. Michael Patrick Gillespie. New York: Norton, 2007. 337–344. Print.

———. *The Picture of Dorian Gray. A Norton Critical Edition*. Ed. Michael Patrick Gillespie. New York: Norton, 2007. Print.

———. "To the Editor of the St. James's Gazette." In *The Picture of Dorian Gray. A Norton Critical Edition*. Ed. Michael Patrick Gillespie. New York: Norton, 2007. Print.

Williams, Kristian. "Pictures of Dorian Gray, Images of Oscar Wilde; Part Two: The Cartoons of Dorian Gray." TCJ.com. Fantagraphic Books, 18 May 2010. Web. 20 January 2014.

———. "Pictures of Dorian Gray, Images of Oscar Wilde; Part Four: The Double Image." TCJ.com. Fantagraphic Books, 20 May 2010. Web. 20 January 2014.

Illustrating the Abyss
An Interview with Catherine Anyango on *Heart of Darkness*

Christine Ferguson

Catherine Anyango's and David Zane Mairowitz's stunning 2010 *Heart of Darkness* is not the first graphic adaptation of Joseph Conrad's fiction,[1] but it arguably demonstrates better than any precedent the unique potential of comics to encompass those aspects of the writer's famed impressionistic style which other media struggle to translate. Previous comics versions such as *Classics Illustrated*'s *Lord Jim* (1957) or Seiho Takizawa's *seinen* manga *Heart of Darkness* (2004) have followed film adaptations of Conrad novels in focusing primarily on the adventure plots of their source texts at the expense of their narratorial nuance.[2] But adapting Conrad solely for plot, as Owen Knowles and Gene M. Moore remind us, is a tricky business that can leave a substantial portion of the original source untapped:

> The difficulty of doing Conrad "as written" is not so much a matter of exotic settings or the technical requirements of gales and typhoons as it is essentially the problem of Conrad's indirect and often ironic narration. Films can present narratives in action, but they have difficulty "showing" the act of narrating from a perspective other than that of the camera, which, as the point from which the pictures are presented, tends to occupy the position of narrator in a fictional work [111].

As a mixed medium, comics has the ability to juxtapose text and visual point of view in ways that thwart the conventional narrative attribution described above; it can also, by presenting images simultaneously on a shared page rather than consecutively in time, break single image-moments into discrete units in a way that resonates with the Conradian technique of delayed decoding so famously explicated by Ian Watt (175). This temporal subdivision is only one of the ways in which Anyango and Mairowitz pay homage to, without slavishly reproducing, their source text's style.[3] Others include the use of a hazy monochrome palette— applied equally, and intriguingly, to both the African and European scenes— which evokes the epistemological uncertainty so central to "Heart of Darkness" (Peters 51).

Not all of the team's creative decisions seem so readily compatible with current critical consensus on the novel's form and import. Their choice to draw the narrating Marlow as Conrad, and to interject the narrative with excerpts from Conrad's *Congo Diary* (1890), has been criticized by some reviewers as a crude reduction of the original's complex narration to biographical reportage.[4] This reaction may have more to tell us about the lingering squeamishness towards putative instances of biographical fallacy than it does about the actual, and far from homogeneous, presentation of differing narrative personae in the graphic novel, but it nonetheless provides an important register of the continuing controversy around the relationship between the personal, the political, and the aesthetic in Conrad's early masterwork.

I sat down with Catherine Anyango at her Dalston studio on July 29, 2013 to discuss the planning, production, and reception of *Heart of Darkness*'s rich and haunting illustrations. A fine artist with no prior experience of graphic novel work, Anyango came to the attention of comics publisher SelfMadeHero in 2009 through her series of single drawings based on "Heart of Darkness," prepared for a competition during her degree study at London's Royal College of Art (fig. 1).[5] This sequence is only one of the many works by Anyango to be inspired by nineteenth-century images and literary texts; others include a film and drawing series based on Jean-Martin Charcot's photographs of hysterics, and a set of illustrations for Henry James's *The Turn of the Screw* (1898). We discussed the enduring importance and adaptive allure of Victorian visual culture to her work, the exciting new *rapprochement* between fine arts and comic art in which SelfMadeHero's *Heart of Darkness* participates, and the creative team's controversial decision to cast Conrad as Marlow and incorporate excerpts from the *Congo Diary* in the context of the novella's vexed postcolonial legacy. For Anyango, this choice was geared not, as Andrew van der Vlies has suggested, to exculpate Conrad from charges of racism "by showing him to have been troubled by what he saw in the jungle" (Vlies 80), but rather to give Conrad credit for presenting a far from flattering version of self-portraiture, if by no means direct autobiography, in Marlow. Indeed, van der Vlies's accusation of retrospective white-washing makes little sense in relation to the selected excerpts from the *Diary*, most of which, far from registering deep unease or ethical indignation at the treatment of the Congolese, simply position Conrad in place and time. Anyango and Mairowitz juxtapose these relatively anodyne records of Conrad's experience—"Wednesday, 2nd July. Country more open. Gently undulating hills. Road good, in perfect order"—with the intricate, lingering, and highly realistic portraits of dying Africans that the diary text cannot or will not verbally incorporate.

If anything, then, the graphic novel uses intertextuality to demonstrate the dissonance between the *Congo Diary* and "Heart of Darkness," while its visual

Figure 1. The Woman outside Kurtz's house. Anyango and Mairowitz, *Heart of Darkness*. SelfMadeHero, p. 87.

depiction of Marlow as Conrad aims to make these contrasting authorial selves, rather than some disembodied, agentless entity of style or the *zeitgeist*, responsible for both the aesthetic accomplishments and ethical blindspots of the original text. Edward Said makes a similarly strategic biographical conflation in *Culture and Imperialism* (1993) when he writes "Conrad could probably never have used Marlow to present anything other than an imperialist worldview, given what was available for either Conrad or Marlow to see of the non–European at the time" (27). Anyango's and Mairowitz's graphic novel aims to be true to the horror of that world-view, exploring in unflinching detail its devastating—if by no means equally so— consequences for colonialism's victims and perpetrators alike. In doing so, it initiates a newly grown-up approach to Conradian comics adaptation,[6] one that eschews the terrain of the boys' adventure story for a complex ethical meditation on the testimonial value of literary and visual art.

CF: *Heart of Darkness* has been out since 2010, and you started working on it in 2009. This was your first time working in the graphic novel medium. Could you just tell me a bit about how you got involved in the project?

CA: SelfMadeHero had worked with Andrezj Klimowski, who is Professor of Illustration at the Royal College of Art, where I also teach. They had the RCA connection already, and actually I had done a series of eight illustrations for "Heart of Darkness" during my time studying at the College for the same competition I did the *Turn of the Screw* work. So I had the illustrations, and [SelfMadeHero] saw them, and then approached me about doing the book.

CF: Are any of those original illustrations in the book?

CA: Yes, because I was running out of time [laughter], so some of them appeared, but they were obviously just single illustrations where the book is more panels-based. But the style was exactly the same; that was good because I could start with a way of working that felt true to the book. So that sort of helped in the beginning; at least I had something to work from.

So what I did was a whole lot of research. I had about eight months to do it in, and I took two months to just do research— historical, costumes, background, politics, that kind of thing to make sure I got everything right. I thought that was very important in terms of the subject matter and the memory of everyone involved. And then I just started drawing.

CF: You'd come to the book independently as a student before you were commissioned. What made you want to work with *Heart of Darkness* in the first place?

CA: For that particular competition they gave us a list of books to work with, and it was just an obvious pick for me. I think I'm quite like you; I enjoy things from that period. Also, I studied literature. After I finished at the RCA I went to University College London to do an M.A. in English Literature and that's something I had lined up before I started my art career. So I've studied the book at school as well. That's also helped me with the preparation because I wasn't coming to it completely cold. It was a well-known text to me.

CF: It sounds like literature is quite important for you as an artist.

CA: Yes, very, very.

CF: Let me then ask you about the working process. You and David [Mairowitz] are obviously in very different parts of the world; how did this collaboration work?

CA: We emailed back and forth—he did the adaptation first, and so basically he took the book and extracted what was going to be used and not used, and laid it out page by page with dialogue. I went through that and came back with my comments about things that I really thought should be included. I also said "I'll work with this as a base, but I might decide to focus the action in a different way and collapse three of your pages into one," for example, because pacing is visually very important. We had that back and forth, and then I would do the roughs, and we'd talk about them; then I would do the final images. I said from the beginning that I would have to be quite independent, because I don't collaborate well [laughs]; I just need to be able to do things how I want them. A couple of times they made suggestions that I didn't really want to take on board so I just ignored them. But when they did say something that I wanted and thought was relevant then I did say yes to that.

CF: That raises a question in terms of what Eye Classics[7] were looking for. Did you get any instructions about how faithful you should be? Did they have a vision of the project in advance?

CA: No, I think it was pretty much up to me. The book is drawn quite realistically, and that was a decision I made because I felt that historically I didn't want to turn it into a caricature, or something ... something not serious, because I was so overwhelmed by the book. And so I thought, keep it looking quite realistic, but then I could take liberties within that.

I think their vision really was just to stick with the style I had already developed and then there were two elements which we discussed with David, which was the combination with the *Congo Diary*, and Marlow as Conrad. Those two things came from David; the *Congo Diary*, definitely he suggested that, so I bought it and read it. I thought that was good. And then from that the idea of using Marlow as Conrad sort of seemed natural. And that was quite fun because, obviously drawing this kind of thing, you need a lot of reference— it became like finding treasures; I'd find a new picture of Conrad from a different angle [laughs]. I can draw him from that angle now!

CF: That is such an interesting choice, for me, to draw Marlow as Conrad, and what that really emphasizes are the autobiographical dimensions of "Heart of Darkness."

CA: Yes— I mean, the novel is based on his trip, and there's a lot of correlation between the *Congo Diary* and the story, so I think it's a thinly veiled autobiography, definitely. Also, the fact that Marlow is not treated as some sort of overarching hero; he has flaws. That's a very brave way to do an autobiography and for that reason I thought, might as well give [Conrad] that kudos.

CF: So the decision was a way of giving integrity to Conrad?

CA: Yes, exactly.

CF: You mentioned that you studied literature and you've worked with Henry James's *The Turn of the Screw* and [Jean-Martin] Charcot's photographs of hysterics; what is it about the nineteenth-century period that draws you?

CA: You know, until you'd asked that, I hadn't even connected these things at all, but it's true; I've started thinking of why that was the case. There's a couple of things: obviously the nineteenth century was a real period of expansion— global expansion, and also in terms of discovery and invention. These [nineteenth-century] books are written with a nod to that; they acknowledge something new and scary. That's definitely there in "Heart of Darkness."

There's also the idea of evidence, because the written word and the photographic image were such strong evidence of fact, because photography had just really started—you know, been invented— and if you had a photograph of something, that was how it was. But already, the medium was being manipulated, and I find that so fascinating that it's just in our nature to use whatever means possible to twist the truth, whether negatively or positively. *The Turn of the Screw,* the hysteria material, and "Heart of Darkness" all deal with fiction and reality; the ghosts in *The Turn of the Screw,* we're not sure if they're real or not. I think that's written quite masterfully into it. It's an era of not knowing, of technological advancement outstripping human imagination. *Jekyll and Hyde* was written at the same time, and that's again extrapolating the idea of what could be. I think that might be missing a little bit from fiction now because we're a little bit more cynical, perhaps. I really like the fact that it was this period where things were new, especially with photography.

I'm very interested in the use of photography and am working on a series of drawings now of crime scenes and I realize that's quite related as well, to this idea of evidence—a photograph being something we look to for clues.

CF: Are they historical crime scenes?

CA: No, they're contemporary ones. I'm drawing them in a way that makes them look like photographic negatives; I'm going to make them really big. They are, in the same way that ["Heart of Darkness"] was a sort of homage to the victims of the Congolese occupation, the crime scenes as well are— we see CCTV images all the time; what these are, are images of the last time you see a certain person before they died. And it's just horrible, some of them. So I'm sort of trying to make that last moment a little bit nicer than just this horrid photo released to the public.

CF: What you're talking about there is a real ethical investment in your art. I think we could talk about that a bit more specifically in regards to your relationship with "Heart of Darkness." Obviously, this is one of the most controversial of all nineteenth-century novels. How did its reputation affect your approach as an artist and a woman of African descent; you knew the controversies about its treatment of race. How were you positioned towards the book when you started, and did that change as you worked through the project?

CA: Yes, I did change as I worked through it because of all the research I did. I started off—because I'd read the book so closely, you know I'd studied it and really studied the lines and nuances, I felt pretty confident in my own assessment of whether I thought it was racist or not. I didn't really mind that there was going to be controversy. In a way, it's a bit like the way I worked with SelfMadeHero and David; I just didn't care if they thought "this isn't really for me" [laughs], so I wasn't too bothered about that. I also wanted to validate that through the writing, so I was very careful to make sure my ideas were validated. I just felt that the way it was written was—it wasn't the nicest portrayal of the Congolese, but I thought it was very honest. It goes back to this whole idea of this as a century of exploration and expansion, and this was the first view of something very new and different. I think it would be a little bit candy-coated to expect someone to go over to the Congo and feel an immediate kinship with a different kind of person. There's plenty of lines in the book that [Marlow] says he feels a strange and remote kinship, and that it wasn't bad, it was just different. Also [Conrad's] portrayal of the white settlers is pretty horrific as well. I really do think that it's a sympathetic portrayal [of the Congolese], and I think, like perhaps Conrad, Marlow goes through stages of revelation, and so maybe starts off thinking "They're very other"; but at the end, he's full of sympathy. There's one quote where [Marlow] is looking at the head outside Kurtz's house and he really then understands; I think he says, "the horrors that made this all possible now broke the daylight." He's just disgusted with everything that's happened. So I really did think it was a very honest portrayal of somebody coming upon something different.

And again back to the idea of evidence—this book and the Casement report brought knowledge of what was happening over there and played a big part in raising awareness of what was going on. That kind of empirical evidence needs to be, in a way … not detached, but … a real report; it was the reality of it, rather than some sort of fictionalized response to make everyone feel better, and I think if [Conrad] had done that then it wouldn't have had the impact it did.

CF: You mentioned the drawing of the head on a stick outside Kurtz's house. For me that's one of the most powerful images in the whole book, because it's right there, up close (fig. 2). Just thought that was a really interesting choice, because there were a few directions you could have went in here. You could have chosen to either not represent it and give us some distance on it, or this closeness—this is not an adaptation that shies away at all from the horrors of the Congolese situation. Why was it important to you to make sure that violence and brutality was so, in your face, as it were?

CA: Firstly with that double spread of the face, the text at that point is showing how [Marlow] and the head are really in the same position; they're both pretty doomed. I wanted to show them as the same size, side by side. I think this is also when Marlow recognizes his kinship, so visually I wanted to relate them. With the violence, I thought, one tactic I had with drawing the book, was that I thought if I make these drawings really rich and really immersive and beautifully textured and full of detail, it will draw the reader in, and then you can hit them much harder when something violent or brutal happens. There's a line in the book as well that says, "It seemed improbable that such horrors could have existed here in the sunshine." To me that was the basis of how to lay it out, how these horrors could exist in such a beautiful setting.

CF: Yes, it's a beautifully drawn book about horrific things.

CA: Exactly. And you could go full-on blood splatters, but I thought, it almost emphasizes the mundanity of how the violence was, there were day-to-day horrors. I thought if I make everything the same level, beauty and horror, it will make my readers really think about it.

CF: You touched there on the impressionistic quality of Conrad's work. Conrad

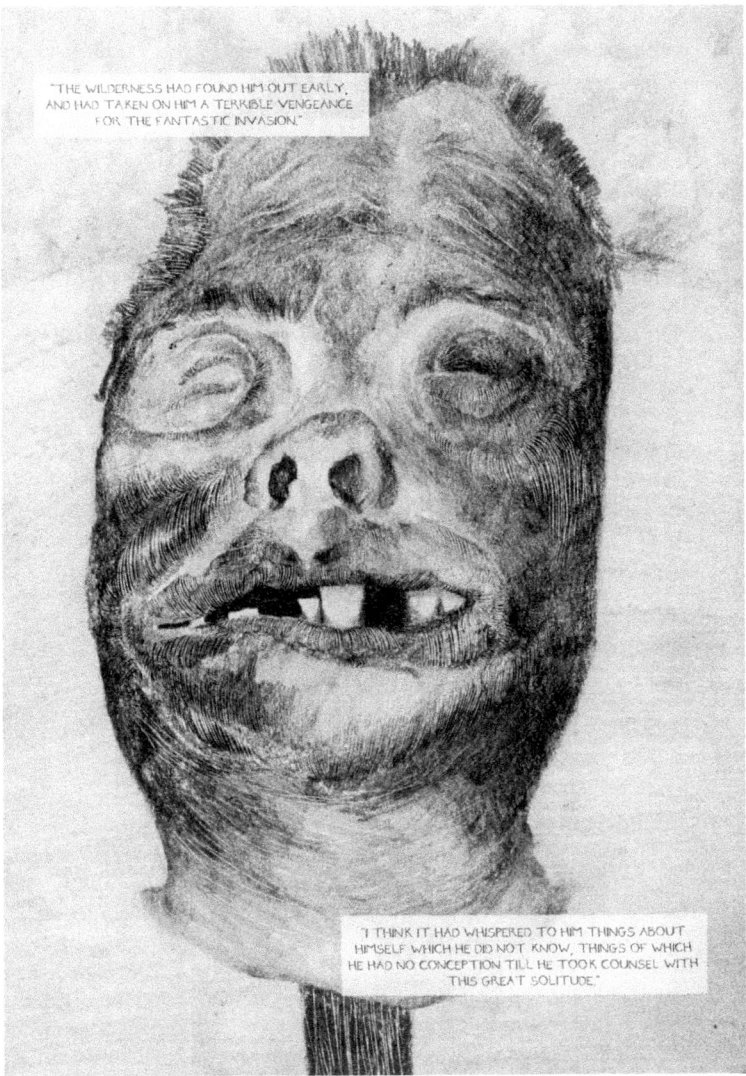

Figure 2. *Congo Diary* entry and image of dead Congolese bearer. Anyango and Mairowitz, *Heart of Darkness*. SelfMadeHero, p. 33.

is known as the great writer of the obscure, which makes him such an interesting challenge for a visual artist. Clearly, you're interested not only in the plot but also in his form, and I'm sure that was one of your starting points; how do you then reproduce this experience of not really being able to see?

CA: "Heart of Darkness," more than any of [Conrad's] other books, is about not really being able to see things; everything is obscure, and it's always foggy and misty and dark and impenetrable. Obviously a lot of that text was cut because the text that remains in there is really about speech and action, so all the description, which I think is the most beautiful part of Conrad's writing, is taken out. But then that gave me the liberty to make those descriptions into images, and use the images to make things obscure. There's a lot of that in the book. Some critics— on Amazon!— say "I can't see what's going, it's too dark!" [laughs]. And actually it has been printed a tiny bit darker than it should have been, but that's fine. Also what I did, as the book progressed, I made the drawings smaller and smaller, so that they would be more fractured when I blew them up. So your mind is disintegrating and so is the pencil mark as we go through the book.

CF: That's what I wanted to ask you—these are all pencil drawings?

AC: Yes, and at points I've used watercolor.

CF: The book is beautifully detailed; it must have taken a long time.

AC: I just was drawing constantly; it was so brutal because I felt so— reading all that history was just, depressing, and drawing the book was so intense. I guess that's good in a way. I got so emotional about everything.

CF: The *Heart of Darkness* year! Could I ask you—I think we saw this in some of the panels; it's in your biographical note at the end, where you talk about the importance of film and cinema to your work and the way you were drawing on those methods. I think it's the interesting the way some of the panels are set up as if they're filmic sequences. *Heart of Darkness* has been made into a really famous film adaptation; were you working with those cinematic precedents when you were drawing?

CA: I was working with cinematic techniques, like of framing and of pacing, because again, a lot was left out of the text so I wanted subliminally for things to be moved along by our knowledge of cinematic tropes. I hadn't seen *Apocalypse Now*; I just didn't want to. Also I guess it's a slightly different story; I just didn't even worry about that. My mum did keep sending other people's visual adaptations of it, but none that I really liked, and also there hadn't been a graphic novel one as such, so I was pretty free from influence.

CF: So the influence then is from cinematic technique and form rather than any particular film version?

CA: Absolutely, yes.

CF: In terms of the framing of the images, one of the things that really strikes me about the book is the way that you draw so many scenes from above; it's a disorienting perspective—we're above the water or above the characters. What made you want to position us in that strange narrative space?

CA: I think that's from the cinema, the use of different points of view. Because it's very intense, and it's a very small world they're inhabiting when you see only a few inches in front of their faces, the reason I did some of those shots was to emphasize scale—not just scale of the situation but scale of the narrative at that point. This was one of the really saddest quotes: "There was the empty immensity of sky and water, there she was a French man of war incomprehensibly firing into a continent." And that is so incomprehensible and epic that I thought, let's remove ourselves for a second and see this as a universal thing than as something that's just about the Congolese situation. Here— [in an overhead spread showing Congolese bearers carrying agents (Mairowitz & Anyango 30–31)]— it was to remove ourselves from the absurdity of the situation because you've got them being carried, and then later on you've got him dying because they're marching. So it was to sort of reinforce that this is happening not just in this late nineteenth-century situation; that this is—I'm not explaining it very well—I wanted to bring the reader out of this very claustrophobic world, to remember that this is a universal, tragic pattern. And it's occurring even now. And also, to not make it boring [laughs].

CF: The Eye Classics *Heart of Darkness* seems part of the closer proximity we've seen between comics artists and fine artists in recent years. You're trained as a fine artist, and this is your first graphic novel; were you aware of that kind of crossover before?

CA: Not so much. This is my only graphic novel and I would call myself a fine artist more than a graphic novelist, so I was coming to it from that perspective. I know of the trend in graphic novels. This book isn't very typical because it's drawn in such detail, and usually [in graphic novels] the style is a bit simpler and fast paced— I knew that I didn't want to do that. I almost didn't think of it like I was doing a graphic novel, because I wanted to make my own mind up about the panels and the sequencing, and make it look like film. That was my approach from the beginning.

I do really like graphic novels but I don't think I've been very inspired by them for this one; I actually see them as something separate. And the ones I like— well, it's more about the writing really, I suppose in graphic novels that I'm interested in. I really like Alison Bechdel. I have been working on my own new graphic novel, but it's taking ages! I keep reading that Donna Tartt took ten years to write her novel after *The Little Friend*, and it's like, ten years, how can that be! [laughs] I mean, life goes on.

CF: What's your new graphic novel about?

CA: It's about—it sounds very banal [laughs]— a corrupt city council and it's an extrapolation of what could happen in that situation. It's a take on things that happened in downtown L.A. where the surface of the earth was undermined so much by digging that they just got all of these sinkholes, and it was partly to do with bad tenders from the council. Also here in Hackney we had a lot of problems with the council destroying housing so that then they could sell it off because it was uninhabitable. I just extrapolated that into a story where the whole city was ruined and people had to move out. There's only two people left and it's their story. He might have killed someone...

CF: Is this a real city; is it set in London?

CA: No, it's a random, everywhere place.

CF: And you're doing the drawings and the text for this?

CA: Yes.

CF: So, you are moving into the graphic novel *auteur* stream then?

CA: I know [laughs]; I'm really happy. This one also looks more like a graphic novel than *Heart of Darkness* because it's simpler, but I'm still playing with the panels and how they connect cinematically. It is really fun.

Notes

1. For ease of distinction, I refer to Conrad's *Heart of Darkness*, first published in book form in *Youth; a Narrative and Two Other Stories* (1902), in quotation marks, while I italicize the title of Anyango's and Mairowitz's adaptation.

2. This approach is likely selected to appeal to these comics genre's male youth target audiences. For more on the origins and audiences for *Classics Illustrated* and *seinen* manga, see Kinsella (2000) and Jones (2011). For more on Conrad and film adaptation, see Moore 1997.

3. See for example the split-frame vista of Marlow's steamboat as he prepares to travel up river in search of Kurtz (20), and of Marlow's encounter with a dying laborer (25).

4. See Der Vlies 2010, Faber 2010, and Francis 2011.

5. Three of these were subsequently incorporated into the graphic novel: see the drawings of the woman outside of Kurtz's house (87), of Marlow at the door of the Intended (116), and of Kurtz's dying "The Horror, the Horror!" speech (109).

6. Soon to follow in this vein is Matt Kish's series of illustrations for "Heart of Darkness," more abstract and less realist than Anyango's, to be published in late 2013. Ten of these are previewed in *The Graphic Canon* (2013).

7. Eye Classics is the series of British graphic novel publisher SelfMadeHero devoted to adaptations of classics of world literature. The publisher also produces specialist lines in Manga Shakespeare, crime classics, and graphic biography.

Works Cited

Anyango, Catherine, and David Mairowitz. *Heart of Darkness*. London: SelfMadeHero, 2010. Print.

Conrad, Joseph. "Heart of Darkness." In *Youth: A Narrative, and Two Other Stories*. Edinburgh: Blackwood, 1902: 49–183. Print.

_____. *Lord Jim*. Classics Illustrated No. 136. New York: Gilberton, 1957. Print.

Faber, Michel. Rev. of *Heart of Darkness* by Joseph Conrad, Catherine Anyango and David Zane Mairowitz. *The Guardian*. 25 September 2010. Web. 3 August 2013.

Francis, Andrew. Rev. of *Heart of Darkness* by David Zane Mairowitz and Catherine Anyango. *The Conradian*. 36.1 (Spring 2011). Web. 5 August 2013.

Jones, William B., Jr. *Classics Illustrated: A Cultural History*. 2d edition. Jefferson, NC: McFarland, 2011. Print.

Kinsella, Sharon. *Adult Manga: Culture and Power in Contemporary Japanese Society*. Richmond: Curzon, 2000. Print.

Kish, Matt. "Heart of Darkness by Joseph Conrad." *The Graphic Canon: Volume 3*. Ed. Russ Kick. New York: Seven Stories Press, 2013: 2–12. Print.

Knowles, Owen, and Gene M. Moore, eds. *Oxford Reader's Companion to Conrad*. Oxford: Oxford University Press, 2000. Print.

Moore, Gene M. ed. *Conrad and Film*. Cambridge: Cambridge University Press, 1997.

Peters, John G. *Conrad and Impressionism*. Cambridge: Cambridge University Press, 2001. Print.

Said, Edward. 1993. *Culture and Imperialism*. London: Vintage, 1994. Print.

Takizawa, Seiho. *Who Fighter with Heart of Darkness*. 2004. Milwaukie, OR: Dark Horse Comics, 2006. Print.

Van der Vlies, Andrew. " 'The Horror!' in Pen and Ink." *Art South Africa* 9.2 (Summer 2010): 80. Print.

Watt, Ian. *Conrad in the Nineteenth Century*. Los Angeles: University of California Press, 1979. Print.

Visualizing the Unrepresentable
Graphic Novel Adaptations of Kafka's *Metamorphosis*

Martha Kuhlman

> As Gregor Samsa awoke one morning from uneasy dreams, he found himself transformed in his bed into a giant insect.
> —Franz Kafka, *The Metamorphosis*

The first line of *The Metamorphosis* is so famous it is easy to forget that in the original German, Kafka does not actually use the word "insect," but rather the more troubling and ambiguous words "ungeheueren Ungeziefer," also translated as "monstrous vermin."[1] It is not, as commonly held, as straightforward as representing Gregor as a cockroach or a beetle, even if his description resembles these insects. In fact, when corresponding with his publisher about the cover, Kafka was adamant that, "the insect itself cannot be drawn" (qtd. in Emrich 127). When we consider graphic novel adaptations of *The Metamorphosis*, the predicament of the ambiguous first line becomes acute since Gregor must inevitably be visually represented. A choice has to be made about how to depict this nightmarish awakening.

How can this apparently impossible representational quandary be solved? This chapter examines and compares possible answers in three graphic novel adaptations of Kafka's text using Thierry Groensteen's concept of *transécriture*. According to this notion, it is important to make specific use of the unique qualities of the medium when transforming a narrative from one form into another. In the case of *The Metamorphosis*, can the graphic novel adaptation evoke similar conflicting sensations of defamiliarization, horror, and humor as the original while simultaneously using the specific idiom of comics? Moreover, to what extent do these graphic adaptations echo or re-envision interpretations in the history of Kafka scholarship on *The Metamorphosis*? The well-known adaptation by Robert Crumb and David Zane Mairowitz (1994) takes a largely mimetic approach but deploys unusual cropping and panel layout. By contrast, Peter Kuper's version (2003) and Czech artist Václav Gatarik's adaptation (*Proměna*, 2009) tend to emphasize the more grotesque and alienating aspects of Kafka's aesthetic. What interests me most in this comparison is the extent to which each artist makes creative use of the expressive potential of comics form. In analyzing these examples, the purpose is not necessarily to cast judgment on one over another, but to look for points in common as well as to appreciate the variety of approaches and referential frameworks used in these successive adaptations.

Critical Interpretations

Given that Kafka is such an opaque and mysterious writer, *The Metamorphosis* has understandably given rise to a formidable archive of scholarly work that has evolved according to currents and trends in literary criticism. The original 1915 story of the salesman who unexpectedly finds himself transformed into a creature and his ultimate demise has yielded historical, biographical, allegorical, religious, and symbolic interpretations. Criticism from the 1930s through the 60s read the story from psychological or psychoanalytic perspectives (Kaiser and Webster), as a representation of alienation (in the context of the modern metropolis, for instance (Emrich) or as a consequence of the inability to integrate into bourgeois life (Richter), and as tragic hero who suffers from a split subjectivity (Sokel). In reaction to this profusion of approaches, other critics called for a renewed attention to language and form, most notably Stanley Corngold's *The Commentator's Despair: The Interpretation of Kafka's Metamorphosis* (1973) and *Kafka: Towards a Minor Literature* (1975) by Gilles Deleuze and Félix Guattari. These works turn away from symbolic interpretations of the text and propose close readings that reflect upon the nature of writing (Corngold) and the subversive potential of a "minority" use of language that opposes official languages and authority given Kafka's marginal status as a German speaking Czech Jew (Deleuze and Guattari).

Twenty-first century approaches to the text draw upon disciplines such as disability studies and animal studies to create new readings of the story. James Metzger argues that there are a number of correspondences between the protagonist and the experience of the disabled: Gregor loses control of his body, has difficulty communicating with his family, feels guilt about his condition, becomes accustomed to his new body, and is oppressed by his family's incomprehension and rejection. Metzger sees the story as potentially functioning as a narrative of resistance because "its overall effect is to elicit sympathy for its alienated and marginalized protagonist" (33). Following a similar line of reasoning, Matthew Powell asserts that in Kafka's animal stories "otherness becomes a subjective point of view to be explored and experienced." In representing this perspective, Kafka's narrative challenges "the notion of a stable, coherent self" and cultivates a grotesque aesthetic "to demonstrate the otherness that lies within the self" (140–141).

"Otherness" is a useful point of departure for examining graphic novel adaptations of *The Metamorphosis* both because it signals the difficulty of representing the complexity of Gregor's narrative position, oscillating as it does between human and non-human perception, and because it alludes to the aesthetic shift entailed in analyzing comics—what Charles Hatfield calls the "otherness" of reading comics:

> The fractured surface of the comics page, with its demarcation into different images, shapes, and symbols, presents the reader with a surfeit of interpretive options, creating an experience that is always decentered, unstable, unfixable [xiii–xiv].

Hatfield's description of the comics page as offering "a surfeit of interpretive options" can just as easily be applied to *The Metamorphosis*. How much more complex, then, becomes the task of adapting a multivalent text into an equally multivalent medium?

Rather than denigrating adaptation as a debasement of some original, auratic text, Linda Hutcheon and Thierry Groensteen argue that the transformation from one medium to another—what Hutcheon terms "transcoding"—can expose new, unexpected aspects of a work that are unique to that particular medium as well as bring another social and historical context to bear on its interpretation.[2] For Hutcheon, adaptation works in three fundamental ways, as: "an acknowledged transposition of a recognizable work; a creative and an interpretive act of appropriation; an extended intertextual engagement with the adapted work" (8). Since Kafka's text poses broader questions about the nature of representation and language, it is an especially fascinating opportunity for thinking about adaptation as metamorphosis in all of these senses.

Crumb's Melodramatic Metamorphosis

As the father of the comics underground, Crumb's reputation for "anti-conformity, cultural alienation, sublimated sex and violence" and his commitment to "complete freedom of content, markedly lacking in concession or self-censorship" (Hignite 6) make him an apt choice for converting *The Metamorphosis* into comics form. The Crumb-Mairowitz version (1994), rendered in Crumb's fine black pen and ink on a white background, is a logical place to start both because it is probably the most well-known and because the adapters explicitly tackle the problem of representation from the beginning. On the first page, they reproduce the 1916 cover by Ottomar Starke which shows a man in a dressing gown striding into a room with his hands obscuring his face below his wildly disheveled hair; behind him, an open door leads into darkness. If Kafka had consented to this cover, one might presume that the metamorphosis is only the delusion of a troubled mind, as a few critics have argued (Beissner 187). But on the next two pages, Crumb depicts partial views of the enormous insect: his spindly legs flail as he lies in his bed, his antennae are placed in the foreground opposite the shocked face of his boss, and the back of his body with legs trailing is wedged into the door as he is expelled from the living room (40–41). By the fourth page, we see the entire creature, shown as a generic beetle. In his concluding notes, Mairowitz also comments that Kafka did not want the insect to be represented, and speculates that "this may have been his way of containing the horror of the transformation." Or, he continues, perhaps it is just that "the line between his feelings about his body in human form and its 'insecthood' was not all that clear" (56).

Be that as it may, Crumb did choose to draw Gregor as a beetle; there is no ambiguity in this. Instead, Crumb insinuates Gregor's otherness through the use of off-kilter panels to show the creature's point of view, in contrast to his family, the boarders or his boss, who are represented in panels at conventional right angles. Gregor's panels are not only presented at an angle, but also appear in irregular patchwork shapes like a narrative puzzle that cannot fit together. Captions and word balloons overlap and exceed the panel boundaries as if they were also separate fragments assembled into a kind of destabilized collage. Crumb's dense crosshatching in combination with the skewed panels produces a cramped, claustrophobic effect. Panel borders are juxtaposed to doors, windows, and picture frames, suggesting Gregor's confinement and desire for escape (44–45). Occasionally Crumb will employ a low-angle view to emphasize Gregor's perspective as when Gregor tries to help his sister Grete find medicine for their mother, or when he hears his sister play the violin. But most of the panels depict the characters interacting in a medium-shot frame consistent with the style he uses in his underground comics; the propulsive force of this version lies elsewhere.

Familial drama and conflict, emphasized with motion lines and sweat

*Visualizing the Unrepresentable—*KUHLMAN 209

beads that vibrate with emotion, take center stage in this adaptation. The most extreme example is at the climax of the story when the father is assaulting Gregor with apples and his mother comes to his defense. In the center of the page, panel borders are swept away by a whirlpool of wavy, agitated lines that center around the figure of the threatening father; the mother and sister are visibly distraught, begging for Gregor's life (50). Gregor, by contrast, is placed

Figure 1. Gregor's mother and sister restrain his father from punishing the unfortunate Gregor any further. Crumb and Mairowitz, *Metamorphosis*. Kitchen Sink Press, p. 50.

at the outer boundaries of the fearsome black hole his presence has provoked, appearing rather diminished and covered in filth in the lower right panel (fig. 1). Mairowitz favors psychological and biographical readings of the text by offering his own interpretation at the end, "What counts most in this great fable is not so much Gregor's suffering, but rather that which he inadvertently inflicts on his parents and sister, mirroring Kafka's own feelings of inadequacy with regard to his family" (56).

Over the course of the seventeen-page adaptation, Mairowitz and Crumb strike an uneasy balance between portions of narration that are rendered in type as third-person omniscient narration and hand-lettered captions, thought balloons, and speech balloons. The entire text, based upon Mairowitz's own translation, condenses the story into short speeches punctuated with added colloquial exclamations and outbursts. These latter inventions seem necessary to move the story along, but switching between the hand-lettered text and the typeset passages can be distracting. Still, this version retains key passages (although in shortened and modified form) such as Gregor's speech when he is late for his job: "I shall now get dressed, pack my samples and be off. I'm so deeply beholden to the boss, as you well know ... I'm in a tight spot, but I shall work my way out of it."[3]

Critics often remark upon the anecdote about Kafka reading his work out loud to friends, "sometimes laughing so hard he could not continue" (Updike xiii). Crumb hints at this humor in his absurd juxtapositions of image and text, as is the case in the other adaptations as well. It is painfully obvious that the insect creature Gregor cannot possibly get to work on time, but in the prose version the reader might try to dismiss the details about his changed body as the residue of a bad dream at that point in the story. The visual representation adds poignancy and humor to the gap between Gregor's self-perception and the way others see him. When Gregor tries to aid his sister, Crumb depicts him in the lower right corner of the bottom panel, looking up at Grete's fleeing skirts; the balloon above him telegraphs his thoughts: "I want to help!" (46). A final layer of irony is included in the Crumb-Mairowitz version since the story is set in the broader context of the book *Introducing Kafka* (1994) that summarizes Kafka's life, works, and contemporary reception. At the time the book was published, Prague was hailed as the "Paris of the 90s" as Americans flocked to this beautiful city where they could live relatively inexpensively. Thus, *Introducing Kafka* satirizes the "Kafka industry" of coffee cups, t-shirts, and kitsch for tourists while at the same time situating itself as part of this trend in popular culture as a comic book (Bruce 244).

The Alienated Gregor

Of the three adaptations under discussion, Peter Kuper's is most self-consciously art historical in its frame of reference. His stark black and white scratchboard technique[4] recalls the style of Frans Masereel and Lynd Ward, woodblock artists whose wordless graphic narratives are social critiques of urban life. Masereel is also a significant intertextual reference since he worked with Karl Wolff, who was also Kafka's publisher, between 1915 and 1925 (MacDonald 64). In his introduction, Kuper also links his adaptation to comics history by citing Winsor McCay's "Dream of the Rarebit Fiend" (1904) as a source of inspiration. This surreal one-page newspaper comic features a main character who falls victim to strange and increasingly threatening scenarios until he or she wakes up only to realize that it was a bad dream provoked by eating rarebit (a cheese and bread concoction) just before bed. Thus, both Kafka and McCay's work exhibit a "genius for rendering the anxious intersection of reality and dreamscape," as Kuper puts it (5).

Recognizing the importance of the first sentence as confusing the border between reality and dream, Kuper creates a suspenseful opening by choosing a simple black page with white typeset text that reads, "When Gregor Samsa awoke one morning from disturbing dreams, he found himself transformed...."[5] On the next page, Kuper decides on a compromise between the literal and figurative interpretations of Kafka's metaphor by depicting Gregor as an insect with a human head. Gregor's split subjectivity is expressed both through the incommensurability between his thoughts (in speech balloons and captions) and his insect incarnation, and through the play between his human facial expressions and his insect body. The decision to use a human head—albeit spiked with antennae—is a savvy one since it allows Kuper to show a range of emotions on Gregor's face as he grapples with his situation.[6] His insect-human hybrid body, drawn with dramatic striations and triangles to emphasize his exoskeleton, contrasts with the memories of his former self as a hapless salesman dressed in a suit in a set of panels above his head (10–11).

Considering the many possible interpretations of the text, Kuper's adaptation is most inclined towards a Marxist reading of Gregor as an alienated worker in the modern world, defeated by the equation of time and money.[7] Kuper emphasizes how Gregor's life is dominated by the tyranny of his boss, his crushing debt, and a constant anxiety about time—a clock appears on six out of the seven first pages. A wide range of inventive page layouts and visual metaphors express his despair: in one instance, Gregor is depicted trapped in an hourglass, just keeping his head above the mass of bills that trickles away beneath him; on another page, he is running around the face of a clock like a hamster in a wheel. His desperate pursuit of money is exposed as futile and worthless when his family manages to survive without him thanks to their thrift and ingenuity, thus rendering his alienation from his job and his family complete.

Kuper adeptly uses the space of the page to create a claustrophobic atmosphere that corresponds to the otherness of Gregor's perception (Pointner and Boschenhoff 95). The page layout physically cramps Gregor, as in a tight sequence of eight rectangular panels early in the story that depict him trying and failing to turn over on his side (9), and later when he tries to hide under the couch (31). These first scenes show Gregor in an adversarial relation to his body, but he eventually adapts to his changed circumstances and behaves more like an insect. To demonstrate this in comics form, the gutter is used as a space for the caption, "for recreation he had taken up the habit of crawling crisscross over the walls and ceiling. He especially enjoyed hanging suspended from the ceiling; it was much nicer than lying on the floor; one could breathe more freely..." (42). Mimicking the path of Gregor, the caption runs down the right hand side of the page, flips upside down, turns around in awkward kinks (fig. 2).

Gregor's alienation from his family is represented in dramatic spatial juxtapositions that emphasize the separation between their two respective spheres of perception. One page is split along a diagonal to form two panels: in the upper left panel, framed in light, Gregor's mother knocks on his door; in the lower panel, framed in black, Gregor is inside his room, struggling to get out of bed (16). His inability to communicate is heightened through the hand-drawn, scraggly lettering used for his speech, which looks markedly different from the typeset captions and speech of other characters. In this way, Kuper develops a number of visual oppositions between Gregor and his family: dark vs. light, inside vs. outside, lower vs. higher, scratchy and unformed lettering vs. neatly printed words. As we near the moment when his family first sees Gregor, Kuper places his mother and the chief clerk in the first two panels coinciding with the upper two panels of Gregor's bedroom door, thus exploiting the visual analogy between the comics panel and this architectural detail (21). The suspense builds in the following two-page spread, with the left hand side representing the scene outside Gregor's door, and the right hand page showing the darkened interior of his room (22–23). When this barrier is finally breached and the assembled crowd sees Gregor, the shock of this contact is expressed in a series of unhinged panels that twist and tilt down the page as the clerk retreats in terror (26–27).

Because Kuper's version is more than four times longer than Crumb's, more space is allotted to text and the development of crucial moments in the

Figure 2. Gregor gradually learns to feel at home in his new body by crawling around the room like an insect. Kuper, *Metamorphosis*. 3 Rivers Press, p. 42.

story. When the father pelts Gregor with apples, a scene that occupies one page in Crumb's version, Kuper plays out the conflict over the course of four pages (47–50). In a dramatic two-page spread, the father's arm extends across the page to occupy the center gutter of the right hand side, demonstrating his strength and dominance (48–49). Kuper gives significant weight to Kafka's third-person narration, as is the case in this scene. While Gregor wonders, "C-Could this be father? The same tired old man?," a block of narration superimposed on black space of the father's back reads: "But Gregor did not dwell on this reflection for he had known from the first day of his new life that his father considered only the harshest measures suitable for dealing with him..." (48). The Crumb-Mairowitz adaptation generally omits passages such as these, focusing instead on dialogue and action to advance the story. Kuper relies upon Kerstin Hasenpusch's translation, which is similar to the standard Muir version, and tends to be formal in tone and is less colloquial than Mairowitz's.[8]

Overall, this adaptation of the *Metamorphosis* is formally complex and has a dimension of social critique in keeping with Kuper's other projects, including an adaptation of Upton Sinclair's *The Jungle* (2004) and his wordless comic *The System* (1997). Gregor is at first the hapless salesman, and then the object of pity and scorn in his transformed state, although the similarities between the two states are suggested by their juxtaposition on the page. Varied page layouts convey Gregor's fragmented and confused perception, sometimes departing from the conventional grid for dramatic effect. Following Gregor's death, right angles and regular panels are reestablished; we now view the landscape of Prague from the family's perspective as they take a tram ride into the country with a sense of relief. Only the small detail of a beetle on a telephone pole in the foreground hints at the loss of Gregor. At every turn, Kuper takes advantage of the specificity of comics layout as a mode of expression, a technique that Groensteen advocates in his discussion of how comics can bring something unique to an adaptation.

The Grotesque Gregor

Gatarik's Czech version, the longest of the three at over one hundred pages, introduces new aspects to the story that render it more of an "an interpretive act of appropriation," to quote Hutcheon, than the prior two examples. A few added details resonate in the Czech context: Gregor's sister Grete becomes "Marketa," who at one point sallies forth to the pub to get a beer. Perhaps to underscore the malleable division between animal and human, the family dotes on their little yippy dog and cat while the outcast Gregor languishes in his room. But the most striking difference is that the entire story is framed by a character who is writing at his desk, looking out the window at the landscape of Prague. Most likely this is supposed to be Gregor in human form, but it's ambiguous; the figure also conjures up the image of Kafka, or perhaps even Gatarik himself. Hunched over the table with his head in his hands, the man in the first panel resembles Kafka's drawing of a stick-figure at a desk, and the haircut as well as the bowler hat seem references to well-known photos of Kafka. His first thoughts reinforce his identity as a writer, "Somehow I can't bring myself to write today and I feel tired. I'll have a glass and go to sleep" [*Nějak mi to psaní dnes nejde a cítím se znaven. Dám si sklenku a půdju spat*] (5). Delaying the original opening of the story with this sequence adds a metafictional dimension to *The Metamorphosis*, obliging us to consider the work's origin and moment of creation. This gesture echoes Corngold's interpretation, which places considerable emphasis on the act of writing and the position of the writer. Gatarik's representation dovetails with understanding the narrative as a kind of allegory about writing itself in which Kafka's identity as an author sets him apart as strange and different from his own family, just like Gregor (Corngold xvi).

The unveiling of the metamorphosis only occurs on the third page, with Gregor gradually peeping his head over the sheets accompanied by the caption "Gregor Samsa awoke from uneasy dreams to find himself transformed into a monstrous beetle" [*nestvůrného bourka*](6). Like Kuper, Gatarik chose to depict Gregor as an insect with a head, although in this case the face is monstrous and grotesque rather than human. Gregor is deliberately ugly, drawn with a frenetic line that varies in thickness and contrasts markedly with the clean edges in Kuper's version or the studied, vibrating lines of Crumb. Both grossly exaggerated and somewhat humorous, the face evokes conflicting reactions in the viewer and recalls Powell's definition of grotesque otherness in Kafka's animal stories as "a subversive aesthetic meant to disturb, shock, and confound its audience" (140–141).

What makes Gatarik's representation of Gregor especially unsettling is the way in which it blurs the distinction between the human and the animal, and reveals "the otherness that lies within the self" (Powell 141). At times, the character can evoke pity, as in the scene when he laments that all he has left are memories. In this flashback, conveyed in a circular panel to distinguish it from the main action in the present, Gregor is depicted presenting money to his grateful parents (33). We see Gregor as his former human self, somewhat resembling portraits of Kafka; in a significant reversal, Gatarik choses to make

Gregor the skilled violinist, with his sister commenting admiringly, "Gregor, you play so beautifully! You should definitely go to the conservatory."[9] Occasionally Gregor is poignant and funny, as in the scene where he tries to cover himself with a sheet in an attempt not to affright his sister; the cloaked figure of Gregor looks ridiculous, like a monster disguised as a ghost for Halloween (37).

Figure 3. Gregor, drawn here to resemble Kafka, remembers his former self as a successful salesman and a talented violinist. Gatarik, *Proměna* [Metamorphosis]. Garamond, p. 33.

Like Kuper, Gatarik often conflates the space of the gutter with a door or partition to underscore the division between Gregor and his family. To distinguish conventional white panel gutters from ones that double as a wall, Gatarik uses a heavy black line (10, 13). In figure 3, when Gregor bangs his head against the door in frustration and thinks "I'm so tired of it all" [*Jsem ze všeho tak unavený*], his father reacts in the adjoining panel: "What's that damn ruckus again?" [*Co tam sakru zase vyvádí?!*]. Although the page layout generally conforms to regular tiers of rectangular panels, characters often burst out of their frames, exclaiming, flailing, gesticulating, and yelling at each other; the effect is one of visual anarchy that threatens to overwhelm the page.

Gatarik occasionally arrests our attention with full-color single-page compositions that invite closer study. One such instance is when Marketa goes to the pub for beer and she is surrounded by leering, grotesque characters that could have stepped out of a George Grosz drawing (31). Implicit in this juxtaposition is a comparison between Gregor's monstrous form and more quotidian kinds of monstrosity in the red-faced, hideous customers in the bar. The last page of the book, also in color, follows the pattern of the prior adaptations and depicts the family out for a ride in a tram with the Prague castle in the background. As in the Kuper version, there is an allusion to Gregor in the small beetle scaling a wall in the foreground. But Gatarik also includes something entirely new: on the sidewalk next to the tram, a mother is pushing her handicapped boy along in a wheelchair. This addition prompts reflection in another direction, suggesting an affinity between Gregor's situation and the condition of being disabled, as Metzger argues.

On the whole, Gatarik takes greater liberties with Kafka's text than the other two adaptations; however this is not necessarily to its detriment.[10] In this case, the focus is not as much on the tone and rhythm of the original since most of the story is filtered through Gregor's thoughts or direct dialogue among characters; captions of straight narration are relatively rare. But Gatarik's version ventures further in adapting the story into a Czech context and prompting reflection about writing, authorship, subjectivity, and disability. It is more a thoughtful appropriation than it is a "faithful" adaptation — a concept that has been called into question by Hutcheon in any case.

The Elusive Gregor

Gregor remains a cipher. Although a number of words circulate around his representation like a negative halo — "vermin," "monstrous," "unclean," "uncanny," "creature,"—nothing will definitively pin down this "opaque sign," as Corngold terms it ("Metamorphosis of the Metaphor" 87). Julia Kristeva's description of the abject is especially applicable here: "It is thus not a lack of cleanliness or health that causes abjection but what disturbs identity, system, order. What does not respect borders, positions, rules. The in-between, the ambiguous, the composite" (4). In these comics adaptations, Gregor *must* be graphically represented. Crumb envisions the ambiguous figure of Gregor as a scrappy, nondescript beetle, while Kuper and Gatarik imagine a composite insect-human creature that is horrible and yet pitiful. There is also the "otherness" of the medium of comics and how the story is told—*metamorphosed*—into graphic narrative form. Most evident in the literal manipulation of panel borders, formal conventions assume symbolic weight, as when gutters and walls are conflated and then breached to dramatize the divide between Gregor and the others. Kuper and Gatarik in particular play with the negative and positive space of the gutters in order to destabilize "borders," "positions" and "rules" within the system of comics.

We have also considered the way in which these artists' interpretations intuit or coincide with a parallel strain of scholarly discourse on Kafka's text. Psychological and Marxist readings are implicit or explicit to some degree in the Crumb-Mairowitz and Kuper versions respectively. Crumb-Mairowitz and Gatarik's adaptations also include the cultural and historical context of Prague, with Gatarik even going so far as to pose visual analogies between Gregor and Kafka. This is not to say that any of these versions is derivative; rather, the variety of graphic interpretations demonstrates how readings of the text change depending upon the time and place. To remain fresh and relevant, Kafka's *Metamorphosis* must be reinvented and transcoded into whatever media audiences consume, testing and experimenting with the limits of these new forms.

NOTES

1. Note that "gigantic insect" is the Muir translation; "monstrous vermin" is Stanley Corngold's translation.
2. In "Le Processus adapatif," [the process of adaptation] Groensteen remarks that it is important to note the historical context of the source text, which he states is "artistic, cultural, social, economic and ideological." He also notes that an adaptation is "necessarily determined by the situation of the medium at a particular historical moment." *Transécriture*, 274.
3. In the Corngold translation, this speech is a lengthy paragraph that takes nearly an entire page. He begins, "Well, I'll get dressed right away, pack up my samples, and go. Will you, will you please let me go? Now, sir, you see, I'm not stubborn and I'm willing to work; traveling is a hardship, but without it I couldn't live..." (16) Bantam edition, 1972.
4. Pointner and Boschenhoff describe this process: "In order to achieve a rough xylographic

(woodcut) effect, Kuper employed black scratchboard from which he scrapped off the ink, since, generally speaking, xylography tends to confine the form finding of an artist to rather crude delineation, which suits his project perfectly" (93).

    5. Kuper explains that this ambiguity would have been extended to the book cover as well if he had had his choice: "In the original design I had for the cover there would've been a translucent paper over the image of Gregor so that the reader would have to remove that in order to see him." Email with the author, Aug 16, 2013.

    6. Kuper states, "It was clear that I had to make Gregor more human since readers would be following him over eighty pages of art. So I decided I would have him be close to human rather than inscrutable insect from the very beginning." Email with the author, Aug 16, 2013.

    7. Tanis MacDonald asserts that this adaptation "invokes the suffocation of being intensely embodied in a mechanized world, favoring critics who claim *The Metamorphosis* as a story about urbanized, mechanized class anxiety" (64).

    8. Kuper collaborated with Kerstin Hasenpusch on her translation, which uses some more contemporary diction than Muir's version but retains the stilted formality of the prose style. Kuper writes: "I always loved the Muirs' translation though and find most modernized translations just don't feel ... *Kafkaesque*." Email with the author, Aug. 16 2013.

    9. Kafka's original text describes how Gregor had wanted to send his sister Grete to the conservatory.

    10. Unfortunately, this edition contains no information about the translation. Presumably Gatarik adapted an existing Czech translation, or perhaps he translated directly from German to Czech himself.

Works Cited

Beissner, Friedrich. "The Writer Franz Kafka." In *The Metamorphosis by Franz Kafka*. Ed. Stanley Corngold. New York: Bantam Books, 1972. 187–188. Print.

Bruce, Iris. "Kafka and Popular Culture." *The Cambridge Companion to Kafka*. Ed. Julian Preece. Cambridge: Cambridge University Press, 2002. 242–246. Print.

Corngold, Stanley. *The Commentator's Despair: The Interpretation of Kafka's* Metamorphosis. Port Washington, NY: Kennikat Press, 1973. Print.

_____. "Kafka's *The Metamorphosis*, Metamorphosis of the Metaphor." *Kafka's The Metamorhposis*. Norton Critical Edition. Trans. and ed. New York: Norton, 1996. 79–107. Print.

Crumb, Robert, and David Mairowitz. *Introducing Kafka*. Northhampton, MA: Kitchen Sink Press, 1994. Print.

Deleuze, Gilles, and Félix Guattari. *Kafka: Towards a Minor Literature*. 1975. Trans. Dana Polan. Foreword Réda Bensmaïa. Minneapolis: University of Minnesota Press, 1986. Print.

Emrich, Wilhelm. "The Animal as Liberating 'Self.'" In *The Metamorphosis by Franz Kafka*. Ed. Stanley Corngold. New York: Bantam Books, 1972. 115–132. Print.

Gatarik, Václav. *The Metamorphosis* [Proměna]. Prague: Garamond, 2009. Print.

Groensteen, Thierry. *La Transécriture: Colloque de Cerisy. Centre Nationale de la Bande Dessinée*. Québec: Éditions Nota Bene, 1998. Print.

Hatfield, Charles. *Alternative Comics*. Jackson: University Press of Mississippi, 2005. xiii–xiv. Print.

Hignite, Todd. "Robert Crumb." *In the Studio: Visits with Contemporary Cartoonists*. New Haven: Yale University Press. 6–39. Print.

Hutcheon, Linda. *A Theory of Adaptation*. New York: Routledge, 2013. Print.

Kafka, Franz. "The Metamorphosis." *Franz Kafka: The Complete Stories*. Trans. Willa and Edwin Muir, Ed. Nahum Glatzer. New York: Schocken Books, 1971. Print.

Kaiser, Hellmuth. "Kafka's Fantasy of Punishment." 1931. *The Metamorphosis by Franz Kafka*. Edwin Muir, Ed. Nahum Glatzer. New York: Schocken Books, 1971. Print.

Kristeva, Julia. *Powers of Horror*. Trans. Leon S. Roudiez. New York: Columbia University Press, 1982. Print.
Kuper, Peter. Correspondence with author. 16 Aug. 2013. Email.
———. *The Metamorphosis*. By Franz Kafka. New York: Three Rivers Press, 2003. Print.
MacDonald, Tanis. "Voice of the Gutter: Comics in the Academy." *From Text to Txting: New Media in the Classroom*. Bloomington: Indiana University Press, 2012. 43–68. Print.
Metzger, James A. "Re-visioning Kafka's *Metamorphosis* Through Illness and Disability." *Journal of the Kafka Society of America*. 2009: 33–34. Print.
Pointner, Frank Erik, and Sandra Eva Boschenhoff. "Classics Emulated: Comic Adaptations of Literary Texts." *CEA Critic: An Official Journal of The College English Association* 72.3 (2010): 86–106. Print.
Powell, Matthew T. "Bestial Representations of Otherness: Kafka's Animal Stories." *Journal of Modern Literature* 32.1 (2008): 129–142. Print.
Richter, Helmut. "The Metamorphosis." 1962. *The Metamorphosis by Franz Kafka*. Ed. Stanley Corngold. New York: Bantam Books, 1972. 192–194. Print.
Sokel, Walter H. "Education for Tragedy." 1964. *The Metamorphosis by Franz Kafka*. Ed. Stanley Corngold. New York: Bantam Books, 1972. 169–186. Print.
Updike, John. "Foreword." *Franz Kafka: The Complete Stories*. New York: Schocken Books, 1983. Print.
Webster, Peter Dow. "Franz Kafka's *Metomorphosis* as Death and Resurrection Fantasy." 1959. *The Metamorphosis by Franz Kafka*. Ed. Stanley Corngold. New York: Bantam Books, 1972. 157–168. Print.

An Unusual Adaptation of F. Scott Fitzgerald's The Great Gatsby

Stephen E. Tabachnick

Given F. Scott Fitzgerald's emphasis on luxurious living by Tom, Daisy, and Gatsby in his novel of the 1920's, *The Great Gatsby*, one expects an adaptation to feature elegant, nicely dressed people, grand houses, elaborate parties, and Long Island beach settings. And that is what one gets in the 1974 film adaptation by Francis Ford Coppola and also in the 2013 film adaptation by Baz Luhrmann. But it is not what appears in the first graphic novel adaptation of this famous novel. Instead Australian artist Nicki Greenberg does something startling: she uses invented creatures rather than people to represent the characters, and she colors all of the panel backgrounds in a brownish-green tint, so that the story looks like it is taking place in a strange land or under the sea, rather than simply near it. Moreover, she has varied the number of panels per page, has put them against a black background, and has photo-like borders on them all, so the reader feels that he or she is looking at old photos in a photo album instead of panels on a page of comics. In fact, in the beginning of the adaptation, we see the Nick Carraway creature putting these "photos" into an album that he is compiling, and toward the end we again see him putting a previously torn but now repaired photo of the Gatsby creature into the album. The adaptation obviously consists of that album, complemented by Fitzgerald's words. So the novel has in effect been transformed into a photo album with words inside the drawings of the photos, and the reader scrolls through this album as he or she reads. On her website, Greenberg comments that "The book is presented in the form of an old photograph

Figure 1. The hulking Tom dwarfs both Nick and the delicate flower, Daisy. Greenberg, *The Great Gatsby.* **Penguin, p. 11.**

album with the snapshots forming the 'frames' of the story. In this way, the reader is invited into the private world of the characters, while sharing the sense of nostalgia and loss that pervades the novel." All told, a more unusual transformation of a literary work is difficult to imagine. Yet, surprisingly, it works, and in some ways better than an elegant, human-populated adaptation would have. This chapter will try to explain why this is the case.

The first reason for its success is that the graphic novel like the original novel and unlike a film remains a reading experience, even in Greenberg's unusual treatment. Given the invented creatures, it might seem similar in approach to an animated film for children, but one must read the pages from left to right and top to bottom, rather than being hurried along as a film would do. We can stop reading the graphic novel whenever we wish, and look forward and backward in it at will. While a film would give us constant movement and the sound of voices, the graphic novel leaves us having to fill in those elements. Although we actually see Fitzgerald's characters as we do not in the original, we must imagine how they sound, and how they move. So although it shares the visual presentation of the characters with a film or theatrical production, our experience with Greenberg's adaptation is more imaginative, intimate, and interactive. This reader involvement fits Scott McCloud's idea in *Understanding Comics*, following Marshall McLuhan's original thought in *Understanding Media*, that comics are a very interactive form that requires the reader's constant involvement because of what McCloud calls closure—the fact that the reader is always imagining what happens between the comics panels (66–72).

Another important difference between the original and the graphic novel allies it to some degree with a film or theatrical production. While we are conscious that Nick is reporting all of the dialogue as in the original, we see the characters speaking and therefore do not always think of Nick as the narrator. He is indeed seen putting the photos into the album at the beginning, he is the one who begins and ends the story and sums it up, and clearly his narrative comments on the action and characters are important throughout—but in the adaptation we are allowed to forget that fact when the characters speak for themselves. So the graphic novel, while a reading experience, also includes a film or stage-like more immediate feeling for the characters than the original does, at least during the fairly frequent junctures when they speak for themselves.

Perhaps because we see the creatures interacting and speaking for themselves, our perceived distance from them is not as great a distance as one might imagine before reading the adaptation. We cannot identify with them physically and as completely as we would with humans despite the fact that they often have clothes and hands and faces. But because they have very understandable feelings and expressive faces, and discuss their needs and inclinations using Fitzgerald's eloquent words, we understand and feel close to them. Surprisingly, because we do not have to identify with people unlike ourselves, but rather with invented creatures that have unusual bodies and recognizable and expressive if not always detailed faces, we can usually identify with the characters even better than we could with human characters. This feeling, too, follows McCloud's idea that because the portrayal of comics characters is usually less specific than fully detailed drawings, that portrayal allows us to put ourselves into comics characters' faces and bodies, however odd, and to identify more completely with them than we do with characters in other media (36).

But perhaps most importantly, Greenberg's creaturely stand-ins for the major characters are each unique like Fitzgerald's characters, and capture the psychological essence of those characters. On her website, Greenberg writes that Daisy, Nick, Tom, Jordan, and Gatsby are rendered true to Fitzgerald's original characterizations. Inhabiting the authentic setting of 1920's New York, they join a throng of other fantastical creatures to play out the drama, the wry humor, and the tragedy of the novel. On her website, Greenberg comments:

> Why not humans? To me, Fitzgerald's characters are so incisively rendered, their personalities, movements and voices so immediate and true, that an ordinary human representation does not capture the essence of the written characters. In imagining the physical form of each creature—Nick's shy antennae and soft body, the lift of Daisy's dandelion head on her slender neck, Jordan's languid tentacles—my aim was to make their physical attributes embody and illuminate their personalities, that 'series of successful gestures' so sharply drawn by Fitzgerald.

Greenberg succeeds in capturing these personality traits throughout the work. Nick Carraway, for instance, is a somewhat mundane-looking (in comparison to the other creatures) lizardly creature with large eyes and antennae, which, as Daniel Worden remarks (233), are suitable for his role as a narrator, who must notice and respond to everything so that he can report it to us convincingly. His relatively straightforward and even soft appearance, though lizardly, convinces us that Nick is indeed a normal if sensitive guy in terms of his attitudes and psychological responses, and that he is therefore a trustworthy narrator. Beyond the fact that Nick is clearly a non-human creature, Greenberg's work makes us feel that only the language of Nick's narration is extraordinary, and that of course is because of Fitzgerald's unique, lyrical style.

Nick, then, resembles something of a usual, natural creature compared to some of the others in this adaptation, a creature that we might see in the real animal world. But Tom and Daisy do not belong to the natural animal world, and indeed Fitzgerald sets them apart from the rest of the characters in the original story. As Nick comments at the end when he is pasting a torn photo of Gatsby together again and is therefore cleaning up a "mess" as it were, "They smashed up things and creatures and then retreated back to their money or their vast carelessness or whatever it was that kept them together ...

and let others clean up the mess they had made" (299).[1] (Amazingly, the word "creatures" in this quotation is Fitzgerald's word in the original and undoubtedly served as an inspiration for Greenberg.) They are richer than everyone else in the story, and their money serves as a shield that protects them from their errors. So, appropriately, Daisy looks very unique, with a thin neck and round head something like a flower's, and a very expressive mouth and eyes (but no nose). She is delicate and sensitive, and fragile, much like a dandelion as Greenberg says on her website. Just as appropriately, she is always wearing a nice dress and sometimes a hat; clearly she is "high class" as it were. Nick describes her face as "sad and lovely with bright things in it, and bright eyes and a bright, passionate mouth," (10) and Greenberg captures that look. As in the original, the reader tries to imagine her voice, which sounds "like money" according to Gatsby.

Tom, on the other hand, while also unique-looking, is anything but delicate or sensitive. Nick describes him as "a sturdy man of thirty with a rather hard mouth and a supercilious manner, a cruel body and shining arrogant eyes" (7). Greenberg's Tom looks something like a tough, powerful lizard, with sharp teeth at the ends of and in the middle of his mouth, a large and humanoid hairy chest and arms, and big, pointed, hairy ears. His eyes are small but accentuated by downward-pointing eyebrows, while his nose is horizontally straight and broad with two nostrils at the ends, giving him an aggressive, insensitive look overall. He wears pants but never a shirt, as if he is always displaying his physical strength. His appearance matches his bullying personality. The delicate flower-like Daisy and the bullying Tom do not fit together physically, which mirrors their mental differences; and as we learn, money seems to be the primary factor that binds them together (fig. 1).

Then there is Jordan Baker, who looks like a bored squid or octopus. She has many tentacles, and uses two of them as arms. Her eyes are half-closed and have large eyelashes, her mouth is often curved downward in discontentment, and she has uneven eyebrows which create the impression of boredom. And her "hair" is a border around her head, which is like two triangles—one above her eyes and one below. She is also given a collar but no other item of clothing or accessories except sometimes a fan (10), accentuating her languid and bored expression. Our impression of her, as in the original, is that she is elegant but vapid, and lacking in energy. We do not see her in action as a golfer, which is her profession, and her bored looks and often reclining posture make her profession seem very contradictory to her character, so that we do not completely trust her and are not surprised when Nick eventually breaks off their relationship.

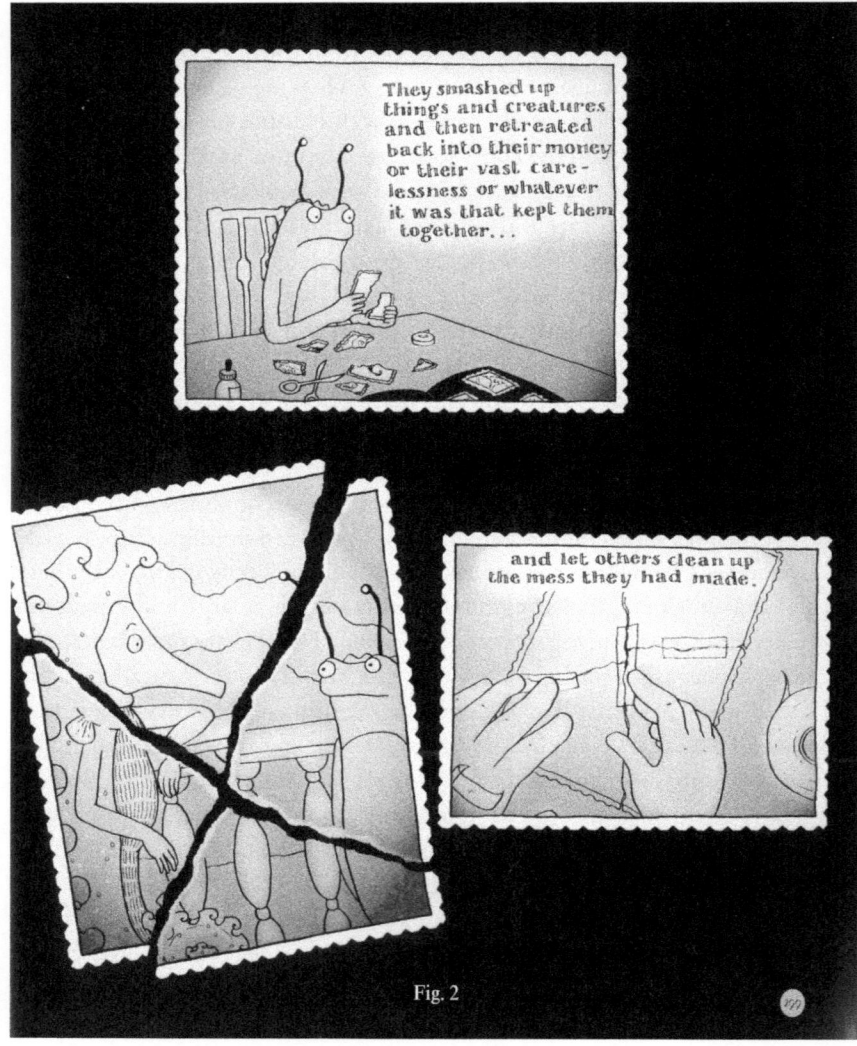

Figure 2. Nick sadly puts together the pieces of his memory of Gatsby. Greenberg, *The Great Gatsby*. Penguin, p. 299.

Tom's mistress, Mrs. Myrtle Wilson, is one of the few major characters who, like him, can be described as outright ugly in Greenberg's adaptation. On page 37, they are shown arm in arm, and they make quite a grotesque pair. She has one eye in the middle of her face with eyelashes all around it. Her nose resembles Tom's, and her mouth seems normal. But that staring eye and her several nipples on each breast poking through her dress do not allow her to appear human, regardless of her hat, dress, curly hair, and human hands and feet. Her human-like characteristics cause surprise when we also look at the eye, which is always prominently displayed. So she disconcerts us, as she does in the original novel, albeit for a different reason. In both novel and adaptation we are disconcerted because she is married and is having an affair with a married man; in the adaptation we are also disconcerted by her looks. When she peers out of her window at Tom and Jordan when they stop at Wilson's garage on their way to New York (205), we see her primarily as a grotesque staring eye and a downturned mouth full of teeth. But while Greenberg is clearly not partial to Myrtle in terms of appearance, she does build sympathy for her. We are told by Nick that "Her expression was curiously familiar. It was an expression I had often seen on women's faces, but on Myrtle Wilson's face, it seemed purposeless and inexplicable." Then Nick understands the reason for her expression, and comments that he "realized that her eye, wide with jealous terror, was fixed not on Tom, but on Jordan Baker, whom she took to be his wife" (206). Notice that he mentions her "eye," not her "eyes" as in the original, which fits the adaptation; otherwise, as always, Greenberg is true to the original text. But as wide as Myrtle's eye opens and as strange as that lone eye seems, her downturned mouth, her hands clasped as if in prayer, and her tear win some sympathy from us for her situation in this scene. Wilson, Myrtle's husband, is a strange, insect-like creature with heavy black and light green coloring unlike any other character. He has bulging eyes, a downturned mouth, a tail like a lobster's, and he is much smaller than Tom, which earns Wilson too, some sympathy, as when we see him on page 204. We also understand that he and Myrtle are not well-suited to one another not only because of Myrtle's affair, which he suspects, and what they say about one another, but because they look so different and clearly belong to completely different species, as do Tom and Daisy, who are also not well-suited except in terms of their love of money.

Among the other major characters is Meyer Wolfsheim, who is given a furry face, hat and shirt complete with collar, tie and cuffs. His eyes and nose are mundane, but he does not seem to have a mouth behind his beard-like facial fur. He sometimes smokes a cigar, and looks like a well-dressed businessman, with an often cagey, realistic look, especially when he tells Nick that he can't get mixed up in Gatsby's funeral (288), although in Greenberg's rendering he does seem a bit regretful about that. Greenberg also does a good job of catching character when she portrays Wolfsheim's secretary, who looks like a shapely young woman with long eyelashes and fish-like fins which stick out of her head and resemble blonde hair. As in the original, the secretary tries to keep Nick from seeing Wolfsheim but in the end to her exasperation she is obliged to let him through (284–285). Greenberg is always able to convey emotion even in these unusual faces. The guests at Gatsby's parties have a variety of looks, including a creature with four eyes, one who looks like a horse with horns, and one vaguely fish-like creature with a long neck, necklace, tiara, bracelet, fan, and dress, who confidentially tells another creature completely composed of black fibers except for her arms, some of the myths about Gatsby that circulate at every party of his (152). In the party guests, we see Greenberg's imagination at its most extravagant, as when she shows us a very odd group of partygoers, to go with Nick's list of names, in twelve small panels per page on pages 58–59. Dr. Webster Civet, who looks something like a rhinoceros, and is therefore one of her more "normal" inventions, contrasts with Newton Orchid, who "controlled Films Par Excellence." He has five eyes, and despite his open bowtie is also bare-chested. On page 60, the adaptation includes a torn notebook page listing the names of the partygoers; as on page 277, where Greenberg gives us Wolfsheim's handwritten letter to Nick declining to come to the funeral, this use of real-looking artifacts helps substantiate the story and makes it seem real.

Even against this background of strange and striking creatures with characteristics adapted from land and sea animals and plants via Greenberg's imagination, Gatsby stands out as entirely unique. As we see him first on page 4, he looks like a sea horse, with a curling tail, and a nose and eyes sticking out from what looks like crenellations surrounding his head and running down his back. He has usual human arms but a tail rather than feet. The crenellations around Gatsby's head make him seem a bit fancy and distinguished. But overall, Gatsby looks sympathetic—his smile is pleasant, he has two eyes and a long nose, and his eyes are expressive. He seems to be a decent guy, however unique his looks. His father, Mr. Gatz, who comes to the house after Gatsby's death and meets Nick (289), also has a nose, mouth and eyes like Gatsby's but also thinning hair and no crenellated equipage. So he looks much more mundane, as well as bereft because of his son's death. The message, fitting the original, is that Gatsby became a much fancier person than his father ever was.

Greenberg's use of narrative framing by using the photo album adds to her descriptions. On page 60, the adaptation includes a torn notebook page listing the names of the partygoers; as on page 277, where Greenberg gives us Wolfsheim's handwritten letter to Nick declining to come to the funeral, this use of real-looking artifacts helps substantiate the story and makes it seem real.

At the beginning of the adaptation Nick places Gatsby's photo in his album (4). The photo is torn, and Nick must put it together with tape—symbolizing Gatsby's death, since his is the only photo that is torn and repaired, as Nick does not put together a photograph of an ex-girlfriend (76). In putting Gatsby together again, Greenberg is showing Nick beginning his story—which amounts to putting Gatsby and all of the events of this story together again so we can study and understand them. As Nick repairs Gatsby's photo again on page 299, this idea frames the story, as he "cleans up the mess" that Tom and Daisy caused, as Nick puts it at the end.

Greenberg comments on her website that:

> ... the images do not give a simple recital of the story, but visually interpret the novel's physical and emotional landscapes: Daisy's face appears in the clouds over the water; guests tumble on a sparkling wave of champagne at Gatsby's party; Dr. Eckleburg's eyes silently shift their gaze. These images are integrated with original text from the novel. Fittingly for the defining novel of the Jazz Age, I like to think of this interpretation in jazz terms—as an energetic and entertaining, but also thoughtful and subtle, "arrangement" of the original piece of music. And I would like it to inspire readers to visit—or revisit—the original book with fresh and curious eyes.

Greenberg successfully accomplished her goals. She has given us an interpretation of the novel by means of her unique characterization of the creatures, her framing techniques, and sometimes by filling in the blanks of a given scene and showing us things not directly stated in the novel.

The words and pictures in Nick's album work very subtly in given scenes, often producing effects unique to the adaptation. This is another important reason for Greenberg's success, and for reading her adaptation even after reading the original. For instance, Tom talks about the book *The Rise of the Coloured Empires* "by this man Goddard," and goes on to comment that "The idea is that if we don't look out, the white race will be utterly submerged" (15). This is ironic, because we are constantly aware that Greenberg's Tom is anything but white or even human. So Greenberg adds to Tom's stupidity in the original by adding his lack of awareness of his own looks (15). Also, on pages 32–33, as Greenberg comments on her website, Dr. T.J. Eckleburg's eyes change their position, giving the eyes a God-like ability to see everything, which is implied in the original but not fully described. And when Nick gets drunk at Tom and Myrtle's apartment in New York, one of the photos on the page appears upside down, including the words in it (42). In these various ways, Greenberg adds to our reading of these scenes.

She also portrays what is in the original text in striking ways that exceed our own imaginations as we read the original. When the party-goers are described by Nick as having "hair bobbed in strange new ways and shawls beyond the dreams of Castile" (55), we see those things, as well as the faces of the strange creatures that wear them; and in Greenberg's rendering Nick is not just using an expression of speech here—they are indeed "strange new ways." Thus Gatsby's crowd of party-goers appears even more exotic than in the original. Furthermore, as Nick names the party-goers, the photos become small, twelve per page instead of the more usual three, or four, or six and one photo is devoted to each person or couple named, forcing us to focus on each one and his or her unique looks (58–59). When everyone leaves the party and Nick comments on Gatsby's aloneness, Greenberg's panel/photo of Gatsby in front of his house allows us to experience that. This is the only panel on the page, and Gatsby appears especially small and far away as he stands on the steps of his large house, waving goodbye (74). The surrounding black page seems empty, emphasizing the emptiness that Nick sees and describes in this scene. In all these ways, Greenberg's adaptation helps us visualize the novel as we could not have done otherwise and accentuates certain elements of it, making them even more striking than they were in the original.

This visual enhancement is especially notable during important scenes. When Gatsby tells Nick a made-up story of his being the son of wealthy Midwesterners, an Oxford man, and a collector of rare objects, we see Nick's face as he says that he "managed to restrain my incredulous laughter" and Gatsby looks at him disconcertedly (87). But when Gatsby produces his medal for extraordinary valor on the battlefield, and a photo of himself at Oxford (89–90), Nick believes him, and so do we because we see these artifacts before our eyes. So Greenberg's visualization reinforces Fitzgerald's attempt to have us believe Gatsby at this point. When Nick, per Gatsby's secret request, invites Daisy for tea, and Gatsby shows up at the door, Nick tells us that Gatsby was "glaring tragically into my eyes" (130), and we see Gatsby's anxiety clearly in the adaptation. This reinforces the original and makes it more powerful.

Visualization of prose descriptions is of course expected in a graphic novel adaptation of a prose text, but Greenberg also adds new elements/visuals to what we are given in the original. What we do not see at all in the Daisy-visits-Gatsby's-house scene in the original novel is how Nick looks, since Nick is the narrator and does not describe himself. But we do see his facial expression in Greenberg's adaptation, as we watch Nick's worried face across six panels (130–131). As he joins Gatsby and Daisy, we see exactly what he sees—a disconcerted Gatsby and a surprised Daisy—since Greenberg has us look directly over Nick's head (132). She again shows us Nick's face after he leaves and is outside worrying (136–37). So we are aware of Nick's role as narrator in the adaptation as in the original (except when the characters speak for themselves or are shown in a panel with no Nick present, as on page 138), but the addition of Nick's facial expressions adds to Nick's authenticity.

The addition of facial expressions also affects the reader's impressions. When Gatsby shows Daisy around his house, and Nick comments that "There must have been moments even that afternoon when Daisy tumbled short of his dreams—not through her own fault, but because of the colossal vitality of his illusion" (148), we see Gatsby looking a bit disappointed, and a bit depressed, as he stares out of a window when her back is turned. Greenberg interprets Fitzgerald's words accurately, but seeing Gatsby's face makes those words more powerfully true, and perhaps makes the adaptation a bit more melancholy than the original.

Sometimes Greenberg's rendition is very subtle. When we hear of Gatsby's association with Dan Cody from the age of seventeen, and see the episode of his involvement with Cody (154–160), Gatsby looks similar to the way he looks when he is older, with one significant difference: his "hair" is different as a boy (the crenellations on his head and back are uncurled rather than curled, as later), and Daisy comments that he never told her that he once had had a pompadour (159), so Greenberg uses this to mark the change in his physical appearance over the years.

Fitzgerald does not specify the young Gatsby's adventures with women, but his youthful dreams of a "universe of ineffable gaudiness" (154–55) are realized very well by Greenberg. The episode with a girl, taking up only two panels, fills in the blanks in his early adventures. The night dreams consist of eight panels on a single page. They show Gatsby in a strange world with palaces, fighting pirates, getting measured for new clothes, and finally sleeping on a half moon; Greenberg's excellent depiction of these dreams bring out Gatsby's youthful adventurousness. When Gatsby remembers kissing Daisy for the first time in Louisville, and the words read "At his lips' touch she blossomed for him like a flower ... and the incarnation was complete" (177), we see Gatsby for the first time in complete bliss, as his closed eye shows. Daisy's tendril is wrapped around one of the crenellations on Gatsby's head. Daisy becomes a heavenly body, like a god, for Gatsby, and Greenberg devotes a small panel just to that (177). When Daisy later kisses Gatsby as they rekindle their affair, her eyes are closed and his eyes stare with wonder— he obviously thinks here that he can indeed repeat the past (188). However, Gatsby looks at Daisy and Tom's little girl with startled surprise because as Nick says, "I don't think he had ever really believed in" the child's "existence before" (189). Again, Greenberg very effectively visualizes the text, which for a reader may be difficult. Seeing the creatures' facial expressions, we connect with them as if they were human, but since they are not, we focus on their emotions rather than on their looks.

Greenberg also adds irony to the original in this scene as Daisy describes her daughter, saying, "She doesn't look like her father. She looks like me. She's got my hair and shape of the face" (190). Greenberg's depiction, however, proves her wrong—the little girl has Tom's ears, nose, and mouth, and they are far more prominent than the girl's dandelion-like hair and round head. A jealous Gatsby would probably see more of Tom than Daisy in the little girl, so we see from Gatsby's point of view here, and understand why he is shocked by the child's appearance. Instead of favoring Daisy in her depiction, Greenberg's choice to favor Tom's appearance discredits Daisy's words and heightens Gatsby's discomfort as we see from his perspective. Greenberg's rendition emphasizes Fitzgerald's point that one cannot go back to the past after all, as Gatsby wants to believe. In this way the adaptation imposes a point of view on the reader, which is something that adaptations do as they interpret the stories on which they are based.

We again get value added when we see the crucial hit and run scene, with Daisy at the wheel. In the original, Gatsby describes this action, but here we see Daisy's shocked expression as she knows she will hit Myrtle, and Gatsby's shock as he feels the impact (242–243). So the adaptation makes the accident more graphic and authentic-feeling, as does Gatsby's sad and startled face when he speaks to Nick after the accident. Of course, the reader imagines these looks as he or she reads the original, but here Greenberg supplies a better envisioning that most readers can do for themselves; and the fact that these are all creatures rather than humans does not seem to matter at all.

The advantage of the adaptation, with all of its value added elements, comes together particularly in fraught scenes, in which there is a good deal of emotional tension. Pages 216–229 offer one such incident, in which Tom, in the Plaza Hotel, confronts Gatsby in front of Daisy, Jordan, and Nick; and then Nick and Jordan become closer as a result. Greenberg's treatment of one of the most emotionally-charged scenes in the novel offers a lesson in the methods and value of graphic novel adaptations.

As Greenberg depicts the scene, she adds impact by displaying facial expressions and manipulating the frames of the narrative sequence. On these pages, for the most part, the photo/panels are large, ranging from four to six per page. This is done so Greenberg can focus on the speakers' faces, allowing us to read their emotions while reading their verbal responses. Tom, aggressively pointing a large finger at Gatsby, asks what kind of a row Gatsby is trying to cause in his house; Gatsby looks happy and confident now that the issue is being raised. Only Daisy, with her downturned mouth, seems hesitant and afraid. It is Tom, though, who has had a series of mistresses and has disregarded the obligations of matrimony and family life, so his aggressive look seems particularly ironic and inappropriate (217). As the scene escalates, and Tom and Gatsby argue over who Daisy loves or has ever loved, Greenberg gives them each a full panel to showcase their faces (218). On the next page, Tom alone figures in three out of the four panels, each one emphasizing his physical bulk, as he states emphatically that Daisy has always loved him. Gatsby, in one smaller photo, looks weaker and smaller as he responds with a simple "No" (220). Urged by Gatsby to deny her love for Tom, Daisy eventually admits, "I did love him once—but I loved you too"(223). We are able to see Gatsby's reaction as Tom confidently responds, "Even that's a lie. She didn't know you were alive. Why, there's things between Daisy and me that you'll never know—things that neither of us can ever forget." Nick tells us that "The words seemed to bite physically" into Gatsby, and we see him looking startled as Daisy covers her eyes and cries (223). But when Gatsby tells Tom that "Daisy's leaving you" and Tom responds "Nonsense," Daisy, still looking hesitant, says "I am, though" (224). As Tom attacks Gatsby as a bootlegger and criminal, we see Nick's observation of Daisy's terror and Gatsby's startled and sad attempt at explanation visualized. Greenberg, effectively capturing the scene's drama, has given us very plausible facial expressions at the appropriate moments. So the scene is at least as convincing as in the original, and a lot more visceral.

Now the attention shifts to Nick's face as he tells Tom and Jordan that it is his birthday. With Tom driving, and Nick sits in the back of the car with Jordan, Nick is worried and looks upset about being "Thirty. The promise of a decade of loneliness ... a thinning list of single men to know, a thinning brief-case of enthusiasm, thinning hair...." Jordan, in her own panel, looks at Nick, and in the next panel embraces him with one of her tentacles, eyes closed, as Nick gently smiles (229). Greenberg's masterful negotiation of the scene provides a positive closure, and the use of photo/panels makes us aware that the events are part of a memory. Although Nick's romance with Jordan did not last, this is a sweet memory for him. Most of all, the portrayal of these events is completely convincing because of the characters' faces and gestures.

In the adaptation, the story exists not only in Nick's memory as in the original, but in the photos we are looking at, which add a feeling of authenticity. We are "borne back ceaselessly into the past," as Nick puts it at the very end of the tale, and so we are continually as we study these photos and turn the pages of the album ourselves. The penultimate panel shows Gatsby in a boat trying to go forward and "beat against the current" (305). Shortly before that, we again see the torn photo of Gatsby (299), which Nick is taping together, attempting to repair Tom and Daisy's damage. Gatsby is forever torn apart and cannot be brought back to life, even if his picture is taped over. Nick is still putting the story together, turning it over in his mind. The reader too is turning the words and the visuals in the story over in his or her mind as he or she gets to the end. Gatsby's dream of Daisy is indeed romantic, even noble, and even after seeing the tragic action and photos we cannot, just as Nick cannot, forget him. We are likely to agree that Gatsby was better than the rest of his crowd put together, as Nick had told him (259); and of course he is the one who suffers a tragic fate as a result.

Nick has learned that a dreamer like Gatsby who believes that one can relive the past, will be abandoned by a cruel world which cares only about the present, and about money. Nick now knows that we cannot recapture past time except in a narrative (or even more nostalgically, in an adaptation's photo album), and some of the final photo/panels in the book show both Gatsby and Nick reaching out into the ocean for that past, which continually recedes. Gatsby, however, wants to relive the past with Daisy, while Nick seems to want to bring Gatsby back and perhaps to reach out to the future as well.

As Daniel Worden writes, "Greenberg's *Great Gatsby* molds Fitzgerald's novel into a narrative about loss and longing" (236). Her adaptation succeeds because it gives us added value—sights from the original that we find it hard to realize in our minds without her help, and sights that are not in the original but which add authenticity, irony, and interpretive meaning. She manages to transform the story by putting it into a photo album, which we look at nostalgically with Nick. With great originality, she forces us to focus on important moments, important faces, and important events and to see the original novel in a completely new way. By means of her very unusual adaptation, she has offered us an outstanding demonstration of the unique value of the graphic novel as an interpretative tool.

Note

1. All page references to *The Great Gatsby* are to Greenberg's adaptation.

Works Cited

Fitzgerald, F. Scott. *The Great Gatsby*. New York: Scribner, 2004. Print.
Greenberg, Nicki. *The Great Gatsby: A Graphic Adaptation*. Toronto: Penguin, 2007. Print.
_____. www.nickigreenberg.com Web.
McCloud, Scott. *Understanding Comics: The Invisible Art*. New York: HarperPerennial, 1994. Print.
Worden, Daniel. "A Salamander and Seahorse in Sepia Tone." *The F. Scott Fitzgerald Review* 8 (2010): 231–37. Print.

Not Telling, but Retelling
From Raymond Queneau's *Exercises in Style* to Matt Madden's *99 Ways to Tell a Story*, and Back

Jan Baetens

Why Exercises in Style *Is Much More Than Just Another Funny Book*

In the Anglophone world, Raymond Queneau (1903–1976) is perhaps best known today as the cofounder, with François Le Lionnais, of Oulipo or *Ouvroir de littérature potentielle* ("Workshop for potential literature"). Since its creation in the 1960s, and more particularly since the success of the Oulipian novels by Georges Perec in the 1970s and 80s, Oulipo's role has become increasingly important in French literary life, to the point that the group and its aesthetics is now considered the very heart of the contemporary canon (Mathews and Brotchie 2005, Baetens 2012, Bloomfield, Lapprand and Thomas 2012). Oulipo was and still is definitely antiromanticist: its emphasis on "procedural" or "constrained" writing (perhaps the most famous example of which is Perec's novel *La Disparition*, in which the letter "e" is never used), happily replaces the romantic confidence in the notion of the inspired genius, and thus makes a radical break with the past. It was also, from the very beginning, forward-looking: its interest in machine writing, collective writing, collaborative writing and, last but not least, intermedial writing, can be seen as anticipations of paths taken by innovative forms of communication in the new media age (Baetens and Poucel 2009 and 2010). Given its experimental and multi-media stance, in all of these debates and transformations Oulipo's influence has rapidly expanded outside of the traditional literary field, as demonstrated by the creation of similar groups in different media, such as the Oubapo, or *Ouvroir de bande dessinée potentielle* ("Workshop for potential comics"), which has existed since 1992. Like Oulipo, which attracted non–Francophone writers such as Harry Mathews and Italo Calvino, Oubapo is open to authors producing literature in other languages. The aim of this chapter is, first, to examine how one of these non–French Oubapo artists, Matt Madden (an invited honorary guest of Oulipo and Oubapo, who has been running an Oubapo workshop for several years now[1]), has reinterpreted a key work produced under the influence of Oulipo, and, second, to show how this new interpretation can be framed in historical terms and what it can teach us about both the graphic novel as a medium as well as about the literary material by Queneau that it reworks.

While he was a founding member of Oulipo, Queneau's position was far from unambiguous. First of all, this avant-garde writer, excluded from the Surrealist group in 1930, did not consider all of his literary productions to be purely Oulipo-based or Oulipo-inspired. Queneau certainly wrote Oulipo texts and novels, and he even invented and illustrated new constraints, but it is important to stress that he always stuck to the original and somewhat restrictive definition of Oulipo's aims, which were: 1) to identify (well known but also completely forgotten) formal constraints and to imagine new ones, exemplifying them if possible (for some of these constraints were so drastic that it was difficult to put textual meat on the conceptual bones), or useful (for some of them were quite banal and hence more interesting as concepts than as actual realizations); and 2) to take advantage of these formal constraints every time that the author experienced a lack of inspiration or, worse, a writer's block, without necessarily claiming that the resulting work had to be totally Oulipian.

These basic principles explain Queneau's vision of the status of the text: for him, Oulipo has to do with brainstorming and the genesis of the text, whereas the completed literary text itself must stand on its own, completely separate from the process of its genesis (or to paraphrase Freud: where Oulipo was, there the text shall be). Hence, Queneau refused to distinguish, in his production of texts, between Oulipian and non–Oulipian works (he continued to write non–Oulipian works after he helped found Oulipo and did not label his Oulipan works as such). Hence, also, his deeply rooted skepticism towards the disclosure of the subtle formal constraints he used during the production of a given work (his favorite metaphor was borrowed from construction work: once the house is finished, one has to remove the scaffold, he liked to say). Both elements—the status of the finished work, which must be judged in itself and the status of the subtle formal constraints he used, which must not be revealed—are typical of Queneau and more generally of the first members of the Oulipo group. Today, however, things have changed in many respects: Oulipo has become a label, and the literal presence and availability of the constraint, open to reuse, is also a general feature of the group's activities, some inevitable exceptions notwithstanding.

In Queneau's oeuvre, *Exercises in Style* (2013 [1947]) occupies a special position. It offers 99 retellings of the same, very simple and banal anecdote, each retelling being made in a different style or relying on the use of a different rhetorical device or figure. *Exercises in Style* is clearly Oulipian in spirit as well as in form. There is an identifiable constraint in each retelling, which is as explicit as possible. Moreover, the book anticipates the body of work produced by Oulipo after its creation while also announcing some of Oulipo's more radical features, such as: 1) the creative commons philosophy (borrowed from Raymond Roussel's *How I Wrote Certain of My Books* (2005 [1933]); 2) the idea of textual "productivity," that is, the idea that a good constraint is a constraint capable of producing an infinite number of texts; and 3) the idea of trans-genre and trans-media reuse (very soon, adaptations into other media appeared). It should not come as a surprise that the success of *Exercises in Style*, which became almost a "genre" in itself, would be repeated within the comics field, more specifically within the Oubapo group.

From Oulipo to Oubapo, and Queneau to Madden

The reasons for this transfer from Oulipo to Oubapo are twofold. On the one hand, the model of *Exercises in Style* has been decisive in the critique of one of the most prevalent features of traditional comics, namely the idea that a comics work should have just one visual style (Groensteen 2013: 112–117), Meesters (215–218). True, author styles can change over time, or styles can change because the work is passed from one author to another, or because there is a difference between a "main author" and "studio assistants," the former drawing, for instance, the characters, and the latter drawing the props (as happens in later works by Hugo Pratt, the creator of *Corto Maltese*). But the idea that a single work should have a single style and that exceptions to this rule have to be seen as "errors" (attributed, for instance, to haste or distraction), is a generalization that has been challenged only recently, and in this process the role of Oubapo, which has always promoted stylistic heterogeneity, has proven key. On the other hand, *Exercises in Style* is also a cutting-edge book in the sense that it contests the even more traditional idea that a book belongs to just one author: Queneau's work ties in with new tendencies toward collective and participative creation, often in media environments outside or beyond the printed book, each with their own constraints and possibilities. Here as well, Oubapo has been a ground-breaker (Menu 431–449).

In comparison with Oulipo, the basic philosophy of Oubapo remains the same, but Oubapo adds a radical key concept. First of all, and completely in line with Oulipo, the aim of Oubapo has always been to identify, invent, exemplify, and implement a repertoire of available formal and narrative constraints. From a theoretical point of view, one has to admit that the taxonomic efforts of the group, mainly thanks to the presence of comics theoretician Thierry Groensteen, have been more innovative than those of Oulipo, as demonstrated for instance by the very helpful distinction between constraints that are "transformative"—that is, which modify and combine existing works—and "productive"—constraints that produce new drawings (Groensteen 1997: 17, 41). Second, and here is the difference, Oulipo is straightforward, while Oubapo has tried to question the very method of producing comics, challenging both commercial group studio work and the *auteur* ideology of the individual creator. For instance, the Oubapo group fostered collective and participative constraints, often structured by very "easy" and "open" time-based constraints ("Do something on this subject in × minutes and pass on the work to the next participant"), which tended to impose a model of improvisation, thus breaking the aesthetics of the "finished" job by the "single" author. This objective is of course not alien to Oulipo itself, but in the case of Oubapo it became much more outspoken, as if the critique of the traditional author's position was one of the core issues of the group's policy in the 1990s.

Yet here as well, the position of Queneau's model is quite complex. *Exercises in Style* is obviously a work that is open to radical appropriations and adaptations. It certainly invites the challenging of all those homogeneities that define classic storytelling in comics: harmony of style and unity of author, but also unity of "text" (during his 99 variations on a story, Queneau does not transform one single material Ur-version; the story remains the same but there is no single text that all the other versions are derived from), and unity of "medium" (for very soon adaptations into other media appeared, some of which were as original as the one created by Queneau himself). However, Queneau's book also allows for very classic forms of adaptation. For instance, it has inspired a spirit of competition and emulation that has allowed for individual brio, which, after all, was common in the original Oulipo gatherings and the eagerness of the first members to prove themselves capable of inventing original constraints (often christened by a reference to the names of their inventors!) and of producing examples of allegedly hyper-difficult, if not unrealizable, constraints.

Since *Exercises in Style* aims at exploring the very many possibilities of literature's medium-specificity, it is of course a real challenge to transfer its own logic to a different field, in this case the world of comics and graphic novels. In the graphic novel domain, the best known reworking of *Exercises in Style* is without any doubt Matt Madden's *99 Ways to Tell a Story* (2005). However, Madden's book is much more than just a transmedial adaptation or reinterpretation of Queneau's book. The author plays with different constraints, and the differences between the set of verbal constraints used by Queneau and the set of visual (or mainly visual) constraints used by Madden, make sense. Besides, nearly six decades separate the original from Madden's reworking. In this period, the face of literature has changed dramatically. Comics and the graphic novel have also evolved very rapidly (the appearance of the graphic novel, for instance, has dramatically restructured the whole field). It is from these various perspectives that one has to take a closer look at *99 Ways to Tell a Story*.

To Start With: The Story

Matt Madden starts his book by explaining—and how right he is to do so!—that his ambition is to foreground the textual embodiment of the story, as well as to exceed once and for all outdated ideas concerning the complete separation of form and content. For Madden, form is content and content is form. This statement, however, does not imply that for the purposes of analysis, story on the one hand and storytelling on the other cannot be envisaged or discussed independently of one another.

Indeed, the most telling difference between *Exercises in Style* and *99 Ways to Tell a Story* that comes to the fore at the moment that Matt Madden's book begins, is the remarkable repositioning of the story world. In the case of Queneau, the story, although entirely banal and seemingly incomplete, is quite captivating. Queneau's narrator gets on the "S" bus in Paris (now no. 84), witnesses an altercation between a man with a long neck and funny hat and another passenger, and then sees the same person two hours later at the Saint-Lazare railway station getting advice on adding a button to his overcoat. This story is intriguing in more than one sense of the word. First, because it constitutes a real script with somebody observing somebody else who appears to be involved in two successive events. The meaning of these events, the possible links between them, the relationship between observer and observed, the status of the narrator, the stylistic and dramatic features of the language used, and so on, make the reader feel both disappointed by the shallowness of the anecdote and curious to know more about it. The text, in other words, creates more than enough tension to make the reader feel keen to learn more about this strange sequence of apparently uneventful events. Moreover, the spatio-temporal details of the narration, as well as the broader context of daily life in Paris, undoubtedly help trigger the narrative expectations of the reader, who already imagines not only the scene, but also Paris. The tiny details the narrator provides have more or less the same function as the ritual formula "once upon a time..."; they prepare us for a story to come even if the story seems to come to an end before it has started.

In the case of Madden, things work differently. To begin with, the story itself is very different *qua* story. The author does not repeat or transform Queneau's basic anecdote, except in one single instance, the "Two in One" variation, where Queneau makes a cameo appearance in pure Hitchcock style (Madden 113). However, even here the original story is strongly modified (for example, through the addition of other characters, including a woman character who would be totally absent in the all-male universe of Queneau, as well as one of Hergé's Thompson and Thompson detectives, who tend to attract all the attention of the reader). Madden's story is not only simpler than Queneau's, it is also less of a story. The narrator, who happens to be Madden himself, takes a break from his work and goes down to the refrigerator in order to get something to eat. But when he opens the refrigerator door, and is perhaps distracted by his wife's question about what time it is, he no longer remembers what he was looking for. End of the story.

At first sight, the initial story of *99 Ways to Tell a Story* is as complete and tellable and as interesting as Queneau's narration. We see various characters, about whose motivations we can speculate. We can ask ourselves questions about the deeper meaning of the story, which seems to have no meaning at all (but as we know, this is often a strong incentive to start looking for one). There is a time (1:15 p.m.), and there is a space. The space is the artist's studio, his home, which seems to be also the place where his wife (or do we suppose too easily that the off-screen voice is that of his wife?) is present. And there is a string of actions and events with a clear beginning, middle, and end. The fact that the basic page layout in this episode is composed of three horizontal tiers functions as a visual echo of this fundamental narrative structure.

At the same time, however, the reader cannot but feel the gulf that separates the two micro-stories by Madden and Queneau. Is it exaggerated to assume that *99 Ways to Tell a Story* does not tell just "any story," as *Exercises in Style* is doing, but a story that sabotages itself? Not in the sense that this story frustrates the reader, although such frustration can be an extremely powerful narrative trigger: to feel that information is missing is often a crucial feature in our decision to continue to read, or to reread, or to start thinking hard and harder about what we have just read. But here we seem to be confronted with a story that discourages these hermeneutic efforts, that does not open new ground for speculation and imagination, that seems to tell us: well, this is a not really a story, but this is all there is; stop looking for more for there is nothing to be found. Besides, and this is quite a difference from Queneau's *Exercises in Style* as well, Madden does not indulge in any appealing variety: the story he tells is, most of the time, really the same, contrary to Queneau, who very rapidly starts making improvisations on his basic script. As mentioned earlier, there is no single formal Ur-version of Queneau's text, whereas *99 Ways to Tell a Story* usually stays much closer to a supposed original version, which may be represented by the photo-strip variation the reader will discover later on (Madden 39).

This is a very audacious strategy. Most authors who tell uneventful stories do their very best to make us understand that there is a gap between the story's surface (boring, uneventful, empty) and the story's actual meaning (whatever that meaning may be). Here, however, there is just the surface, there is just the non-story. Yet it is not too difficult to see why Matt Madden adopts this very radical position.

The decision to keep the basic storyline of *99 Ways to Tell a Story* so straightforwardly simple and elementary is part of the challenge that Matt Madden, in a traditionally Oulipian emulation spirit, poses for himself. By choosing a story that is rather weak in tellability, he wants to reinforce his claim that stories cannot exist independently from their telling. In that perspective, the uneventfulness of the story is a structural necessity: the emptier the story, the stronger the demonstration that storytelling is not just the narrative expansion of a given story, but the story itself. In a more implicit manner, the author also suggests that by starting from so shallow a storyline he is capable of doing at least as well, if not better, than his model, Queneau's *Exercises in Style*. Not only because he invents another story to tinker with, which helps avoid any charges of plagiarism or lack of creativity, but also because he invents one that makes the constraint more difficult and for that reason more rewarding to realize: since the story itself is so dramatically simple and insignificant (at least at first sight), the proper role of the constraint and the proper merit of the author capable of executing them will draw all the attention as well as the admiration of the reader.

But there is more to say about the story, which is only deceptively simple. For both Queneau and Madden do not invent a story for the mere sake of their demonstrations. Their stories do not come out of the blue, but are unmistakably context-bound. Queneau's story is a manifest parody of a *fait divers* or news item, the kind of story one found in the inconsequential *chiens écrasés* ("dogs that were run over") sections of French popular newspapers of that time; but perhaps it is also an indirect and ironical critique of the dominant existentialist and politically committed strand in postwar French literature, where there was no longer any room for this kind of populist newspaper entertainment. Similarly, Madden's non-story, so to speak, also has critical and ironical undertones. We can see in it a twisted version of what has come to define storytelling in the contemporary graphic novel, with its double emphasis on autofiction or semi-autobiography, as a narrative regime, and boredom, as a thematic center of gravity. Often, contemporary graphic novels focus on boredom as their main thematic thread. They foreground both the absence of tellable events and at the same time, the excess of the non-tellable, boring, dull, empty moments and feelings of daily life (Schneider, forthcoming). In his book, Madden establishes an evident dialogue with these kinds of stories. At the same time, contemporary graphic novels sometimes include a documentary mode (reportage, history) or an autofictional one, and *99 Ways of Telling a Story* participates without any doubt in the latter. It does so in an ironical mode, however, for the autobiographical or semi-autobiographical story told by a narrator who is also the real author of the work is not a testimony about a traumatized youth or a troubled life, as is the case in most of these autofictional narratives, but a cunning hint at the emptiness of much biographical material and therefore simultaneously a contrasting statement about the depth of fiction, invention, and imagination.

These singularities shed a new light on Madden's story, which ceases then to be seen as empty of meaning and whose gaps and blanks and frustrating emptiness become doubly meaningful, and are understood by the reader to be both contextually and structurally motivated. In other words: in order to define his own position—and even more his own achievement!—in comparison with his historical model (Queneau) and his modern competitors (the graphic novelists), Madden has to do what he is, in fact, doing. He has to embrace a minimalist story in order to obtain a maximalist effect. A more complete or interesting basic story would have made the comparison with *Exercises in Style* less exciting, while cutting it off from the bulk of graphic narratives produced and read today.

To Continue: The Storytelling

Similar remarks apply to the aspects of storytelling. Madden definitely refuses to copy his model in a servile, unimaginative way. There are hardly any overlaps between the constraints used by Queneau and those used by Madden, and even when there seems to be a direct link between both, such as in the "subjective" variations, it is the difference between Queneau's verbal storytelling and Madden's graphic storytelling that come to the fore. The use of "subjective" variations in *Exercices in Style* (and there are several of them, including "Le côté subjectif," "Autre subjectivité," and "Moi je") means, in the very first place, that a strong emphasis is put on the personal presence of the narrator, whose language, point of view, ideology, and so on are overwhelmingly present in the story, at the expense of the story matter itself. In Madden's book, the "subjective" constraint is interpreted in strictly visual terms: it establishes a way of telling that imposes a strictly subjective point of view (comparable to the one that characterizes Robert Montgomery's 1947 film adaptation of Raymond Chandler's *The Lady in the Lake*), in which Madden is present in every episode without, however, modifying the story itself. As might be expected, Madden reaches explicitly for medium-specific constraints. Instead of mechanically adapting Queneau's verbal constraints, he invents new visual ones, a shift that becomes very clear in the way he plays with intertextual models. Whereas Queneau rewrites his story in, for instance, "free verse" (with a strong nod to post–Verlaine impressionist writing), Madden retells his story using the model of a map (95), the single panel comic (37), or (101) the style of George Herriman's *Krazy Kat* (among many other examples). *99 Ways to Tell a Story* also stresses the complex and hybrid character of a comic, drawing attention to its genetic particularities, as in the "Storyboard" variation (121), which is very different from a literary draft version. Madden even creates what seems to be a purely textual (with no pictures) comic, as in the "Calligram" variation (125). But even in that variation we do get a picture as well as the text, because the story is printed in the shape of a question mark, as in concrete poetry, and so it qualifies as a comic.

The most striking feature at the formal level is, however, Madden's strong refusal to indulge in any form of aestheticism. This attitude can be described at two levels. First of all, Madden brings into play a very "basic," straightforward, efficient style, a style that is immediately recognizable, so that the reader can easily follow the transformations from one variation to another without being distracted from the demonstration that is going on. The rather minimalist take on most variations therefore obeys a structural logic: the drawings need to remain slightly conceptual, stylistically speaking, in order to enhance the idea that the author is creating on the page. Second, Madden also declines the temptation to copy the stylistic features of the intertextual models and examples that he appropriates in his work. Let's take, for instance, the case of Tintin,

Figure 1. "Ligne Claire" variation. Matt Madden, *99 Ways to Tell a Story. Exercises in Style*. Chamberlain, p. 92.

symptomatically called the "Clear Line" (and not "Hergé" or "Tintin") variation (Madden 91). Following very closely the style and page layout of the opening variation of the book, the "Ligne Claire (Clear Line)" plate (see fig. 1) offers the reader as much as it denies him.

The page is an example of what the Clear Line drawing style means; yet it is not, despite the identifiable presence of Tintin (for the aficionados, there may be even an allusion to a scene in *The Secret of the Unicorn*), an example of what it means to draw like Hergé (those readers who might have expected a kind of pastiche will be disappointed). It is clear that the relative absence of Hergé is not a question of drawing skill. Other variations of *99 Ways to Tell a Story* amply demonstrate the outstanding technique of Matt Madden (see for instance the "Cento" variation [Madden 111], with clever and perfectly executed imitations of David Mazzucchelli, Ben Katchor, Chester Brown, Marc-Antoine Mathieu, Daniel Clowes, Art Spiegelman, Julie Doucet and Gary Panter [see fig. 2]). Here the reason that Matt Madden does not try to "copy" Hergé refers to the overall strategy of the book. Madden does not want us to admire his capacity to compete with the maker of Tintin, he wants us to judge the way in which he manages to implement the set of constraints that he is applying to the basic story. In addition, the author of *99 Ways to Tell a Story* takes also into account that any exaggerated attention to Hergé would harm the global decision to keep the storyline as simple as possible. Madden's stance is here perfectly in line with what he is doing elsewhere in his book. Just as he refrains from "thickening" his story, he refrains from "aestheticizing" his style, while keeping this style as recognizably "Madden" as possible, and this as well is in perfect accordance with the contemporary graphic novel field, where authors are less keen to make "nice" or "smooth" drawings than to enforce their own personal styles.

To End With: Oulipian Madden

A suggested above, it is not enough to simply describe the origin and model and the formal program as well as the technical and intellectual achievement of *99 Ways to Tell a Story*. One can, of course, examine in detail the creative appropriation of Queneau's book by Madden's new variations, but a mere formal analysis would miss the historical meaning of Madden's publication, which did not appear in a historical void. After all, 60 years lay between the first publication of *Exercises in Style* and its remake by Matt Madden in a new medium. This remake is a historical event, to which it is necessary to pay attention.

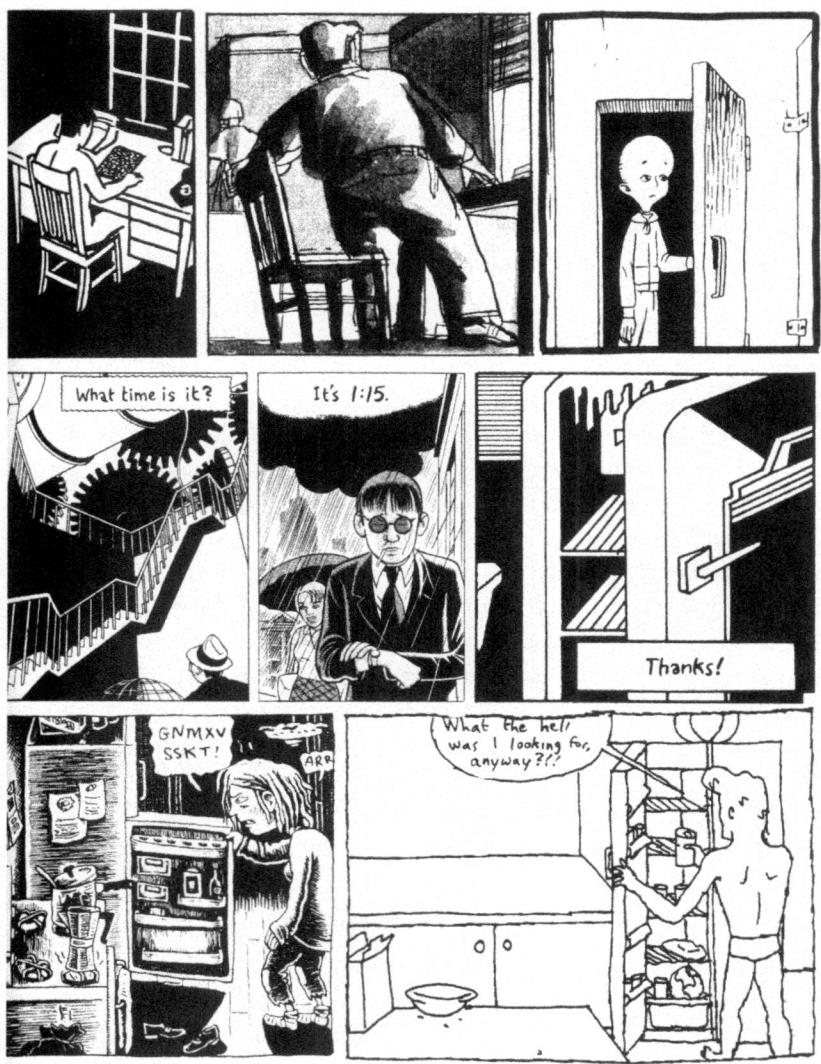

Figure 2. "Cento" variation. Matt Madden, *99 Ways to Tell a Story. Exercises in Style.* Chamberlain, p. 112.

First of all, it is crucial to stress here that Madden's book, although directly inspired by the work of the Oubapo group, represents also a return to one of the founding fathers of the Oulipo and, more importantly perhaps, to a certain interpretation of what the Oulipo stood for. True, Madden does not advocate a return to an Oulipian use of constrained literature, in which the rule was at least as important as its realization and in which the members of the group, rather than catering to a broad audience, entered into a playful internal competition with their peers. In contrast to that model, Matt Madden is definitely in sympathy with the general orientation of the Oubapo group, eager to share its findings and experiments with a large audience, and more interested in the realization of actual works than in the invention of sometimes very byzantine constraints. However, Madden's position is no less complex than that of Queneau, for *99 Ways to Tell a Story*, which can be seen as a love song addressed to the comics medium, is visibly nearer to the graphic novel universe, with its strong insistence on *auteur* philosophy and on certain thematic and narrative keywords such as "boredom" and "semi-autobiography," than to some radical experiments of the Oubapo group, which question the position of the individual author as well as the status of comics as sequential drawings on paper and eventually in print. *99 Ways to Tell a Story* should therefore be considered a classic book, not because it adopts a classic aesthetic, but because within its modern approach it defends certain values and ideas (author, work, and clarity, for instance) that are not necessarily shared by all those who, like Matt Madden, appropriate Oulipo's heritage. Perhaps the notion of "modern classic" might be the proper label for a book like this.

Note

1. For more information on the artist and his multiple activities, see http://www.mattmadden.com/.

Works Cited

Baetens, Jan. "OuLiPo and Proceduralism." *The Routledge Companion to Experimental Literature*. Ed. Bray, Joe, Alison Gibbons, and Brian McHale. New York: Routledge, 2012. 115–127. Print.

―――, and Jean-Jacques Poucel, eds. "The Writing of Constraint (I)." *Poetics Today* 30:4 (2009). Print.

―――. "The Writing of Constraint (II)." *Poetics Today* 31:1 (2010). Print.

Bloomfield, Camille, Marc Lapprand, and Jean-Jacques Thomas, eds. "Oulipo@50. L'Oulipo à 50 ans." *Formules* 16 (2012). Print.

Groensteen, Thierry. "Premier bouquet de contraintes." *Oupus* 1. Paris: L'Association, 1997, 13–59. Print.

―――. *Comics and Narration*. Transl. Ann Miller. Jackson: University Press of Mississippi, 2013 (original publication in French: 2011). Print.

Madden, Matt. *99 Ways to Tell a Story*. New York: Chamberlain Bros, 2005. Print.

Mathews, Harry, and Alistair Brotchie. *The Oulipo Compendium,* revised edition. Los Angeles and London: Make Now Press and Atlas, 2005. Print.

Meesters, Gert. "Les Significations du style graphique: *Mon fiston* d'Olivier Schrauwen et *Faire semblant c'est mentir* de Dominique Goblet." *Textyles* 36–37 (2010). 215–233. Print.

Menu, Jean-Christophe. *La Bande dessinée et son double*. Paris: L'Association, 2011. Print.
Queneau, Raymond. *Exercises in Style*. Transl. Barbara Wright. New York: New Directions, 2013 (first publication in French: 1947). Print.
Roussel, Raymond. *How I Wrote Certain of My Books*. Transl. Trevor Winkfield. Boston: Exact Change, 2005 (First publication in French: 1933). Print.
Schneider, Greice. *What Happens When Nothing Happens: Boredom and Everyday Life in Contemporary Comics*. Leuven: Leuven University Press, forthcoming. Print.

Illustrated Man
Ray Bradbury, Comics and the Authorized Graphic Novels

Darren Harris-Fain

In *Fahrenheit 451* (1953), Ray Bradbury's dystopian depiction of a future in which books are banned and burned, the protagonist, a "fireman" named Guy Montag, is visited by his supervisor, Beatty. Montag has shown a spark of interest in books, and Beatty lectures him on how society reached this state. One key cause, he explains, is that publishers avoided offending anyone and simplified their product for the masses:

> Books, so the snobbish critics said, were dishwater. No *wonder* books stopped selling, the critics said. But the public, knowing what it wanted, ... let the comic books survive. And the three-dimensional sex magazines, of course. There you have it, Montag. It didn't come from the Government down. There was no dictum, no declaration, no censorship, to start with, no! Technology, mass exploitation, and minority pressure carried the trick, thank God. Today, thanks to them, you can stay happy all the time, you are allowed to read comics, the good old confessions, or trade journals [57–58].

Given Bradbury's negative depiction of this book-burning society and his valorization of the written word, one might expect that Bradbury is critiquing not only censorship but also the dumbing down of literature as comic strips and books.

However, Bradbury *loved* the comics, and had since childhood. In numerous essays and interviews, he recalled how the debut of *Buck Rogers in the 25th Century* impacted his nine-year-old self and his career. In "Predicting the Past, Remembering the Future" (2001), he wrote, "Two amazing things happened in my ninth and tenth years." One of them was the discovery of

Edgar Rice Burroughs's third John Carter novel, *The Warlord of Mars*, serialized between 1913 and 1914 and published as a novel in 1919. The other was the launch of *Buck Rogers* in October 1929. "That one strip's concussion shook me into a new life.... That one strip transported me into the future. I began to collect Buck Rogers adventures and never returned from that long journey into tomorrow" (36–37). Not only did he collect the strip: he obsessed over it. In a 1975 interview, he said, "...when Buck Rogers came along, instantly, within the very first strip I just went absolutely crazy. I'd just started with the most *amazing* thing I'd ever seen; I could barely *wait* through each day. That's the way I lived. I lived hysterically, waiting for that hour every afternoon when Buck Rogers came into the house" (Dorf 86). He talked about the strip with his schoolmates, and when they teased him for being childish, he tore up his collection. He soon regretted his impulsive reaction and decided to ignore his peers and pursue his passions, becoming once again an avid reader and collector of the strip (Weller 45–47). He would often say later that *Buck Rogers* was responsible for his later career in science fiction, as in his introduction to *The Collected Stories of Ray Bradbury* (1980), republished in his 1996 book *Zen in the Art of Writing* ("Drunk, and in Charge of a Bicycle" 52).

But *Buck Rogers* was not the only strip Bradbury read and collected. As he relates in his introduction to the first volume of *The Ray Bradbury Chronicles* (1992):

> From *Buck Rogers* I moved to collecting the huge Sunday color pages of *Buck* and *Tarzan* and, a few years later, *Flash Gordon*. I collected *Prince Valiant* for more than 30 years and wrote love letters to Harold Foster, its creator, naming him as the top comics illustrator of my entire life. For a reward, Foster sent me two giant full-page Sunday *Prince Valiant* originals, which I will let go of only on my last day on Earth.
>
> I still have everything from 1929 on. All the strips, panels, books, collections and super-collections. *Mickey Mouse. Major Hoople. Popeye. Out Our Way. Brick Bradford*. You name 'em, I got 'em.
>
> And I still read *Andy Capp, The Far Side, B.C.,* and *The Wizard of Id* every day [5–6].

Although he sounds a more critical tone in his foreword to *The Autumn People* (1965), he still credits comics with influencing him as a writer and confesses to loving them despite critical dismissals, saying:

> Without all this splendid mediocrity, this sublime and wondrous trash in my background, I don't think I would be any sort of writer today.
>
> I have no patience with the literary snob who turns his back on his root-system, what he was, what he once loved with all his heart.
>
> Now that I am older, I will not be a turncoat to my old and deepest affections. Part of me, buried away, still loves Major Hoople and Dale Arden [n.p.].

In an interview a year later, Bradbury listed among his heroes Buck Rogers, Flash Gordon, and Alley Oop and among his influences "all the comic strips ever produced" (Burton 37). Nor did his childhood involvement with comics end here. At twelve, Bradbury pestered a local radio station to let him work there. After proving himself a tireless gofer, they offered him a chance to do a show, and he chose to read newspaper comics with a group of other kids, complete with sound effects (Dorf 87). When asked in 1975 why he loved comics, Bradbury cited their humor and said that "they criticize the total society and not just a part of it" (Dorf 94). He added, "But I admire illustration and always did, and I suppose I always will. I get a kick out of well-drawn comic-strips when you're dealing with storytelling, as in the case of 'Prince Valiant,' or well-drawn comic-strips which deal with humor..." (Dorf 94).

Given his youthful interests, Bradbury naturally tried his hand at the medium himself. In his 1975 interview with Shel Dorf, he says he began to write as a child and illustrated his stories (87). He tried creating a comic strip at twelve, heavily inspired by Foster's *Tarzan,* which he greatly admired (87). However, he found his artistic abilities were limited. "I never got very good at it," he said. "I'm still a doodler and a Sunday painter, but not good enough to do that incredible work which influenced me" (Dorf 87). He may have decided that drawing a comic strip was beyond him, but through his long career he toyed with the idea that he might eventually write one. For instance, in his foreword to *Tomorrow Midnight* (1966), he talks about his comic strip collections and how he still enjoys contemporary strips, adding, "Someday, I would like to have the leisure time to write my own Sunday panel..." (n.p.). And in the mid 1970s, he worked with artist Doug Wildey to develop a Sunday strip based on his collection *The Martian Chronicles* (1950), but the strip never advanced past the planning stages (Weist 185).

Even if Bradbury never wrote comics, he often maintained that his early immersion in the medium helped him create imagery in his writing (Dorf 95). Not only was this true of his prose fiction, he claimed, but also for his work in Hollywood. As he says in his introduction to the second volume of *The Ray Bradbury Chronicles,* "I could not help but storyboard my screenplays in my mind as if they were Sunday comics panels. So while other screen-writers were cudgeling their brains for visual images, ... mine came naturally from a childhood of *Tarzan, Mandrake the Magician, The Katzenjammer Kids,* and *Brick Bradford*" (5).

It is little wonder, then, that Bradbury would welcome comics adaptations of his fiction. However, his first encounter with such an adaptation came as a surprise. In the early 1950s, EC Comics, published by William Gaines and edited by Al Feldstein, published three stories clearly based on stories by Bradbury: "A Strange Undertaking" (*The Haunt of Fear* #6, March/April 1951) was obviously drawn from "The Handler" (1947); "What the Dog Dragged In" (*The Vault of Horror* #22, December 1951/January 1952) was an abridgement of "The Emissary" (1947); and "Home to Stay" (*Weird Fantasy* #13, May/June 1952) combined elements of "Kaleidoscope" (1949) and "The Rocket Man" (1951). In all three cases, Bradbury was not credited as the author. According to Jerry Weist, Gaines and Feldstein routinely raided pulp magazines and books for story ideas and must have encountered Bradbury's stories in this fashion (90).

Rather than sending Gaines and Feldstein a cease and desist letter or contacting an attorney, Bradbury sent them a bill. Writing on April 19, 1952, he said:

> Dear Sir:
> Just a note to remind you of an oversight. You have not yet sent on the check for $50 to cover the use of secondary rights on my two stories THE ROCKET MAN and KALEIDOSCOPE which appeared in your WEIRD-FANTASY May-June '52 #13, with the cover-all title of HOME TO STAY. I feel this was probably overlooked in the general confusion of office-work, and look forward to your payment in the near future [Weist 90].

This was rather clever on Bradbury's part, asking for what would have been a decent sum for the reprint rights, with the realization that surely EC stood to lose much more if sued for copyright infringement. Bradbury's humorous letter offered a winning proposition for both parties.

Further, Bradbury's realized that EC could provide another market for his work and appended a postscript to his letter:

> P.S. Have you ever considered doing an entire issue of your magazine based on my stories in DARK CARNIVAL, or my other two books THE ILLUSTRATED MAN and THE MARTIAN CHRONICLES? I'd be very interested in discussing this with you for some future issue. I think we could do an outstanding job here [Weist 90].

In their April 25, 1952 reply, Gaines and Feldstein did not admit that Bradbury's work was the basis of the story but nonetheless sent him the requested fifty dollars. They also expressed an interest in working with him as he had suggested (Weist 91). Bradbury replied three days later, sending them copies of *The Martian Chronicles* and *The Illustrated Man* (1951) and suggesting that they adapt *The Martian Chronicles* in its entirety, "with a few deletions here or there..." (Weist 93). In effect, he was proposing a comics adaptation of his linked Martian tales—what we would today call a graphic novel. He adds, "I am vitally interested in seeing my book become a single comic-book issue because I believe it is the first step toward starting the younger readers on their way to reading my work later..." (Weist 93). In Gaines's May 16, 1952 response, he said that it would be impossible to adapt any of Bradbury's books as a 28-page comic book. He added that this would be a risky venture for EC, since most of their readers would be unfamiliar with Bradbury and because "the titles aren't 'punchy' enough!" (Weist 94). Instead, Gaines proposed adapting individual horror or science fiction stories on a regular basis, including story credit, $25 per story, and title credit (Weist 95).

Thus began a partnership that resulted in six-to-eight-page adaptations of dozens of stories, including a few from *The Martian Chronicles*, in *Weird Fantasy, Weird Science, Weird Science-Fantasy, Vault of Horror, Haunt of Fear, Tales from the Crypt, Crime Suspenstories,* and *Shock Suspenstories* (see fig. 1). The adaptations employed the standard EC style, with ample verbiage (often drawn directly from Bradbury's own writing) in most panels. One might assume this was done because Feldstein wanted to pay homage to Bradbury's prose, but actually this was typical of EC's comics in general. As Mike Benton says, "The EC horror stories were wordy—full of descriptive captions and mood-setting monologues. Feldstein consciously created a unique style of writing for the EC horror comics that was rich, rhythmic, and evocative" (16). That Bradbury's style matched Feldstein's simply made the latter's job easier.

Bradbury was delighted with the adaptations, both because he was exposing a new audience to his work exposed while getting paid in the process and because of his long-time love of comics. However, he was not entirely uncritical. On August 18, 1952, Bradbury wrote to Gaines commending Jack Davis and Joe Orlando for their work on "The Coffin" and "The Long Years," and in response to Gaines's request for criticism he said, "...I have only one minor gripe, which may or may not please you to hear about. For what it is worth, here it is. Would there be any chance, in the future, of cutting down on the exclamation points?!!!!!!!" (Weist 97). Throughout 1952, he continued to compliment EC on their adaptations, and in a November 17, 1952 letter to Wally Wood and Jack Kamen praising their work on "Mars Is Heaven" and "Zero Hour," he wrote, "It seemed to me that again and again you both achieved the exactly right atmosphere and angle in carrying out the story" (Weist 99–100).

In a January 25, 1953 letter to Gaines, Bradbury wrote, "Your adaptations of my work have been faithful and exact, you have utilized my narrative and my dialogue. I have had no reason to feel that you have laid rough hands on any of my work..." (Weist 101–102). However, in the same letter Bradbury said he had received criticism in certain circles because of his association with

Figure 1. Bradbury's mechanical house survives the bomb in a story included in *The Martian Chronicles,* adapted for EC Comics by Feldstein and Wood. From *Weird Fantasy* #17 (January–February 1953).

comics, and in particular having his name displayed on EC's sensationalistic covers, and thus asked that EC remove his name from future covers for fear of harming his sales (Weist 102–103). This was a special concern for Bradbury, who was trying to transition from the pulp magazines to the slicks and also hoped to work for Hollywood.

The success of EC Comics was short lived. In *Seduction of the Innocent* (1954), Fredric Wertham's attack on comic books, EC was singled out for its often gruesome imagery, and the company also found itself under assault in congressional hearings that same year on purported connections between juvenile delinquency and comics. Gaines encouraged other publishers to unite to fend off government censorship, resulting in the Comics Code Authority. Ironically, Gaines found the Code too restrictive, since its self-imposed structures would prevent publishing the very type of material for which EC was known. When distributors refused to carry EC's horror titles, Gaines decided to terminate them in the fall of 1954. Further battles with the Code, as well as additional distributor woes, led to the end of EC's comics in February 1956. So even if Bradbury had not begun to balk at their partnership, it would have soon ended anyway.

Despite Bradbury's concerns in the 1950s, when Ballantine Books republished sixteen of these adapted stories as mass-market paperbacks—eight horror stories in *The Autumn People* (1965), eight science fiction stories in *Tomorrow Midnight* (1966)—Bradbury not only assented to their publication but also wrote forewords for each. In *The Autumn People*, he comments on his love of comics and says that "having these comic adaptations of my stories reprinted in book form is a good and happy experience for me. Intellectual snobs will no doubt be shocked. Those with widespread, happy tastes will accept, as I accept, this new form—faithfully, and in many cases beautifully done—of some of my old stories. " Similarly, in *Tomorrow Midnight* Bradbury talks about his comic strip collections and how he still enjoys contemporary strips.

Although American comics experienced a resurgence in the 1960s, with many titles focusing on science fiction themes in the wake of the space race and the atomic age, Bradbury was not involved in comics during this decade. Still, he remained an avid fan, especially of newspaper comics, and was sympathetic toward new developments in comic books. Asked in 1975 about the increasing sophistication of comic books since the 1960s, he said, "We need comics to exist at every level for every kind of age group and intellectual group" (Dorf 95). Whereas in the 1950s he seemed to regard comic books as juvenile, accepting an arrangement with EC in part to develop a new generation of readers, now it seemed he was open to the idea that comics weren't just for kids.

Not only were mainstream comics reaching older readers in the 1960s, but also the independent comix pushed the boundaries of content and expression, serving as an important precursor to the development of the graphic novel in the 1970s. Comics veteran Will Eisner launched the term's popularity with his 1978 collection *A Contract with God*, and by 1982 the Marvel Graphic

Novel series had begun. Their competitor followed suit in 1983, first with their DC Graphic Novel series and then with their DC Science Fiction Graphic Novel series starting in 1985. The latter consisted of adaptations of classic stories by established writers such as Harlan Ellison, Frederik Pohl, Robert Silverberg—and Ray Bradbury.

The third book in the series was Klaus Janson's *Frost and Fire* (1985), an adaptation of a 1946 Bradbury novella. First published in the magazine *Planet Stories,* "Frost and Fire" is set on an alien planet where an interstellar exploration has crashed. Although it has a breathable atmosphere and edible plants, its rapid rotation has dramatically altered the survivors and succeeding generations, so that people live and die of old age in only eight days. The planet's harsh environment, with scorching sun by day and freezing temperatures at night means that the humans must spend most of their brief lives in caves. The protagonist, Sim, sees a ship off in the distance, but the devastating environment makes it too difficult to travel. Yet Sim, with the encouragement of his community's despised scientists, decides to try anyway, joined by Lyte, the young woman with whom he has fallen in love.

Bradbury's story has ample action and adventure, and this, along with its novella length, made it an appropriate choice for DC's 24-page format. Janson makes a few minor changes in the story's details but otherwise offers a faithful adaptation. He had inked *Daredevil* in the late 1970s and early 1980s, eventually working with artist (and later writer) Frank Miller, and he later inked Miller's *Batman: The Dark Knight Returns* (1986). The similarity of their styles is apparent in *Frost and Fire*: the artwork is heavily lined, which contributes to the story's feeling of hardness, and he also effectively conveys heightened emotions as well as violence and movement. Even so, the artwork appears rushed in places, no doubt because Janson took on the job of scripting, penciling, inking, and coloring the book, as short as it is, in addition to his ongoing work in monthly comics. Yet the colors are rich and vibrant, reflecting new processes in color separation and reproduction that emerged in the 1980s.

Frost and Fire enjoyed respectable sales yet was not a groundbreaking graphic novel in the same way that DC's *Batman: The Dark Knight Returns* and Alan Moore and Dave Gibbons's *Watchmen* (1987) later were. Also, the growing trend in graphic novels was for original work rather than adaptations. So it is unsurprising that Bradbury's dream of seeing *The Martian Chronicles* adapted as a book-length comic, let alone any of his other works, was not realized until near the end of his life.

Before that, however, once again he was given the opportunity to have selected short stories adapted as comics. Between 1992 and 1993, Byron Preiss published six volumes of adapted Bradbury stories as *The Ray Bradbury Chronicles*. These included new adaptations as well as a few of the EC adaptations, newly colored for these books. Preiss also published eight issues of *Ray Bradbury Comics*. Artists included Gibbons, P. Craig Russell, Richard Corben, and Matt Wagner. In addition to his introductions for these volumes, Bradbury also wrote individual introductions for each story.

Bradbury was one of the first writers to break out of the science fiction "ghetto" and receive something approaching mainstream respectability. Therefore it is perhaps appropriate that, when his dream of adapting his books finally happened, it came through a respected literary publisher. Hill and Wang started as an independent publishing house in 1956 and was acquired by another reputable publisher, Farrar, Straus and Giroux, in 1971. Hill and Wang gained attention in graphic novel publishing with the first book in their graphic novel series, *The 9/11 Report: A Graphic Adaptation* (2006). They have since published other nonfiction graphic novels, but they also commissioned three adaptations of books by Bradbury, each published as "the authorized adaptation": Tim Hamilton's *Fahrenheit 451* (2009), Ron Wimberly's *Something Wicked This Way Comes* (2011), and—fifty-nine years after first proposing the idea to William Gaines—Dennis Calero's *The Martian Chronicles* (2011).

Regrettably, the latter is the weakest of the three. The artwork is often impressive but just as often sketchy, and Calero frequently repeats the same image, which may be intended to suggest stillness and thought but nonetheless gives the impression of laziness. But the biggest problem has to do with the nature of the text and the limitations of the adaptation's 151-page format. *The Martian Chronicles* is an example of what is known in science fiction as a "fix-up": a collection of related, previously published stories gathered as a book. Sometimes fix-ups can be shaped into novels, but *The Martian Chronicles* is still a collection of twenty-eight stories about the colonization of Mars. According to Stefan Dziemianowicz, the narrative structure of the book is loose. "Nevertheless, the stories are organized to fit a clearly determined arc and evoke an elegiac tone" (1167). Calero's adaptation strives to present this arc and this tone in only fourteen stories, but even with the original's loose structure, one senses too much has been omitted for the adaptation to cohere. The reader feels that important story elements have been skipped in a way untrue of Bradbury's original. Consequently, Calero's adaptation reads more like a set of independent stories rather than as a unified graphic novel. The stories themselves are not necessarily bad, but the impression of something lacking is nevertheless present.

By contrast, the other two books are examples of adaptations whose creators have merged appropriate artistic styles to faithful, complete renditions of their sources. *Fahrenheit 451* is drawn in a realistic style with ample shadowing, reflecting the dark tone of Bradbury's novel and the intellectual and moral darkness from which its protagonist emerges. The dark hues also dramatically contrast with the flames used against books and, at times, people. At the same time, whenever we see Montag's young neighbor who nudges him from his dogmatic slumber, the palette is lighter. Hamilton also uses imagery effectively. In Part One, Montag feels threatened by the station's "mechanical hound," designed to dispatch lawbreakers, and Montag comments that he wouldn't want to be its next victim. Beatty replies, "Why? You got a guilty conscience about something?" (Bradbury 27; Hamilton 30). A few pages later in the novel Beatty asks Montag if he has books at home. He says no, but "in his mind, a cool wind started up and blew out of the ventilator grille at home..." (34). In the graphic novel, when Beatty asks if Montag feels guilty, Hamilton juxtaposes this with an image of the grille itself—behind which, readers later learn, Montag indeed has hidden forbidden books. Thus Hamilton intensifies Bradbury's use of foreshadowing with a visual connection. Another skillful juxtaposition comes with Beatty's lecture to Montag. In talking about the simplification of reading material, Beatty says, "Classics cut to fill a two-minute book column." Yet the images that accompany this part of Beatty's speech include, rather ironically given the fact that this is a graphic novel adaptation of a classic science fiction novel, *Classic Comics* adaptations of *Moby Dick* and *Treasure Island* (Hamilton 47).

Hamilton's visual storytelling is also apparent in his layouts, as in the scene in which Montag and his colleagues report to the home of a woman who refuses to leave her books. After spreading kerosene, the firemen prepare to ignite it, but then the woman reveals a match. The standoff continues through the recto side of the book, and in the last two panels she strikes the match (see fig. 2). Readers must turn the page to see the devastating results—a skillful development of dramatic tension and resolution through the printed page (Hamilton 35–40). He employs a similar technique when Montag later confronts Beatty (114–116).

Wimberly's adaptation of Bradbury's 1962 novel *Something Wicked This Way Comes* looks very different but also is an effective graphic novel and adaptation. Whereas Hamilton's book is in color, Wimberly's is black, white, and shades of gray—a suitable choice for a story that deals with good and evil and the moral struggles one faces throughout life's stages. Hamilton's technique is realistic; Wimberly's is cartoonish and impressionistic, often employing

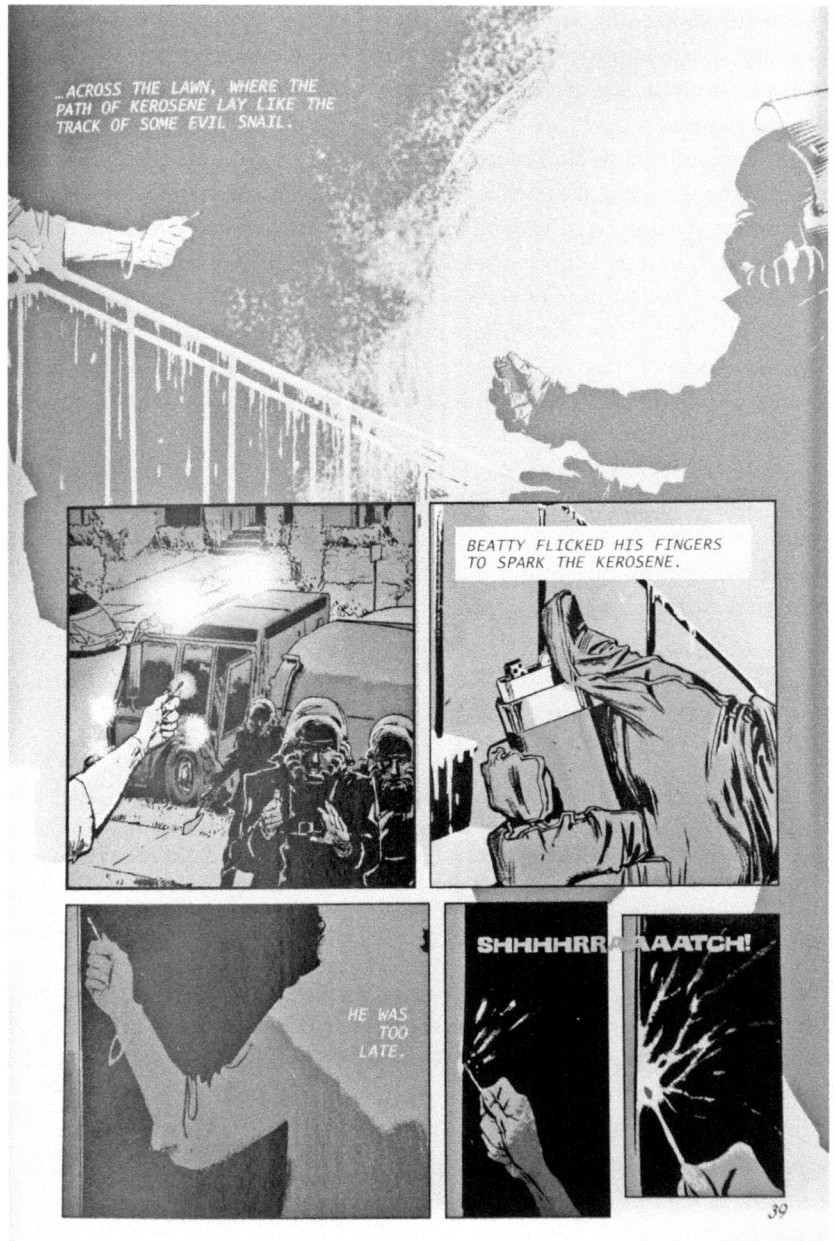

Figure 2. Creating dramatic tension visually and verbally: a confrontation between "firemen" and a lover of banned books, not to be resolved until the reader turns the page. From Hamilton, *Ray Bradbury's Fahrenheit 451*. Hill & Wang, p. 39.

extreme foreshortening and unusual angles—again an appropriate choice, since this story of the temptations of an evil carnival is conveyed mostly through the impressions of one of its two young protagonists and because of the tale's fantastic nature.

Like Hamilton in *Fahrenheit 451*, Wimberly periodically uses narration from Bradbury's original to convey information or mood, but he does not simply produce an illustrated version of the story, using, like Hamilton, images, dialogue, and thought balloons to tell the story instead. Given the more expansive format of the graphic novel—Hamilton's adaptation is 150 pages, Wimberly's 130—both artists have more room for visual storytelling than the EC adaptations, where often the story feels cramped due to all the verbiage. Hamilton and Wimberly also use Bradbury's words, but more selectively, letting the pictures tell the story as well.

Also, at times Wimberly uses the visual format to make explicit what is only hinted at in Bradbury's novel. This is especially the case with Bradbury's seventh chapter. The main characters, thirteen-year-old boys named Will and Jim, are fast friends, but Will is uncomfortable with Jim's desire to spy into a house they call the Theater:

> ... it was the one house with a window at the side and this window, Jim said, was a stage, with a curtain—the shade, that is—up. And in that room, on that strange stage, were the actors, who spoke mysteries, mouthed wild things, laughed, sighed, murmured so much; so *much* of it was whispers Will did not understand....
> And Will, hanging to the limbs of the tree, tight-pressed, terribly excited, staring in at the Theater, that peculiar stage where people, all unknowing, flourished shirts above their heads, let clothes fall to the rug, stood raw and animal-crazy, naked, like shivering horses, hands out to touch each other.
> What're they *doing!* thought Will. Why are they laughing? What's wrong with them, what's *wrong!?* [Bradbury 21–22]

What Bradbury suggests through Will's naïve viewpoint, Wimberly shows—not in explicit detail, but enough to show what Bradbury hints at. Wimberly also uses juxtaposed panels to show Will and Jim's different responses to what they see (16–17).

Wimberly also uses visual storytelling effectively in other ways, as with the first appearance of the carnival's appropriately named ringleader, Mr. Dark. At first he is seen in shadows in the background. In the next panel, when he speaks, readers see his face, eyes still shaded, in a close-up occupying nearly half the page (38; see fig. 3). More symbolic imagery occurs during a conversation between Jim and Will. Jim examines an apple, only to find a worm within—evoking both the Edenic myth that relates to the novel's theme of

Figure 3. The dramatic introduction of Mr. Dark. Two boys, their dark and light natures revealed in the colors of their hair and clothes, run afoul of an evil carnival and meet its master. From Wimberly, *Ray Bradbury's Something Wicked This Way Comes*. Hill & Wang, p. 38.

innocence and experience as well as the novel's themes of good and evil and the deceptiveness of appearances.

The fact that these three adaptations were authorized by Bradbury, who also supplied introductions for each volume, provided a fitting capstone to the career of an author with a lifelong love of comics. The last two appeared a year before his death in 2012, nine years after the passing of his wife, Marguerite. As a sign of their love, he honored her at her funeral by recognizing her favorite author, Marcel Proust (Weller 6). Unable to place the multivolume *Remembrance of Things Past* in her casket, instead, he sent her to her final rest with a graphic novel adaptation of Proust's masterpiece (328–329).

Works Cited

Benton, Mike. *Horror Comics: The Illustrated History*. Dallas: Taylor, 1991. Print.
Bradbury, Ray. "Drunk, and in Charge of a Bicycle." *Zen in the Art of Writing*. Santa Barbara: Joshua Odell, 1996. 47–66. Print.
_____. *Fahrenheit 451*. New York: Ballantine/Del Rey, 1988. Print.
_____. Foreword. *The Autumn People*. Adapted by Albert B. Feldstein. New York: Ballantine, 1965. N.p. Print.
_____. Foreword. *Tomorrow Midnight*. Adapted by Albert B. Feldstein. New York: Ballantine, 1966. N.p. Print.
_____. Introduction. *The Ray Bradbury Chronicles*. Vol. 1. New York: Byron Preiss–Bantam, 1992. 4–6. Print.
_____. Introduction. *The Ray Bradbury Chronicles*. Vol. 2. New York: Byron Preiss–Bantam, 1992. 4–6. Print.
_____. "Predicting the Past, Remembering the Future." *Bradbury Speaks: Too Soon from the Cave, Too Far from the Stars*. New York: William Morrow–HarperCollins, 2005. 35–42. Print.
_____. *Something Wicked This Way Comes*. Toronto: Bantam, 1983. Print.
Burton, Pierre. "Ray Bradbury: Cassandra on a Bicycle." *Conversations with Ray Bradbury*. Ed. Steven L. Aggelis. Jackson: University Press of Mississippi, 2004. 31–38. Print.
Calero, Dennis. *Ray Bradbury's* The Martian Chronicles. New York: Hill & Wang, 2011. Print.
Dorf, Shel. "The Bradbury Chronicles." *Conversations with Ray Bradbury*. Ed. Steven L. Aggelis. Jackson: University Press of Mississippi, 2004. 85–99. Print.
Dziemianowicz, Stefan. "*The Martian Chronicles* by Ray Bradbury (1950)." *The Greenwood Encyclopedia of Science Fiction and Fantasy: Themes, Works, and Wonders*. 3 vols. Ed. Gary Westfahl. Westport, CT: Greenwood, 2005. 1166–1168. Print.
Hamilton, Tim. *Ray Bradbury's* Fahrenheit 451. New York: Hill & Wang, 2009. Print.
Janson, Klaus. *Frost and Fire: A Story by Ray Bradbury*. New York: DC Comics, 1985. Print.
Weist, Jerry. *Bradbury: An Illustrated Life—A Journey to Far Metaphor*. New York: William Morrow–HarperCollins, 2002. Print.
Weller, Sam. *The Bradbury Chronicles: The Life of Ray Bradbury*. New York: William Morrow–HarperCollins, 2005. Print.
Wimberly, Ron. *Ray Bradbury's* Something Wicked This Way Comes. New York: Hill & Wang, 2011. Print.

Bibliography

Selected Books, Theses and Dissertations about the Graphic Novel

Assouline, Pierre, and Charles Ruas. *Hergé: The Man Who Created Tintin*. Oxford: Oxford University Press, 2009. Print.

Barker, Martin. *Comics: Ideology, Power and the Critics*. Manchester: Manchester University Press, 1989. Print.

Baetens, Jan, and Hugo Frey. *The Cambridge Introduction to the Graphic Novel*. Cambridge: Cambridge University Press, 2014. Print.

Beineke, Colin. "Towards a Theory of Comic Book Adaptation." MA thesis. The University of Nebraska, 2011. Web.

Bell, Roanne, and Mark Sinclair. *Pictures and Words: New Comic Art and Narrative Illustration*. New Haven: Yale University Press, 2005. Print.

Bettley, James. *Art of the Book: From Medieval Manuscript to Graphic Novel*. London: V and A Publications, 2001. Print.

Brauer, Stephen Michael. "Containing the Criminal: American Crime Narratives, 1919–1941." PhD Diss. New York University, 1999. Print.

Carlin, John, Paul Karasik, and Brian Walker. *Masters of American Comics*. New Haven: Yale University Press, 2005. Print.

Carrier, David. *The Aesthetics of Comics*. University Park, PA: Penn State University Press, 2001. Print.

Chute, Hilary. *Graphic Women: Life Narrative and Contemporary Comics*. New York: Columbia University Press, 2010. Print.

Duncan, Randy, and Matthew J. Smith. *The Power of Comics: History, Form and Culture*. New York: Continuum, 2009. Print.

Eisner, Will. *Graphic Storytelling and Visual Narrative: Principles and Practices from the Legendary Cartoonist*. New York: W.W. Norton, 2008. Print.

Gardner, Jared. *Projections: Comics and the History of 21st Century Storytelling*. Palo Alto: Stanford University Press, 2011. Print.

Gravett, Paul. *Graphic Novels: Everything You Need to Know*. New York: Harper Collins, 2005. Print.

Green, Matthew J.A., ed. *Alan Moore and the Gothic Tradition*. Manchester: University of Manchester Press, 2013. Print.

Groensteen, Thierry. *The System of Comics*. Trans. Bart Beaty and Nick Nguyen. Jackson: University Press of Mississippi, 2007. Print.

Hatfield, Charles. *Alternative Comics: An Emerging Literature*. Jackson: University Press of Mississippi, 2005. Print.

Heer, Jeet, and Kent Worcester, eds. *A Comics Studies Reader*. Jackson: University Press of Mississippi, 2009. Print.

_____. *Arguing Comics: Literary Masters on a Popular Medium*. Jackson: University Press of Mississippi, 2005. Print.

Inge, M. Thomas. *Comics as Culture*. Jackson: University Press of Mississippi, 1990. Print.

Jones, William B., Jr. *Classics Illustrated: A Cultural History, with Illustrations*, 2d edition. Jefferson, NC: McFarland, 2011. Print.

Kick, Russ, ed. *The Graphic Canon: The World's Great Literature as Comics and Visuals*. 3 vols. New York: Seven Stories Press, 2012, 2013. Print.

Kovacs, George, and C. W. Marshall. *Classics and Comics*. Oxford: Oxford University Press, 2011. Print.

Martin, George Ira. "Secondary English Students' Responses to *Classics Illustrated* Comic Books." Diss. University of Virginia, 1992. Web.

McCloud, Scott. *Understanding Comics: The Invisible Art*. Lettering by Bob Lappan. New York: HarperPerennial, 1994. Print.

Sabin, Roger. *Adult Comics: An Introduction*. London and New York: Routledge, 1993. Print.

_____. *Comics, Comix and Graphic Novels: A History of Comic Art*. New York: Phaidon, 1996. Print.

Saltzman, Esther Bendit. "Comics as Criticism: Graphic Novel Adaptations as Interpretive Discourse." MA thesis. The University of Memphis, 2011. Print.

Schodt, Frederik L., and Osamu Tezuka. *Manga! Manga! The World of Japanese Comics*. Oxford: Oxford University Press, 1997. Print.

Steiling, David A. "Icon, Representation and Virtual Reality in Reading the Graphic Narrative." PhD Diss. University of South Florida, 2006. Web.

Tabachnick, Stephen E. *The Quest for Jewish Belief and Identity in the Graphic Novel*. Tuscaloosa: University of Alabama Press, 2014. Print.

_____, ed. *Teaching the Graphic Novel*. New York: The Modern Language Association of America, 2009. Print.

Tondro, Jason William. "An Imaginary Mongoose: Comics, Canon, and the Superhero Romance." PhD Diss. University of California Riverside, 2008. Web.

Versaci, Rocco. *The Book Contains Graphic Language: Comics as Literature*. New York: Continuum, 2008. Print.

Warshow, Robert. *The Immediate Experience: Movies, Comics, Theatre, and Other Aspects of Popular Culture*. Cambridge: Harvard University Press, 2002. Print.

Witek, Joseph. *Comic Books as History: The Narrative Art of Jack Jackson, Art Spiegelman and Harvey Pekar*. Jackson: University Press of Mississippi, 1989. Print.

Wolk, Douglas. *Reading Comics: How Graphic Novels Work and What They Mean*. New York: Da Capo, 2007. Print.

Wright, Bradford W. *Comic Book Nation*. Baltimore: Johns Hopkins University Press, 2001. Print.

BOOKS ABOUT ADAPTATION THEORY

Cutchins, Dennis, Lawrence Raw, and James M. Welsh, eds. *Redefining Adaptation Studies*. Lanham: Scarecrow Press, 2010. Print.

Hutcheon, Linda. *A Theory of Adaptation*. New York: Routledge, 2006. Print.

Sanders, Julie. *Adaptation and Appropriation*. London: Routledge, 2006. Print.

BOOKS ABOUT FILM AND GRAPHIC NOVEL ADAPTATIONS

Booker, M. Keith. *"May Contain Graphic Material": Comic Books, Graphic Novels, and Film*. Westport, CT: Praeger, 2007. Print.

Gordan, Ian, Mark Jancovich and Matthew McAllister, eds. *Film and Comic Books*. Jackson: University Press of Mississippi, 2007. Print.

ARTICLES ABOUT GRAPHIC NOVEL ADAPTATIONS

Blackmore, Tim. "*300* and Two: Frank Miller and Daniel Ford Interpret Herodotus's Thermopylae Myth." *International Journal of Comic Art* 6.2 (2004): 325–349. Print.

Carrier, David. "Proust's *In Search of Lost Time* : The Comics Version." In *The Art of Comics: A Philosophical Approach*. Eds. Aaron Meskin and Roy T. Cook. Malden,

MA: Wiley-Blackwell, 2012. 188–202. Print.

Castaldo, Annalisa. "'No More Yielding than a Dream': The Construction of Shakespeare in *The Sandman*." *College Literature* 31.4 (2004): 94–110. Print.

Ferguson, Christine. "Steam Punk and the Visualization of the Victorian: Teaching Alan Moore's *The League of Extraordinary Gentlemen* and *From Hell*." In *Teaching the Graphic Novel*. Ed. Stephen E. Tabachnick. New York: MLA, 2009. 200–207. Print.

Ferstl, Paul. "Novel-Based Comics." In *Comics as a Nexus of Cultures*. Eds. Mark Berninger, Jochen Ecke, et al. Jefferson, NC: McFarland, 2010: 60–69. Print.

Finlayson, J. Caitlin. "The Boundaries of Genre: Translating Shakespeare in Anthony Johnston and Brett Weldele's *Julius*." In *Teaching the Graphic Novel*. Ed. Stephen E. Tabachnick. New York: MLA, 2009. 188–199. Print.

Fishelov, David. "Dialogues with/and Great Books: With Some Serious Reflections on *Robinson Crusoe*." *New Literary History* 39.2 (Spring 2008): 335–353. Print.

Gal, Ana G. "The Social Modes of Heroization and Vilification in *Stoker's Dracula, a Graphic Novel by Roy Thomas and Dick Giordano*." *International Journal of Comic Art* 12.1 (Spring 2010): 200–214. Print.

Heuman, Josh and Richard Burt. "Suggested for Mature Readers? Deconstructing Shakespearean Value in Comic Books." In *Shakespeare after Mass Media*. Ed. Burt. New York: Palgrave, 2002. 151–172. Print.

Jensen, Michael. "The Comic Book Shakespeare." *Shakespeare Newsletter* 56.3 (2007): 2; 57.2 (2007): 47. Print.

Kuhlman, Martha. "Teaching Paul Karasik and David Mazzucchelli's Graphic Novel Adaptation of Paul Auster's *City of Glass*." In *Teaching the Graphic Novel*. Ed. Stephen E. Tabachnick New York: MLA, 2009. 120–128. Print.

Perret, Marion D. "More than Child's Play: Approaching Hamlet through Comic Books." In *Approaches to Teaching Shakespeare's Hamlet*. Ed. Bernice W. Kliman. New York: MLA, 2001. 151–164. Print.

_____. "'And Suit the Action to the Word': How a Comics Panel Can Speak Shakespeare." In *The Language of Comics: Word and Image*. Eds. Robin Varnum and Christina T. Gibbons. Jackson: University Press of Mississippi, 2001. 123–144. Print.

_____. "Not Just Condensation: How Comic Books Interpret Shakespeare." *College Literature* 41.4 (2004): 72–93. Print.

Pointner, Frank Eric. "Classics Emulated: Comic Adaptations of Literary Texts." *Critic* 72.3 (2010): 86–106. Print.

Royal, Derek. "'Meddling with 'hifalut'n foolishness': Capturing Mark Twain in Recent Comics." *The Mark Twain Annual* 7 (2009): 22–51. Print.

_____. "Sequential Poe-try: Recent Graphic Narrative Adaptations of Poe." *Poe Studies/Dark Romanticism* 39–40 (2007–2008): 55–67.

_____. "Visualizing the Romance: Uses of Nathaniel Hawthorne's Narratives in Comics." *Nathaniel Hawthorne Review* 39.2 (2013). 126–153. Print.

Saltzman, Esther Bendit. "Lady Macbeth: Graphic, but Not Comic: Lady Macbeth as Early Modern Mother." In *Re-Told Feminine Memoirs: Our Collective Past and Present*. Ed. Gabriela Mádlo. Oxford: Inter-Disciplinary Press, 2013. ebook.

Smith, Don G. "Lovecraft in Comic Books." In *H.P. Lovecraft in Popular Culture: The Works and Their Adaptations in Film, Television, Comics, Music and Games*. Jefferson: McFarland, 2006. 137–145. Print.

Stam, Robert. "Beyond Fidelity: the Dialogics of Adaptation." In *Film Adaptation*. Ed. James Naremore. New Brunswick: Rutgers University Press, 2000. 54–76. Print.

Tabachnick, Stephen E. "The Graphic Novel and the Age of Transition: A Survey and Analysis." *English Literature in Transition: 1880–1920* 53.1 (2010): 3–28. Print.

_____. "The Gothic Modernism of T.S. Eliot's *Waste Land* and What Martin Rowson's Graphic Novel Tells Us About It and Other Matters." *Readerly/Writerly Texts* 8.1–2 (2000): 79–92. Print.

Tondro, Jason. "Camelot in Comics." In *King Arthur in Popular Culture*. Eds. Elizabeth S. Sklar and Donald Hoffman. Jefferson, NC: McFarland, 2002. 169–179.

Websites

The Center for Cartoon Studies, www.teachingcomics.org

Comic Art Collection, Michigan State University Libraries, www.lib.msu.edu/spc/collections/comic

Comic-Con International, www.comic-con.org

ComicsResearch.org (Comics Scholarship Annotatied Bibliographies), www.comicsresearch.org

Comics Research Bibliography, www.rpi.edu/-bulloj/comixbib.html

Comix-Scholars Discussion List, www.english.ufl.edu/comics/scholars

ImageTexT, www.english.ufl.edu/imagetext

International Bande Dessinée Society, www.arts.gla.ac.uk/ibds

About the Contributors

Jan **Baetens** is a professor of literary and cultural studies at the University of Leuven (Belgium) and has published widely on word and image studies. He is the co-editor of a double issue of *Poetics Today* on the topic of constrained writing and the author of a chapter on the French literary movement Oulipo in a forthcoming book on avant-garde writing.

Eric L. **Berlatsky** is an associate professor of English at Florida Atlantic University in Boca Raton. He specializes in narrative theory and postmodern and postcolonial fiction. Recently his focus has been on comics and graphic novels. He is the author of *The Real, the True, and the Told: Postmodern Historical Narrative and the Ethics of Representation* (Ohio State University Press, 2011) and the editor of the Eisner-nominated *Alan Moore: Conversations* (University Press of Mississippi, 2011).

Christine **Ferguson** is a lecturer in English literature at the University of Glasgow, where she specializes in Victorian and contemporary literature. Her publications include the books *Determined Spirits* (Edinburgh University Press, 2012) and *Language, Science, and Popular Fiction in the Victorian Fin-de-Siècle* (Ashgate, 2006), and articles in *Neo-Victorian Studies, SEL: Studies in English Literature,* and *LIT: Literature Interpretation Theory*.

J. Caitlin **Finlayson** is an assistant professor of English at the University of Michigan–Dearborn. She has a doctorate from the University of Toronto. Her research interests include Renaissance pageantry and the history of the adaptation of Shakespeare. She is particularly interested in the adaptation of his plays to graphic novels, television commercials, and popular digital media. She teaches the courses "Shakespeare on Stage, Page and Screen" and "Adaptations of Literary Texts."

Ana G. **Gal** has an M.A. in Irish studies from Babes-Bolyai University, Romania, and a Ph.D. in literary and cultural studies from the University of Memphis. She has published articles on vampires in literature and graphic novels in the *International Journal of Comic Art* and *Dracula Studies*.

Matthew J. A. **Green** is an associate professor of English literature at the University of Nottingham. In addition to articles published on William Blake, Lord Byron and graphic novelist Alan Moore, he is the author of *Visionary Materialism in the Early Works of William Blake* (Palgrave Macmillan, 2005) and editor of *Alan Moore and the Gothic Tradition* (Manchester University Press, 2013).

Simon **Grennan** is half of the collaborative artists' team known as Grennan & Sperandio, and well-known as a pioneer of interventionist, New Genre and post-relational practice through his work in publishing, television and social action projects. He has also been director of Viewpoint Photography Gallery, Salford and director of Public Art Forum (now IXIA). He has a Ph.D. and is a research fellow in fine art at the University of Chester. Grennan & Sperandio are at www.kartoonkings.com.

Darren **Harris-Fain** is chair of the English and Philosophy Department at Auburn University at Montgomery. His publications include *Understanding Contemporary American Science Fiction: The Age of Maturity, 1970–2000* (University of South Carolina Press, 2005); contributions to the *Dictionary of Literary Biography* (Gale Research); and essays on science fiction, fantasy, horror, comics and graphic novels, and film and television in more than twenty books.

Martha **Kuhlman** is an associate professor of comparative literature in the Department of English and Cultural Studies at Bryant University where she teaches courses on the graphic novel, Central European literature and critical theory. She coedited *The Comics of Chris Ware: Drawing Is a Way of Thinking* (University Press of Mississippi, 2010) with Dave Ball. In addition, she has published articles on comics in *The Journal of Popular Culture, European Comic Art,* and the *International Journal of Comic Art.*

Eric S. **Rabkin** is the Arthur F. Thurnau Professor at the University of Michigan at Ann Arbor where he teaches English language and literature as well as art and design. His teaching and research interests include graphic narrative, fantasy, science fiction, and technology and the humanities. He is the recipient of many awards for teaching and the Science Fiction Research Association's Pilgrim Award for lifetime contributions to fantasy and science fiction criticism.

Derek Parker **Royal** is a comics scholar and the editorial director of the Brown Books Publishing Group. He is also the co-host of "The Comics Alternative" podcast and blog. His books include *Philip Roth: New Perspectives on an American Author* (Praeger, 2005), *Unfinalized Moments: Essays in the Development of Contemporary Jewish American Narrative* (Purdue University Press, 2011), and *Visualizing Jewish Narrative: Essays on Jewish Comics and Graphic Novels* (forthcoming, Bloomsbury Publishing).

Esther Bendit **Saltzman** is a Ph.D. student at the University of Memphis. She completed her master's thesis on graphic novel adaptations, and has spoken on adaptations of *Macbeth* and *A Christmas Carol* at conferences in the Czech Republic and the U.K., respectively. Her dissertation is on graphic novel adaptations of literary classics in relation to their adapted texts and corresponding book illustrations.

David **Skilton**, emeritus professor in English at Cardiff University, was general editor of the Trollope Society/Folio Society edition of Trollope's novels (48 vols., 1998–2000). His books include *Anthony Trollope and His Contemporaries* (St. Martin's Press, 1972) and *The English Novel: Defoe to the Victorians* (David and Charles, 1977). He has written on the art and literature of London and on literary illustration, and he is founding editor of the *Journal of Illustration Studies.*

Paul D. **Streufert** holds the George F. Hamm Chair in Arts and Humanities at the University of Texas at Tyler, where he directs the honors program and teaches world literature. He has published articles on a variety of ancient and modern authors, such as Aeschylus, Euripides, and graphic novelist Frank Miller. Along with Jonathan Walker, he is the co-editor of *Early Modern Academic Drama* (Ashgate, 2008).

Stephen E. **Tabachnick** is professor of English literature at the University of Memphis. The author or editor of many books on Victorian and modern British literature, he is also the editor of the Modern Language Association's *Teaching the Graphic Novel*, which includes thirty-four essays by university teachers in the U.S., the U.K., and Europe. He is the author of *The Quest for Jewish Belief and Identity in the Graphic Novel* (The University of Alabama Press, 2014).

Jason **Tondro** is an assistant professor of English at the College of Coastal Georgia. He earned a Ph.D. at the University of California, Riverside, and is the author of *Superheroes of the Round Table* (McFarland, 2011). He has taught and written on *Beowulf* for years; an abridged version of his essay "A Book on Fire: An Exploration of *Beowulf* in the Media" appears in the production notes for Neil Gaiman's 2007 *Beowulf* film. He blogs at doctorcomics.blogspot.com.

Dirk **Vanderbeke** studied German and English literature at the University of Frankfurt/Main, where he received a Ph.D. in English literature. He has published on a variety of topics, including Joyce, Pynchon, Milton, science fiction, self-similarity, evolutionary theory, vampires and graphic novels. He holds a professorship of English literature at the Friedrich Schiller University in Jena, Germany, and a permanent guest-professorship at the University of Zielona Góra.

Index

Numbers in **_bold italics_** indicate pages with photographs.

A la recherche du temps perdu (*Remembrance of Things Past*) 99, 262
Abbate, Carolyn 155; *Unsung Voices* 155
Acclaim Books (*Classics Illustrated*) 100; graphic novel adaptation of *Moby-Dick* 100
Action Comics 88
Adaptation (journal) 7
adaptation studies 7–9, 110–111, 114; adaptation as a form of parody 82–95; adaptations and fidelity to the original 7–9, 12, 34, 42, 43, 60–62, 64, 67, 68, 71, 72, 74, 76, 79, 79n3, 86, 96–97, 99, 110, 113, 166, 197, 198, 217, 224, 227, 253, 255, 256, 257, 258; and film 1, 3, 8, 10, 12, 33, 36, 39–40, *41*, 52, 54, 58, 60, 68, 82, 83, 87, 94, 96, 97, 98, 101, 103, 104, 108n6, 140, 157, 173, 194, 195, 202, 203, 204n2, 221, 223, 228, 243; traditional, casual and instrumental adaptation 82–95
The Adventures of Luther Arkwright 116
Aeschylus 21
Africa 76, 163, 195, 196, 199
Alanguilan, Gerry 67; "The Black Cat" 67
Aldiss, Brian 91
Alice in Sunderland: An Entertainment (graphic novel adaptation of Carroll's *Alice in Wonderland*) 14, 110–125
Alice in Wonderland 14, 110, 111, 112, 113, 114, 119–125; *Classics Illustrated* 110–111, 112, 116, 125, 125n1; *Illustrated Classic* 111, 112, 125
Alice's Adventure Underground 113, 114, ***118***, ***119***, 120, 121, 122
Alice's Adventures in Wonderland 113, 120
Alixe, Pascal 98, 101, 103, 104; graphic novel adaptation of *Moby-Dick* 98, 101, 103, 104
Allen, Chris 49

Allen, Graham 114, 115; *Intertextuality* 114, 115
Alley Oop 251
Amazon (online bookseller) 202
Andy Capp 250
"Annabel Lee" 64
Antarctica 153
Anyango, Catherine 15, 147, 194–204; graphic novel adaptation of *Heart of Darkness* 15, 147, 194–204; illustrations for *Turn of the Screw* 195, 197
Apocalypse Now (film) 202
Appignanesi, Richard 47, 49; *Manga Shakespeare Othello* 47, 49–54, 55, 58
Arata, Stephen D. 163; "The Occidental Tourist" 163
Ardizzone, Edward 157
Aristotle 22
Asia 163
Asma, Stephen T. 25; *On Monsters* 25
Attwood, Fiona 174; *Mainstreaming Sex* 174
Australia 153, 157
An Autobiography (Trollope) 153, 155
Avary, Roger 39, 40, ***41***, 44; film adaptation of *Beowulf* 39, 40, ***41***, 44
Avengers 89
Azpiri, Alfonso 97; *Lorna: Leviathan* 97

Baetens, Jan 16, 225, 235; "OuLiPo and Proceduralism" 235; "The Writing of Constraint (I)" 235; "The Writing of Constraint (II)" 235
Bakhtin, Mikail 8, 115, 125
Bakshi, Ralph 34; *Lord of the Rings* film adaptation 34
Ballentine Books 255
Baltimore 64
Banshee Isles (Philippines) 103

Index

Barnes, Hazel 143*n*5; "The Biographer as Literary Critic" 143*n*5
Barthes, Roland 152; *The Responsibility of Forms* 152
Batman 36, 108*n*8
Batman: The Dark Knight Returns 256
Battaglia, Dino 147; graphic novel adaptations of Guy de Maupassant stories 147
Baudelaire, Charles 129, 131, 143*n*5
Beard, Henry 88; "Dr. Jekyll and Mr. Heckle" 88
Beardsley, Aubrey 84–86; *The Rape of the Lock* illustrations 84–86
Beaty, Bart 151; *Comics versus Art* 151
B.C. 250
Bechdel, Alison 203
Beinike, Colin E. 98, 105, 108*n*4, 108*n*8; *Towards a Theory of Comic Book Adaptation* 98, 105, 108*n*4, 108*n*8
Beissner, Friedrich 208; "The Writer Franz Kafka" 208
Beizer, Janet 143*n*2; *Ventriloquized Bodies* 143*n*2, 143*n*3
Benjamin, Walter 148; *Illuminations: Essays and Reflections* 148
Benson, Carol 26
Benton, Mike 253; *Horror Comics* 253
Benveniste, Émile 149; *Problems in General Linguistics* 149
Beowulf 12, 33–45
Beowulf: Dragon Slayer 33, 36–37
"Berenice" 67, 80*n*10
Berkley First **106**
Berlatsky, Eric L. 14, 184
Berner, David 70; graphic novel adaptation of "The Oval Portrait" 70
Berry, Rob 99; web comic adaptation of *Ulysses* 99
Berthold, Michael C. 97, 98; "Color Me Ishmael: *Classics Illustrated* Versions of *Moby-Dick*" 97
Biber, Douglas 149; *Register, Genre and Style* 149
Bible 102; King James 91
Bingham, Jerry 33, 34–36, 38, 39, 40, 44; *Batman: Son of the Demon* 34; *Beowulf* graphic novel adaptation 33, 34–36, 38, 39, 40, 44; "*Beowulf:* A Lot of Mileage Since 1984" 34, 35, 36; Facebook page and blog 35; wins first Kirby Award 34
Birken, Lawrence 129, 143*n*3, 143*n*9; "Madame Bovary and the Dissolution of Bourgeois Sexuality" 143*n*3, 143*n*9
"The Black Cat" 67, 69, 71, 74, 79*n*4
"Blonde Eve" 90–92
Blondie 90–91
Bloomfield, Camille 235; "Oulipo@50" 235
Bluestone, George 8; *Novels into Film* 8
Blum, Alex 113; *Classics Illustrated* 113, 125*n*1
Boitard, François 59*n*2
The Book of Sequels 88
Booth, Bradford Allen 155; *Anthony Trollope* 155
Boschenhoff, Sandra E. 110, 125, 212, 218*n*4; "Classics Emulated: Comic Adaptations of Literary Texts" 110, 125, 212, 218*n*4
Bradbury, Marguerite 262
Bradbury, Ray 16, 249–262; *The Autumn People* 250, 255; "The Coffin" 253; *The Collected Stories of Ray Bradbury* 250; *Dark Carnival* 252; "The Emissary" 252; *Fahrenheit 451* 16, 249, 257, 258, **259**, 260; "Frost and Fire" 256; "The Handler" 252; *The Illustrated Man* 252; "Kaleidoscope" 252; "The Long Years" 253; *The Martian Chronicles* 251, 252, 253, **254**, 256, 257; "Predicting the Past, Remembering the Future" 249–250; *The Ray Bradbury Chronicles* 250, 251, 257; *Ray Bradbury Comics* 257; "The Rocket Man" 252; *Something Wicked This Way Comes* 257, 258, 260–262; *Tomorrow Midnight* 251, 255; *Zen in the Art of Writing* 250
Bragard, Véronique 125; "Conrad's Two Visions" 125
Brannon, April 20, 31
Brick Bradford 250, 251
Bronfen, Elizabeth 143*n*3, 144*n*10; *Over Her Dead Body* 143*n*3, 144*n*10
Brontë, Emily 12, 89, 92, 94; *Wuthering Heights* 12, 92–95
Broodthaer, Marcel 147; *Un Coup de dés jamais n'abolira le hansard* 147
Brooks, Marilyn 143*n*3, 144*n*10; "*Madame Bovary:* Becoming a Heroine" 143*n*3, 144*n*10
Brotchie, Alastair 235; *The Oulipo Compendium* 235
Brown, Chester 245
Brusco, Giulia 184; graphic novel adaptation of *The Picture of Dorian Gray* 177–193
Buck Rogers 250, 251
Buck Rogers in the 25th Century 249
Budapest 163
Buitron-Oliver, Diana 26
Burroughs, Edgar Rice 250; *Tarzan* 250, 251; *The Warlord of Mars* 250
Burton, Pierre 251; "Ray Bradbury" 251
Buscema, John 34
Butler, Samuel 20
Byerly, Alison 183

Index 273

Calero, Dennis 257; graphic novel adaptation of *The Martian Chronicles* 257
Calvino, Italo 236
Cambridgeshire 153, 157
Campfire 100, 103; *Moby-Dick* graphic novel adaptation 100, 103
Candlewick 37, **38**, 39
Capstone 72
Carroll, Lewis 14, 110–125; *Alice in Wonderland* 14, 110–125; *see also* Dodgson, Charles
Casement, Roger 200
"The Cask of Amontillado" 71, 77, 79n5, 92
CCTV 199
Cervantes, Miguel D. 98; *Don Quixote* 98, 99
Chamberlain (publishers) **244**, **246**
Chandler, Raymond 243; *The Lady in the Lake* 243
Charcot, Jean-Martin 195, 198
"The City in the Sea" 75, 76
Clarke, Catherine 44n3
Classic Comics 107n2, 258; *Moby Dick* 258; *Treasure Island* 258
Classical Comics 161–176; *Dracula: The Graphic Novel* 161–176
Classics Illustrated 4, 65, 72, 79n7, 98, 104, 107n2, 110, 111, 116, 125, 125n1, 204n2; graphic novel adaptation of *Alice in Wonderland* 110–111, 112, 116, 125, 125n1; graphic novel adaptation of *Lord Jim* 194; graphic novel adaptation of *Moby-Dick* 97–98, 104; graphic novel adaptation of *The Strange Case of Dr. Jekyll and Mr. Hyde* 87–88
Classics Illustrated Deluxe (Papercutz) 74, 79n7; *The Murders in the Rue Morgue and Other Tales by Edgar Allan Poe* 74–75
Cliff Notes 62, 72
Cloonan, Becky **167**; *Bram Stoker's Dracula: The Graphic Novel* **167**
Closs, Adolph 55
Clowes, Daniel 245
Cobley, Jason **171**; *Dracula: The Graphic Novel* **171**
Cohen, Beth 26, 27, 31
Colet, Louise 127, 128, 143n2
Comico 34
Comics Code Authority 36, 255
The Comics Journal 191n1
comics studies 5–7
Common Core standards 43
Conan the Barbarian 20; Conan 34, 36
Congo 196, 200
Congo Diary 195, 196, 198, **201**
"The Conqueror Worm" 75, 76, 80n10

Conrad, Joseph 13, 15, 147, 194–204; *Congo Diary* 195, 196, 198; *Heart of Darkness* 13, 15, 147, 194–204; *Lord Jim* 194; *Youth; A Narrative and Two Other Stories* 204n1
Conrad, Susan 149; *Register, Genre and Style* 149
Constable, Liz 128; "Consuming Realities" 128
Coppola, Francis Ford 221; film adaptation of *The Great Gatsby* 221
Corben, Richard 75–79, 80n9, 80n10, 257; *A Corben Special: House of Usher* 75; *Edgar Allan Poe's The Conqueror Worm* 75; *Edgar Allan Poe's The Fall of the House of Usher* 75, **78**; *Edgar Allan Poe's Haunt of Horror* 75; *Edgar Allan Poe's Morella and the Murders in the Rue Morgue* 75; *Edgar Allan Poe's The Premature Burial* 75, 77; *Edgar Allan Poe's The Raven and the Red Death* 75; *Edgar Allan Poe's Spirits of the Dead* 75; graphic novel adaptation of "Alone" 75; graphic novel adaptation of "The Assignation" 75, 76; graphic novel adaptation of "Berenice" 75; graphic novel adaptation of "The Casque of Amontillado" 77; graphic novel adaptation of "The City in the Sea" 75, 76; graphic novel adaptation of "The Conqueror Worm" 76; graphic novel adaptation of "The Fall of the House of Usher" 77–**78**; graphic novel adaptation of "The Haunted Palace" 77; graphic novel adaptation of "The Masque of the Red Death" 77; graphic novel adaptation of "Morella" **78**; graphic novel adaptation of "The Premature Burial" **78**; graphic novel adaptation of *Ray Bradbury Comics* 257; graphic novel adaptation of "Shadow" 75, 76; graphic novel adaptation of "The Sleeper" 75
Corngold, Stanley 206, 215, 217, 218, 218n1, 218n3; *The Commentator's Despair* 206, 215; *The Metamorphosis of Franz Kafka* 218n3; "The Metamorphosis of the Metaphor" 218
Cornhill Magazine 151
Costa Book Award 154
Coulthart, John 15, 178, 183, 185, **186**, 189, 190–191, 192; graphic novel adaptation of *The Picture of Dorian Gray* 15, 177–193
County Durham (England) 117
Un Coup de dés jamais n'abolira le hansard 147
Courbet, Gustave 157
Creepy (magazine) 75
Crumb, Robert 15, 144n19, 206 207–210, 212, 214, 215, 218; graphic novel adapta-

tion of *The Metamorphosis* 15, 206, 207–210, 212, 214, 215, 218; "Drawing Cartoons Is Fun" 144*n*19; *Introducing Kafka*, 207–210, 212, 214, 215, 218

Culbard, I.N.J. 15, 178, 181, ***182***, 183, 184, 188, 189, 190, 191, 192; graphic novel adaptation of *The Picture of Dorian Gray* 15, 177–193

Culler, Jonathan 143*n*3, 143*n*7, 144*n*11; "The Uses of *Madame Bovary*" 143*n*3, 143*n*7, 144*n*11

Cunningham, John W. 96; "The Tin Star" 96

Daily Chronicle 192*n*9
Dalston (London) 195
Dambrusi 59*n*2
Danahy, Michael 143*n*3, 144*n*9, 144*n*11; "*Madame Bovary*: A Tongue of One's Own" 143*n*3, 143*n*9, 143*n*11
Dante Alighieri 89
Danube 163
Dark Carnival 252
Dark Horse 75, 78, 80*n*10
Dark Horse Presents 75
Daumier, Honoré 14, 157
Davis, Jack 253; "The Coffin" 253; "The Long Years" 253
Day of the Dead (Mexico) 71
"Days of Bagnold Summer" 154; nominated for Costa Book Award 154
DC Comics 34, 36, 37, 79*n*8, ***105***, 256; *Arkham Asylum. A Serious House on Serious Earth* ***105***; *House of Mystery* 36
de Gaultier, Jules 143*n*6
Delano, Jamie 68; graphic novel adaptation of "The Tell-Tale Heart" 68–69
Deleuze, Gilles 206; *Kafka* 206
Delvaux, A. 59*n*3
de Man, Paul 156
Despeyroux, Denise 74, 79*n*4; *Dark Graphic Tales by Edgar Allan Poe* 79*n*4; graphic novel adaptation of "The Gold Bug" 74; graphic novel adaptation of "The Fall of the House of Usher" 74; graphic novel adaptation of "The System of Dr. Tarr and Professor Fether" 74
Dickens, Charles 152, 158; *Barnaby Rudge* 158
Dickie, George 151; *Art and the Aesthetic* 151
Din, Susurrus 71
Disney studios 34
Dispossession (*Courier deux lièvres*) 147–160
D'Israeli 69; graphic novel adaptation of "The Murders in the Rue Morgue" 69

Dr. Jekyll and Mr. Hyde 199
Dodgson, Charles 110–125; *Alice in Wonderland* 110–125; *Alice's Adventure Underground* 113, 114, ***118***, ***119***, 120, 121, 122; *Alice's Adventures in Wonderland* 113, 120; *Through the Looking Glass, and What Alice Found There* 113; *see also* Carroll, Lewis
Don Quixote 98, 99
Dorf, Shel 250, 251, 255; "The Bradbury Chronicles" 250, 251, 255
Doucet, Julie 245
Dougherty, Dan 67; "William Wilson" 67
Dracula 14–15, 161–176
Drawn & Quarterly 90, 93
Ducis, Jean François 59*n*2
Duke, Alice 69; graphic novel adaptation of "The Tell-Tale Heart" 69
Dziemianowicz, Stefan 257; "*The Martian Chronicles* by Ray Bradbury (1950)" 257

East Texas 19
EC Comics 79*n*8, 92, 251–253, ***254***, 255, 260; *Crime Suspenstories* 253; *The Haunt of Fear* 252, 253; "Home to Stay" 252; *Shock Suspenstories* 253; "A Strange Undertaking" 252; *Tales from the Crypt* 92, 251, 253; *Vault of Horror* 252, 253; *Weird Fantasy* 252, 253, ***254***; *Weird Science* 253; *Weird Science-Fantasy* 253; "What the Dog Dragged In" 252
Eclipse Comics 34
Edelman, Lee 156; "I'm Not There" 156
Edginton, Ian 15, 178, 181, ***182***, 183, 184, 188, 189, 190, 191, 192; graphic novel adaptation of "The Murders in the Rue Morgue" 69; graphic novel adaptation of *The Picture of Dorian Gray* 15, 177–193
Eerie (magazine) 75
Eisner, Will 5, 6, 101, 104, 255; *Comics and Sequential Art* 6; *A Contract with God* 255; graphic novel adaptation of *Moby-Dick* 98, 101, 102, 104; *Graphic Storytelling and Visual Narrative* 6
Eisner Award 44*n*2
"Eldorado" 79*n*6
Elfquest 72
Ellis, Steward March 155; *The Hardman Papers* 155
Ellison, Harlan 256
Emrich, Wilhelm 205, 206; "The Animal as Liberating Self" 205, 206
England 133, 153, 157, 162, 168, 169, ***171***; *see also* Great Britain
Enslow Publishers 74; *Chilling Tales of Horror: Dark Graphic Short Stories* 74; *Dark Graphic Novels* 74

Erkilla, Betsy 76
Eureka Productions 65, 67, 68
Europe 163, 195
Evergreen, Nelson 67
Eye Classics (SelfMadeHero) 198, 203, 204n7

Faber, Michel 204n4; revised of Anyango and Mairowitz graphic novel adaptation of *Heart of Darkness* 204n4
"The Facts in the Case of M. Valdemar" 67
Fago, Dorothy Calhoun 49
Fahrenheit 451 16, 249, 257, 258, 259, 260
Fajardo, Alexis 42–43, 44; *Kid Beowulf* 42–43, 44
"The Fall of the House of Usher" 69, 70, 71, 74, 75, 77, **78**, 79n4, 75n5, 80n10; *Mad Trist* by Launcelot Canning 71
The Far Side 250
Farrar, Straus and Giroux 257
Feldstein, Al 108n6, 252, 253, **254**; "Morbid Dick" 108n6; *see also* EC Comics
Ferguson, Christine 15, 197–203
Ferguson, Frances 143n3, 144n20; "Emma, or Happiness (or Sex Work)" 143n3, 144n20
Fiction House 125n1
film *see* adaptation studies
Finlayson, J. Caitlin 13; *Othello* 46–59; *Shakespeare on Page, Stage and Screen* seminar 53
First Comics 34, 35, 36
Fitzgerald, F. Scott 16, 221–234; *The Great Gatsby* 16, 221–234
Fitzgerald, Robert 20
Fiumara, Sebastian 15, 178, 179, **180**, 181, 183, 184, 188, 189, 190, 191, 192; graphic novel adaptation of *The Picture of Dorian Gray* 15, 177–193
Flash Gordon 250, 251
Flaubert, Gustave 14, 127–144; *Letters* 127, 128; *Madame Bovary* 14, 127–144
Fletcher, James 69; "The Black Cat" 69
Folger Shakespeare Library 46, 47, 59; Digital Image Collection 59; *Picturing Shakespeare* project 46
Foreman, Carl 96; *High Noon* (film) 96–97
Foster, Hal (Harold) 34, 250; *Prince Valiant* 250, 251; *Tarzan* 251
Foucault, Michel 69
France 14, 42, 128, 133, 144n20
Francis, Andrew 204n4; revised edition of Anyango and Mairowitz graphic novel adaptation of *Heart of Darkness* 204n4
Frazetta, Frank 34
Frost, Robert 82; "Stopping by Woods on a Snowy Evening" 82

Furst, Lilian 143n3, 143n4, 144n9; "The Power of the Powerless" 143n3, 143n4, 144n9

Gaiman, Neil 33, 39, 40, **41**, 42, 44, 108n9; "Bay Wolf" poem in *Smoke and Mirrors* anthology 39; film adaptation of *Beowulf* 39, 40, **41**, 42, 44; *The Monarch of the Glen* in *Fragile Things* 39; *The Sandman. Endless Nights* 108n9
Gaines, William 253, 255, 257; *see also* EC Comics
Gal, Ana G. 14–15
Gaines, William 251, 252
Garamond (publisher) **216**
Garden of Eden 188
Gardner, Jared 7
Gardner, John 36; *Grendel* (novel) 36–37
Gardner, Martin 121; *The Annotated Alice* 121
Gatarik, Václav 15, 206, 214–217, 218, 219n10; *Proměna*, graphic novel adaptation of *The Metamorphosis* 15, 206, 214–217, 218
Gauguin, Henri 59n2
Gelder, Ken 163; *Reading the Vampire* 163
Gemma Bovery 14, 127–144
Genette, Gírard 83, 114, 147; *Palimpsests: Literature in the Second Degree* 83, 114, 147
Gerrard, Lisa 144n9, 144n11; "Romantic Heroines in the Nineteenth Century Novel" 144n9, 144n11
George Frederick Watts Gallery (Guildford, UK) 3
Gibbons, Dave 256, 257; *Ray Bradbury Comics* 257; *Watchmen* 256
Gillespie, Michael Patrick 177, 183, 187–188; *Oscar Wilde and the Poetics of Ambiguity* 177, 183, 187–188
Ginsburg, Michal 144n12, 144n14, 144n16; "Narrative Strategies" 144n12, 144n14, 144n16
Giordano, Dick 15, 101, 104, 164, 168, **170**; *Dracula* graphic novel adaptation 15, 161–176; *Moby-Dick* graphic novel adaptation 98, 100, 101, 102, 104
Gilberton (publisher) 125n1
Girl's Romances 86
Gleiser, P.M. 21
Godwin, Vincent 49
"The Gold-Bug" 74
Goodwin, Sarah Webster 143n3, 143n8, 144n15, 144n20; "Libraries, Kitsch, and Gender in *Madame Bovary*" 143n3, 143n8, 144n15, 144n20

The Graphic Canon 5, 178, 204n4
Graphic Classics (Eureka Productions) 65, **66**, 67, 68, 70, 79n5, 79n6; *Edgar Allan Poe* 65, 66, 67, 68, 70, 79n5, 79n6; *Edgar Allan Poe's Tales of Mystery* 67, 70
Graphic Universe (Lerner Publishing) 21
Great Britain 115, 151; British Empire 163; British history 123, 125; *see also* England
The Great Gatsby 221–234
Green, J.A. Matthew 14
Greenaway, Kate 189; *The Language of Flowers* 189
Greenberg, Nikki 15–16, 221–234; graphic novel adaptation of *The Great Gatsby* 16, 221–234
Grell, Mike 36; *Warlord* 36
Grennan, Simon 14, 147–160; *Dispossession (Courier deux lièvres)*, graphic novel adaptation of *John Caldigate* 14, 147–160
Groensteen, Thierry 7, 205, 207, 214, 218n2, 237, 238; *Comics and Narration* 237; "Premiere bouquet des contraints" 238; *The System of Comics* 7; *La Transécriture* 205, 207, 214, 218n2
Grove, Valerie 154
Grosz, George 217
Grummere, Francis B. 37, 39
Guardian (newspaper) 128
Guattari, Félix 206; *Kafka* 206
Gulliver's Travels 98
Gypsies 163–164

Hackney (London) 203
Haines, Robin 154; *Life and Death in the Age of Sail* 154
Halloween 216
Hamilton, Tim 257, 258, **259**, 260; graphic novel adaptation of *Fahrenheit 451* 258, **259**, 260
Hamlet 19
Harris-Fain, Darren 16
Harvey Award 44n2
Haschenpusch, Kerstin 214, 219n8; translation of *Metamorphosis* 214, 219n8
Hatfield, Charles 207; *Alternative Comics* 207
"The Haunted Palace" 70, 71, 77
Hawthorne, Nathaniel 89
Heaney, Seamus 33, 37, **41**
Heart of Darkness 13, 147, 194–204
Heart of Empire 116
Heer, Jeet 5; *A Comics Studies Reader* 5
Hergé 240, 245; Thompson and Thompson detectives, 240; *The Secret of the Unicorn*, 245; *Tintin*, **244**, 245
Herholz, Bert M. 71; *The Casque of Amontillado*, 71

Herman, David, 7
"Hernando's Hideaway" (song from *Pajama Game*) 82
Herriman, George 243; *Krazy Kat* 243
Heuet, Stéphane 99; graphic novel adaptation of *A la recherche du temps perdu* 99
Hignite, Todd 208; "Robert Crumb" 208
Hill and Wang 257; *Fahrenheit 451*, 257, 258, **259**; *The Martian Chronicles* 257; The *9/11 Report: A Graphic Adaptation* 257; *Something Wicked This Way Comes* 257, **261**
Hinds, Gareth 12, 20, 22, 23, 24, 25, **28**, **29**, 37–39, 40, 43–44; *Beowulf* graphic novel adaptation 33, 37–39, 40, 43–44; *The Odyssey* graphic novel adaptation 12, 20, 22–23, 27, **28**, **29**, **30**, 31
Hitchcock, Alfred 240
Hollywood 33, 40, 97, 166, 168, 251, 254
Homer 12, 19–32; *The Iliad* 19, 98; *The Odyssey* 98; *The Odyssey*, books 9–12, "travels of Odysseus" 20–32
Hontiveros, David 65, 68; "The Pit and the Pendulum" 65–67, 68
House of Mystery 36
Huston, John 97, 103, 104; film adaptation of *Moby-Dick* 97, 103, 104
Hutcheon, Linda 8–9, 13, 16n1, 61, 64, 65, 67, 70, 71, 72, 79n3, 115, 116, 148, 173, 207, 214, 217; *A Theory of Adaptation* 8–9, 115, 116, 148, 173, 207, 214, 217
Huyssens, Andreas 143n3, 143n8; *After the Great Divide* 143n3, 143n8
Hyman, Gwen 169; *Making a Man* 169

IDW 33, 39, 44n4
Iger, Jerry 125n1
The Iliad 19, 98
Illustrated Classic 111, 112, 125; graphic novel adaptation of *Alice in Wonderland* 111, 112, 125; graphic novel adaptation of *Othello* 49, 59n4
The Illustrated Man 252
"The Imp of the Perverse" 79n5
Inge, M. Thomas 60, 79n1, 98, 100, 104, 107n2; "From Ahab to Peg-Leg Pete: A Comic Cetology 97, 104; *Incredible Mr. Poe* 60; "Melville in the Comic Books" 97, 98, 107n2; "Poe and the Comics Connection" 79n1

Jackson, Henry 51
James, Henry 195; *Turn of the Screw* 195, 197, 198, 199
Janson, Klaus 256; *Batman: The Dark Knight Returns* 256; *Daredevil* 256; *Frost and Fire* 256

Japan 162
Japan Sea 102
Jazz Age 229
Jew 206
Jimenez, Jim 71; graphic novel adaptation of *The Fall of the House of Usher* 71–72, 79n4
John Caldigate 14, 147–160
Jolie, Angelina 44
Jolley, Dan 12, 20, 21, **30**, 31 ; *Odysseus: Escaping Poseidon's Curse* 12, 20, 21, 25, **30**, 31
Jonathan Cape (publisher) **117**, **118**, 124
Jones, Hobby 71; graphic novel adaptation of "The Black Cat" 71
Jones, William B., Jr. 113, 125n1, 204n2; *Alice in Wonderland* introduction 113, 125n1; *Classics Illustrated: A Cultural History* 204n2
Joubert, Joseph 134; *Pensées* 134
Joyce, James 99; *Ulysses* 99
The Jungle 214

Kafka, Franz 15, 205–220; *The Metamorphosis* 15, 205–220
Kaiser, Hellmuth 206; "Kafka's Fantasy of Punishment" 206
Kamen, Jack 253; "Mars Is Heaven" 253; "Zero Hour" 253
Kani, John 52
Kanter, Albert 4, 98, 100; *Classics Illustrated* 4, 98; *Classics Illustrated* graphic novel adaptation of *Moby-Dick* 100
Kapoor, Sucheta 143n3, 144n9; "Transgressing Limits" 143n3, 144n9
Katchor, Ben 245
Katholieke Universiteit Leuven 148
The Katzenjammer Kids 251
Kelly, Dorothy 143n3; *Fictional Genders* 143n3; *Reconstructing Woman* 143n3
Kent, Rockwell 104
Kick, Russell 5, 178, 185, 189; *The Graphic Canon* 5, 178, 185, 189, 204n6
Kid Beowulf (graphic novel adaptation of *Beowulf*) 33, 42–43, 44; *Kid Beowulf and the Blood-Bound Oath* 42–43; *Kid Beowulf and the Song of Roland* 42; *Kid Beowulf and the Rise of El Cid* 42
"King Pest" 79n6
King's Men (1610 Oxford *Othello* performance) 51
Kinsella, Sharon 204n2; *Adult Manga* 204n2
Kirby, Award 34, 36, 44n2
Kish, Matt 204n6; illustrations for *Heart of Darkness* 204n6

Kitchen Sink Press **209**
Klimowski, Andrezj 197
Knowles, Owen 194; *Oxford Reader's Companion to Joseph Conrad* 194
Kotz, Dean 64, 65; *Poe* 64
Krazy Kat 243
Kristeva, Julia 83, 110, 114, 115, 125, 218; *Desire in Language* 110, 114, 115, 125; *Powers of Horror* 218
Kuhlman, Martha 15
Kuper, Peter 15, 206, 211–214, 215, 217, 218, 219n4, 219n5, 219n6, 219n8; graphic novel adaptation of *The Jungle* 214; graphic novel adaptation of *The Metamorphosis* 15, 206, 211–214, 215, 217, 219n5, 219n5, 219n6; *The System* 214; translation of *The Metamorphosis* 217, 218, 219n8

LaCapra, Dominick 131, 143n7, 144n12, 144n14; *Madame Bovary on Trial* 131, 143n7, 144n12, 144n14
The Lady in the Lake 243
Lake District (England) 116
Lamb, Robert Paul 108n5; "Fast Fish and Loose Fish" 108n5
Lapprand, Marc 235; "Oulipo@50" 235
Larson, Gary 98
Lasch, Christopher 143n8; *The Culture of Narcissism* 148n8
Lavery, David 97, 99; "Melville's *Moby-Dick* and Hollywood" 97
Lawler, Donald 187, 188, 190, 192n6; *An Investigation* 187, 188, 190, 192n6
Lefévre, Pascal 7
Lehrer, Tom 82–83, 84; "Oedipus Rex" 82–83, 84
Leitch, Thomas 8, 96; "Adaptation at a Crossroads" 96; "Twelve Fallacies in Contemporary Adaptation Theory" 8
Le Lionnais, François 235
Leney, William Satchwell 55; 59n2
Levine, Jeffrey 107n2; "Illustrated Editions of *Moby-Dick*" 107n2
Lichtenstein, Roy 86, 87, 88; *The Kiss V* 86, 87, 88
Liddell, Alice 111, 112, 113, 120, 121
Liddell sisters 113, 120
The Life and Opinions of Tristram Shandy, Gentleman 99
"Ligeia" 92
Lincoln, Andrew 152; "Walter Scott, Politeness, and Patriotism" 152
Lipscomb, George D. 125n1
The Little Friend 203
Livingston, Michael 44n3
Lombardo, Stanley 22, 25–26

London 15, 68, 116, 128, 132, 141, 162, 168, 169, *171*, 172, 183, 195, 197, 203
Long Island 221
Lord Jim 194
Los Angeles 203
Lott, Rod 67; "The Black Cat" 67
Lovecraft, H.P. 79n1
Lubbock, Percy 144n17; ["The Craft of Fiction in *Madame Bovary*"] 144n17
Lugosi, Bela 162
Luhrmann, Baz 221; film adaptation of *The Great Gatsby* 221

MacDonald, Tanis 211, 219n7; "Voice of the Gutter" 211, 219n7
MacPherson, Dwight L. 63–64, 65; *The Surreal Adventures of Edgar Allan Poo* 63–64, 65
MAD 108n6
Madame Bovary 14, 127–144
Madden, Matt 16, 235–248; *99 Ways to Tell a Story* 16, 235–248
Magyars 163, 175n2
Mairowitz, David 15, 194–204, 206, 207–210, 214, 218; graphic novel adaptation of *Heart of Darkness* 15, 194–204; graphic novel adaptation of *The Metamorphosis* 15, 206, 207–210, 214, 218; *Introducing Kafka* 207–210, 212, 214, 218
Major Hoople 250
Malory, Thomas 98; *Le Morte d'Arthur* 98
"The Man of the Crowd" 68
Mandrake the Magician 251
Manga Shakespeare 204n7; *Manga Shakespeare Othello* 47, 49–54, 55
Manning, Matthew K. 71; graphic novel adaptation of *The Fall of the House of Usher* 71–72, 79n4
Marder, Elissa 143n4; "Trauma, Addiction, and Temporal Bulemia in *Madame Bovary*" 143n4
Margopoulos, Richard 75; *Edgar Allan Poe's Haunt of Horror* 75; work for *Creepy* and *Eerie* 75
Marion, Phillipe 144n18
Market Theatre (Johannesburg) 1989 *Othello* performance 52
The Martian Chronicles 251, 252, 253, **254**, 256, 257
Martinet, Jeanne 86–87; parody of *Girls' Romances* #36, 86; *Truer Than True Romance* 86–87
Marvel Comics 11, 15, 20, 21, 34, 36, 75, 100, 161–176, 177–193, 256; *Conan the Barbarian* 20; *Edgar Allan Poe's Haunt of Horror* 75; *Moby-Dick* graphic novel adaptation 98, 100; *The Odyssey* graphic novel adaptation 20, 21; *The Picture of Dorian Gray* graphic novel adaptation 11, 178–193; *Stoker's Dracula*15, 161–176; *Tomb of Dracula* 36
Masereel, Franz 211
"The Masque of the Red Death" 61, 69, 72–74, 77, 79n6
Masterpiece Comics 13, 88–95
Mathews, Harry 235, 236; *The Oulipo Compendium* 235
Mathieu, Marc-Antoine 245
Matthew, Book of (New Testament) 91
Mazzucchelli, David 245
McCloud, Scott 6–7, 33, 75, 223, 224; *Making Comics* 33; *Understanding Comics: The Invisible Art*, 6–7, 223, 224
McEachern, Patricia A. 143n3, 143n4; "True Lies" 143n3, 143n4
McFarlane, Brian 8; *Novel into Film* 8
McKay, Winsor 211; "Dream of the Rarebit Fiend" 211
McKean, Dave 105; *Arkham Asylum. A Serious House on Serious Earth* **105**; *The Sandman. Endless Nights*, 108n9
McLuhan, Marshall 9, 223; *Understanding Media* 9, 223
Meesters, Gert 237; "Les Significations du style graphique" 237
Melville, Herman 13, 14, 79n1; *Moby Dick*, 13, 96–107
Menu, Jean-Christophe 238; *La Bande dessineé et son double* 238
Meredith, George 155
The Metamorphosis 15, 205–220
Metz, Christian 154; *Psychoanalysis and Cinema* 154
Metzger, James A. 206, 207, 217; "Re-envisioning Kafka's *Metamorphosis*" 206, 207, 217
Mickey Mouse 250
Mikkonen, Kai 137, 140, 144n17; "The Implicit Narrator in Comics" 137, 140, 144n17
Millais, John Everett 152, 156
Miller, Elizabeth 175n2; *Dracula: Sense and Nonsense* 175n2
Miller, Frank 256; *Batman: The Dark Knight Returns* 256
Miller, Harry G. 125n1
Miller, J. Hillis 3
Mitchell, J. Barton 64, 65; *Poe* 64
Moby-Dick 13, 96–108
Moench, Doug, et al. 108n8
Monnin, Katie 43
Montgomery, Robert 243

Moore, Alan 5, 256; *Watchmen* 256
Moore, Gene M. 194, 204*n*2; *Conrad and Film* 204*n*2; *Oxford Reader's Companion to Joseph Conrad* 194
Moore, Leah 69; "The Black Cat" 69
"Morella" 75, 77, 78
Morrison, Grant 105; *Arkham Asylum. A Serious House on Serious Earth* **105**
Le Morte d'Arthur 98
Muir, Edwin 214, 218*n*1, 219*n*8; translation of *Metamorphosis* 214, 218*n*1, 219*n*8
Muir, Willa 214, 218*n*1, 219*n*8; translation of *Metamorphosis* 214, 218*n*1, 219*n*8
"The Murders in the Rue Morgue" 67, 69, 70, 74–75
Murnau, F.W. **106**; *Nosferatu* (film) **106**
"The Mystery of Marie Roget" 74

National Museum (Warsaw, Poland) 26
Neill, Michael 49, 53
"Never Bet the Devil Your Head" 79*n*5
New Bedford 100
New South Wales 153, 158
New York 227, 229
Nickel, Phillip 175; "Horror and the Idea of Everyday Life" 175
Nieves, Rafael 67; "William Wilson" 67
1984 (Orwell) 68
99 Ways to Tell a Story (graphic novel adaptation of Queneau's *Exercises in Style*) 16, 239–247
Nino, Alex 101, 102, 103, 104; graphic novel adaptation of *Moby-Dick* 101, 102, 103, 104, 128
Normandy (France) 128, 132, 137, 148
Nyberg, Amy 36; *Seal of Approval* 36

Oakley, Shane Ivan 69; graphic novel adaptation of "The Fall of the House of Usher" 69
O'Brien, Geoffrey 65
The Odyssey (Homer) 12, 19, 98; books 9–12, 24; Telemachy, 20; "travels of Odysseus" 20–32
Odysseus: Escaping Poseidon's Curse (graphic novel adaptation of *The Odyssey*) 12, 20, 21, 25
Oedipus Rex 82, 84
Old King Hamlet 42
Oldman, Gary 162
Orlando, Joe 253; "The Coffin" 253; "The Long Years" 253
Orley Farm 156
O'Rourke, John 125*n*1
Orr, Mary 143*n*3, 143*n*5; *Flaubert: Writing the Masculine* 143*n*3, 143*n*5

Orwell, George 68; *1984* 68
Osada, Ryuta 47, 48, 51, 52, 53, 54, 55, 58; *Manga Shakespeare Othello* 47, 49–54, 55, 58
Othello (Shakespeare) 13, 46–59
Oubapo (Ouvroir de bande dessineé potentialle) 236–248
Oulipo (Ouvroir de littérature potentialle) 16, 235–248
Out Our Way 250
"The Oval Portrait" 70, 77, **78**, 79*n*6, 80*n*10
Oxford (city) 52, 113, 116, 119
Oxford (university) 112, 230

Pace, Jean 143*n*2, 143*n*3, 143*n*8; "Flaubert's Image of Woman" 143*n*2, 143*n*3, 143*n*8
Pacific Comics 75; *A Corben Special: House of Usher* 75
The Pajama Game 82; "Hernando's Hideaway" 82
Panter, Gary 245
Pantheon (publisher) **138**, **139**
Papercutz 74–75, 79*n*7
"A Parasite" (painting) 3
Paris 132, 239, 240
Parker, Oliver 52, 53, 54, 58; 1995 film of *Othello* 52, 53, 54, 58
parody 13, 82–95, 108, 242; adaptation as a form of parody 13, 79, 82–95
Payne (recipient of letter from Oscar Wilde) 177
Peck, Gregory 103, 104
Pendulum Press 100, 103; graphic novel adaptation of *Moby-Dick* 100, 103
Penguin Books 222, 226
Perec, Georges 16, 235; *La Disparition* 235
Perret, Marion 9–10; "Not Just Condensation: How Comic Books Interpret Shakespeare" 9
Peters, John G. 195; *Conrad and Impressionism* 195
Petruso, Michael 129, 143*n*4; "Madame Bovary in a Consumer Society" 129, 143*n*4
Philadelphia 71
The Picture of Dorian Gray 11, 13, 1, 177–193
Pini, Richard 72; *Elfquest* 72
Pini, Wendy 72; *Elfquest* 72; webcomic adaptation, *Masque of the Red Death*" 72–74
"The Pit and the Pendulum" 65–68
Planet Stories 256
Poe, Edgar Allan 13, 60- 81, 92; "Alone" 75; "Annabel Lee" 64; "The Assignation" 75, 76; "Berenice" 67, 80*n*10; "The Black Cat"

67, 69, 71, 79n4; "The Cask of Amontillado" 71, 79n5, 92; "The City in the Sea" 75, 76, 77; "The Conqueror Worm" 76, 80n6; "Eldorado" 79n6; "The Facts in the Case of M. Valdemar" 67; "The Fall of the House of Usher" 69, 70, 77, 79n4, 79n5, 80n10; "The Haunted Palace" 71, 77, *78*; "Hop-Frog" 79n6; "The Imp of the Perverse" 79n5; "King Pest" 79n6; "Ligeia" 92; "The Man of the Crowd" 68; "The Masque of the Red Death" 61, 72–74, 77, *78*, 79n6; "Morella" 75, 77, 88; "The Murders in the Rue Morgue" 67, 69, 70; "The Mystery of Marie Roget" 74; "Never Bet the Devil Your Head" 79n5; "The Oval Portrait" 70, 77, *78*, 79n6, 80n10; "The Pit and the Pendulum" 65–68; "The Premature Burial" 75, 77, *78*, 79n5; "The Raven" 80n10; "Shadow" 75, 76, 80n10; "The Sleeper" 75; "The System of Doctor Tarr and Professor Fether" 74; "The Tell-Tale Heart" 68, 69, 79n5, 92; "William Wilson" 67, 68
Poe, Virginia 63, 64, 65
Poe, William Henry Leonard 64
Pohl, Frederik 256
Pointer, Frank E. 110, 125, 212, 218n4; "Classics Emulated: Comic Adaptations of Literary Texts" 110, 125, 212, 218n4
Pomplun, Tom 65; "Berenice" 67; editor, Graphic Classics (Eureka Productions) 65, 79n6; *Graphic Classics: Edgar Allan Poe* 65–67, 79n5; *Graphic Classics: Edgar Allan Poe's Tales of Mystery* 67, 68
Pope, Alexander 84–86; *The Rape of the Lock* 84–86
Popeye 250
Poucel, Jean-Jacques 235; "The Writing of Constraint (I)" 235; "The Writing of Constraint (II)" 235
Powell, Matthew T. 207, 215; "Bestial Representations" 207, 215
Powerpop Comics 71
Prague 210, 214, 215, 217, 218
Pratt, Hugo 237; *Corto Maltese* 237
Preiss, Byron 256–257; *The Ray Bradbury Chronicles* 257; *Ray Bradbury Comics* 257
"The Premature Burial" 75, 77, 78, 79n5
Prince Valiant 34, 250, 251
Prosser, Adam 69; graphic novel adaptation of "The Masque of the Red Death" 69
Proust, Marcel 99, 262; *A la recherche du temps perdu (Remembrance of Things Past)* 99, 262
Puffin Books 161–176; *Bram Stoker's Dracula* 161–176

Pugh, Steve 68; graphic novel adaptation of "The Pit and the Pendulum" 68–69

Queneau, Raymond 16, 235–248; *Exercises in Style* 16, 235–248
Quinn, Prof. Patrick 97

Rabkin, Eric S. 13, 83; *Narrative Suspense: "When Slim Turned Sideways...."* 83
Raby, Peter 185
Rainey, Rich 68; graphic novel adaptation of "The Man of the Crowd" 68
Rangel, Erik 69; graphic novel adaption of "The Masque of the Red Death" 69
The Rape of the Lock 84–86
"The Raven" 75, 80n10
Reed, Gary *167*; *Bram Stoker's Dracula: The Graphic Novel* *167*
Reeder, Ellen D. 26
Reppion, John 69; graphic novel adaptation of "The Black Cat" 69
Rhodes, Richard 59n3
Richter, Helmuth 206; "The Metamorphosis" 206
Rieu, E.V. 20
Riffaterre, Michael 143n3, 143n8, 144n10; "Flaubert's Presuppositions" 143n3, 143n8, 144n10
Robertson, W. Graham 183
Roddam, Franc 97; film adaptation of *Moby-Dick* 97
Roditi, Edouard 185–*186*, 192n5; *Oscar Wilde* 185–187, 192n5
Rodriguez, Gabriel 39; graphic novel adaptation of Gaiman and Avary's filmadaptation of Beowulf 39–*41*
Rodríguez, Pedro 72; graphic novel adaptation of "The Black Cat" 72, 79n4
Ronell, Avital 143n4, 144n9; *Crack Wars* 143n4, 144n9
A Room of One's Own 129
Rosenbach Museum and Library 175n2
Rouen 132
Round, Julia 113, 115–116, *119*, 120, 123 ; "Contrariwise! Breaking Rules in Bryan Talbot's *Alice in Sunderland*" 113, 115–116, *119*, 120, 123
Roussel, Raymond 237; *How I Wrote Certain of My Books* 237
Rowson, Martin 99; graphic novel adaptation of *The Life and Opinions of Tristram Shandy, Gentleman* 99
Royal, Derek Parker 13; "Sequential Poetry" 79n2
Royal College of Art (London) 195, 197
Russell, P. Craig 257; *Ray Bradbury Comics* 257

Ryall, Chris 39; graphic novel adaptation of Gaiman and Avary's film adaptation of *Beowulf* 39–*41*

Sabiston, Elizabeth 143*n*3, 144*n*9, 144*n*11; "The Prison of Womanhood" 143*n*3, 144*n*9, 144*n*11
Saddleback Illustrated Classics 49, 59*n*4, 72
Said, Edward 196; *Culture and Imperialism* 196
St. James's Gazette 192*n*7
Salomé 183
Salter, William 55, 59*n*3; *Othello's Lamentation* 55
Saltzman, Esther Bendit 15
Sandells, Natalie 70; graphic novel adaptation of "The Oval Portrait" 70
Sanders, Julie 3, 8, 83, 114; *Adaptation and Appropriation* 7, 83, 114
Sargent, John Singer 183
Sartre, Jean-Paul 143*n*5; *The Family Idiot* 143*n*5
Saxons 163
Schmitz-Emans, Monika 97–98; "Helden-Tum und Helden-Comic, Adaptionen von Herman Melville's *Moby-Dick*" (chapter of book, *Literatur-Comics*) 97–98
Schneider, Greice 242; *What happens when nothing happens"* 242
Schor, Naomi 134, 143*n*1, 143*n*3, 144*n*11; *Breaking the Chain* 134, 143*n*1, 143*n*3, 144*n*11
Schultz, Elizabeth A. 97, 98 100, 101, 108*n*9; "Illustrations of Altered Editions of *Moby-Dick*" chapter in her book *Unpainted to the Last. Moby-Dick and Twentieth Century American Art* 97, 98, 100, 101, 108*n*9
Schwartz, Lew Sayre 98, 102, 100, 104; graphic novel adaptation of *Moby-Dick* 98, 100, 102, 104
Scots Observer 192*n*3
Scott, Walter 151–52
seinen manga 194, 204*n*2
SelfMadeHero (publisher) 51, 195, 197, 199, *201*, 204*n*7; Eye Classics 198, 203, 204*n*7
Sequels Illustrated (parody of *Classics Illustrated*, "The Strange Case of Dr. Jekyll and Mr. Heckle") 88
Serratosa, Miquel 74; *Dark Graphic Tales by Edgar Allan Poe*, 79*n*4; graphic novel adaptation of "The Fall of the House of Usher" 74; graphic novel adaptation of "The Gold-Bug" 74; graphic novel adaptation of "The System of Dr. Tarr and Professor Fether" 74
Seven Stories (publisher) 186

Shakespeare, William 12, 13, 19, 88; *Hamlet* 19; *Othello* 46–59
Shapiro, Irwin 101, 102, 103, 104; graphic novel adaptation of *Moby-Dick* 101, 102, 103, 104
Siemon, James 48
Sienkiewicz, Bill 98, 101–102, 103, 104, **105**, **106**, 107, 108*n*4, 108*n*8, 108*n*9; *Batman* cover 108*n*8; *Classics Illustrated* adaptation of *Moby-Dick* 98, 101–102, 103, 104, **105**, **106**, 107, 108*n*4; *The Sandman. Endless Nights* 108*n*9
Sikoryak, R. 13, 83, 89, 92, 94; *Blonde Eve* (parody of *Blondie*) 90–91; "The Crypt of Brontë" (parody of *Wuthering Heights*) 83, 92–95; *Masterpiece Comics*, 13, 88–95; "X-Ray Pics" (parody of "X-Ray Specs") 89–90, 91
Silver Age (DC Comics) 33
Silverberg, Robert 256
Simmonds, Posy 14, 127–144; *Gemma Bovery* 127–144; graphic novel adaptation of *Madame Bovary* 14
Sinclair, Upton 214; *The Jungle* 214
Singh, Lalit Kumar 98, 100, 101, 102, 103, 104; graphic novel adaptation of *Moby-Dick* 98, 101, 102, 103, 104
Skilton, David 14, 151, 155; *Anthony Trollope and His Contemporaries*, 151, 155
Slater, Jeremy 69; "The Tell-Tale Heart" 69
Small, Helen 129, 143*n*3; "Feminist Theory and the Return of the Real" 129, 143*n*3
Smith, Jeremy 40
Sokel, Walter H. 206; "Education for Tragedy" 206
Something Wicked This Way Comes 257, 260, **261**
Sophocles 19, 84; *Oedipus Rex* 84
Spacks, Patricia Meyer 143*n*3, 144*n*11; "Women and Boredom" 143*n*3, 144*n*11
Spain 42
Spiegelman, Art 5, 245
Stahlberg, Lance 98, 101, 102, 103, 104; graphic novel adaptation of *Moby-Dick* 98, 101, 102, 103, 104
Stam, Robert 16*n*1, 96; "Beyond Fidelity: The Dialogics of Adaptation" 16*n*1, 96
Star Trek 116
Star Wars 116
Starke, Ottomar 208
Sterling (publisher) 182
Sterne, Laurence 99; *The Life and Opinions of Tristram Shandy, Gentleman* 99
Stevenson, Robert Louis 87–88; *The Strange Case of Dr. Jekyll and Mr. Hyde* 87–88, 199

Stewart, Patrick 103; 1998 *Moby-Dick* television mini-series 103
Still, Judith 114; *Intertextuality: Theories and Practices* 114
Stoker, Bram 14, 161–176; *Dracula* 14, 161–176
"Stopping by Woods on a Snowy Evening" 82
Storey, Barron 108*n*9; *The Sandman. Endless Nights* 108*n*9
The Strange Case of Dr. Jekyll and Mr. Hyde 87–88, 199
Streufert, Paul D. 12
Suez Canal 154
Sunderland (England) 110–125
Surdiacourt, Stephen 144*n*18; "Can You Hear Me Drawing?" 144*n*18
Sutliffe Sanders, Joe 152; "Chaperoning Words" 152
Sutton, John William 44*n*3
Sutton, Ronn 68; graphic novel adaptation of "The Tell-Tale Heart" 68
Sutton Hoo 38
Suzman, Janet 52, 53; director of Market Theatre Othello performance 52, 53
Swan Lake (ballet) 122
Swift, Jonathan 98; *Gulliver's Travels* 98
"The System of Doctor Tarr and Professor Fether" 74
Szekelys 163, 175*n*2

Tabachnick, Stephen E. 9, 10, 15–16, 178, 182–183, 187; (ed.) *Teaching the Graphic Novel* 9; "The Graphic Novel and the Age of Transition" 10, 178, 182–183, 187
Takizawa, Seiho 194; manga adaptation of *Heart of Darkness* 194
Talbot, Bryan 14, 110–125; *The Adventures of Luther Arkwright* 116; *Alice in Sunderland: An Entertainment* 14, 110–125; authorial personas 122; *Heart of Empire* 116; *The Tale of One Bad Rat* 116
Talbot, Mary 122
The Tale of One Bad Rat 116
Tales from the Crypt 92, 253
Tanner, Tony 143*n*4; *Adultery in the Novel* 143*n*4
Tartt, Donna 203; *The Little Friend* 203
Tarzan 36, 250, 251
Taylor, Charles 59*n*2
Teare, Brad 68; graphic novel adaptation of "The Man of the Crowd" 68
"The Tell Tale Heart" 68, 69, 79*n*5, 92
Tenniel, John 113, 117, 120, 121
Thackeray, William 152
TheComic.Com 37, 38

Thomas, Jean-Jacques 235; "Oulipo@50" 235
Thomas, Roy 11, 12, 20, 21, 23–24, 25, 27, 29, **30**, 31, 101, 104, 164, 168, ***170***, 178, ***180***, 181, 183, 184, 188, 189, 190, 192; *Conan the Barbarian* 20; *Dracula* graphic novel adaptation 15, 161–176 ; introduction to *Moby-Dick* graphic novel adaptation 100, 101; *Moby-Dick* graphic novel adaptation 98, 100, 101, 102, 103, 104; *The Odyssey* graphic novel adaptation 12, 20, 21, 23–25, 27, **28**, **29**, **30**, 31; *The Picture of Dorian Gray* graphic novel adaptation 11, 15, 178–193
Thompson, G.R. 66, 67, 77; "Development of Romantic Irony" 67; *Poe's Fiction* 66, 67, 77
Thon, Jan-Noël 144*n*18; "Who's Telling the Tale" 144*n*18
3 Rivers Press ***213***
Through the Looking Glass, and What Alice Found There 113
Toccini, Greg 12, 20, 21, 23, 24, 27, **28**, **29**, **30**, 31; *The Odyssey* graphic novel adaptation 12, 20, 21, 23–25, 27, **28**, **29**, **30**, 31
Tolkien, J.R.R. 35
Tomb of Dracula 36
Tomorrow Midnight 251, 255
Tondro, Jason 12, 44*n*4
Tonson, Jacob **47**, 59*n*2; 1709 edition of Shakespeare **47**, 59*n*2
Torregrosa, Michael 44*n*1
Transylvania 162, 163, 164, 169
Trollope, Anthony 14, 147–160; *An Autobiography* 153, 155; *John Caldigate* 14, 147–160; *Orley Farm* 156
Turn of the Screw 195, 197, 198, 199
Twain, Mark 79*n*1
Twilight (vampires) 14, 161, 166
Twitchell, James 21

Ulysses 99
University College London 197
Updike, John 210; "Foreword" *Franz Kafka* 210
Uslan, Michael 36; *Batman* 36; *Beowulf: Dragon Slayer* 36–37

Van Dam, Frederik 155; *The Man Without Style* 155
Vanderbeke, Dirk 13; "It was the best of two worlds, it was the worst of two Worlds" 108*n*3
Van der Vlies, Andrew 195, 204*n*4; "The Horror! In Pen and Ink" 195, 204*n*4
Vandervolk, William C. 143*n*3, 144*n*16; "Writing the Masculine" 143*n*3, 144*n*16

Veitch, Rick 97; *Abraxas and the Earthman* 97
Vergara, Carlo 65, 68; graphic novel adaptation of "The Pit and the Pendulum" 65–67, 68
Vicatan 49
The Victorian Web **85**
Vidaurri, S.M. 71; graphic novel adaptation of "The Black Cat" 71
Villamonte, Ricardo 36; *Beowulf: Dragon Slayer* 36–37; *Power Man & Iron Fist* 36
Vinken, Barbara 143n4; "Loving, Reading, Eating" 143n4
Vlad the Impaler 166, 168, 175n2
Voltaire 89

Wagner, Matt 257; *Ray Bradbury Comics* 257
Wagner, Richard 34
Wallachs 163, 166, 168
Ward, Lynd 211
The Warlord of Mars 250
Warren Publications 79n8
Watchmen 256
Waters, Karen Colland 169; *The Perfect Gentleman* 169
Watt, Ian 195; *Conrad in the Nineteenth Century* 195
Wearmouth Bridge **119**
Webster, Peter Dow 206; "*Metamorphosis* as Death and Resurrection Fantasy" 206
Wedeck, Harry E. 175n1; *Dictionary of Gypsy Life and Lore* 175n1
Weinberg, Joanna 52
Weist, Jerry 251, 252, 253, 254; *Bradbury: An Illustrated Life* 251, 252, 253, 254
Weller, Sam 250, 262; *The Bradbury Chronicles: The Life of Ray Bradbury* 250, 262
Wertham, Frederic 88, **254**–255; *Seduction of the Innocent* 88, **254**–255
Whitehead, Dan 69; editor, *Nevermore: A Graphic Adaptation of Edgar Allan Poe's Stories* 68–69; graphic novel adaptation of "The Fall of the House of Usher" 69
Whitson, Roger 116; "Engraving the Void and Sketching Parallel Worlds 116
Wild, Peter 154; "Two Costa nominations" 154
Wilde, Oscar 11, 15, 177–193; "The Critic as Artist" 178; *The Decay of Lying* 183; Letters 177–178, 183, 187, 192n2, 192n3, 192n7, 192n9; *The Picture of Dorian Gray* 1, 11, 13, 15, 177–193; *Salomé* 183
Wildey, Doug 251
"William Wilson" 67, 68
Williams, Kristian 179, 184–185, 192n1; "Pictures of Dorian Gray" 179, 184–185, 192n1
Williams, Tony 143n3, 144n9; "Gender Stereotypes in *Madame Bovary*" 143n3, 144n9
Wimberly, Ron 257, 258, 260, **261**; graphic novel adaptation of *Something Wicked This Way Comes* 257, 258, 260, **261**
Winchell, James 144n9; "Reading (in) *Madame Bovary* 144n9
Winterhart, Jeff 154; "Days of Bagnold Summer" 154; nominated for Costa Book Award 154
The Wizard of Id 250
Wolf, Susan L. 143n3, 143n8; "The Same or M(O)ther" 143n3, 143n8
Wolff, Karl 211
Wollstonecraft, Mary 136
Wood, Wally 253, **254**; "Mars Is Heaven" 253; "Zero Hour" 253
Woolf, Virginia 129; *A Room of One's Own* 129
Worcester, Kent 5; *A Comics Studies Reader* 5
Worden, Daniel 224, 234; "A Salamander and a Seahorse in Sepia Tone" 224, 234
Workman Publishing **57**
Worton, Michael 114; *Intertexuality: Theory and Practices* 114
Wright, John Massey 59n2
Wuthering Heights 13, 83, 92–95

xenia (Greek, "hospitality") 20, 22, 25, 26, 27

Yeates, Thomas 12, 20, 21; *Odysseus: Escaping Poseidon's Curse* 12, 20, 21, 27, **30**, 31

Zansky, Louis 98, 100, 107n2; *Classics Illustrated* adaptation of *Moby-Dick* 98, 100, 107n2
Zarate, Oscar 47, 48, 54, 55, 56, **57**, 58; *Othello* graphic novel adaptation 47, 54–58
Zinneman, Carl 96; *High Noon* 96–97

www.ingramcontent.com/pod-product-compliance
Ingram Content Group UK Ltd.
Pitfield, Milton Keynes, MK11 3LW, UK
UKHW041928140426
5217IPUK00014B/372